Employee Relations

SECOND EDITION

John Gennard is the IPD Professor of Human Resource Management at Strathclyde Business School and has written extensively on employee relations and industrial relations institutions. His most recent research looks at the role of personnel directors in devising and developing corporate strategy, and the career routes whereby people become personnel directors. He is Chief Examiner (Employee Relations) for the IPD and a Fellow of the IPD.

Graham Judge is Head of Personnel for the Adscene Group plc, a major publisher of regional newspapers employing over 900 people. He has held a number of personnel and training posts within printing and packaging, and was a director of the British Printing Industries Federation. He is also an Associate Lecturer in Human Resources Management at the University of East London and an Associate Examiner (Employee Relations) for the IPD.

ß

Other titles in the series:

*Core Personnel and
Development*
Mick Marchington and
Adrian Wilkinson

Employee Development
Rosemary Harrison

Employee Relations
John Gennard and
Graham Judge

Employee Resourcing
Stephen Taylor

Managing Activities
Michael Armstrong

*Managing Financial
Information*
David Davies

*Managing in a Business
Context*
David Farnham

*Managing Information
and Statistics*
Roland and Frances Bee

Managing People
Jane Weightman

Personnel Practice
Malcolm Martin and
Tricia Jackson

The Institute of Personnel and Development is the leading
publisher of books and reports for personnel and training
professionals, students, and all those concerned with the
effective management and development of people at work. For
details of all our titles, please contact the Publishing
Department:
tel 020 8263 3387
fax 020 8263 3850
e-mail publish@ipd.co.uk
The catalogue of all IPD titles can be viewed on the IPD
website:
www.ipd.co.uk

P

PEOPLE AND ORGANISATIONS

Employee Relations

SECOND EDITION

JOHN GENNARD AND GRAHAM JUDGE

INSTITUTE OF PERSONNEL AND DEVELOPMENT

First edition published in 1997 (ISBN 0 85292 654 5)
Reprinted 1998

Second edition published in 1999

Design by Curve

Typeset by Fakenham Photosetting Ltd, Fakenham, Norfolk

Printed in Great Britain by
The Cromwell Press, Trowbridge, Wiltshire

British Library Cataloguing in Publication Data
A catalogue record of this book is available from the British Library

ISBN 0-85292-818-1

INSTITUTE OF PERSONNEL
AND DEVELOPMENT

IPD House, Camp Road, London SW19 4UX
Tel: 020 8971 9000   Fax: 020 8263 3333
Registered office as above. Registered Charity No. 1038333
A company limited by guarantee. Registered in England No. 2931892

Contents

Editors' foreword

People hold the key to more productive and efficient organisations. The way in which people are managed and developed at work has major effects upon quality, customer service, organisational flexibility and costs. Personnel and development practitioners can play a major role in creating the framework for this to happen, but ultimately they are dependent upon line managers and other employees for its delivery. It is important that personnel and development specialists gain the commitment of others and pursue professional and ethical practices that will bring about competitive success. There is also a need to evaluate the contribution that personnel and development approaches and processes make for organisational success, and to consider ways of making them more effective. Such an approach is relevant for all types of practitioner – personnel and development generalists and specialists, line managers, consultants and academics.

This is one of a series of books under the title *People and Organisations*. The series provides essential guidance and points of reference for all those involved with people in organisations. It aims to provide the main body of knowledge and pointers to the required level of skills for personnel and development practitioners operating at a professional level in all types and sizes of organisation. It has been specially written to satisfy new professional standards defined by the Institute of Personnel and Development (IPD) in the United Kingdom and the Republic of Ireland. The series also responds to a special need in the United Kingdom for texts to cover the knowledge aspects of new and revised National and Scottish Vocational Qualifications (N/SVQs) in Personnel and Training Development.

Three 'fields' of standards have to be satisfied in order to gain graduate membership of the IPD: (i) core management (ii) core personnel and development and (iii) any four from a range of more than 20 generalist and specialist electives. The three fields can be tackled in any order, or indeed all at the same time. A range of learning routes is available: full or part-time educational course, flexible learning methods or direct experience. The standards may be assessed by educational and competence-based methods. The books in the series are suitable for supporting all methods of learning.

The series starts by addressing *core personnel and development* and four generalist electives: employee reward, employee resourcing, employee relations and employee development. Together, these cover the personnel and development knowledge requirements for graduateship of the IPD. These also cover the knowledge aspects of training and development and personnel N/SVQs at Level 4.

Core Personnel and Development by Mick Marchington and Adrian Wilkinson addresses the essential knowledge and understanding required of all personnel and development professionals, whether generalists or specialists. Practitioners need to be aware of the wide range of circumstances in which personnel and development processes take place and consequently the degree to which particular approaches and practices may be appropriate in specific circumstances. In addressing these matters, the book covers the core personnel and development standards of the IPD, as well as providing an essential grounding for human resource management options within business and management studies degrees. The authors are both well-known researchers in the field, working at one of the UK's leading management schools. Professor Marchington is also a chief examiner with the IPD. *Employee Reward* by chief examiner Michael Armstrong has been written specially to provide extensive subject coverage for practitioners required by both the IPD's new generalist standards for employee reward and the personnel N/SVQ Level 4 unit covering employee reward. It is the first book on employee reward to be produced specifically for the purposes of aiding practitioners to gain accredited UK qualifications. *Employee Relations*, by chief examiner Professor John Gennard and associate examiner Graham Judge, explores the link between the corporate environment and the interests of buyers and sellers of labour. It also demonstrates how employers (whether or not they recognise unions) can handle the core issues of bargaining, group problem-solving, redundancy, participation, discipline and grievances, and examines how to evaluate the latest management trends. *Employee Development*, by chief examiner Rosemary Harrison, is a major new text which extends the scope of her immensely popular earlier book of the same name to establish the role of human resource development (HRD) and its direction into the next century. After reviewing the historical roots of HRD, she considers its links with business imperatives, its national and international context, the management of the HRD function, and ways of aligning HRD with the organisation's performance management system. Finally, she provides a framework that sets HRD in the context of organisational learning, the key capabilities of an enterprise and the generation of the new knowledge it needs.

These books, like Stephen Taylor's *Employee Resourcing*, are tailored to the new IPD and N/SVQ standards, whereas Malcolm Martin and Tricia Jackson's *Personnel Practice* is focused on the needs of those studying for the Certificate in Personnel Practice. This also gives a thorough grounding in the basics of personnel activities. The authors are experienced practitioners and lead tutors for one of the UK's main providers of IPD flexible learning programmes.

In drawing upon a team of distinguished and experienced writers and practitioners, the People and Organisations series aims to provide a range of up-to-date, practical texts indispensable to those pursuing IPD and N/SVQ qualifications in personnel and development. The books will also prove valuable to those who are taking other human resource management and employment relations courses, or who are simply seeking greater understanding in their work.

Mick Marchington – Mike Oram

Acknowledgements

We would like to thank the following individuals for their help and assistance with this book: Mike Oram for his encouragement in the early days of this project, and Geoff Hayward, the associate examiner, for his contribution, and especially for the material on Europe (Chapter 3); Richard Goff, who provided invaluable comment and feedback; Debbie Campbell, who put together the final document and also did much of the word-processing. Family and friends also made a huge contribution with their encouragement: John would like to thank Anne for her support, while Graham knows that without Kim the book would never have been finished.

John Gennard
Graham Judge
August 1999

Part 1

INTRODUCTION

THE BOOK'S MAJOR THEMES

There are a number of key themes associated with this book. The major ones are these:

- An IPD qualification is different in perspective from an academic qualification.

- Employee relations are just as relevant in non-union environments as unionised ones.

- The unforeseen impact of changes in the corporate environment on the balance of bargaining power between the employers and employees and on the employee relations policies adopted by an organisation.

- The importance of management behaving in a fair and reasonable and consistent manner.

- The need to evaluate whether new employment practices introduced into one organisation can be successfully transplanted into another.

- The day-to-day grind of intra- and inter-management negotiations.

The IPD Graduate Professional Qualification is not an academic qualification. It indicates to employers that its holders can be reasonably expected to be aware, informed and to understand prevailing trends, topics and management techniques deployed in employee relations and can display an acceptable level of proficiency in terms of operational skills. An IPD qualification indicates the competence of personnel managers to solve people management problems by the application of their acquired knowledge and understanding using appropriate management skills. Knowledge and understanding is essential but limited if managers lack the practical skills to apply it. Holders of an IPD professional qualification should be capable of entering a personnel department and operating without causing mayhem when asked to undertake tasks with little or no supervision.

University degree/diploma qualifications have a different curricular balance between theoretical and vocational needs of students than the IPD graduate professional qualification. University degrees require students to be aware of the plurality of perspectives on issues and themes. IPD professional qualifications are management qualifications and students seeking IPD qualifications should be taught from a management perspective. IPD graduates must be capable of demonstrating an ability to identify, define and explain the significance of employee relations managers possessing specific skills to solve people-management problems. This book is written solely from a professional management perspective and draws on the experience of practising personnel professionals operating in both unionised and non-union environments. It explains why personnel managers require specific skills. It is a 'how to do it' book in which the importance of proceeding on the basis of best practice is to the fore.

But, and this is important, it should not be the only book that you should read. You need to use a range of materials, from the more academic texts through to journals such as *People Management*. It is important to be aware of current trends, ideas and research in the field of personnel management.

It is an acute misunderstanding to believe employee relations is only a relevant management activity if the organisation deals with trade unions. In non-union environments, as in unionised ones, collective relationships exist. In non-union firms there are employee representative bodies (for example, Employee Councils, Works Councils, Joint Consultative Committees) and just as in unionised environments employee grievances have to be resolved, disciplinary matters processed, procedures devised, implemented, operated and monitored. In addition, in non-unionised situations, as well as unionised ones, the support and loyalty of one's management colleagues, at all levels of seniority, has to be gained by using, amongst other things, negotiating, interviewing and communication skills. Employee relations knowledge, understanding and skills acquisition are just as relevant to non-union environments as unionised environments.

As we shall explain, an important employee relations concept is the relative balance of bargaining power between the buyers and sellers of labour services and that important determinants of this relationship are external to the organisation, for example, government economic and legislative policies. One result of this is that the key employee relations policies and practices can be rendered irrelevant, illegal or more expensive to operate because of legislative intervention, for example, the changes in representational rights in grievance and disciplinary procedures or the new statutory recognition procedures contained in the Employment Relations Act 1999. The professional personnel manager has to be capable of offering advice as to how their organisation might deal with such situations that stem from decision-making sources over which companies have no direct control. This book is designed to help in this regard.

Changes in the corporate environment influencing the balance of bargaining power help explain changes over time (for example, the 1990s relative to the 1970s) in the employee relations behaviour of employees and employers in terms of processes used, the subject of rules, regulations and agreements and their authorship. In the 1970s when the corporate environment was very different from today, trade unions grew steadily, strike action was more frequent and higher wage increases were gained by employees from their employers. In today's corporate environment trade union membership has fallen, strike action has fallen, employers are able to decide unilaterally on the rules and regulations governing employment and, courtesy of low inflation, wage increases are much smaller. Personnel managers/professionals require an understanding of the impact of changes in the corporate environment on management employee relations strategy, policies and agreements in order to predict the impact of possible external changes on the organisation's employee relations and how they might seek to mitigate it.

In conducting their employee relations activities, professional managers should behave in a fair and reasonable manner and seek to persuade their management colleagues to behave in a like manner. This means acting with just cause (for example, having a genuine reason to dismiss a worker or for selecting an employee for redundancy) and behaving in procedural terms via a series of stages where behaviour is compatible with the standards of natural justice, for example, a statement of the complaint against the individual is given, a proper investigation is carried out, the accused is given the opportunity to cross-examine witnesses, there is sufficient time made available for the accused to prepare their defence, an appeals procedure exists and different individuals are involved at the different stages in the operation of the procedure.

It is important personnel managers appreciate that the underlying principle of employee relations procedures is that they establish standards of behaviour which will pass the tests of reasonableness. However, personnel managers must not only appreciate what constitutes fair and reasonable behaviour but why such best practice is essential to protecting and advancing management's interests, namely the avoidance of adverse financial consequences through the payment of compensation to individuals wronged by such action and damaging the organisation's labour market image in the eyes of the sellers of labour services. As we have already indicated, managers by behaving in a fair and reasonable manner (best practice) help to add value to the business. This is a key theme of the book.

Change and innovation in employee relations policies and practices to gain a competitive advantage or to deliver a service at a higher quality is essential in a modern competitive economy. New and developing management practices (for example, performance-related pay, single-union no-strike agreements) of the 1980s have been successfully introduced into organisations. However, personnel managers cannot assume that such practices can automatically be transferred successfully to their own organisation which may be operating in very different environments. They need to be able to evaluate whether practices introduced in one organisation can be successfully transplanted into their own. Organisations cannot change policies and practices constantly without any reference to organisational needs or existing practices. A further assumption of this book is that 'new initiatives' in management practice have to be evaluated in a rational manner as to whether they can be introduced with equal success into another organisation.

A further theme of this book is the importance of personnel managers understanding why negotiating skills are necessary for the effective solution of people-management problems. They need to be able to identify the different negotiating situations (grievance handling, bargaining, group problem solving) in which managers may find themselves, appreciate the different stages through which a negotiation proceeds and the skills required in different negotiation situations.

THE INFLUENTIAL MANAGER

If personnel/HRM managers, at any level of seniority, are to be pro-active and to have influence in an organisation, then they must demonstrate certain abilities (see Figure 1). First, they require a successful record of professional competence in the personnel/HRM field which is recognised by their managerial colleagues both within and outside the personnel function. Second, they must demonstrate an understanding of the personnel/HRM function as a whole and how its separate components integrate. Third, they must understand the interests of the business/organisation as a whole and that these take preference over those of any management function as a whole or their component parts. Fourth, they need to develop a network of contacts with managers, both within and outside the personnel/HRM function, in their own organisation and with managers in other organisations, including employers' associations and professional bodies such as the Institute of Personnel and Development (IPD) and the British Institute of Management (BIM). Fifth, they should build fruitful relationships with their superiors and possess excellent interpersonal skills, particularly with respect to communications and team-building. Each of these five abilities is a necessary condition for an effective and influential personnel/HRM manager, but each is insufficient on its own.

All people-managers, regardless of their seniority (personnel assistant, officer, manager, executive, etc), need to understand the nature of the business of the organisation in which they manage in terms of its mission, objectives, strategies and policies. In the private sector the effective and influential personnel/HRM manager will understand the 'bottom line' for the business and be able to contribute constructively, at the appropriate level of decision-making (department, section, management team, working party etc), to discussions on how the business might be developed and expanded. In the public sector the effective and influential personnel/HRM manager will understand

Figure 1 Necessary conditions for an effective and influential personnel manager

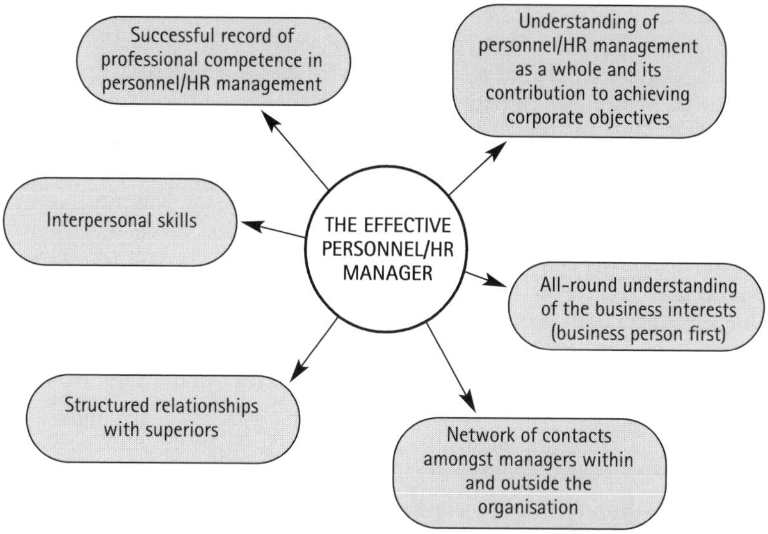

```
┌─────────────────────┐              ┌──────────────────────┐
│  Successful record of│              │  Understanding of    │
│  professional competence in│       │  personnel/HR management│
│  personnel/HR management│          │  as a whole and its  │
└─────────────────────┘              │  contribution to achieving│
                                     │  corporate objectives│
                                     └──────────────────────┘

┌──────────────────┐      ╭──────────────╮
│ Interpersonal skills│    │ THE EFFECTIVE│    ┌──────────────────────┐
└──────────────────┘      │ PERSONNEL/HR │    │ All-round understanding│
                          │   MANAGER    │    │ of the business interests│
                          ╰──────────────╯    │ (business person first)│
                                              └──────────────────────┘

┌──────────────────────┐         ┌──────────────────────┐
│ Structured relationships│       │ Network of contacts  │
│ with superiors       │         │ amongst managers within│
└──────────────────────┘         │ and outside the      │
                                 │ organisation         │
                                 └──────────────────────┘
```

the objectives of efficiency, effectiveness, economy, 'value for money' and the quality of service-delivery to the customer or client.

The effective personnel/HRM manager understands how the people-management function contributes to the achievement of the organisation's commercial or social objectives, or both. They are capable of explaining to other managers, particularly outside personnel/HRM, how the function's strategies and policies help the business to develop and grow, 'add value' to the business as a whole and help provide a higher quality of service to the customer or client. In a nutshell, the personnel/HRM manager can explain to the other managers how the activities of the personnel/HRM function match with the objectives of the organisation as a whole. This is vertical integration of a management function with the overall business objectives.

In addition, the effective personnel/HRM manager can explain how the various components of people management – resourcing, development, reward and relations – contribute to the achievement of the objectives of the personnel/HRM function. This involves their understanding fully how the strategies and policies of the components of the personnel function link together to achieve the goals of the function. This horizontal integration of the personnel/HRM function will not be new to you, because it was a central theme in your core personnel and development studies. It is important during your employee relations studies that you understand vertical and horizontal integration.

The effective personnel/HRM manager in a management team has a proven competence recognised by their management colleagues in employee relations as well as employee resourcing, training and development, and pay and reward. It is essential, therefore, if personnel managers are to be effective, that they have an adequate knowledge and understanding of employee relations and have acquired the appropriate skills to apply that knowledge and understanding to solve employee relations problems in order to enable the organisation to achieve its commercial or social objectives, or both. An implication of this statement is that not only existing, and prospective, personnel managers need to acquire employee relations knowledge, understanding and skills, but so do all managers, regardless of their seniority or specialism.

The personnel/HRM manager who lacks professional competence in employee relations will be a less effective manager. The trend in many organisations to devolve their personnel/HRM function across management teams reinforces this view. Devolution often means that the services of a personnel manager with a specialism will not always be required. However, the activities of the employee relations function (for example, communications policy, handling employee grievances, dealing with disciplinary matters and the adjustment of the size of the workforce) nevertheless must be delivered to the management team. Generalist personnel managers with employee relations skills are essential to any management team. Specialist personnel managers are less attractive to a management team.

This book therefore aims to provide the generalist personnel/HRM manager, and any other managers who have to manage people, with the appropriate employee relations knowledge, and to provide them with the understanding and skills they require to apply that knowledge and understanding to solving people-management problems. This in turn will contribute to the organisation achieving its commercial and/or social objectives. It will have the additional advantage of enhancing the creditability of the personnel/HRM manager in the eyes of their managerial colleagues both within and outside the personnel/HRM function.

A central theme of the book is that 'best practice' in the delivery of the personnel/HRM strategy and policies adds value to the business and thereby contributes to the achievement of the corporate-organisational economic and social objectives. It explains not only what constitutes the best practice (that this is acting with just cause and behaving fairly and reasonably) but why operating to best-practice standards is sound business practice, for example avoidance of falling foul of employment tribunal decisions in terms of having 'bad' practices exposed and thus embarrassing the organisation. The book also aims to help personnel managers/professionals develop and acquire skills, not only to solve people-management problems, but also to develop and improve their interpersonal skills and thereby the quality of their relationships with superiors.

If personnel managers are to be effective and influential, they require to be 'generalist' personnel managers. Generalist personnel managers require an adequate knowledge, understanding and skills of employee relations. If they neglect these and concentrate exclusively on development, resourcing and reward they will be less effective managers.

EMPLOYEE RELATIONS ACTIVITIES

The purpose of employee relations activity is to reconcile the different interests of the buyers of labour services (employers) and the sellers of labour services (employees) and in so doing assist the organisation achieve its business and/or social objectives. This difference of interests revolves around the 'price' (including the quality and quantity) at which labour services will be bought and sold. Although there is this difference of interests, both management and employees have a common interest in reconciling these differences. The alternative is mutual destruction of the organisation. The closure of the enterprise is of no benefit to employers or employees. There is mutual advantage to both employers and employees in resolving their differences as buyers and sellers of labour market services. They accommodate their respective interests by making agreements, rules and regulations by the use of various employee relations processes – employee involvement, collective bargaining, unilateral imposition by management, joint consultation, arbitration, mediation and conciliation and Parliamentary legislation.

The agreements, rules and regulations express the price at which labour services will be bought and sold and are made at different levels (workplace, company, industry) and have different degrees of authorship. Some are written solely (imposed) by the employer with little or no influence from the employees whilst others, usually as a result of collective bargaining, are jointly authored by the employer and representatives of their employees. Agreements, rules and regulations cover two broad ranges of issues. One is substantive issues (pay, holidays, hours of work, incentive schemes, pensions, sick pay, maternity leave, family-friendly policies, etc) whilst the other is procedural issues. Employee relations procedures provide fair and reasonable standards of behaviour to resolve in a peaceful manner issues over which employers and employees have differences. Such procedures normally cover issues such as employee complaints against the behaviour of employers (known as grievances), employer complaints about the behaviour of employees (referred to as disciplinary matters), the need to reduce the size of the workforce (redundancy), employee claims that the responsibilities of their job have increased (job grading) and employee requests for union representation (union recognition procedures).

The content of agreements, rules and regulations and the employee relations processes used to secure them reflect the relative balance of bargaining power between employers and employees. This balance is heavily influenced by changes in the corporate environment in which an organisation undertakes its employee relations activity. The major facts of shaping the external corporate environment are the economic and legal policies of national governments and European Union political decision-making institutions. In an attempt to enhance their economic interests, both employers and employees, via representative organisations, spend relatively large sums of money on the political lobbying process to persuade the government to introduce appropriate economic and legal policies. A further factor in the external corporate environment influencing employee relations is the implementation, by employers, of technological change.

The balance of bargaining power is a central concept that needs to be understood by employee relations managers. It helps explain the constraints in which managements can exercise their power. Abuse of power to obtain one's aims is not professional behaviour. It will inevitably lead to pressure for legal restraints to be imposed to curb the abuse. Unprofessional behaviour in the sense that 'might is right' will result in employees behaving in that way when the balance of bargaining power shifts away from management towards the employees. Professionalism means tackling matters in a systematic and careful manner. The fact that the state of the balance of bargaining power means that management can 'succeed' without behaving in this way is no excuse for managers not to behave in a professional way. Best practice dictates they behave in a professional manner gaining consent by discussion, consultation, negotiation and involvement, not the crude exercise of power.

However, personnel managers/professionals require more than just knowledge and understanding of employee relations parties, processes, agreements, rules and regulations and the external environment in which these activities take place if they are to solve effectively people-management problems. Employee relations problem-solving also requires the development and application of certain skills of which the most significant are communication (oral and written), interviewing, listening, negotiating, evaluating and analysis.

This book therefore widens and develops the employee relations knowledge and understanding you acquired in your core personnel and development studies. It provides sufficient knowledge, understanding and skills for personnel managers and those who manage people in other management functions, to operate as professional people-managers in a number of different situations, including both union and non-union environments. The book also aims to introduce you to the importance of personnel managers/professionals, becoming effective and influential in the organisation by understanding the concepts of best practice and the balance of bargaining power and acquiring and developing the general management skills referred to above.

THE BOOK AND THE IPD STANDARDS

The Indicative Content of the Professional Qualification Scheme covers five areas – employee relations management in context; the parties in employee relations; employee relations processes; employee relations outcomes and employee relations skills.

The employee relations management in context section covers the corporate environment in which organisations undertake their internal employee relations activities. A growing and important part of this external environment is the evolution of the 'social' dimension (Social Chapter, Social Charter) of the European Union. This section of the syllabus also covers the role of the national government as an economic manager and as a law-maker as well as 'state agencies' such as the Advisory Conciliation and Arbitration Service (ACAS) and the Employment Tribunal system. The employee relations management in context part of these standards is covered by Chapter 1 (Employee

Relations: An Overview), Chapter 2 (the Corporate Environment) and Chapter 3 (The European Union).

The parties in the employee relations section of the standards deals with management objectives and styles, employee relations strategies, gaining employee commitment and participation, and managing with or without unions. It also covers the changing role and functions of employers' associations (such as the Confederation of British Industry (CBI) and the Engineering Employers' Federation) and management associations organised at the level of the European Union. The parties section of the syllabus, which covers employee organisations (trade unions, professional associations, staff/employee associations, etc), is dealt with in Chapter 4 (Employee Relations' Institutions). Chapter 5 looks at management strategy and policies together with issues such as management style and the management of change.

There is a wide range of employee relations processes which impact on employment relationships in organisations: joint consultation, employee involvement schemes, third party intervention (arbitration and conciliation), collective bargaining, industrial sanctions (lock-outs, suspension, collective dismissals) and parliamentary legislation. This part of the syllabus is covered by Chapters 4, 5 and 6.

The outcomes component of the syllabus covers the various dimensions of agreements (both collective and individual), their types (substantive and procedural), their authorship (joint or singly by employer), the levels at which they are concluded and their scope (subjects covered by agreements, rules and regulations). This section of the standards is dealt with in Chapter 4.

The employee relations skills section of the standards covers the definition of negotiations, the different types of negotiating situations and the various stages involved in the negotiating process. It also covers the skills required by managers in preparing for and conducting bargaining, in presenting claims/offers and counteroffers, in searching for the common ground, in concluding the negotiations and in writing up the agreement.

The standards also cover the skills required by a manager (or management team) in handling employee complaints against management behaviour (commonly referred to as grievances), in handling disciplinary proceedings and in managing a redundancy situation. It also covers management skills and knowledge and understanding required in devising, reviewing and monitoring procedural arrangements.

Chapter 7 deals with negotiation in general terms (that is, its definition, its different types and its component stages) whilst Chapter 8 deals with handling disciplinary proceedings, including the importance of management behaving in a fair and reasonable manner (good practice), and with the preparation of evidence to defend management's behaviour before an Employment Tribunal. Chapter 9 covers grievance handling whilst Chapter 10 deals with bargaining collectively with the workforce. Both these chapters stress the skills required of management in the preparation stages, of grievance handling and bargaining and in particular identifying the common ground with the other party via the use of techniques like 'if and then' and the 'Aspiration Grid'.

Chapter 11 centres on managing redundancy situations and the devising, reviewing and monitoring of redundancy procedures.

Chapter 12, the concluding chapter, offers help and advice to students in preparing for the Professional Qualification Scheme employee relations examination. Some specimen case studies and questions are discussed.

We hope you enjoy reading this book. If you can acquire and develop a deep understanding and appreciation of its contents you have an excellent chance of gaining an IPD professional qualification.

Part 2

EMPLOYEE RELATIONS: AN OVERVIEW

1 Employee relations: an overview

Some people view employee relations as being about trade union behaviour, collective bargaining, industrial disputes and UK Government–trade union relationships. Trade unions are seen as workplace adversaries negotiating with employers and also as social partners expressing an 'employee view' on economic and social matters, particularly through the Trades Union Congress, to governments. Although the extent to which this 'employers propose/unions oppose' approach squares with reality can be questioned, there is no doubt the perspective is seen of lesser relevance to today's employment relationship. The institutions of trade unions, collective bargaining procedures and arrangements, strikes and tripartism have declined steadily over the last two decades. Indeed, the 1998 Workplace Employee Relations Survey reported that 47 per cent of workplaces have no union members at all.

There is no doubt that attitudes to work and relationships at work have changed since the late 1970s. The driving forces for this have been increased competition, rapidly changing technologies and customer demands for the highest quality of service or product at the lowest price available. In this changed environment of the last 20 years relative to the previous 20, many employers now view employee relations as having a greater focus on the individual employee rather than on the employees as a collective body and on partnership between employees and employers. Such partnership is seen as based on:

- the success of the enterprise

- building trust and greater employee involvement

- recognising the legitimate role of the partners.

These changing attitudes are reflected in the management-led changes in communication methods (for example, team-briefing), in work organisation (quality circles, teamworking and single status), changes in payment systems (for example, performance-related pay), employees' representative systems (business-focused consultation arrangements), recognition of the employees' need for employment security (training and development of employees) and attitudes towards trade union recognition. Employee relations is a study of managing employees both as individuals and as a collective group with the priority given to the individual as opposed to the collective relationship varying between companies depending on the values of their management.

An IPD Position Paper (1997) advocates an employee relations system built on higher skills, better skill utilisation, greater co-operation within the workplace and the use of initiatives to develop higher added value through differentiated goods and services. In this model of employee relations, organisations succeed by:

• raising the skills of their employees

• the provision of high quality services and products

• excellent customer service.

These result in high profits, high earnings and a relatively more secure future for employees. In practical terms, the model embraces effective performance, good people-management practices, a knowledge and understanding of employees' aspirations and attention to the 'employee voice' obtained through a variety of channels (for example, employee involvement and participation and trade union representatives).

Employee relations systems' components
Employee relations systems in any organisation will have a number of components. These are shown in Figure 2. First, there is that of the 'players' in employee relations activities. The principal 'players' are:

• individual employers

• individual employees

• employee representative bodies (staff associations, trade unions, works councils, etc)

• employers' associations

• private companies

• public bodies

• voluntary organisations (for example, Save the Children Fund).

These 'players' operate in a labour market in which they attempt to protect and advance their respective economic interests relative to each other. Although sellers (employees) in the labour market have different interests from buyers (employers), both have a common interest in finding a buyer and a seller. Both employees and employers have a common interest in the survival of the employing enterprise even though they may differ over how any surplus generated by the sales of its products or services should be divided amongst themselves. They have mutual interest in resolving this problem because not to do so will

Figure 2 **Employee relations: reconciliation of interests**

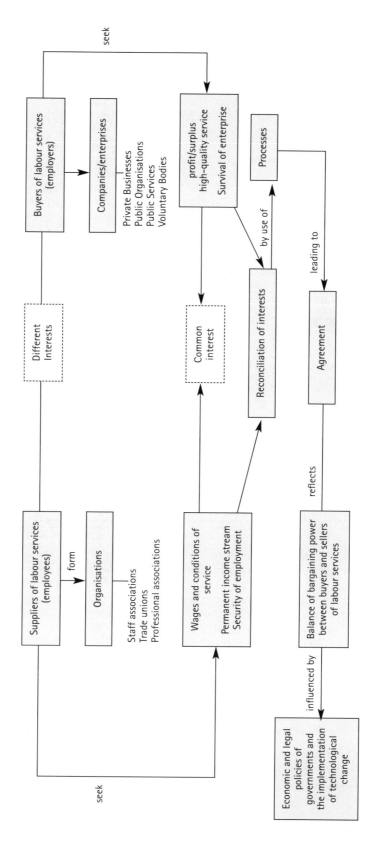

result in mutual destruction. An analysis of the interests of the players in an employee relations system is thus a central concern of employee relations.

The employee relations 'players' also have expectations as to how each will behave towards the other. This is referred to as the 'psychological contract' which has been described by Schein (1978) as a 'set of unwritten, reciprocal expectations between an individual employee and the organisation'. It is based on the assumption that, in addition to the formal employment contract, employees develop a set of informal unwritten assumptions and expectations from their employing organisation. These may concern a range of issues such as job security, career progression, workloads and fair treatment by the employer. It is a concept that enables conclusions to be drawn about the state (quality) of the employment relationship in the UK (IPD, 1998).

Secondly, there are mechanisms available to the buyers and sellers of labour services to accommodate their different economic interests. These mechanisms include:

- consultation

- employee involvement

- communication processes

- collective bargaining

- legal regulation by the UK Parliament and the European Union.

The third component is the agreements, rules and regulations governing the employment relationship for an individual and/or group of employees which result from the use of these mechanisms. These agreements are also a statement of the rights, responsibilities and obligations employers and employees have towards each other.

The external environment
The selling and buying of labour services also takes place in the context of an external environment. The UK Government, through its economic and legislative policies, and increasingly the European Union through its legal instruments, set minimum standards of behaviour for the buyers and sellers of labour services. Employment legislation sets out the redress one party can seek from the other if they step outside these standards of behaviour. The UK Government's economic and legal policies influence, at the macro level, the relative bargaining power between the buyers and sellers of labour services which influences the choice of employee relations mechanisms used as well as the outcomes from their use. If UK government economic and legal policies are more favourable to the interests of employees (for example, by pursuit of full employment policies) then this will be reflected in the content of the 'agreements' rules, and regulations governing the employment relationship.

The mechanism used and the output of an employee relations system in any organisation are also influenced by the balance of bargaining power at the sector and enterprise level. This involves the employee relations specialist analysing variables such as the strategic position workers hold in the production or service provision process and the availability of an alternative workforce to the one currently employed. If a group of workers who have the power to stop an organisation's activities are willing to exercise that power, and have exercised it successfully in the past, then they will have relatively greater bargaining power than their employer and will be able to obtain a 'price' for their labour services which is closer to their ideal economic objectives than to those of the employer. This concept of the relative bargaining power between the buyers and sellers of labour services is the fourth component of any employee relations systems in any organisation.

This chapter introduces you to the components of any employee relations system in any organisation, namely:

- the different, and common, interests of employers (the purchasers of labour services) and employees (the suppliers of labour services) in the labour market

- the mechanisms (processes) available to employers and employees to accommodate their differing interests

- the terms (the 'price') of that reconciliation as expressed in 'agreements', rules and regulations

- the relative balance of bargaining power between employers and employees.

So by the end of this chapter, you will understand the components of an employee relations system.

EMPLOYERS' INTERESTS IN THE LABOUR MARKET

The rationale for employee relations is to solve the problem that in a labour market the buyers (employers) and sellers (employees) have an endemic conflict of interests over the 'prices' at which they wish to exchange their services. Employee relations is a management problem-solving activity designed to reconcile the problem of the 'price' at which they will purchase labour services. The word 'price' is in inverted commas because employers seek to secure labour services on the most advantageous terms they can through offering a package of employment conditions which contain monetary (pay, paid holidays, etc) and non-monetary (opportunities for career development, good work colleagues) advantage and disadvantage aspects.

The employer's employment package
The monetary considerations taken into account by an employer in purchasing labour services include:

- pay

- hours of work

- paid holidays

- sick pay schemes

- incentive schemes

- pension arrangements

• provision of family friendly policies such as childcare facilities.

In return for provision of these items, employers expect their employees to provide, depending on the skill and status of the job:

• flexibility between tasks (functional flexibility)

• minimum standards of competency in the task for which they are being hired as expressed in qualifications, training received and the employee's experience

• a willingness to change (aptitude and adaptability)

• an ability to work as a member of a team

• a capability to show initiative

• a talent to give discretionary effort

• a demonstrable commitment to the organisation's objectives.

In recruiting labour services, the employer trades off items in a package of conditions. A management, for example, which would like to hire and fire labour services at will (numerical flexibility) may be willing to offer potential employees, depending on the state of the labour market, a higher financial reward to compensate for the lower job security. However, if jobs are scarce to come by, an employer may not have to make such a trade-off. Employers who prefer to deploy any labour services they purchase, thereby requiring flexibility between various tasks, are likely to offer a higher package of financial rewards to attract employees who can adapt relatively easily to change.

If an employer wishes to purchase high quality labour services in terms of skills, attitude, etc then they will offer a package of financial rewards which is more advantageous than those offered by employers who are happy to purchase lower quality labour services. In every sector of the economy there will be those employers who are prepared to invest in better employment conditions than their competitors. The argument is that the higher financial rewards to the employees are offset by the increased productivity, lower labour turnover, greater motivation, etc resulting from purchasing higher quality labour services.

In purchasing labour services, the employer cannot ignore the longer-term interests of the organisation. Although employers may like to hire and fire employees at will, they nevertheless require a core of permanent employees to provide continuity and some stability if they are to survive in the marketplace. The size of this core workforce, in relation to those hired and fired at will, is a matter for commercial judgement by the organisation.

The package offered and accepted by the suppliers of labour services may be minimal, consisting of low wages, long hours, few opportunities to acquire and develop skills and little employment security. The suppliers of labour services may be prepared to accept such a package because the alternative is unemployment. However, suppliers of labour services working under such an employment package are likely to have low morale, perform at standards below their capabilities and feel no commitment or loyalty to the purchaser of their labour services. Low morale and low commitment have adverse consequences for an organisation's economic performance and/or the quality of service offered to customers. In the long run, the employment of 'poor' quality labour services will increase the organisation's costs, reduce its competitiveness in the product market and put at risk its very survival.

In purchasing labour services, the package of conditions the buyers will have to offer is influenced by the relative balance of bargaining power between the buyers and sellers. If the relative bargaining power favours the buyers then they will purchase labour services for a lesser package of conditions than if the power relationship were reversed. Should, however, the buyers of labour services abuse this market power by offering unacceptably low wages and conditions, then pressures will develop for the State to restrain – by legal regulation – the use of such power. It was such behaviour, admittedly on behalf of a small number of employers, that led to the imposition by UK Government, from 1 April 1999, of a national minimum wage which must be paid to all those in paid employment who are aged over 21. So in offering a package of conditions to employees employers should have regard to longer-term considerations and not merely to what can 'be got away with' in the short term.

Employee interests in the labour market
In the labour market, the sellers of labour services seek from employers (buyers) the best possible available package of monetary and non-monetary employment conditions. The monetary aspects include wage/salary rates, hours of work, paid holidays, pension schemes, sick pay arrangements, incentive schemes and childcare facilities. The non-monetary elements will involve items such as:

- employment security

- the opportunity to work with good colleagues in a social atmosphere

- the potential for advancement and promotion

- access to training and development opportunities to upgrade skills, acquire new skills, etc

- being treated as a human being not merely as a commodity

- job satisfaction in relation to job design, degree of control over the job (empowerment)

- family friendly employment policies (eg childcare facilities) which enable a balance to be achieved between being a family person and the need to take paid employment to provide for that family

- fair and consistent treatment by managers relative to other employees

- influence on day-to-day operations at the workplace and policy level.

Like the buyers of labour services, the sellers also give different weight to the items in the 'package' of employment conditions on offer. They may, for example, be prepared to work for 'lower' wages if this is compensated by greater employment security. Some employees may, for example, stay with an organisation that pays below the market rates because it practises employment involvement and empowerment by vesting decision-making with the frontline or promotes self-managing teams.

It is impossible to predict the 'standard mix' of benefits sought from employment by employees. Motivation theory postulates that each individual is stimulated by his or her own package and that as their economic and social conditions change, the pressures on employees alter with them. The balance between the various items in the package depends on many factors, including age, family circumstances, local and industry-specific employment conditions and the national scene. Nevertheless, employees, like any seller in a marketplace, seek the best possible package of monetary and non-monetary employment conditions.

> What is your monetary and non-monetary package of employment conditions? Which are the most important to you, and why?

THE EMPLOYMENT RELATIONSHIP

The employment relationship has some similarities with all transactions. A 'golden rule' of buying is to purchase goods or services of acceptable quality, at the lowest price obtainable. A seller wishes to sell at the highest possible price. To reach agreement they need to accommodate each other's interests and establish an appropriate price.

However, the employment relationship is more stable and longer term than that between the buyer and seller of a commodity such as a house or piece of equipment or furniture. In these activities, the buyers and sellers engage in a one-off and immediate exchange relationship. The parties involved in the labour market, on the other hand, are entering what is expected to be a long-term relationship with terms they review periodically and amend if appropriate. In short, a particular feature of the employment relationship is that it has a future.

DIFFERENT INTERESTS WITHIN MANAGEMENT

There are differences of interest within management at all levels of an organisation, including the workplace. Although working to a common end, management is not a united whole. Managers have differences which, like those between the buyers and sellers of labour services, have to be reconciled if corporate objectives are to be achieved.

In larger organisations, common management activities are divided into different functions, for example, marketing, production operations, personnel and finance. These management interest groups have a common interest in the survival and growth of the business but often have different and competing interests at the same time. While the common aim is to ensure the products or services reach the market place at the right time, at the right place and at the right quality, internal power struggles (management politics with a small 'p') and competition for shares of a finite budget often play off one management interest against another.

The main aim of production operations management is usually the achievement of production targets and to this end they may consider the organisation's best interests are served by employment policies which permit freely the hire and fire of labour and the granting of employee demands to prevent production service disruptions. This approach conflicts with that of people managers who see the organisation's interests best served by employees being recruited, selected and dismissed in accordance with good personnel practices and being rewarded on objective criteria rather than the expedient consideration to meet market demand at all costs.

Differences between interest groups within management are resolved by negotiation between themselves or by arbitration by a more senior manager. By use of argument and by making constructive compromises, managers seek to gain the commitment of their managerial colleagues to their proposed course of action. Should managers at the same level of seniority be unable to settle their differences by negotiation then a senior manager will arbitrate and decide the appropriate course of action to be adopted.

Employee relations managers cannot take it for granted that what is proposed by them will not be opposed by other managers. However, differences between managers have to be reconciled in a constructive, not a destructive, manner. Most management differences over how to solve problems are resolved quickly. As an employee relations specialist, you will find yourself frequently negotiating with your management colleagues (at the same, lower or higher level of seniority) to resolve differences over what constitute the 'best' employee relations policies and practices to be implemented if the organisation is to achieve its objectives.

> When did you last have a difference with a colleague over how a problem should be resolved? What was the problem about? What were the differences between you? What was the resolution of the difference? Why was there a difference in the first place?

Different interests within employees
Just as there is a plurality of interests within and between groups of managers, so there is with groups of employees. In a workplace, different types of employees (technical, clerical, administrative, craft manual, semi-skilled and unskilled, etc) are employed and have different interests from each other. Non-manual employees usually expect a positive employment conditions differential over manual workers. Craft manual workers see their interests, relative to those of less skilled workers, best served by pay differentials expressed in percentage terms. If this percentage figure is reduced then craft workers usually demand improvements in pay and conditions to re-establish accepted percentage differentials.

Less skilled manual workers (who also tend to be low paid) view their interests relative to craft manual workers are best served by pay differentials expressed in money terms. They oppose percentage increases in pay on the grounds that such increases widen monetary differentials. To date, these differences between different groups of employees continue. They are particularly acute in the public sector. In 1999 school teachers expressed fierce opposition to the Government's proposal to make teaching a more attractive profession by the creation of a more highly paid 'super teacher'. Differences of interests between different groups of employees often make it difficult for them to support each other in differences with employers.

Recognition of different interests

Employee relations aims to resolve differences between the various interest groups regardless of whether these groups are different categories of managers or employees. The bottom line is that the activity of the organisation has to continue and the behaviour to make this happen alters, depending on the current situation and the underlying climate of employee relations. In organisations, whether non-union or unionised, where the emphasis is on problem-solving, consultation and communications procedures these differences of interests between employers and employees are formally recognised in written statements of policy and procedures or in collective agreements with trade unions, or both. For example, Clauses 2.3 and 2.4 (General Principles) of a Recognition Procedural Agreement between Kingsmead Carpets Ltd, Cumnock and the Scottish Carpet Workers Union signed in 1997 state:

> 2.3 The union recognise management's responsibility to plan, organise and manage the company's operation.
>
> 2.4 The company recognises the union's responsibility to represent the interests of their members and to maintain or improve their terms and conditions of employment and work within the constraints imposed on the plant by corporate policy and finance.

Another example can be drawn from a Recognition and Procedural Agreement between a food manufacturer and the Amalgamated Engineering and Electrical Union signed in 1995, which states in its preamble:

> The company recognises the union as the sole collective bargaining agent in respect of the categories of employees coming within the scope of this agreement.
>
> The union recognises management's responsibility to manage its establishments and accepts that the company must continue with new and improved methods of work and that the company must be able to make free and intelligent use of its labour force to achieve the highest quality of service and obtain maximum efficiency.

Yet another example of the recognition of the difference of interests between employers and employees is seen in the recognition agreement between Volex Powercords and the Transport and General Workers Union which contains the following:

3 General Principles

(a) the company has the right to manage the business and direct its affairs and workforce in the efficient pursuit of the organisation's business

(b) the company recognises the union's responsibility to manage its affairs and to represent the interests of its members

(c) both parties agree the need to maintain open and direct communications with all employees on matters of mutual interest and concern.

The aim of employee relations is to resolve areas of conflicting interests and to identify and pursue areas of common interest so as to maintain the business organisation. We now turn to these common interests.

EMPLOYER-EMPLOYEE COMMON INTERESTS

Unless the organisation keeps running, there is nothing to manage, no profit to be made, no service to provide and no pay for work done. Although, as buyers and sellers of labour services, employers and employees have different interests, they have a common interest in ensuring their different interests are reconciled. There are strong economic pressures on employers and employees to accommodate each other's interests rather than to perpetuate their differences.

Costs to employers
If employers fail to reconcile their different interests with their employees then a number of costs arise:

• The employer has no goods/services to sell in the market place.

• The employer cannot earn profit or provide services at value for money.

• Goods and services cannot be supplied to the market place at the right price, at the right time and at the right quality.

• Customer needs cannot be satisfied.

• Plants, offices and shops lie idle or close down.

• Customers take their business to competitor firms.

Costs to employees
The consequences for employees who fail to resolve their different interests from employers are equally obvious:

• They do not gain employment.

• They do not receive a steady income stream.

• They have no power as consumers.

• They cannot enter into long-term financial commitments (eg mortgages, bank loans, hire purchase contracts).

• They accumulate no employment benefits based on continuity of employment (eg paid holidays and sick pay entitlement).

• There is no certainty as to their future level of income.

If employees gain no income from employment they become dependent on the State for a minimum level of income to satisfy their basic needs of housing, heating, lighting, food, etc.

Recognition of common interests

Both employers and employees have an enlightened self-interest in ensuring their differing interests are reconciled. Enlightened self-interest also helps produce a bottom line, beyond which it is not worth pushing for one's own self-interest against the efforts of the other party. Interest reconciliation brings mutual gain. Employers secure the survival of their enterprises, gain profit or provide services at value for money, and satisfy the needs of their customers. Employees obtain job security, income security, consumer power and status from being employed. Both employers and employees have a common interest in ensuring companies and enterprises are successful. However, there are occasions when this common interest might not seem very common to employees, especially when told by management they are to be made redundant as cost cuts are required to re-establish the viability of the enterprise.

The recognition of this common interest is so important that it is normally formally stated in agreements between employers and employees. For example, the 1998 National Agreement between the Scottish Print Employers Federation and the Graphical, Paper and Media Union says:

> 2. Unit Cost and Competitiveness
>
> The parties recognise that the whole basis of the market for printed products is changing rapidly, posing new challenges for everyone engaged in the industry. It is of fundamental importance that those challenges are met with a positive response from employers and employees in order to secure the future of Scottish printing in the face of intensifying domestic and international competition. The parties willingly accept the need for companies to attain the highest standards in meeting customers' requirements, in particular the need for continuous improvement in increasing efficiency at reducing unit costs.
>
> It is therefore agreed that at individual company level, management and chapel representatives will co-operate fully in identifying, discussing and implementing any changes necessary to achieve increased output and lower unit costs through the most effective use of people, materials and machines.
>
> It is further agreed that where practical, managements and chapels will agree and implement efficiency and productivity measures sufficient to offset in full additional costs arising from the national wages and conditions settlement. Such measures can be wide ranging in scope.
>
> No person will be made redundant as a direct result of implementing this clause.

Similarly, the Constitution and Memorandum of Agreement between the Transport and General Workers Union and the Road Haulage Association Ltd for the Road Haulage Industry (Hire and Reward) contains the following paragraph:

> Objects and Functions:
>
> 3. The objects of the Council should be to promote joint action for their mutual benefit by organisations of employers and working people.

Clauses 6.2 and 6.3 of Section 6 entitled 'Competitive Advantage' of the Pay and Conditions agreement between Scottish Power, Power Systems, Scotland and the Amalgamated Engineering and Electrical

Union, GMB, the Transport and General Workers and UNISON state:

> 6.2 A key part of the competitive advantage strategy will be continuous improvement in all Power Systems activities to ensure that changing business demands can be rapidly met and best working practices, identified through benchmarking and other means, are safely implemented within the normal joint processes so that competitive advantage can be developed and maintained.

> 6.3 The Division and the Trade Unions agree that to achieve and maintain competitive advantage, continuous improvement and the changes which will result will be implemented on an ongoing basis, subject to the normal joint processes.

The common interest between employers and employees to reconcile their different interests to mutual advantage was stressed in the Trade Union Congress document, *Partners for Progress: Next Steps for the New Unionism*, in the following paragraph:

> 3. The theme of this statement is partnership, a recognition that trade unions must not be seen as part of Britain's problems but as part of the solution to the country's problems. At the workplace, social partnership means employers and trade unions working together to achieve common goals such as fairness and competitiveness; it is a recognition that, although they have different constituencies, and at times different interests, they can serve these best by making common cause wherever possible. At the national level, partnership means government discussing issues with employers and trade unions on a fair and open basis where a common approach can reap dividends, for example, attracting inward investment and promoting training and equal opportunities.

One of the methods by which the different labour market interests of employers and employees are accommodated is by negotiation, which involves two parties (employers and employees) coming together to make an accommodation (agreement) by purposeful persuasion (the use of rational argument) and by making constructive compromises (identifying the common ground for a basis for agreement) towards each other's position. There are different types of negotiating situations (see Chapters 7 and 9) but the most common involving employers and employees are:

- grievance handing to resolve a complaint by an employee against management behaviour

- bargaining during which employers and employees 'trade' items within a list of demands they have made of each other

- group problem-solving in which the employer settles the details upon which the employees will co-operate with a request from management to assist in obtaining information to help solve a problem of mutual concern.

Why do you think it is essential for employees and employers to reconcile their differences?

Alternative interest resolution mechanisms

There are, however, other ways in which the conflict of interest is accommodated. In some cases, individuals finding their aspirations (for example, for promotion or for higher pay) cannot be met with their present employer, resign their employment and go to work for another organisation where their interests can be, or are more likely to be, better accommodated. Although labour turnover represents a peaceful method of resolving the differences of interests between employers and employees, management has to keep voluntary disengagements to manageable proportions since labour turnover is not without cost to the employer.

In other circumstances accommodation is achieved by the employer dismissing the employee. Here the employer says it is not in the interest of the company to continue to employ the individual concerned. The employee, however, holds the opposite view and sees his or her interest best advanced by continuing in employment with that employer. However, these differing interests cannot be resolved so the employer forces the issue by dismissing the employee who then is likely to respond by complaining to an Employment Tribunal that they have been dismissed unfairly. The Tribunal then decides in favour of either the employer or the employee, a decision which may take the form of re-instatement, re-engagement or financial compensation. Ultimately, the Tribunal resolves differences of interest between the employer and the employee.

WHERE ARE LABOUR SERVICES EMPLOYED?

Workplace size

The 1998 Workplace Employment Relations Survey found that the smallest workplace (25–49 employees) accounted for 52 per cent of all workplaces but only 17 per cent of all workplace employees. On the other hand, the largest workplaces (employing 500 or more) accounted for only 3 per cent of all workplaces but almost a third of all workers, with the remaining two thirds fairly evenly distributed across other size bands (see Table 1).

Table 1 Distribution of workplaces and employment by workplace size

Workplace size	% of all workplaces	% of all employees
25–49 employees	52	17
50–99 employees	25	16
100–199 employees	12	16
200–499 employees	8	22
500 or more	3	30

Source: 1998 Workplace Employment Relations Survey

Sector distribution

Table 2 shows the extent to which labour services are purchased by sectors of the economy. Eighteen per cent of workplaces were in the manufacturing sector which was predominately privately owned. This same pattern existed for wholesale and retail distribution. Marked differences were apparent in the workforce composition across the groups (see Table 2).

Workplaces making or doing different things had differing skill requirements and there were substantial differences in occupational composition by industry. For example, almost all education workplaces

Table 2 Distribution of workplace: By industry and sector

Industry	Workplaces in private sector (%)	Workplaces in public sector (%)	All workplaces
Manufacturing	99	1	18
Electricity, Gas & Water	85	15	0
Construction	88	12	4
Wholesale & Retail	99	1	18
Hotel & Restaurants	96	4	6
Transport & Communications	78	22	5
Financial Services	100	0	3
Other Business Services	87	13	9
Public Administration	–	100	6
Education	13	87	14
Health	57	43	13
Other Community Services	71	29	4
All Workplaces	72	28	100

Source: 1998 Workplace Employment Relations Survey

employed professional people but few employed plant and machine operatives who were mostly found in manufacturing. The 1998 Workplace Employment Relations Survey reported that some 29 per cent of workplaces employed largely women employees in that at least three quarters of their employees were female. Twenty-seven per cent of workplaces employed mainly male labour services and 44 per cent employed both male and female employees. Under a quarter of private sector workplaces had a largely female workforce compared to nearly a half in the public sector. Women employees dominated workplace employment in health (84 per cent) and education (63 per cent) whilst males dominated construction (85 per cent), transport and communications (71 per cent) and electricity, gas and water (70 per cent).

Part-time workers, defined as those working fewer than 30 hours per week, accounted for a quarter of all jobs in workplaces with 25 or more employees. Sixteen per cent of workplaces employed no part-time workers whilst in 26 per cent of workplaces, part-timers formed the majority of the workforce. Substantial proportions of workplaces in manufacturing, the public utilities and construction used no part-timers at all while similarly high proportions of workplaces in wholesale and retail, hotel and restaurants, education and health employed a majority part-time workforce.

The number of employees in September 1996 (Labour Market Trends 1998) was 22.3 million of which 4 million (18 per cent) were employed in the manufacturing sector. In 1971, manufacturing employed 8.1 million (36.3 per cent) of the workforce. In 1996, the service sector employed 16.5 million which was 76 per cent of the total workforce. In 1971, the share of service sector employment was almost

53 per cent. In 1996, 5.6 million (more than in the whole of manufacturing) were employed in public administration, education and health, 4 million in banking, finance and insurance and 5 million in retail and wholesale distribution, hotel and restaurants.

INTEREST-ENHANCING INSTITUTIONS

Employers

The buyers of labour services seek to maintain and enhance their interests by organising themselves into companies or enterprises of which there are four main types:

- private businesses, in which a distinction can be made between:

  - the private company owned by either an individual or family and which has no shareholders. Such companies retain control of the decision whether to sell themselves to another company.

  - the private company owned by shareholders but controlled by managers. Such companies can be acquired by other companies with the agreement of the shareholders, irrespective of the views of the managers.

- public corporations

- central and local government

- voluntary bodies.

Private businesses employ some 18 million people. Although there are large numbers of small incorporated businesses, the most common form of organisation is the registered company. A major feature of the corporate sector is the concentration of output into a small number of very large private limited companies (many of which have production or service capacity in more than one country) alongside a substantial but growing number of much smaller private firms serving local 'niche' markets. This concentration of output into fewer enterprises is the result of corporate mergers within countries and across national boundaries.

There is, in large, private sector businesses, a divorce of ownership by individual and institutional shareholders such as banks and pension fund managers and management control which lies with a team of professional managers who are accountable to the owners for the performance of the company. Corporate strategy and its associated policies are normally decided by an executive group selected by the chief executive/managing director. This strategy is then taken to the plc board of directors for approval, modification or rejection. Senior, middle and junior managers are appointed to implement the policies to achieve the corporate strategy. In private corporations, the authority chain is from the top downwards through management structures.

Public sector organisation can be divided into public corporations, central government and local authorities. Public corporations which include organisations such as the Royal Mail and NHS Trusts employed in 1996 some 1.5 million people (see Table 3). In the same year central government employed just under 1 million people, of which half worked for the Civil Service. The numbers employed in local authorities in 1996 was some 2.7 million. By 1996, employment

Table 3 Numbers employed in the public sector – 1979, 1991 and 1996 (Thousands)

		1979	1991	1996
Public corporations				
Nationalised Industries		1,849	516	335
NHS Trusts		–	124	1,201
Other		216	107	75
	Total	2,065	747	1,512
Central government				
Armed Forces		314	297	221
NHS		1,152	1,092	90
Civil Service		738	580	534
Other		183	208	142
	Total	2,387	2,177	987
Local authorities				
Education		1,539	1,416	1,183
Social Services		344	414	408
Construction		156	106	79
Police		176	202	207
Other		782	810	774
	Total	2,997	2,948	2,651
	GRAND TOTAL	7,749	5,872	5,150

Source: derived from *Economic Trends*

in the public sector had fallen to its lowest level in the post-Second World War period.

Voluntary bodies are usually small, privately owned organisations with social rather than economic objectives. They include organisations such as Oxfam, Save the Children Fund, The British Heart Foundation and local housing associations. The voluntary sector also contains worker or producer co-operatives where the enterprise is owned and controlled by its members.

Employers' associations were also established by employers to protect and advance their interests. The Annual Report of the Certification Officer, 1998, reports that in 1997 there were 107 such associations. Some of these were national bodies covering a whole industry (for example, the Engineering Employers Federation), others were specialised bodies representing a segment of an industry (for example, the Newspaper Society which represents the interests of provincial newspaper employers in England, Wales and Northern Ireland) and yet others were local associations representing geographically based industrial interests (for example, the Blackburn District Textile Manufacturers Association). Employers associations' major activities can be divided into the following areas:

• assistance to member firms in the resolution of disputes

• general help and advice on employee relations matters

• representation of members' views to political decision-makers at all levels

• representation of members at Employment Tribunals

• in some cases, negotiation of collective agreements with trade unions.

The ways in which employers' associations can assist the employee relations specialist in their everyday job are discussed in Chapter 4.

Employees

Some employees attempt to strengthen and enhance their interests in the labour market by presenting a collective face to the employer. In an attempt to even up their influence relative to employers, employees form organisations to determine, on their behalf, minimum conditions on which they will supply their labour services to the employers. The most common employee labour market organisations are:

• professional associations

• staff associations

• trade unions.

In enterprises where such organisations do not exist, employers often create a collective employee organisation (sometimes called an Employee Council, a Works Council or a Representative Committee) so they can obtain a collective and representative voice from their employees. It is only in very small firms that a truly individual and personal relationship can exist between an employer and employee. Once an organisation grows, in employment terms, beyond a critical size, the views of the employees are best collected (in time and efficiency terms) through some representative organisation. It becomes too time-consuming to talk to each separate employee. Employers' interests, therefore, can be enhanced by their employees having a representative body. However, employers' attitudes vary as to what form of collective employee organisation best serves the company's interests.

Professional associations

Professional associations are not central employee relations agencies. They usually control the education and training of new members to the profession by acting as 'qualifying associations'. They also establish, maintain and review professional and ethical standards for their members. In addition, they advance the standing and status of the profession in the wider community. However, some professional associations, especially those whose members are mainly employed in the public sector, also protect and improve their members' employment interests in pay bargaining. In the health service, for example, there are groups of professional employees, such as nurses and midwives, who use their professional associations in the dual capacity of a professional and negotiating body.

Staff associations

Staff associations are in some cases the creation of employers who wish to keep their business non-unionised. The majority, however, are independent of the employer. Despite low membership subscriptions and lack of militancy, staff associations can, and do, provide an acceptable alternative to trade unions. This is particularly true of certain white collar groups. Nevertheless, most staff associations are characterised by weak finances and a narrow membership base confined to a single employer.

Larger staff associations tend to acquire their own staff and premises and rely less on the employer for services and facilities. In 1998, the Certification Officer's list of Employee Organisations contained 62 staff associations concentrated mainly in the financial sector of which 30 were recognised to be independent of employer influence and domination. These staff associations are characterised by high membership density often exceeding 75 per cent.

Trade unions

Trade unions are the best known form of employee organisation. They were formed to protect and advance the interests of their members against employers and members of other trade unions. In the UK, trade unions have different recruitment strategies. Craft and occupational unions (for example, AEEU, GPMU) focus on recruiting employees performing certain jobs. Some unions confine their recruitment to all grades of employees employed in a particular industry. These are referred to as industrial unions. General unions, such as the T&GWU and GMB, organise workers across the boundaries within and between industries. They will take into membership any worker regardless of the job they do and the industry in which they do it. This contrasts with Germany where trade unions are organised on industrial lines and Japan where unions, in organisational terms, are company based.

In the UK, trade union organisation is characterised by a large number of small unions co-existing with a very small number of large trade unions. In 1997, 73 per cent (177) of the total number of trade unions registered with the Certification Officer had memberships of less than 5,000. On the other hand, 7 per cent (17) of the unions had memberships in excess of 100,000.

Unions represent different interests in terms of jobs, types of workers, industries, services and public and private sectors of the economy. They also have different interests within them (skilled, unskilled, non-manual workers, etc) but these are accommodated through their decision-making procedures which are based on the principle of representative democracy. Trade unions in the UK:

- are job-centred, not class-centred

- prefer to achieve their objectives by industrial methods (for example, collective bargaining) rather than political means (for example, industrial action against government measures they dislike)

- motivated by pragmatism rather than principle.

Trade unions are discussed in more detail in Chapter 4.

EMPLOYEE RELATIONS PROCESSES

The accommodation of the interests of employers and employees is achieved by the use of employee relations processes (mechanisms) of which the most important are:

- unilateral action
- employee involvement and participation schemes
- collective bargaining
- third party intervention
- industrial sanctions.

In addition to these processes, the State can interfere in the buying and selling of labour services by establishing minimum terms that the buyers must offer the sellers. This is known as legal regulation. Unlike the other processes listed above, management has no direct control over what legal regulation the Government and/or the European Union will introduce. However, management does try to influence this matter via its political lobbying activities. For example, in 1998 employers succeeded in persuading the Labour Government alter its proposal in its White Paper 'Fairness at Work' that there should be no limit on the amount of compensation that could be awarded to an individual who is unfairly dismissed by his or her employer. As a result of employer pressure, the government decided to raise the limit on such compensation from £12,000 to £50,000.

Unilateral action
Unilateral action is where the employer is the sole author of the 'agreement' which the employees accept by continuing to work in accordance with its terms. In deciding employment conditions by this method, the employer pays little or no attention to the views (voice) of the employees. This process was usually associated with non-union companies but in the last 20 years there has been a resurgence of employers stressing the need for business efficiency, claiming management's right to manage and to impose decisions ง their employees. However, even in highly unionised organisations (for example, commercial television companies and the NHS Trusts) there have been examples of unilateral changes by management on issues such as overtime opportunities and changes in job descriptions. In the extreme, managers who impose unilateral changes to their employees' employment conditions take the line 'accept these new terms or consider yourself dismissed'. Take it or leave it.

Another area where employers exercise unilateral action is the devising of company rules, which are applicable to all employees and set out in the company handbook/rule book. If employees breach these rules, then serious consequences, including dismissal, can arise. The subject of such rules usually includes the obligation on employees to report to the employer a change of address, what steps are to be followed in the event of an accident, security, safety, hygiene and dress code.

It is difficult to know the extent of management-imposed changes to the employment conditions of employees since there is no source of such information. However, the general impression is that in the 1980s and 1990s the use of unilateral action by employers increased. One of the reasons for this view is that in the past 15 years, the number of workplaces having no union members at all has increased. The 1990 Workplace Industrial Relations Survey (WIRS) showed that 36 per cent of workplaces had no union members at all. The corresponding figure in the 1998 Workplace Employee Relations Survey was 47 per cent. In making a unilateral change to the employment contract, the employer risks being sued for breach of contract or for constructive dismissal. However, such behaviour has gone unchallenged because in the past 20 years the relative balance of bargaining power has been in favour of the employer.

Employee involvement

Employee involvement is a broad term which covers the complete range of processes which help to engage the support, understanding and optimum contribution of all employees to the objectives of the organisation. This includes all communication and consultation processes and financial participation. Communication includes a range of different activities by which information flows through organisations including top down, lateral and upward flows of information and comment, feedback, employee surveys, written and spoken briefings, staff videos and e-mail.

Consultation is different from communication because it invites the participation of staff by seeking views, involving individuals in the decision-making process and delegating power through empowerment. Consultation can take place either directly with staff or through a representative forum such as a works council, or some other form of joint consultation machinery.

Each of the elements of the employee involvement mix is linked. It is not always clear where communication ends and consultation begins. Organisations which pursue employee involvement will typically use a wide range of differing activities to develop the mix needed to achieve success in the marketplace. Employee involvement is analysed in greater detail in Chapter 6.

In joint consultation, management seeks views, feelings and ideas from employees and/or their representatives prior to making a decision. Although joint consultation may involve discussion of mutual problems, it leaves management to make the final decision. There is no commitment to action on the employees' views. Issues dealt with by joint consultation vary from social matters, such as the provision of canteen or sports facilities, to issues such as the scheduling of production.

The Workplace Employee Relations Survey (1998) provides information on the extent of joint consultative arrangements in establishments employing 25 or more employees. It revealed that 28 per cent of workplaces had a Joint Consultative Committee in operation at the workplace meaning there had been no change in their overall incidence since 1990. Twenty-five per cent of workplaces had no workplace committee but did have a committee which operated at a higher level in the organisation. Workplace committees are much more frequent amongst large workplaces and higher level committees are more frequent in larger organisations. All in all, some 67 per cent of employees are in workplaces with joint consultative arrangements at either the workplace or a higher level in the organisation.

Collective bargaining

Collective bargaining is a method of determining the 'price' at which employee services are bought and sold, a system of industrial governance whereby unions and employers jointly reach decisions concerning the employment relationship. It involves employees, via their elected representative and unions, participating in the management of the enterprise. Collective bargaining is a problem-solving mechanism but can only exist if employees are organised and if the employer is prepared to recognise the trade union(s) for collective bargaining purposes.

In practice, the outcome of collective bargaining is not confined to union members. Unionised companies apply collectively bargained terms and conditions of employment to their non-union employees as well as their unionised ones. Companies that do not recognise unions have regard to collectively bargained rates in their industry or comparator firms when deciding on their own employees' employment conditions if they are to remain competitive in the labour market. Many non-unionised companies (for example Marks and Spencers, IBM, Mars) seek to retain union-free workplaces by paying above the union-negotiated pay and other employment conditions. This means that such companies must have an interest in the outcome of collective bargaining although they are not direct parties to it.

Over the period 1984–1990 inclusive, the coverage of workers by collective bargaining declined. The 1990 WIRS revealed the overall proportion of employees covered by collective bargaining had fallen from 71 per cent in 1984 to 54 per cent in 1990. In the public sector, it had fallen from 95 per cent to 75 per cent whilst in private manufacturing, it had been reduced from 64 per cent to 51 per cent.

> What are the main processes used to determine employment conditions in your organisation? Why are these processes used rather than others?

Third-party intervention

In situations where the employer and employees are unable to resolve their collective differences, they may agree voluntarily to seek the assistance of an independent third party. Third-party intervention can be in one of three forms:

• conciliation

• mediation

• arbitration.

In the case of disputes between an employer and an individual employee over unfair dismissal, non-payment of a termination of employment payment or commission and sex, race, equal pay and disability discrimination, the law requires the Advisory, Conciliation and Arbitration Service (ACAS) to attempt a conciliated settlement before the claim can proceed to an Employment Tribunal.

In conciliation, the role of the third party is to keep the two sides talking and assist them to reach their own agreement. The conciliator acts as a link between the disputing parties by passing information, which the parties will not pass directly to each other, from one side to the other until either a basis for agreement is identified or both parties agree there is no basis for an agreed voluntary settlement to their problem. Conciliation permits each side to re-assess continually their situation. The conciliator plays a passive role and does not impose any action or decision on the parties.

The mediator listens to the argument of the two sides and makes recommendations as to how their difference(s) might be resolved. The parties are free to accept or reject these recommendations. Arbitration removes from employers and employees control over the settlement of their differences. The arbitrator hears each side's case and decides the solution to the parties' differences by making an award. Both parties, having voluntarily agreed to arbitration, are morally but not legally obliged to accept the arbitrator's award. Pendulum arbitration is a specific form of arbitration which limits the third party to making an award which accepts fully either the final claim of the union or the final offer of the employer. It reduces arbitration to an all or nothing, win or lose, outcome. By creating an 'all or nothing' expectation, pendulum arbitration is said to provide the incentive for bargainers to moderate their final positions and reach a voluntary agreement.

Third-party intervention is facilitated by ACAS, established as a Royal Commission in 1974 and put on a statutory basis by the Employment Protection Act 1975. Mediation and arbitration are undertaken by an independent person(s) selected jointly by the parties to the dispute from a list held by ACAS of competent arbitrators made up of academics, trade union officers and employers. The members of this list are all experienced and knowledgeable in employee relations. There is also the Central Arbitration Committee (CAC) which is a standing independent arbitration body. It was originally established as the Industrial Court in 1919. It can deal with issues relating to industrial disputes, a single employer or a particular employee group. It provides voluntary arbitration in trade disputes. It determines claims by trade unions for disclosure of information for collective bargaining purposes and has an important role in the operation of the statutory trade union recognition procedure contained in the Employment Relations Act (1999). The role of ACAS is discussed more fully in Chapters 4 and 10 and that of the CAC in Chapters 4 and 5.

The number of completed collective conciliation cases handled by ACAS fell from 2,284 in 1979 to 1,166 in 1997. Mediation is rarely used. In the whole of 1997, there were only 11 mediation hearings arranged by ACAS. Throughout the 1990s, the number of arbitration hearings arranged by ACAS fell. In 1990, there were 200 such hearings but in 1997 there were only 60. Third-party intervention is a little-used employee relations process. It is discussed and analysed in detail in Chapter 4.

Industrial sanctions

The use of industrial sanctions is generally a last resort as it is costly to both sides to impose them on each other. The main sanctions available to the employer are:

• locking out some or all of the workforce

- closing the factory

- relocating operations to another site

- dismissing employees participating in industrial action.

The main industrial sanctions employees can impose on employers are:

- banning overtime

- working to rule

- imposing a selective strike

- holding an all-out strike.

The threat of the imposition of industrial sanctions is important in bringing about a reconciliation of the different interests of employers and employees. The threat that one side might impose industrial sanctions, with their ensuing costs, on the other is as important as sanctions actually being imposed. It is this threat effect that makes the parties adjust their position and negotiate a peaceful settlement. Both parties are reluctant to impose industrial sanctions because of their associated costs. However, their existence means the parties have to have regard to them and adjust their behaviour accordingly.

Employers have to think carefully before imposing or threatening to impose industrial sanctions. There is little to be gained in imposing industrial action if it is unlikely to be successful given that economic pressures may quickly mount as the organisation's product market competitors take advantage of its industrial problems to poach its customers. It is pointless to relocate operations to another site unless an alternative competent workforce is available (or can be recruited) at the new site. To impose sanctions that fail to bring further concessions from the other party undermines, at a future date, the credibility of the threat to use them.

Extent of industrial action
In the UK, official statistics on the use of industrial sanctions relate only to strikes. They measure three dimensions of strike activity – their numbers (frequency), their size (number of workers involved) and their duration (number of working days lost). This last measure is often distorted by a few big strikes. For example, in 1979 an engineering industry-wide strike accounted for 55 per cent of the 29.5 million working days lost in that year. In 1997, the number of working days lost in the UK was 230,000, the lowest in any year since records began in 1891.

However, disputes still happen, such as the series of one day stoppages in 1996 in the Royal Mail over the employer's attempt to introduce major changes in working practices in order to remain competitive in the light of the growth of alternative communication systems (such as faxes and e-mail) to letters. In 1997, a high profile dispute took place between British Airways and the British Airline Steward and Stewardesses Association (part of the T&GWU).

Although dispute levels have declined in the 1990s, there are signs some managers have been performing inadequately in managing their

Table 4 Industrial stoppages in the UK 1979-95

Year	Number of stoppages in progress	Number of workers involved (000s)	Number of working days lost (000s)
1979	2,125	4,608	29,474[1]
1980	1,348	834	11,964[2]
1981	1,344	1,513	4,266
1982	1,538	2,103	5,313
1983	1,364	574	3,754
1984	1,221	1,464	27,135[3]
1985	903	791	6,402[4]
1986	1,074	720	1,920
1987	1,016	887	3,546
1988	781	790	3,702
1989	701	727	4,128[5]
1990	630	298	1,903
1991	369	176	761
1992	253	148	528
1993	211	385	649
1994	205	107	278
1995	234	173	415
1996	244	364	1,303
1997	216	130	235
1998	166	93	282

Notes:

(1) 54 per cent of total accounted for by a strike of engineering workers
(2) 74 per cent of total accounted for by national steel dispute
(3) 83 per cent of total accounted for by coal mining strike
(4) 63 per cent of total accounted for by continuing miners' strike
(5) 49 per cent of total accounted for by strike of council workers

Source: Annual Report on Labour Disputes in Department of Employment *Gazette* and *Labour Market Trends*

employee relations in that there has been a dramatic growth in the number of complaints by employees against employers' behaviour to Employment Tribunals. In the 1980s, the number of complaints reported to ACAS averaged about 45,000 per annum but the number has increased in every year in the 1990s. In the 1990s the annual average exceeded 100,000. This would suggest a rising sense of individual grievances amongst people at work.

Legal intervention

The processes described above are private means whereby the interests of employers and employees are accommodated. Employers have some choice over which of these processes they will use. However, on occasions, the State interferes in these private relationships and sets minimum employment conditions that employers must provide for their employees. Although employers have no control over parliamentary legislation, they can, by political lobbying, attempt to influence the details of proposed legislation to maximise its positive effects on their economic interests or to minimise its negative impact on their interests.

UK Parliament regulation

In the UK today, legal intervention comes from two sources – the UK government and the European Union. The Labour Government, elected in 1997, introduced new minimum standards of protection for employees at the workplace. In April 1999, a national minimum wage of £3.60 for those over 21 and of £3 (rising to £3.20 in 2001) for those aged 18 to 21 inclusive, was introduced. The Employment Relations Act 1999 enabled employees to have a trade union recognised by their employer where the majority of the relevant workforce wish it, created the right for employees to be accompanied by a fellow employee or trade union representative during grievance and disciplinary procedures over serious matters, and gave employees rights to extended maternity absence.

The European Union

The European Union is committed to establishing a 'level playing field' of social regulation in its Single European Market in which goods, capital, people and services can move freely. In 1997, the UK government accepted that more social measures can be harmonised between member states, by the use of the EU's qualified majority voting procedure. One implication of this is that a personnel professional in the UK can expect to experience increasing legal regulation from the European Union (see Chapter 3).

An important piece of legal regulation that came from the European Union is the Working Time Regulations of 1998. These introduced a range of significant new rights and entitlements for employees including:

- a limit of 48 hours on average weekly working time

- a minimum of three weeks' paid leave (rising to four from November 1999) subject to a 13-week qualifying period

- entitlements to a daily rest period of 11 consecutive hours, a weekly rest period of 24 hours and a daily 20 minute rest period where the working day is longer than six hours

- a limit of an average of eight hours work in each 24 hour period for night workers and an actual limit of eight hours in each 24 hour period for night workers whose work involves 'special hazards' or heavy physical or mental strain

- the right to a 'health assessment' before being required to perform night work and at regular intervals thereafter.

AGREEMENTS, RULES AND REGULATIONS

The outcome of the use of employee relations processes is an 'agreement' which establishes the conditions upon which labour services will be bought and sold. These agreements may relate to a group of employees, in which case they are referred to as a collective agreement. On the other hand, the agreement may be the result of bargaining between an employer and an individual employee in which case it is referred to as a personal contract. The distinguishing characteristic of such contracts is that none of its terms have been bargained collectively. The employee has negotiated as an individual although they may have received assistance from a third party, including a trade union.

However, in practice, few personal contracts are genuinely individualised. At British Telecom, for example, all terms and

Table 5

AGREEMENT BETWEEN:

UNION OF SHOP, DISTRIBUTIVE AND ALLIED WORKERS
(USDAW)
&
ABC LIMITED

The following has been agreed between USDAW and ABC Limited, regarding the 1995/96 Pay and Conditions claim.

The following are the rates of pay which now apply for a 39-hour week and are effective from Monday 5 June 1995.

Rates of pay

Boners	£170.82
Butchers	£156.47
M/c Op/Prep	£151.23
Gen Worker 'A'	£146.66
Gen Worker 'B'	£146.66
Drivers	£152.57

Nightshift premiums
    Will be increased from their present levels to 18.5% of basic hourly rate

Working hours – with immediate effect to become:

Dayshift	Monday to Friday	6.00 am until 2.30 pm
	or	8.00 am until 4.30 pm
Nightshift	Sunday to Thursday	9.00 pm until 5.18 am

Breaks – During each shift the following breaks will apply:
    1 × 30 minute lunch break
    1 × 15 minute tea break
    2 × 10 minute tea breaks

Service-day holidays
    Qualification periods for 5 days' holiday to be reduced to 13 years.

Death in service
    Sum assured benefit increased to £10,000

Holidays
    5 days of public holiday to become part of annual holiday commencing 1 April 1996.

---

conditions for senior managerial staff were standard across all personal contracts. The only difference was that pay was determined 'individually' with no published rates or transparency in the criteria by which pay increases were given to individuals.

Types of agreement
It is traditional to divide agreements into two broad types. First, there are substantive agreements which cover the money aspects of employment conditions (pay, hours of work, paid holidays, shift premiums, etc). An example of a substantive agreement is shown in Table 5.

Secondly, there are procedural agreements which set standards of conduct to be met by employers and employees in resolving their differences over the issue which is the subject of the procedure. In this sense, they provide the 'law and order' for the workplace. They provide tests by which reasonable, fair and consistent behaviour by employers can be judged by employees and outside institutions, such as Employment Tribunals. They provide quick and informal methods for resolving disputes. Procedures also send a message to all employees as to how they will be treated should the issue covered by the procedure arise.

In practice, employers will have in their enterprises a wide range of procedural arrangements and agreements covering issues such as:

- disputes

- employee grievances

Table 6

CLERICAL STAFF PROCEDURE AGREEMENT

SECTION FIVE – APPEALS AGAINST GRADING

1 Individual right to appeal

Where an employee is dissatisfied with the decision of the University at the annual review concerning an application for regrading on the grounds of increased duties and responsibilities, then he/she may apply in writing within three weeks to the Director of Personnel to have his/her case considered by an Appeals Panel constituted as below

2 Appeals panel – membership

The Appeals Panel shall consist of five members, as follows:

(a) Two members nominated by the University
(b) Two members nominated by the Association
(c) One member, who shall act as Convenor, acceptable to the University and the Association

Procedure for appeals

(i) Persons Involved in the Hearing

(a) The appellant
(b) A colleague or Trade Union representative of the appellant if he/she wishes
(c) A Personnel Officer
(d) The Head of Department or his/her nominee

(ii) Prior to the Hearing

(a) The Panel shall have available to it all the original documentation
(b) Each party shall make available a written statement of case to the Panel
(c) Written statements and supporting documents, if any, should be in the hands of the Personnel Officer eight working days prior to the hearing. These together with copies of all the original documents will be circulated to the members of the Panel four working days prior to the hearing.

(iii) Hearing of the Appeal

(a) The appellant or his/her representative may, if they wish, present a short summary of the case to the Panel.
(b) The members of the panel may then ask questions of any of those present.
(c) The appellant will withdraw from the hearing.
(d) The Personnel Officer will be asked to present the University's case.
(e) The Head of Department of his/her nominee will be asked to present the departmental view of the merits of the case and the members of the Panel may ask questions.

(iv) Consideration of the Appeal

(a) The Panel will then consider its decision after all parties have withdrawn.
(b) The decision will be by a simple vote of the Panel. The decision of the Panel is binding on all parties.

- discipline

- redundancy

- union recognition

- grading

- health and safety

- promotion

- staff development and career review.

An example of a procedural agreement (Appeal Against Grading) is shown in Table 6. The 1998 Employee Relations Workplace Survey reported that in 92 per cent of establishments surveyed there was an individual grievance procedure with a similar proportion of workplaces operating formal disciplinary procedures.

> Select three procedures which operate in your organisation. Explain how they demonstrate that management behaves fairly and reasonably in operating these procedures.

Legal status of collective agreements

Collective agreements have a unique status in the UK in that they are not legally binding on the parties who have signed them. If either the union or management acts contrary to the agreement, the other party cannot enforce its rights outlined in the agreement via the Courts. Collective agreements are binding in honour only. In almost every democratic society, collective agreements between unions and employers are legally binding and enforceable through the Courts.

A consequence of non-legally binding collective agreements is that they are not comprehensive and their wording can be relatively imprecise. This reinforces the requirement for employers to have a disputes procedure to resolve differences with their employees as to whether the agreement is being applied properly. The style of UK collective agreements also reflects that they are normally subject to review and re-negotiation on an annual basis.

Dimensions of agreements

Agreements can be analysed by their dimensions. The main ones are:

- scope (ie subjects covered)

- formality (written/unwritten)

- level

- bargaining units (employees covered).

The scope (ie the subjects covered) of both collective agreements and personal contracts varies widely but normally covers some or all of the following:

- pay levels and structure

- overtime and shift payments

- incentive (bonus/performance-related pay) payments

- hours of work and paid holidays

- working arrangements and productivity

- training and re-training opportunities

- the means of resolving disputes, individual grievances, etc.

It is traditional for pay rates and working arrangements to be reviewed and amended annually by the signatories to the agreement. Hours of work and paid annual holidays are normally reviewed and changed at less frequent intervals. Procedural arrangements can remain unchanged for many years.

Agreements can also be analysed in terms of their formality. The vast majority of collective agreements have their contents written down but there are some which do not exist in written form. These are referred to as 'Custom and Practice'. The employees (or employers) have operated the working practice for many years. Management (employees) have gone along with this behaviour although they have never formally agreed it with their employees (management). The practice has become accepted and if management (employees) were to try to change it, the employees (employer) are likely to expect something in return.

Agreements are concluded at different levels. Some apply only to the place where those covered by it work, others apply to all workers in the company (referred to as company agreements) such as in the Ford Motor Company and ICI. Some agreements cover a group of workers in an enterprise whilst others relate to all (or certain grades of) workers in an industry; these are commonly referred to as national or industry-wide agreements. Over the past 15 years, many employers have withdrawn from operating under national agreements, often supplemented by local bargaining, preferring to bargain collectively (especially over pay) with their employees at a more de-centralised level; they consider this necessary to recruit, motivate, retain and reward the right calibre of employees if the success of the business is to be secured.

Agreements, rules and regulations can also be analysed in terms of the number of workers they cover. In the case of collectively bargained agreements, this is referred to as the size of the bargaining unit. In some unionised organisations, management operates by concluding separate agreements with separate trade unions representing different groups of employees and thus has a multiplicity of bargaining units and collective agreements. This is the classic multi-union situation.

However, other unionised companies prefer to have a single agreement covering all relevant groups and thus have one bargaining unit covering significant numbers of employees and possibly a different number of trade unions. This is referred to as single table bargaining, in which all recognised trade unions sit at the same table with the employer. Yet other managements may see the business objectives as more achievable if they have one bargaining unit in which all employees are represented by a single union (a single union agreement situation).

Non-union companies, like unionised ones, will have substantive and procedural agreements but they will have been written by the employer; only the most professional of these will have consulted with their workforce in doing so. In non-union companies, agreements, rules and regulations can also be analysed in terms of their scope (ie issues covered by information and consultation arrangements) and the number of workers covered. Some information and communication systems apply to all workers in the enterprise whilst others apply to some groups. Quality circles on the other hand, are usually confined to small groups from the same work area or who do similar job tasks and activities. Performance-related pay schemes often will apply to certain occupational groups (eg managers in strategic positions) within an enterprise or workplace. Financial participation schemes will again vary in terms of the workers covered. Some will embrace all employees (eg profit sharing and profit-related pay) whilst some will be confined to certain occupational groups (eg share option schemes).

Workforce agreements
The Working Time Regulations 1998 have given rise to a new form of agreement entitled 'Workforce Agreements'. The Regulations allow for some of the measures to be adopted through agreements between workers and employers so as to allow flexibility to take account of the specific needs of local working agreements. Employers and workers are expected to agree which of three types of agreement – collective agreements, workforce agreements and relevant agreements – are the most appropriate for their circumstances.

Workforce agreements permit employers to agree working time agreements with workers who do not have any terms or conditions set by a collective agreement. Workforce agreements allow employers to agree on how to use the flexibilities permitted in the implementation of the Regulations. A workforce agreement may apply to the whole of the workforce or a group within it. Where it is to apply to a group of workers, the group must share a workplace function or organisational unit within a business.

THE BALANCE OF BARGAINING POWER

Whether the contents of agreements are closer to satisfying the interests of the employers or the employees is influenced heavily by the relative balance of bargaining power between them. Issues relating to the relative balance of bargaining power are relevant to employers who bargain individually with their employees as well as to those who bargain collectively with their workforce. The balance of bargaining power is a key employee relations concept which influences, inter alia, the employer's preferred relations process, the subject matter of agreements, whether agreements are jointly authored by employers and employees or solely written by one of the parties, and the actual terms of the agreements, rules and regulations.

The macro level
The external environmental factors influencing the relative balance of bargaining power between employers and employee are:

• economic

- legal

- technological.

The government's economic and legal policies have major implications for the outcome of employee relations activities. If economic policies are directed towards the creation of full employment and the maximising of economic growth, this weakens the bargaining power of the employer relative to that of the employees. In an expanding economy the demand for labour services increases causing its price to rise. On the other hand, if macro economic policies are directed at restraining economic growth then the demand for labour services falls, resulting perhaps in redundancies and increasing unemployment. In such circumstances the balance of bargaining power of the employer is strengthened relative to that of the employees.

If the government introduces legislation favourable to employers' interests, for example, by restricting the circumstances in which trade unions can instruct their members to undertake industrial action without employers being able to resort to the Courts for redress (for example, compensation to cover economic losses from lost sales, etc) then the bargaining power of employers relative to employees is strengthened. The Conservative Governments of the period 1979–97 inclusive enhanced employer bargaining power by passing nine pieces of parliamentary legislation which progressively more tightly regulated the labour market activities of trade unions.

If a government introduces legislation favourable to the interests of individual employees and trade unions then the bargaining power of employees relative to employers is increased. The Labour Government via its Employment Relations Act 1999, which introduced statutory trade union recognition, enhanced employee/trade union bargaining power relative to the employer.

The implementation of new technology also impacts on the relative bargaining power between employees and employers. Technological developments based on computers, lasers and telecommunications have in some sectors of the economy destroyed jobs (for example, compositors – typesetters – in the printing industry), de-skilled jobs, blurred demarcation lines between existing jobs and industries and created for employers an alternative and lower paid workforce. These impacts have increased the bargaining power of the employer relative to the employee.

However, in other sectors of the economy, by creating new jobs, new skills and making some industries more capital-intensive, the implementation of technological change has strengthened the bargaining power of employees relative to the employer. For example, the growth of telephone banking services has created a new business, which in part replaces the jobs lost in traditional banks.

The economic and legal environment surrounding an employee relations system influences the relative bargaining power between employers and employees at the macro level. This is why employer and employee organisations spend large sums of money in lobbying political decision-makers.

The micro level

An analysis of the relative bargaining power at the macro level cannot explain why some groups of employees retain their bargaining power vis-à-vis the employer despite recession and high unemployment or why some employers are in a relatively weak bargaining position despite depressed economic activity. This is the relative bargaining power at the micro level.

At this level the balance of bargaining power is influenced by some of the following factors:

- Can the employees inflict costs on the organisation?

- Is there an alternative workforce available to the employer?

- Is the group of employees aware of its potential power?

- Has the group of employees exercised its power?

- If the group has exercised its power, was the outcome favourable to them?

For example, in assessing the relative bargaining power of a group of its employees management has to consider how crucial the group is to the production/service supply process. The more central the group is to the workflow, the greater is its potential power within the organisation. In many organisations computer staff, for example, are now in strategic positions to disrupt workflow.

The bargaining power of a group of employees relative to management is strengthened if there is a lack of an appropriate alternative workforce available to undertake the group's work on an individual or a departmental basis. In short, a group of workers difficult to substitute has greater bargaining power relative to the employer than a group whose services are easily replaceable.

EMPLOYEE RELATIONS SKILLS

Employee relations professionals need knowledge and understanding as well as competency in the necessary skills to apply that knowledge and understanding to solve employee relations problems. The core skills required and why will be described in more detail in the appropriate ensuing chapters. The core skills required of an employee relations professional are:

- information gathering, analysis and review

- communications (written and oral)

- planning, monitoring and reviewing

- interviewing

- listening

- negotiating

- assertiveness

- team building.

Communication skills include note-taking, letter and report writing and public speaking. Managers do not always communicate effectively yet they rely heavily upon the spoken word in making notes (often in small group discussion, negotiating situations and to capture accurately the sequence of events), in writing reports to colleagues and senior managers (ie putting ideas and possible policies onto paper against tight deadlines), in sending letters and in making presentations to other managers and to employees. Communicating well is a skill. To perform it effectively managers must acquire and develop its techniques.

Information gathering, analysis and review are essential skills when establishing the facts of a situation or researching the background to a bargaining situation. It is crucial all information is collected and sifted so that any differences in perception are cleared up. In some situations it is possible to centre on hard information and make definitive conclusions. However, hard facts are not always available. Frequently the personnel professional is dealing with people's recollection of what they saw and interpretations of what they experienced. Going into a negotiating or interviewing situation without having all the facts is unwise. This makes the information gathering and interpretation skills vital weapons in the 'kit bag' of the employee relations professional.

Interviewing skills are important for managers who spend time gaining appropriate information to deal with complaints by employees against management behaviour (employee grievances), and with complaints by the employer about employee behaviour (discipline). In negotiating situations, management requires information to confirm expected areas of agreement and/or whether they need to be re-assessed in the light of information received from the employees' representatives. In all these situations, management obtains the relevant information by word of mouth from interested parties. The effective manager will be more than competent in interviewing skills.

Listening Skills – Management cannot operate by issuing instructions. Managing people requires contact with them. A major source of information, even more important than reading reports, is listening to what individuals are saying. Listening skills involve concentration on what is being said. The ability to listen is often taken for granted but effective listening skills have to be acquired and developed. They require attention (watching for body language, etc), comprehension ('thinking ahead of the speaker') and absorption (making notes of what is heard). The effective manager has competency in listening skills. A failure to listen carries a high risk of missing a vital piece of information.

Negotiating Skills – Managers are frequently meeting with other management colleagues, employees and employee representatives to solve problems by making an agreement by purposeful persuasion and constructive compromise. The competent negotiator requires a number of skills, for example information gathering and analysis, communication, interviewing, listening, anticipating how the other party might react to arguments and proposals, interpreting body language and judgement (is the solution the best that can be reached in the circumstances?).

Evaluation Skills – Managers are frequently approached by their line manager and asked why a management practice that is reported to have been successfully introduced into one organisation should not be adopted in their company or organisation. It is important that employee relations managers have the evaluation skills to determine why the practice has been successful in one organisation and assess whether it could (or could not) be transplanted successfully into their organisation. Evaluation skills are also crucial if employee relations managers are successfully to monitor, review and amend the working of existing management policies, practices and procedures. The effective employee relations manager will be competent in evaluation skills.

Planning, Monitoring and Review – Employee relations professionals have to think on their feet and take fairly fast decisions. Unconsidered and ill thought out actions can lead to long-term damage and a breakdown in relations. Most actions and initiatives need careful planning and attention to detail. This involves the use of planning skills whereby definite objectives are established and everyone involved has a clear view of who is doing what, by when and why. Once the planned action has been implemented, progress has to be monitored and reviewed so that the objective remains in sight and the project does not stray off course.

Assertiveness – This is an essential skill for a personnel professional if they are to help any organisation to run effectively. Assertiveness allows an individual to retain self-control when dealing with difficult situations and people, to hear and respect what another person is saying, to express their own feelings, opinions and views and to achieve a reasonable compromise between those with differing interests. Assertiveness is very different from being aggressive and from being passive. It is a philosophy rather than a set of easy techniques.

Teams – a team brings something extra to an employee relations situation such as a negotiation or a problem-solving session. A team provides a breadth of experience and knowledge and a range of different and complementary skills. Teams enable processes where plans can be integrated, ideas can 'spark' and develop and different strands of action can be started and maintained simultaneously. Team development is a series of special skills, of setting common goals, identifying the range of skills and roles in the team, sharing the planning progress and monitoring process and development.

SUMMARY

In this chapter we have identified the four main components of an employee relations system in an organisation, economy or sector. First, we identified the interests of the players (employees/employers) in such systems. We saw that as buyers (employers) and sellers (employees) of labour services they have different economic interests. Employers want to purchase labour services for the lowest price whilst employees want to sell their labour services for the highest price. We noted that in an attempt to achieve this employees form organisations, the most common of which are trade unions and staff associations.

However, it was also noted that although sellers and buyers in the labour market have different interests they have a common interest in finding a buyer and a seller. Employees and employers have a common interest in the survival of the enterprise even though they may differ over how any surplus generated by the sales of its products or services should be divided amongst themselves. It was explained how economic pressures on business and sellers of labour services lead them to accommodate each other's interests. They have a common interest in resolving their differences since not to do so leads to mutual destruction.

Second, we identified the processes available to employers and employees to accommodate their different economic interests. These included:

- employee involvement

- communication processes

- collective bargaining

- third party intervention (conciliation, mediation, arbitration)

- industrial sanctions

- legal regulation by UK Parliament and European Union.

Third, we noted that the use of these processes resulted in agreements, rules and regulations (the output of the system). These govern the employment relationship for an individual and/or group of employees and express the prices at which labour services are exchanged. It was also pointed out that agreements, rules and regulations provide rights, responsibilities and obligations for employers and employees. Rules, regulations and agreements, it was noted, can be analysed in terms of their scope (subjects covered), formality (written/unwritten), type (substantive/procedural), level (industry, company, plant, department) and types of workers covered.

Finally, we noted that whether the price at which labour services are exchanged is closer to those of the interests of the buyers (employers) or the interests of the sellers (employees) is determined by the relative balance of bargaining power of the parties. We saw how at the macro level the balance of bargaining power is influenced by the Government's economic and legal policies; for example, in an expanding economy the demand for labour services increases causing their price to rise. Employee relations does not take place in a vacuum and the corporate (external) environment surrounding it is a crucial factor in understanding management behaviour.

It was noted that at the micro level the relative balance of bargaining power is influenced by questions such as: 'Can employees inflict costs on the organisation?' and 'Is there an alternative workforce available to the employer?' For example, the balance of bargaining power of a group of employees is strengthened if there is a lack of an appropriate alternative workforce available to undertake the group's work on an individual or a departmental basis.

REFERENCES AND FURTHER READING

ADVISORY, CONCILIATION AND ARBITRATION SERVICE *Annual Reports.*

ADVISORY, CONCILIATION AND ARBITRATION SERVICE *The Company Handbook.*

BEARDWELL I. (ed.) *Contemporary Industrial Relations: A critical analysis.* Oxford, Oxford University Press. Chapters 1, 3 and 7, 1996.

CENTRAL ARBITRATION COMMITTEE *Annual Reports.*

CERTIFICATION OFFICE FOR TRADE UNIONS AND EMPLOYERS' ASSOCIATIONS *Annual Reports of the Certification Officer.*

CULLY, M. *et al The 1998 Workplace Employee Relations Survey: First findings.* London, Department of Trade and Industry/Economic and Social Research Council/The Advisory, Conciliation and Arbitration Service/Policy Services Institute, 1998.

DEPARTMENT OF TRADE AND INDUSTRY *Fairness at Work*, Cm 3968, May 1998.

DEPARTMENT OF TRADE AND INDUSTRY *National Minimum Wage Regulations*, September 1998.

FARNHAM D. *Employee Relations in Context.* London, Institute of Personnel and Development. Chapters 1, 2, 3, 6, 8 and 10, 1997.

FOWLER, A. *Negotiating, Persuading and Influencing.* London, Institute of Personnel and Development. Chapter 1, 1998.

FOWLER, A. *The Disciplinary Interview.* London, Institute of Personnel and Development. Chapter 3, 1998.

HONEY, P. *Improve Your People Skills* (2nd edn). London, Institute of Personnel and Development. Pages 2, 8, 32, 80, 83, 93, 104, 124 and 144, 1997.

INSTITUTE OF PERSONNEL AND DEVELOPMENT *Employment Relations into the 21st Century: An IPD Position Paper*, December 1997.

INSTITUTE OF PERSONNEL AND DEVELOPMENT *Fairness at Work and the Psychological Contract*, 1998.

INVOLVEMENT AND PARTICIPATION ASSOCIATION *Towards Industrial Partnership: New ways of working in British companies*, February 1997.

MACKAY I. *Listening Skills.* London, Institute of Personnel and Development. Chapters 1 and 2, 1998.

MARTIN R. *Bargaining Power.* Oxford, Oxford University Press. Chapter 3, 1992.

TRADES UNION CONGRESS *Partners for Progress: Next Steps for the New Unionism*, Undated.

Part 3

CONTEXT, INSTITUTIONS, PROCESSES AND POLICIES

2   The corporate environment

INTRODUCTION

The IPD statement on Employee Relations (1997) drew attention to the need for every organisation to improve continually its performance because of the challenges constantly being imposed on them by the corporate environment. Whether those challenges come from intensifying market competition or from the tight spending controls which characterise the public sector, the pressure is much the same for all organisations. It is unlikely, in the short term, to reduce.

The most important thing to note is that these pressures are external to the organisation and this chapter examines those factors which, when taken together, are referred to as the external corporate environment in which all organisations have to operate. It matters not whether the organisation is a large multi-national, a National Health Service Trust or a medium-sized service company; their employee relations are influenced and shaped by the way in which the external corporate environment impacts on the workplace.

CONTEXT

In Chapter 1 we saw that the corporate environment consisted of three contexts:

- the economic
- the political/legal
- the technological.

These elements are important to understanding employee relations and why organisations choose to adopt particular policies and how such policies have changed and might change over time.

The business environment in which employee relations practitioners operate is constantly changing and it is important for them to be aware not only of specific shifts in employee relations policies resulting from such changes, but to monitor the environment to anticipate possible changes and developments and draw up a plan to deal with these expected changes if and when they arise. Employee relations policies devised and implemented in this context have both a reactive and a proactive role – a strategic role that is central to the organisation's growth and survival.

Although each of the elements is crucial in determining the employee relations practices of individual employers, the response of each to the impact on their own business or organisation is likely to be different. For example, a traditional non-union company such as Marks and Spencer is unlikely to have responded in the same way to the legislative changes introduced during the 1980s as a company that was traditionally heavily unionised. Equally, non-union organisations may react in a completely different way to the Employment Relations Act 1999. Its statutory rights on automatic recognition provision will require a fundamental re-think in attitudes towards collectivism and the role the workforce may play in the process of change. In the 1980s, changes to the laws on strikes, picketing and closed shops opened the door to employers who wanted to force through change, as was evidenced by the radical transformation that occurred in the newspaper industry. Many employers now have real fears that the gains made in the last 20 years in eliminating outdated working practices may be eroded if the introduction of statutory recognition procedures encourages a resurgence of workforce militant behaviour.

Change in Organisations

Employers have their own objectives, their own styles of employee relations and their own structures of organisations and associations. These structures have changed in recent times and it is important the employee relations specialist keeps up to date with new trends and developments. For example, the role of employers' organisations has declined in recent years in response to moves to decentralise the levels at which collective bargaining takes place. In the private sector there is now little national bargaining while in the public sector some local authorities have decentralised traditional systems of bargaining in favour of local wage determination.

Organisational structure has changed in both the public and private sectors. The growth of individual NHS Trusts is one example. Changes have also occurred in respect of employees and their organisations. As we shall see later in this chapter, the UK government economic policy and changes in legislation alter the relative balance of bargaining power between employers and employees. This can explain *inter alia* changes in the level of membership of unions causing individual unions to change their strategies to protect and advance their members' interests. These included merging with other unions (eg UNISON), creating in their wake a number of 'super unions'. These issues are discussed in greater detail in Chapter 4.

The role of the state has also changed. It has always been a major employer in its own right and the post-war expectation was that it would be a 'model employer', by:

- encouraging collective bargaining

- ensuring the pay of its employees was in line with that of the private sector

- resolving differences with its employees by arbitration and not by the use of industrial sanctions.

This concept has now changed. The whole nature of public sector employment has altered, with former civil servants now working for quasi-private sector employers such as Training and Enterprise Councils. The growth of executive agencies such as the Prison Service and the Benefits Agency, outsourcing of local authority services and the spread of privatisation have further diluted the concept of the public servant.

Most of this change resulted from the objective of successive Conservative administrations during the 1980s and 1990s to reduce the influence of government on people's lives. They, therefore, saw the role of the UK government as staying outside the employee relations arena. Although the requirements of compulsory competitive tendering have been changed and the state remains a large employer, it no longer views collective bargaining, pay comparability and arbitration as central to its employee relations policies. There continues to be a strong encouragement to relate pay increases of government employers to improvements in individual performance. Whilst the present government is not as anti-union as its Conservative predecessors, there is no suggestion it will actively promote an increase in collective bargaining in its employee relations policy towards those employees whose terms and conditions of employment it directly or indirectly finances.

All this change has impacted on the nature and style of employee relations processes. As the impact of collective bargaining, and thus collective agreements, has declined, there has been a growth in the use of other employee relations processes. Joint consultation has undergone a resurgence and employee involvement schemes (for example, two-way communication, encouraging employees to contribute their knowledge and experience to operational decisions) have become much more important.

In Chapter 1 the concept of the balance of bargaining power and how important it is to the selection by the employer of appropriate employee relations processes was introduced. This balance is conditioned by changes in the economic, political and technological elements which taken together make up the corporate environment. In this chapter the concept is examined in greater detail and linked directly to the economic, legal and technical environment in which organisations exist and compete. The concept of the balance of power is also significant in helping to explain changes in the employee relations system over time; for example, why employee relations behaviour as we enter a new millennium is different from how it was in the 1970s. When you have completed this chapter you should be able to:

a) describe how the UK government in its role as economic manager influences employee relations

b) understand the two principal economic theories that have been applied to the management of the economy since the Second World War

c) explain how changes in the Labour Market have impacted on employee relations

d) explain how the legislative system, including laws emanating from Europe, influences employee relations

e) explain how the corporate environment affects the relative balance of bargaining power

f) explain what impact new technology has on the working environment.

ECONOMIC MANAGEMENT

The economic environment is influenced by the macro-economic policies that a particular government chooses to implement. In the context of the UK, government policies regarding the levels of:

• employment

• inflation

• taxation

• interest rates

have a direct effect on employee relations. This is because they have an impact on the relative balance of bargaining power between the buyers and sellers of labour services and thereby on the prices at which they are exchanged.

However, it would be a mistake to assume the UK government has a completely free hand in deciding what economic policies to implement. Like businesses, they are affected by external events. For example, the devaluation of sterling in 1992, which was caused by the UK's withdrawal from the European Exchange Rate System, created severe repercussions for the economy as a whole. More recently, the economic crisis affecting the Asian and Brazilian economies has impacted adversely on both export and home markets. Decisions by Japanese and Korean businesses not to proceed with planned new investment in the UK are examples of this.

In addition, UK macro-economic policy will be affected by any decisions the UK government makes regarding European Monetary Union. However, now that the Euro is a reality, irrespective of whether the UK joins or stays out, our economy will not be immune from its impact. Many organisations have made arrangements to deal in Euros and have set up systems that will allow their employees to be paid in the new currency. Some banks are establishing Euro accounts for customers who want them. All of this will inevitably feed down into employee relations practices and policies at the workplace.

However, whatever the degree of outside influence, the UK government has the role of an economic manager. While different political parties may have different ideologies and policies, the objectives of economic management, whichever party is in power, have been broadly similar. These have been:

• price stability

• full employment

• economic growth

• balance of payments surplus.

However, the priorities given to these four objectives has differed between governments. The Conservative governments (1979–1997) gave the greatest priority to price stability whilst Labour governments (1974–1979) put the greatest emphasis on the full employment objective. Although the two main political parties when in government had the same economic objectives, the policies they implemented to achieve these objectives were different. The employee relations specialist needs therefore to understand that the economic policies of a Conservative government are likely to differ from those of a Labour government and that these distinctions in policy can have differing impacts on the relative balance of bargaining power. There are some politicians who believe Britain should follow a policy of full employment and that the achievement of this goal justifies a degree of direct UK government intervention into the affairs of public and private enterprises. When this approach has been adopted, the outcome has been to give organised labour an advantage in the balance of relative bargaining power.

An important issue of economic policy, therefore, surrounds public expenditure. All UK governments seek to keep public borrowing under some control because of the impact on inflation of not doing so. The International Monetary Fund (IMF) has repeatedly warned that financial market confidence and long-term interest rates are adversely affected if governments pay insufficient attention to the need to reduce the public sector borrowing requirement. Translated into employee relations terms, this usually means keeping a tight control over increases in public sector pay. Amongst private sector employers, there is always concern over the possibility of any government taking a soft line on public sector pay. For example, the desire to improve rewards for groups such as nurses in response to public opinion creates a 'knock on' effect across the board. If government is unwilling, or unable, to keep a tight control over public sector pay settlements, then any appeals to the private sector to show restraint will fall on deaf ears. That is why one of the most important skills of the employee relations manager/professional is the art of scanning the political and environmental landscape to establish the extent to which policy shifts may have an impact on employee relations in the future.

The present government has repeatedly stated it wants the UK to be a 'knowledge-based economy', and that human capital, in the form of employees, help to create wealth. Therefore it is of fundamental economic importance to create significant numbers of new jobs. If, through initiatives like the 'New Deal', the government is successful in reducing the numbers of unemployed and creating a significant number of new skilled jobs then there could, as we examine later in this chapter, be a swing in the balance of power towards employees and away from employers. Pressure on wage rates could increase as unemployment decreases, particularly if skill shortages increase, and this may be exacerbated if there is an upsurge of trade unionism.

> What occupational types, either within your own organisation or externally, could be in short supply in such circumstances? Do you think your organisation has planned sufficiently far ahead in respect of its manpower requirements?

There is evidence that many organisations have, over time, failed to invest sufficiently in training. Once the pool of available labour reduces, its 'price' goes up. Clearly these and other effects are not necessarily the immediate results of a change of UK government, but over time the needs of economic management change and shift. The strategic employee relations specialist monitors and anticipates such changes, to support and inform the organisation's future plans and objectives.

In economic terms, a further impact on employee relations comes from the growth in multinational companies and the expansion of the global marketplace. In a world of multinationals, the intricacies of international finance have effects on employee relations at the local level. Indeed, they can influence the location of new employment opportunities and, in some cases, the underlying culture of employee relations practices. The debate in early 1999 over whether BMW would continue to invest in Rover's Longbridge plant or relocate some of its manufacturing elsewhere is evidence of this.

Multinationals see wage rates, expansion and investment in the context of the global market, in much the same way that a national company makes decisions after taking into account subsidies from enterprise areas, development corporations and so on. International competition affects employee relations in other ways. Firms from the USA and Japan who set up in the UK look for qualities such as flexibility and adaptability. This has caused some of the traditional demarcation lines in industry to become blurred or removed. The negotiation of such methods of working makes them important in the area of employee relations.

To understand how the UK government's role of economic manager can have an effect on employee relations and on the relative balance of bargaining power between employers and employees, it is important to review and understand the two principal economic theories that have been applied to the management of the UK economy since the end of the Second World War, not least because a reversal of the economic policies that are currently being applied could result in a high wage, high inflation economy.

The full employment/economic growth era

For nearly 30 years after the Second World War, successive UK governments, regardless of their political complexion, were committed to a policy of full employment. During this period economic management was heavily influenced by the ideas of the economist John Maynard Keynes, whose basic ideas included:

- The general level of employment in an economy is determined by the level of spending power in the economy.

- The overall spending power in the economy depends upon the amount of consumption and investment undertaken by individual households and employing organisations as well as UK government expenditure on health, education, social security, defence, industrial assistance, etc.

- Full employment is achieved by the government regulating overall spending power in the economy by its fiscal (tax), monetary (interest rates) and public expenditure policies.

- If unemployment rises, due to a lack of overall spending power in the economy, then the government should inject spending power by reducing taxes on incomes, property, expenditure (VAT, excise duties), by lowering interest rates or by increasing its own expenditure.

Application of the Keynesian model of economic management led to economic growth, increased public provision (in such areas as housing, education and the national health service) and personal prosperity for the majority of households. From the perspective of trade unions, full employment provided them with increased bargaining power which, in many instances, led employers to concede inflationary wage settlements. Many of the craft unions, for example printers and engineers, operated policies aimed at restricting the number of new entrants to their particular craft to delay introduction of new working methods or technology. This behaviour created labour shortages in certain occupations and led to overstaffing in others. Attempts to resolve this problem resulted in considerable organisational conflict and a perception that management was unable to implement effective policies to counteract many of these restrictions. This led, inevitably, to a worsening of management and union relationships.

However, notwithstanding the increase in the overall standard of living, the general level of performance of the British economy was one of slower economic growth than its major competitors. As Pettigrew and Whipp report, 'in the three decades after the Second World War, the British economy showed the lowest rate of growth (an average of two and a half per cent per annum) of the major industrialised countries'. This relative economic underperformance had many negative effects, of which less than constructive employee relations was certainly one.

By the latter part of the 1960s the effect of high wage settlements, together with union defensive attitudes and poor management, caused many commentators to take the view that this deterioration in competitiveness was a direct consequence of poor workplace industrial relations (Nolan and Walsh, 1995). This view was supported by the report in 1968 of the Royal Commission on Trade Unions and Employers' Associations which was established in 1965 under the chairmanship of Lord Donovan. Thus, the reform of workplace industrial relations became a major public policy priority. However, opinions on the type of reform, and how best to implement it, differed particularly under the role of the law as a catalyst for bringing back change. Nonetheless, the need for reform was not questioned.

So, by the mid-1960s, the concerns about the prevailing system of employee relations and its adverse impact on economic competitiveness via relatively higher UK prices than those of our economic competitors made the issue central to the political agenda. The Labour government under Harold Wilson, which was elected in 1964, decided to try to re-establish UK economic competitiveness by direct interference into the outcome of employee relations through a productivity, prices and incomes policy designed to control inflation by ensuring income increases were linked to increases in productivity and not to changes in the rate of inflation or what other workers were receiving.

According to Keynesian economics, if creating full employment gave rise to inflation then the implementation of an incomes policy was necessary. Because wage costs account for such a significant proportion of employers' total costs, excessive rises in wage levels affect the inflation spiral. As inflation rises, economic policy makers are tempted to regulate economic activity by stifling demand which, in turn, can lead to rises in unemployment. Keynes argued that increasing unemployment to control inflation could be avoided and full employment maintained by the introduction of an incomes policy.

The history of incomes policies over the period 1948–1979 shows that in the short run they were successful but ultimately broke down, usually in the face of a strike in support of a pay increase in excess of the policy. By the 1970s such policies were proving politically explosive. Such attempts to limit wage settlements were seen by some as a deliberate attempt to shift the balance of bargaining power towards the interests of employers and were resisted by the unions to the point of industrial disputes, the most famous of which were the miners' strikes of 1972 and 1973/74 and the 'winter of discontent' in 1978/79.

Management was not always impressed by the arbitrary imposition by the UK government of pay norms and was often happy to work with employees to find ways round them. Private-sector employers were more interested in continuation of production and some were prepared to pay higher wages to avoid industrial action. While we now live in a highly competitive world economy, where maintaining some form of competitive advantage is essential for most businesses, this was not always the case in the three decades after the Second World War. During that period a much greater proportion of an organisation's customer base was static relative to today and therefore they had a much greater ability to pass on increased wage costs in the form of increased prices. In the case of the public sector, there was no serious long-term attempt to limit the growth in public expenditure and therefore companies and enterprises learned to live with high inflation and its consequent impact on wages and prices.

'Irresponsible union' behaviour

Circumventing pay norms was but one example of a wider malaise. By the beginning of the 1960s the balance of power was firmly with the trade unions and particularly in the motor car industry where shop stewards at plant level were increasingly exercising this power. They were reluctant to abide by disputes procedures and to subject themselves to control by full-time officials, particularly those national trade union leaders who were prepared to co-operate with some form of pay restraint. Some industries, like shipbuilding, motor car manufacture and the ports, had their own agendas which tended to be parochial, and in the opinion of many employers, were based on political and not industrial objectives. Many employers also questioned whether shop stewards, in calling unofficial and unconstitutional strikes, truly represented the wishes of all their members. Such views about the internal democracy of trade unions were given credence in that many industrial action decisions were based on voting by a show of hands at mass meetings, rather than by a secret ballot of those being asked to become involved.

One common theme of the 1960s and 1970s was the perception, partly based on strike statistics, and on the trade unions links with the Labour Party and therefore Labour governments, that trade union leaders were more powerful than UK government ministers. Because poor workplace industrial relations were judged to have had a negative impact on economic performance, unions and their alleged 'irresponsible' use of power were seen as major contributors to the UK's relative lack of economic competitiveness. If businesses were not investing sufficiently, this, it was claimed, was the fault of the unions. If new technology was not embraced sufficiently quickly, again the unions were seen as the basis of the problem. If inflation was out of control, it was the fault of the unions. Although any objective examination of industrial relations during this period would show the unions having to accept a large part of the blame, weak management performance during the period was also a contributory factor. There was insufficient investment in training and development and then, as now, insufficient investment in innovation and research. The debate about skill levels within UK organisations relative to our international competitors is still ongoing. Despite the investment in Training and Enterprise Councils, National Vocational Qualifications and the National Curriculum, there is still concern that some employers have failed to see the value of investing in people (Nolan and Walsh, 1995).

The rise of monetarism

The 1978/79 so-called 'winter of discontent', when low-paid public-sector employees took strike action to gain pay increases in excess of the then Labour Government pay increase norm, coincided with the end of the five-year electoral cycle. The incumbent Labour government knew it had to call a General Election during 1979 and, although it sought to postpone this for as long as possible, an election was duly held in May 1979. The Conservative Party fought the election promising better management of the economy, lower income taxes, less Government expenditure and curtailment of union power, all of which it claimed would help the UK economy regain competitiveness. It committed itself to introducing legislation designed to ensure that trade unions acted responsibly.

During its period in opposition (1974–1979) a growing faction within the Conservative party began to question the ability of Keynesian economic policies to provide price stability (commonly referred to as sound money). Instead, what Keegan (1984: p66) refers to as the 'economic evangelicalists' began to embrace the concept of monetarism as the means to control inflation and improve economic competitiveness. While monetarism can mean different things to different people its basic propositions are:

• if the general level of purchasing power in the economy as a whole grows more quickly than the increase in the general level of goods and services produced in the economy as a whole then firms and households will have more money to purchase goods and services than are available in the economy as a whole.

• this could lead to a situation where there is 'too much money chasing too few goods and services'; demand is greater than supply. Shortages arises and market prices start to increase as consumers compete with each other for this reduced supply.

• increasing inflation increases expectations of future inflation rates which will be even higher resulting in (a) higher wage demands and settlements and (b) a wages–prices inflationary spiral resulting in an increase in the general level of unemployment as the competitiveness of firms declines and workers 'price themselves out of jobs'.

• to prevent inflation the increase in overall level of purchasing power in the economy as a whole must match the rate of increase in the general output of goods and services in the economy as a whole.

• if the increase in the economy-wide level of purchasing power exceeds the increase in the general level of the supply of goods and services in the economy as a whole, spending power (demand) must be decreased by raising interest rates and reducing the level of UK government (public) expenditure.

For monetarists, unemployment will only fall, in the longer term, if the productive capacity of the economy is increased. Measures to achieve such an increase are usually referred to as 'supply-side' economics. The key to reducing unemployment and controlling inflation is enhancing the ability of the economy to increase the supply of goods and services to the market more efficiently by:

• creating an environment conducive to private enterprise

• creating incentives for individuals to work

• creating incentives for firms to invest, produce goods and services and employ workers

- liberalising product markets

- privatising publicly-owned enterprises

- reducing taxation

- deregulating labour markets.

The Conservatives won the 1979 election and under the premiership of Margaret Thatcher began the process of applying monetarist policies to the management of the UK economy. These policies have now been applied in one way or another since that time and are being continued by the present government. However, it believes competitive advantage comes from quality and added value rather than price. It may be that the application of economic policy is now less doctrinaire than in the past. There is a view that New Labour endorses and understands the concept of human capital much more than the Conservatives. By spreading opportunities through education and injecting more social justice into the equation it hopes the UK can become a 'knowledge-based economy' capable of competing with the best.

LABOUR MARKET CHANGES

The make-up of the UK economy has changed radically in the last quarter of the 20th century. One of the visible results of this, for the employee relations specialist, has been a much more deregulated labour market. The reforms to the labour market have seen a move from employment in manufacturing to employment in the service industry, which has accounted for an increase in non-manual jobs at the expense of manual ones. Part-time employment has increased while full-time employment has decreased. The rise in part-time employment, when converted to full-time equivalents, does not compensate for this downturn in full-time work. While it would be an over-simplification to blame all the changes in the labour market on monetarist policies, those policies were the engine by which the reforms were driven. The consequences of higher unemployment than in the 1960s and 1970s have had a major impact on employee relations. While trade union influence is lower and industrial disputes have declined, there has been a growth in employee insecurity and, if the number of cases being dealt with by ACAS and Employment Tribunals is any guide, a rise in the number of workplace grievances. High levels of employee insecurity are not helpful if, as we saw at the beginning of the chapter, organisations need to improve continually their performance.

The feelings of insecurity expressed by many employees are a major concern to employers and thus employee relations specialists. In your organisation have you identified a rise in grievances, individual or collective, as a consequence of such insecurity? If insecurity exists, but grievances have not risen, how does the concern over insecurity manifest itself?

The labour market

Some commentators have argued that the relative growth in jobs in the service sector compared to the manufacturing sector has led to an increase in 'McJobs' – part-time, badly paid and with low status – which has contributed to the decline in trade union membership and influence. It is argued that the lack of security offered by this type of employment has made people less inclined to join trade unions as they are afraid to challenge their employer. Clearly, the decline in traditional union strongholds such as mining and shipbuilding has had an effect, but as with most things in employee relations, the reality tends to be more complex.

If we are to understand the significance that the labour market has on employee relations we need to understand more about the composition of the UK workforce. The 1998 Workplace Employee Relations Survey (WERS) provides useful data. As its authors point out, 'commentators looking at the British labour market often highlight the issue of flexibility' and they therefore considered it valid to look at the 'extent to which workplaces contract out different services ... [because] if the extent of contracting out has been on the increase, it may have led to a reduction in direct employment in workplaces'.

The Survey asked whether workplaces had contracted out services which would previously have been undertaken by people directly employed in the organisation and found that a third of respondents said this was the case. Furthermore, one third were using former employees of the workplace as the contractors. They found that 11 per cent of employers had transferred some employees to a different employer in the five years preceding the publication of their report and that this proportion was far higher (22 per cent) in the public sector than in the private sector (6 per cent).

Another area which has had a major impact on the labour market is non-standard employment. This is generally defined as anything that is not permanent full-time work and embraces part-time working, the use of freelancers, outworkers and temporary and fixed-term contract employees.

Critics of labour market reforms have argued there has been a growth in the use of part-time labour to the detriment of full-time jobs. The WERS provides information on the extent of part-time employment which is defined as anybody working fewer than 30 hours per week. The Survey found part-time workers accounted for a quarter of all jobs in workplaces with 25 or more employees, but that their distribution varied enormously across workplaces of different kinds. As Table 7 (opposite) shows, 16 per cent of workplaces employ no part-timers, while in 26 per cent of workplaces, part-timers form a majority of the workforce, a figure that shows a 10 per cent increase since 1990.

The WERS revealed the use of freelancers (13 per cent) and outworkers (6 per cent) is reasonably significant, but provided some revealing data about temps and fixed-term contract employees. There has been a widely-held perception that employers have placed a greater reliance on the use of temporary and fixed-term contract employees.

Table 7 Use of part-time employees, by industry

Industry	No part-time employees	Most employees part-time
	% of workplaces	% of workplaces
Manufacturing	36	1
Electricity, gas and water	51	0
Construction	39	0
Wholesale and retail	14	43
Hotels and restaurants	3	55
Transport and communications	23	4
Financial services	20	5
Other business services	23	7
Public administration	9	1
Education	0	40
Health	1	50
Other community services	8	51
All workplaces	16	26

Base: all workplaces with 25 or more employees.
Figures are weighted and based on responses from 1,914 managers.

Table 8 (below) shows this is not the case and the majority of workplaces do not use temps or employ people on fixed-term contracts.

Whatever the statistics, there is no doubt 'the ability of managers to adjust the size of their workforces in line with requirements and demand – usually referred to as "numerical flexibility" – appears to be widespread'. The figure below shows that during the 1990s there has been an increase in the use of non-standard employment.

Whatever type of organisation you work in, the impact of the labour market changes will have affected the way you do your job. In organisations that still rely on a greater proportion of traditional permanent full-time employees there is likely to be pressure for

Table 8 Use of temporary agency workers and fixed-term contracts, by occupation

Occupation	Temporary agency workers	Fixed-term contracts
	% of workplaces employing	% of workplaces employing
Managers and administrators	1	6
Professional	5	15
Associate professional and technical	5	6
Clerical and secretarial	17	13
Craft and related	2	3
Personal and protective service	2	5
Sales	0	4
Plant and machine operatives	4	2
Other occupations	5	6
None of these workers used	72	56

Base: workplaces with 25 or more employees.
Figures are weighted and based on responses from 1,921 managers.

Figure 3 Change in the use of different forms of labour over the past five years

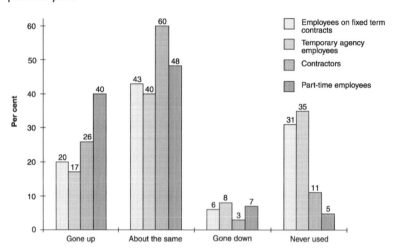

Base: all workplaces that are five or more years old with 25 or more employees.
Figures are weighted and based on responses from 1,706 managers.

change. Employment costs are still, for most businesses, the most significant item in the management accounts and provide one of the better opportunities to make savings. In the near future, as competition heightens, some form of the 'flexible firm' will have to become a reality for all organisations; this is not necessarily bad news, although the pessimistic view of the reformed labour market is the 'McJobs' thesis. Two 1999 reports suggest the reality more encouraging.

A report by the Institute for Employment Research at Warwick University (IER) predicts that over the period 1997 to 2006, 1.4 million new jobs will be created. As this figure is higher than the expected increase in the population of working age, it will allow unemployment to stay low. While the report acknowledges that many of the new jobs will be part-time and employ women, some of the biggest increases in demand will be for professional and technical staff.

The second report by the Institute for Fiscal Studies (IFS), assesses the Government's changes to the tax and benefits system and the introduction of the national minimum wage. It concludes that the package of measures will make work pay by between £7 and £13 a week extra. The two reports suggest that we are about to witness a labour market where employers are creating new jobs and people are more willing to take them.

JOB CREATION

Although it is acknowledged that part-time jobs will account for most of the net job creation and that the proportion of women in the workforce will continue to rise, it would be wrong to interpret this as the creation of a second-class labour market. A closer look at the forecasts contained in the two reports shows job creation is taking place in two broad categories. One is 'personal and protective services', which includes security guards and carers. While this could be made to fit the pessimistic thesis, the impact of the minimum wage and the working time regulations should help to mitigate some of the abuses of long hours and low pay.

The second category is in managerial, professional and technical jobs, demanding high levels of education and skill. On average it is predicted there will be 171,000 more jobs a year in these categories between now and 2006, compared to 77,000 a year in the personal and protective services category. The IER predicts big increases in retailing and tourism which, while they will require plenty of part-time labour, are also in the process of upskilling available jobs. For example, hotels and restaurants are having to train staff to meet higher standards of food hygiene, make more use of information technology and fill more demanding managerial roles; chefs have to be involved in budgeting, for example, and reception staff need to work the computer booking system and respond to customer demands.

GREATER FLEXIBILITY

But what does all this structural change in the labour market mean at the level of the individual firm. What is its impact on employee relations? Many of the changes that have taken place over the last two decades have been driven by the increase in the global marketplace and by the need to develop organisations that can respond flexibly to the rapidly changing demands of that market. This has given rise to the concept known as the 'flexible firm', but the data from WERS indicates that the movement towards changing work patterns is at best mixed. Stredwick and Ellis (1998) identify a number of surveys that 'throw light on the reality of the movement towards flexible working'. They conclude that 'the evidence is strong all round that the move to greater flexibility is gathering pace, and that organisations see it as a means of achieving competitive advantage'.

Evidence concerning the employees' attitude to flexible working arrangements is thin, but Emmott and Hutchinson (1998) note that 'generally they are perceived as a "good thing" ... [but] that there are negative implications'. This ties in with Stredwick and Ellis's conclusion that 'employees are not always fully co-operative in these ventures' and it is this lack of co-operation that is likely to present the greatest challenge to the employee relations specialist. If, as Stredwick and Ellis state, employees are given little choice about embracing flexibility, this will have a major impact on their sense of security and well being. Furthermore, if they are right that few organisations are embracing flexibility for strategic reasons, they could enhance the ability of trade unions to recruit workers as a means of resisting change. We shall consider this strategic aspect more fully in Chapter 5.

The State as an employer pre-1979

In this and the sections that follow, we look at some of the policy initiatives of the past 18 years, and how they have contributed to the change in employment relationships. During the post Second World War period, the State always sought to give a lead to the private sector as a model and good employer. Collective bargaining was considered a good and desirable activity and union membership was encouraged. When industries were taken into public ownership both after the Second World War and then in the 1970s (for example, shipbuilding), there was an obligation on the public corporation created to recognise, consult and negotiate with trade unions. The State also sought to ensure its staff received comparable pay and conditions to those doing the same or similar work in the private sector. Comparability was thus the basis of wage claims and adjustments. For example, in the Civil Service the civil servants were given a Pay Research Unit to look at rates of pay, to compare pay with private-sector employees and to provide information to the negotiators.

Increasing the supply side

Conservative Governments post-1979 had a different approach to economic management and pursued a twin-track policy to achieve their objectives. They eschewed the prevailing post-war consensus in areas such as the welfare state, UK Government intervention in industry, incomes policy, tripartite discussions and keeping unemployment in check even at the risk of inflation rising. Instead they made clear their intention of letting the market decide.

Monetarist policies were introduced as a means of reducing inflation which meant sharp increases in interest rates and in indirect taxes (especially VAT) and cuts in public expenditure. The impact was large increases in unemployment, especially in the country's manufacturing industries such as shipbuilding, motor cars and steel. By allowing unemployment to rise, the UK Government was making it clear radical measures were needed if the British economy was to re-establish its competitiveness.

In addition, Conservative Governments sought the encouragement of an enterprise culture by the deregulation of product and labour markets, the privatisation of nationalised industries and the regulation of trade unions' industrial activities. As Blyton and Turnbull (1994: p145) saw it, 'the objectives of UK Government policy in the 1980s can be simply stated: namely, to encourage enterprise through the deregulation of markets, especially the labour market'. They noted that the foundations of Conservative government policy under Mrs Thatcher can be found in the writings of free market economists such as Milton Friedman and in particular Friedrich Hayek. Of the UK economists who subscribe to the monetarist philosophy, the work of Patrick Minford is a good indicator of why the policy agenda has developed as it has. Minford argues that trade unions use their power to raise wages above the market rate which then causes price inflation which in turn causes further rises in unemployment. This process, he argues, reduces both the efficiency of individual firms and the economy as a whole through the imposition of restrictive practices, demarcation, etc. For the monetarists then, if employment is to increase, the labour market behaviour of trade unions needs to be regulated. Trade unions need to be restrained from abusing market power. It was for this reason that the Conservative administration over the period 1979–1997 introduced legislation to free labour markets from trade union influence.

The restriction on trade union behaviour was two-pronged. The Conservatives made it clear that they were no longer prepared to promote the government's traditional role as a 'model employer'. The idea that the state should be a model to the private sector remained, but the notion of what constituted a 'model employer' changed. In 1981 the government ended the civil service comparability agreement which had operated since 1951. This led to industrial action in the security services, which in turn resulted in the UK Government ending union recognition (which was not reversed until 1998) from its highly secret communications headquarters (GCHQ).

The UK Government became less favourably disposed to collective bargaining and instead argued that employees should be rewarded as individuals. They sought to act against the collective voice, because they subscribed to the view that it led to overpriced jobs and consequently unemployment. The state ceased to encourage people to become members of trade unions or to take part in collective bargaining. Conversely, they also discouraged the traditional role of employers' federations in national wage bargaining. Comparability of pay for public sector employees was terminated because it was thought pay increases should be related to the ability to pay and availability of labour resources. Thus, the pay of an occupational group should not necessarily be the same in different parts of the country. Differentials should reflect the scarcity of that labour. Thus, wage negotiation at operating unit levels, where the ability to pay and scarcity of labour factors could more easily be taken into account, was encouraged and the traditional 'going-rate' argument discouraged.

> Are any of these principals incorporated into the reward structure within your organisation? If yes, what is the impact on employee relations?

PUBLIC EXPENDITURE

The UK Government argued inflation was the result of money supply increasing faster than the increase in output of goods and services in the economy. Money supply is the total spending power in the economy as a whole, but a major component in this is public expenditure. Given that the UK Government was responsible directly or indirectly for the wages of one third of the employees in the country, and given that pay is an important part of public sector expenditure, UK Governments cannot adopt a neutral stance on public sector settlements. Therefore, although the UK Government made it clear that a formal incomes policy with norms and enforcement agencies was not on its agenda, it was prepared to ensure effective controls over the pay rises for public sector employees by the simple expedient of limiting the rise in public expenditure. This approach brought the UK Government into conflict with a number of public sector unions, for example school teachers, who had their collective bargaining rights removed by Act of Parliament.

The labour market reforms over the past twenty years have seen a progressive diminution of the welfare safety net for unemployed workers. Governments considered that overgenerous welfare provision meant people had less incentive to work and, therefore, remained unemployed for longer than is necessary. This so-called dependency culture was tackled by changing the basis on which an individual was eligible for unemployment benefit and by reducing the length of time such benefit was payable. Because of the fear of unemployment such changes in the welfare system meant employees became less resistant to employer control and were less likely to seek reviews of their terms and conditions of employment for fear of losing their jobs.

THE STATE AS LAW-MAKER

Otto Kahn-Freund, in his classic book *Labour and the Law* (1977) outlined three functions of the law in regulating employee relations. These were:

- The auxiliary function, where the law is designed to promote private behaviour (for example, collective bargainers) towards certain ends or else the law, in the last resort, will force them to behave in this way. A good example of the statutory trade union recognition procedure is the Employment Relations Act 1999.

- The regulatory function, where the law regulates management behaviour towards its employees and trade union officers behaviour towards their members. This is the area of individual employment rights and the rights of individual trade union members.

- The restrictive function, where the law establishes the 'rules of the game' when employers and employees are in the process of making agreements. This type of legislation effectively lays down the circumstances in which employers and trade unions can impose industrial sanctions on each other without the parties having redress to the legal system.

The idea that the law was used to promote collective bargaining was anathema to Margaret Thatcher and the 1980 Employment Act repealed a statutory trade union recognition procedure introduced in the Employment Protection Act 1975. The auxiliary function of the law as described by Kahn-Freund did not figure highly in her legislative programme during her period in office. The Employment Relations Act 1999, with its provisions for statutory recognition and opportunities for trade union representation at discipline and grievance hearings, reverses this process.

The regulatory function of the law

Statutory rights for individual employees relative to their employer began to emerge in the early 1960s. Parliament justified providing such rights on the grounds that private arrangements (for example, by collective agreement) had failed to provide an adequate minimum level of protection to individual employees against certain behaviour by their employers. At the same time it sent a clear message to employers that they must act with just cause and be 'fair and reasonable' in the treatment of their employees on those matters where statutory minimum standards were being established for their employees.

Individual employees enforce these rights relative to their employer via Employment Tribunals which are independent judicial bodies set up to deal with claims quickly, informally and cheaply. They have a legally qualified chair who sits with two other members, each of whom is drawn from panels appointed by the Secretary of State, one after consultation with employee organisations, the other after consultation with employers' organisations. The floor of legal rights was created by UK Governments sympathetic to the view there should be a basic level of employment protection, below which no employer should be permitted to fall. These minimum levels can be enhanced by private agreements, for example, via collective bargaining.

However, Conservative Governments post-1979, although accepting the principle of employment protection, argued the minimum standards were too high and were a disincentive for employers, particularly small and new firms, to recruit labour. To counteract this disincentive, they introduced measures that exempted small firms from certain aspects of the law and increased the qualifying period for obtaining employment rights in the case of unfair dismissal and redundancy to two years.

A statutory floor of rights for trade union members relative to their trade union was considerably extended under the post-1979 Conservative Governments. This has been justified on the grounds that trade unions needed to be more democratic and more accountable to their members and to exercise their power more responsibly. The UK Government believed trade union leaders were, without collecting the views of their members, coercing them to undertake labour market activities (for example, undertaking industrial action) harmful to their employment security.

This view resulted in the enactment of a series of measures to provide positive rights for union members to participate in or restrain union decision-making on specific issues. The main trade union member rights are:

- the opportunity to participate in regular secret post ballots, at least once every 10 years, to decide whether or not their union should establish, or retain, a political fund financed by political fund contribution, independent of the normal union subscription

- to elect all voting members of their union's executive (including its President and General Secretary) by secret postal ballot at least once every five years

- to participate in a secret ballot before a union takes organised industrial action against an employer

- not to be called upon to participate in industrial action not supported by a properly conducted secret ballot

- not to be disciplined unjustifiably by their union

- to inspect their union's accounting records.

As a means of helping individual union members enforce their rights the Commissioner for the Rights of Trade Union Members (CRTUM) was created under the Employment Act 1988 and had two sets of powers. The first was to grant assistance to union members considering or taking legal action against their union. The second was to give assistance when a union member claimed his or her union had failed to observe the requirements of its own rule book. The Commissioner also acted as the Commissioner for Protection against Unlawful Industrial Action and could help those third party individuals who wished to challenge the lawfulness of industrial action. These institutions have now been abolished and the powers of the 'Certification Officer' have been extended to incorporate the powers formerly held by the Commissioner.

The restrictive function of the law
Ever since 1871 trade unions have, except when they were undermined by the Taff Vale decision in 1901, enjoyed immunity from actions for civil damages. The basic immunity framework was contained in the Trade Disputes Act 1906 and this remained in force until 1971 when the Conservative Government introduced the Industrial Relations Act. This limited trade union immunity by the introduction of the concept of 'Unfair Industrial Practices' which if committed by the unions, gave those affected by the action the right to sue for damages.

The Trade Union and Labour Relations Act 1974 repealed the Industrial Relations Act 1971 and re-established the trade unions' immunities position back to that provided by the Trades Disputes Act 1906. The Trade Union and Labour Relations (Amendment) Act 1976 extended trade union immunity to the breach of all contracts for which trade unions were responsible when they called their members out on industrial action. This gave trade unions licence to persuade their members to take secondary industrial action. Secondary action is that taken against an employer with whom the trade union has no dispute, but who might, for example, be a key customer of an employer with whom they currently do have an industrial dispute. By taking this type of industrial action the union hopes the secondary employer will put pressure on the employer involved in the main dispute to settle the dispute on terms which are more favourable than those presently on offer.

By 1976, trade unions had a very wide immunity from legal action in the case of industrial disputes. They could call, without a legal liability arising, for industrial action in connection with any kind of industrial dispute, no matter how remote those taking the action were from the original dispute. Nobody seriously challenged this union legislative position until 1979, after which things began to change.

Legislation came at regular intervals and between 1980 and 1993 there were seven Acts of Parliament designed to restrict trade union activity and behaviour:

- The Employment Act 1980 removed the unions' immunity if their members engaged in picketing premises other than their own place of work.

- The Employment Act 1982 narrowed the definition of a trade dispute, outlawed the practice of pressuring employers not to include non-union firms on tender lists and enabled employers to sue trade unions for an injunction or damages where they were responsible for unlawful industrial action.

- The Trade Union Act 1984 introduced pre-strike ballots.

- The Employment Act 1988 effectively outlawed the closed shop.

- The Employment Act 1990 removed union immunity if they organised any type of secondary action in support of an individual dismissed for taking unlawful action.

- The Trade Union and Labour Relations (Consolidation) Act 1992 brought together in one piece of legislation much of the law relating to collective provision.

- The Trade Union Reform and Employment Rights Act 1993 made some amendments to existing requirements, most particularly in relation to ballots for industrial action.

These pieces of legislation increased substantially the grounds on which legal action can be taken against a union by an employer. The circumstances in which unions can claim immunity from civil action have been tightened and now include provisions which require full-time officials to repudiate the actions of lay officials if they take actions which are contrary to the legislation. If immunity is to be maintained such repudiation has to be meaningful and the courts can require unions to present evidence as to the steps they have taken to bring their members within the law.

There is now less argument that these reforms were both necessary and timely. Requiring unions to hold a pre-strike ballot of their members prior to taking industrial action is not seriously questioned any more. Nor is the requirement that full-time officials should be subject to periodic re-election.

THE IMPACT OF TECHNOLOGY

All organisations operate within certain technological constraints which impact on their size and structure. In turn, the size and structure of an organisation will undoubtedly have an influence on its culture. As culture affects relationships between people, it can be seen that technology and technological development are important factors in employee relations.

It is important employee relations specialists understand the term 'technology'. If it merely implies some form of process or engineering, does it have any relevance outside manufacturing? Technology is more than an engineering process. From the perspective of an organisation it is about the application of skills and knowledge. It is therefore both relevant and necessary to understand it.

It is possible to identify three perspectives from which to view the impact of new technology on employee relations. One is that new technology, because of its impact on traditional skills, acts as both a de-skilling agent and a creator of unemployment. The second perspective is that new technology is a positive force in that it creates new opportunities for employees who have the chance to learn new skills. A third perspective sees technology as the means whereby previously unpleasant or repetitive tasks can be eliminated. For example, the introduction of robotics into the car industry removed the need for employees to carry out mundane operations with a consequent improvement in the climate of employee relations in an industry previously dogged by labour problems. Each of these three perspectives is, to some degree, correct, but the impact of new technology varies from industry to industry and from organisation to organisation.

While most people acknowledge that, in general terms, technological development has reduced the demand for certain types of labour, it is clear it has presented some significant opportunities for job creation. One example is the large growth in the use of call centres, particularly in the financial services sector. Call centres now employ nearly 300,000 people and this figure is forecast to rise further over the next decade. They are clearly technology-driven and rely on a combination of complex computer-driven communications technologies.

Technological development based on computers, lasers and telecommunications not only has the capacity to de-skill jobs; it can:

• blur demarcation lines

• create for an employer an alternative lower paid workforce

• provide the impetus for changes in work patterns.

It is important for the employee relations specialist to recognise where technology requires changes in working patterns or processes and to identify appropriate and available training opportunities.

A commonly held view about the impact of technological change is that it creates problems, particularly where trade unions are represented in the workplace, and is often resisted. These views are given added credence by the way in which the media report such issues. The News International dispute at Wapping in 1986 is famous for the attempts by the print unions to resist the takeover of their jobs by fellow trade unionists, the electricians. It provided a useful opportunity to present old craft unions (Printers) as resistant to change, with 'reformist' unions like the electricians being the acceptable face of collectivism. There was no real attempt by the media to address the real employee relations issues that such a dispute raised. When change is on the agenda, both trade unions and employees generally have fears over job losses, de-skilling and increased management control. The skill of the employee relations specialist lies in understanding these concerns and seeking ways of mitigating them. Personnel specialists should have a vested interest in the management of change, not just the imposition of change.

> Some commentators argue that the pace of technological change must, inevitably, slow down. Do you think this is a fair statement? If not, where do you see change happening, and how is it likely to impact on your organisation?

Whenever the subject of technology is discussed the question of de-skilling arises; the debate concerning the long term impact on skill levels applicable to technological change has raged for decades, much of it being conducted by means of case study investigations. One investigation, the Social Change and Economic Life Initiative (SCELI), provided the first systematic survey data with which to assess the nature of skill change in Britain. As Ashton and Felstead (1995) report, the information collected was gathered from interviews with over six thousand individuals in six areas. Those interviewed were asked to compare their current jobs with what they were doing five years earlier, in terms of the level of skill and responsibility required. Over the period, 52 per cent experienced an increase in the skills that they required, compared to only 9 per cent who saw their skills decline. This common experience of upskilling was true for all occupational categories, but was more prevalent among those already in highly skilled occupations.

A further survey, 'Employment in Britain' indicated that the trends identified by the SCELI investigation have continued into the 1990s. Again, this survey, conducted during 1992, demonstrated that higher level qualifications are now required for jobs which some years earlier were not rated so highly (Ashton and Felstead, 1995). While these surveys were carried out some time ago, their conclusions are still valid. We have already noted that organisations such as hotels and restaurants need to enhance the skills of their employees and the IER report showed more skilled jobs than unskilled jobs being created.

Whatever skills organisations require in the future, the employee relations specialist will have to recognise that changes in the balance of skills will have a significant impact on their work. In some organisations investment in improved technology may lead to both staff development and redundancies. In some organisations such investment can cause difficulties in recruiting sufficient skilled labour with the consequent pressure that this can bring, particularly in respect of unit labour costs. Overall it is important to remember that new technology varies in its impact. This is based on a number of variables including the nature of the product or service, the type of organisation involved, the management strategy employed and the attitude of trade unions (where they are represented) and employees.

THE BALANCE OF BARGAINING POWER

In chapter one we introduced the concept of the 'balance of bargaining power' and said that it was this balance that determines whether employers or employees feel that their interests have been satisfied. We also said that this balance in bargaining power operates at both a macro and a micro level. At the macro level the combination of economic management and political, legislative and technological change influences the overall conduct of employee relations, while at the micro level these factors can have totally different impacts.

The government's economic and legal policies have major implications for the outcome of employee relations activities. If economic policies are directed towards the creation of full employment and the maximising of economic growth, this weakens the relative bargaining power of the employer but strengthens that of the employee. A high level of demand for goods and services in the economy as a whole generates demand for labour to produce/provide those goods and services. If the demand for labour services increases relative to their supply (ie shortages develop) then the 'price' employers will have to pay to secure those services will increase.

If, on the other hand, government economic policies give the highest priority to reducing inflation by lowering household and corporate spending and reducing public expenditure, then the demand (spending power) in the economy will fall and as a consequence so will that for labour. The result will be labour 'surpluses' giving rise to redundancies and increased unemployment. The effect of the supply of labour exceeding demand is downward pressure on the 'price' of labour services or, if labour prices are inflexible downwards, less labour will be employed than previously at the same price (leading to unemployment). In such situations, the relative balance of bargaining power of employers will be strengthened and that of the employees weakened.

If the government introduces legislation favourable to employers' interests then the bargaining power of employers relative to employees is strengthened. This, as we stated above, is what Conservative Governments did during the period 1980–97 by introducing a series of labour law reforms. If a government introduces legislation favourable to the interests of employees and trade unions then the bargaining power of employees relative to employers is strengthened. Some employers have real fears that the introduction of the statutory recognition procedures contained in the Employment Relations Act 1999 will swing the balance of power towards trades unions, particularly in industries like media and communications. Legislation, by setting standards of behaviour by employers to regulate the relationship between an individual employee and their employer (for example, the right not to be unfairly dismissed), also influences the relative balance of bargaining power between employers and individual employees.

The implementation of new technology also impacts on bargaining power. For example, developments in communications have helped to produce global markets which have increased product market competition. This can lead to downward pressure on the 'price' of labour services and a shift in bargaining power towards the employer. The reverse can also be true. By creating new jobs, new skills and making some industries more capital intensive, the implementation of technological change has strengthened the bargaining power of employees. One only has to look at the advertised vacancies for a whole range of Information Technology jobs to identify one sector where this is true.

The influence on bargaining power of the wider economic and legal environment surrounding an employee relations system cannot be underestimated and in this regard the decision-making bodies of the European Union have become increasingly important. The role of the UK Government and European Union Council of Ministers (see Chapter 3) in this context means that representative bodies of employers and employees need to participate in the political lobbying process to persuade the political decision-makers to introduce economic and legal policies favourable to their interests.

The micro level

So far, the relative bargaining power between the buyers and sellers of labour services has been analysed on the macro level. However, analysis at this level cannot explain why some groups of employees retain their bargaining power *vis à vis* the employer despite low growth or high unemployment and why some employers are in a relatively weak bargaining position despite the economic climate being in their favour. In many respects, what matters for the employer is their bargaining power relative to particular groups of workers at the enterprise level. This is the relative bargaining power at the micro level.

Consider a situation where the national picture is unfavourable to employees in general. Unemployment is rising steeply, redundancies are occurring every day, employers are seeking to restrict wages and general employment conditions and new, small firms are replacing more established businesses. However, your organisation could be in a sector where the product or process has a limited shelf life. If you also have a collective relationship with a well-organised trade union they would be aware of how a trade dispute could have an immediate and costly effect on customer confidence or income generation. Alternatively, your company could be non-union, but very high-tech and experiencing rapid expansion. It requires highly skilled, highly trained and committed employees to produce its products. However, these skills are in short supply because the major employers in the area are in the information industry and other new companies seeking the same skilled labour are continuing to move into the area.

In both these situations employees would perceive that, notwithstanding the national (macro) picture, the relative balance of bargaining power was very much in their favour. This situation could be made even worse if the management of the business had no clear employee relations strategy or policies and procedures were non-existent or out of date.

Consider the work groups in your organisation. Which have the most potential power to disrupt the organisation? What is the basis of the power? Do they realise they have this power? If not, why not? Do you think they would be willing to use their power?

BARGAINING POWER AND MANAGEMENT BEHAVIOUR

In general terms, the balance of bargaining power has been in favour of employers over the past years because of the legislative and economic policies of successive governments. When this is the case it is important that power is exercised in a responsible and not an arbitrary manner.

If the balance of bargaining power favours management, it may achieve its objective despite adopting a management style that is unprofessional and based on an attitude of 'take it or leave it', 'go and work for somebody else' and 'there are plenty of other people who would be only too willing to work here'. In such situations the workforce complies with, but is not committed to, management's actions and policy. The employees are cowed, have no respect for management and store up grievances that will come to the surface with a vengeance when the relative balance of bargaining power turns in favour of the employee.

Managing in this fashion is not sustainable in the longer term. It is a crude abuse of power, which in the long term will be detrimental to the business which, in turn, will experience high labour turnover, low employee morale and commitment and depressed productivity levels. The personnel professional manages on the basis of just cause for action, consults and discusses with employees and treats them in a fair, reasonable and consistent manner. Managing on this basis regardless of the relative balance of bargaining power between employers and employees normally gains the respect of the latter even though management invariably gains what it wants.

A further reason why a personnel professional should not act in an arbitrary manner is that, if the bargaining pendulum can swing one way, it can swing back. If you fail to exercise power responsibly when it is in your favour then you should not expect responsible behaviour from employees when they have the advantage. Bargaining power, as we have noted, is influenced by economic policy and legal intervention. If those policies are changed a number of variables may be affected. For example, if the predicted increase in managerial, professional and technical jobs becomes a reality and employers do not invest sufficiently in skills training, skill shortages will raise the price of certain types of labour. Statutory rights to union recognition could provide employees with greater bargaining power.

> Where does the relative balance of bargaining power lie in your organisation? Do you see this balance as static, or is there potential for a significant shift in power?

SUMMARY

This chapter has examined the role of the UK Government as an economic manager in terms of the objectives of macroeconomic policy and how employee relations is affected by the way in which that policy is implemented. In particular we examined the contrast between the Keynesian and monetarist approaches to economic management and the impact that the change to monetarism has had on the UK economy since 1979. We have looked at the role that the State plays in developing the legal framework in which employee relations has to operate and how the combination of a changed economic system and reforms to labour law have caused trade union power and strike activity to decline. These changes have clearly had a marked effect on the balance of bargaining power in that they have made employers more confident and given them a belief in their 'right to manage'. The confidence that managers have stems from a number of factors, but one of them is a growing realisation among trade unions that industrial action is not necessarily in the best interests of their members. That change, in one form or another, is inevitable if employment opportunities are to be protected. Therefore it makes more sense for that change to be negotiated. However, it is important for the employee relations specialist to appreciate that the wheel can turn full circle. Although it is widely acknowledged that requiring trade unions to ballot their members before taking industrial action is a positive step forward, it can be a double-edged sword. The legitimacy that such a ballot provides can actually give the union more bargaining power, not less. Notwithstanding this, most employers would say that the legislation is supportive and has helped to tilt the balance of bargaining power in their favour.

We have looked at the role of UK Government as an employer and discussed the way in which the concept of UK Government as a 'model employer' has changed over time. In the immediate post-Second World War years there was encouragement of collective bargaining and an attempt to ensure comparability of pay between the public and private sectors. From 1979 the emphasis was on a more individual approach to the employment relationship with a clear discouragement of national pay bargaining.

Finally, we looked at the impact of technological change on the corporate environment and acknowledged that it influences employee relations in a number of ways. It can create unemployment, it can provide the opportunity for employees to learn new skills and it can generally improve the working environment.

From whatever perspective you view the corporate environment there is no doubt that over the last twenty years there has been a radical change in our system of employee relations. This change has manifested itself in changes to working practices and changes in the labour market with an increase in part-time and temporary working. Reward systems have also changed, with issues like performance-related pay, reward for teams and profit-related pay becoming more prevalent. The common theme running through all these changes is the need for them to be negotiated. Negotiation, as we discuss in Chapter 6, is one of the key employee relations skills and is an absolute necessity for any employee relations specialist who is going to operate in a constantly evolving corporate environment.

REFERENCES AND FURTHER READING

ASHTON D. *and* FELSTEAD A. 'Training and development', in Storey J. (ed.), *Human Resource Management: A critical text*. London, Routledge, 1995.

BLYTON P. *and* TURNBULL P. *The Dynamics of Employee Relations*. London, Macmillan, 1994.

DONALDSON P. *and* FARQUHAR J. *Understanding the British Economy*. London, Penguin, 1991.

EMMOTT M. *and* HUTCHINSON S. 'Employment flexibility: threat or promise?' in Sparrow P. and Marchington M. *Human Resource Management: The new agenda*. London, Financial Times/Pitman Publishing, 1998.

FARNHAM D. *The Corporate Environment*. London, Institute of Personnel and Development, 1995.

INSTITUTE FOR EMPLOYMENT RESEARCH. *Review of the Economy & Employment 1998–1999*.

INSTITUTE FOR FISCAL STUDIES. *Entering Work & The British Tax and Benefit System*.

KAHN-FREUND O. *Labour and the Law*. London, Stevens, 1977.

KEEGAN W. *Mrs Thatcher's Economic Experiment*. London, Penguin, 1984.

LEWIS D. *Essentials of Employment Law*. 5th edn. London, Institute of Personnel and Development, 1997.

NOLAN P. *and* WALSH J. 'The structure of the economy and labour market' in Edwards (ed.), *Industrial Relations – Theory and practice in Britain*. Oxford, Blackwell, 1995.

STREDWICK J. *and* ELLIS S. *Flexible Working Practices: Techniques and innovations*. London, Institute of Personnel and Development, 1998.

3 The European Union

THE IMPORTANCE OF THE EUROPEAN UNION

Developments in the European Union (EU) impact on personnel/HR management in the UK in a number of ways. First, EU employment and social legislation designed to harmonise gradually employment legislation in the Member States has been adopted and implemented into the UK. The extent of EU originating legislation is considerable. Collective redundancies, transfers of undertakings, acquired rights, written proof of employment relationship, pregnancy and maternity leave and payment, paternity leave, working time and equal opportunities are all areas where EU legislation directly impinges on the everyday work of the UK personnel professional. Further impacts can occur even after their implementation. Cases brought before the European Court of Justice can result in decisions which have direct impact upon a UK-based organisation's personnel/HR policies, even though the case may have been brought by and involved companies and individuals in another State of the EU.

Second, the amount of EU-initiated employment and social legislation that will be transposed into UK legislation in the immediate future will increase. By 2001, EU-originated legislation covering young people at work, part-time work, burden of proof in sex discrimination cases, fixed-term contracts, transnational and possible national-level information and consultation arrangements, and the posting of workers to employment in other Member States will have been the subject of UK legislation.

Third, increased competition and business opportunities from the free movement of goods, services, capital and labour resulting from the development and enlargement of the European Single Market have caused a number of UK companies to expand their operations into other Member States and vice versa. One impact of this is that an increasing number of UK personnel/HR professionals have, for the first time, been subject to experiences from other employee relations systems and personnel cultures. They need to acquire and develop a knowledge and understanding of these systems. This can be acquired through consulting publications such as *Industrial Relations and Collective Bargaining* (IPD, 1996) and Hyman and Ferner *Changing Industrial Relations in Europe* (1998).

Four, it is likely, subject to a referendum, that early in the new millennium the UK will join the European Single Currency. In the UK, there has been debate on the economic and political merits and impacts of the Euro but very little attention has been given to its potential effects on employee relations, even though much of the economic debate has focused on the implications of entry into the single currency for the labour market. Over the foreseeable future, personnel/HR professionals will increasingly have to think about the employee relations impacts of joining (or not joining) the Euro (see Cressey, 1998). In organisations where collective relationships exist these will include, *inter alia*, issues such as: what will happen to collective bargaining? Will negotiations centralise or de-centralise? Will bargaining take place at company, sector, branch, national or even supranational level? And what will be the impact of low inflation, sound fiscal policy, stable exchange rates and interest rates on employee relations?

THE DEVELOPMENT OF THE EUROPEAN UNION

The origins of the European Union date back to 1951 and the revulsion following the devastating World Wars. In that year Germany, Italy, France, Belgium, the Netherlands and Luxembourg created the European Coal and Steel Community (Treaty of Paris), whose fundamental aim was to allow these six countries to control jointly production, development and distribution of coal and steel, which were still prerequisites for waging war.

The Institutions' powers and procedures of the Coal and Steel Community provided a model for the establishment, via the Treaty of Rome 1957, of two further European Communities – the European Atomic Energy Community and European Economic Community (EEC) which was commonly referred to as the 'Common Market' and aimed to develop close co-operation on economic matters.

In 1967, the three Communities and their institutions were merged by a Merger Treaty which created the European Communities (EC). In 1973, the UK, Ireland and Denmark joined the EC, followed by Greece in 1981 and Spain and Portugal in 1986. The EC became the European Union (EU) in 1993 when the Maastricht Treaty on the European Union revised and widened the remit to include inter-governmental co-operation between Member States on common foreign and security policy and on justice and home affairs. In 1995, Sweden, Finland and Austria joined the EU. The 15 Member States of the EU constitute the largest economic unit in the world with a population of over 372 million and a labour force of about 146 million.

Iceland, Norway and Liechtenstein are part of the European Single Market. They are subject to all EU Single Market legislation under the European Economic Area Agreement (EEAA) including some employment legislation. However, they are not full EU members.

Aims of the European Union
The principal aims of the European Union are to:

• preserve and strengthen peace in Europe

• enable Member States to compete more effectively, both between themselves and together in the world marketplace by removing barriers to free trade and creating a Single European Market

- bring its members closer together politically, economically and socially

- ensure that, wherever joint European action would be more effective than separate action by Member States in achieving a common objective, a common approach is taken.

The basic objectives, structure and operation of the EU are defined in a series of Treaties (see below). They are the constitution of the EU and provide a legal basis for legislation and other measures. All members have to abide by these Treaties and the legislation agreed under them.

When there are changes to the Treaties, they have to be ratified by all Member States. This is done in two ways. In Denmark, Ireland and Portugal, any Treaty changes have to be approved in a referendum of their citizens. In the other 12 Member States, ratification is achieved by a majority vote in their national parliaments. In both cases, the people, or their representatives, have the last word. However, there is always a price to democracy, namely 'delay'. Ratification normally takes about 18 months to two years. Changes brought about by Treaties do not become binding on Member States until the ratification process has been completed.

The Treaty of Rome 1957
The founding Treaty of the EU is the Treaty of Rome (the European Economic Community Treaty) of 1957 which provided for the creation of a free trade area by removing barriers to the free movement of goods, labour, capital and services (the so-called four great freedoms) between Member States. By integrating the economies of the Member States, it was hoped healthy competition would stimulate innovation, technological development, increased productivity and increased demand. It was envisaged consumer prices would fall, stimulating even further demand for goods and services. The 'European Economy' would thus be firing on all four cylinders and this 'virtuous circle of prosperity' would result in real benefits for everyone within the Common European Market.

Whilst the bulk of the Treaty of Rome was concerned with removing the barriers to free trade, it did contain two chapters which related to employment. The 'Free Movement of Workers' chapter enshrines the fundamental right of EU citizens to live and work wherever they wish in the EU without discrimination on grounds of nationality except for limited reasons connected with public security.

The 'Social Chapter' (Articles 117–122) provides for closer co-operation in the 'social field' between Member States and has as one of its objectives

> to promote improved working conditions and an improved standard of living for workers so as to make possible their harmonisation while the improvement is being made.

The Chapter also enshrines, as one of its principles, the right to equal pay for equal work between men and women (Article 119).

Table 9 **The Development of the European Union**

- 1957 The Treaty of Rome

  a) creation of a 'Common Market'
  b) contains two social measures
     - freedom of movement of labour
     - harmonisation of social conditions (the Social Chapter)

- 1987 The Single European Act

  a) introduced the Qualified Majority Vote (QMV) procedure
  b) health and safety to be harmonised on the basis of QMV

- 1993 The Treaty on the European Union

  c) provided for a common currency (Euro) from 1 January 1999
  d) Social Policy Agreement containing Social Protocol extending the social issues to be harmonised by QMV
  e) greater involvement of social partners in the EU decision-making machinery

- 1999 The Treaty of Amsterdam

  f) introduced an Employment Chapter
  g) Social Policy Agreement incorporated into the Treaty of Rome as the Social Chapter
  h) further measures to combat discrimination based on sex, sexual orientation, disability, age, religious belief and racial/ethnic origin
  i) EU institutions required to encourage social dialogue on issues such as employment, right to work, training, etc.

The founders of the EU were not just creating a free trade area but a community in which there would be harmonisation of social conditions. There would be free competition within the free trade area but this would be within the constraints of minimum social standards across Member States. Unlike any other free trade agreement (for example the North America Free Trade Association) the EU has always had a social dimension.

The Single European Act 1987
Progress in moving towards a free market was slow largely because each proposal to achieve this objective required the unanimous agreement of all Member States. There was always at least one Member State which objected, therefore a way had to be found to prevent any single Member State preventing the rest from getting on with the job of completing the establishment of a free trade market. In 30 years, the Council of Ministers (see below) had hardly been able to adopt a single important measure designed to achieve the Single Market.

In 1985, the Commission (see below) proposed that Member States should speed up the creation of the common market and by 31 December 1992, adopt 282 necessary measures to achieve the free movement of goods, capital, labour and services between Member States. To achieve this, the Single European Act amended the Treaty of Rome in three important ways.

First, for the first time a deadline – 31 December 1992 – was set for finally achieving the four freedoms.

Second, it introduced a new legal basis to allow Member States to agree measures by Qualified Majority Vote (QMV) rather than unanimous vote. Under this system Member States were given a number of votes relating to their populations:

- France, Germany, Italy and the UK each have ten votes

- Spain has eight votes

- Belgium, Greece, the Netherlands and Portugal each have five votes

- Sweden and Austria each have four votes

- Denmark, Finland and Iceland each have three votes

- Luxembourg has two votes.

A Qualified Majority is 62 of the total 87 votes available. To block proposals a Member State must gather together 26 votes. Put another way, there must be opposition from at least three Member States to block a proposal. Two large States (for example, France and Germany together) cannot veto proposals. In the absence of at least 26 votes against, a proposal becomes accepted and even the Member States who abstain or voted against it have to implement it into their national law.

Third, the Act introduced another innovation by formalising the EU's commitment to involve the 'Social Partners' (employers and trade unions) in its decision-making machinery (see below).

The Single European Act also amended the Social Chapter. It provided that health and safety regulations across the EU Member States could be harmonised on the basis of qualified majority voting (Article 118A). This health and safety 'fast track' has been used lavishly (see IPD *Europe*, October 1998) and was the basis of the Working Time Directive 1993 which was then transposed into UK employment law via the Working Time Regulations 1998 (see below).

The impact of the Single European Act cannot be overestimated. By removing the veto of a single Member State to proposals, it was radical and revolutionary. It meant Europe would never be the same again. It meant the EU law-making mechanisms could actually start to work as envisaged by the authors of the Treaty of Rome. Above all, it meant employee relations specialists had to take Europe seriously as it was now possible to influence the drafting of new EU laws in a way unthinkable within national Parliaments.

The Treaty on the European Union 1993
In December 1991, the heads of Member States met in Maastricht to negotiate further changes to the Treaty of Rome to provide for greater political, economic and monetary union. The eventual outcome was the Treaty on the European Union 1993 which formally changed the name of the EC to the European Union (EU) and provided for the creation of a common currency (the Euro) from 1 January 1999 with national currencies being taken out of circulation by the year 2002. The Treaty also restated the principle of subsidiarity which gives the EU competency to act only when common objectives can be better achieved by harmonised EU action than by Member States acting unilaterally.

The Treaty on the European Union also made two important changes to the Social Chapter. First, all Member States (excluding the UK) accepted proposed extensions of issues in employment and social legislation to be harmonised by QMV. As the UK objected, no new 'social provisions' were incorporated into the main Maastricht Treaty. However a compromise agreement was reached whereby Member States other than the UK could use EU institutions to introduce additional binding legislation within the social field, but any such legislation would not apply to the UK. This is whence the term 'the UK's opt-out from the Social Chapter' comes. This was done under a separate Social Policy Agreement which listed the specific social issues that the rest of the Member States could legislate on. This Agreement was attached to the Social Protocol annexed to the main Treaty spelling out the arrangements just described.

The second innovation was the introduction of Article 118(b) which formalised the EU's commitment to involve the 'Social Partners' (see below) directly in its decision-making machinery. It provided for compulsory consultation with the Social Partners on EU Commission social proposals and permitted them to agree voluntarily to negotiate a Framework Agreement on the issue and for that agreement to be then made binding on Member States by the Council of Ministers issuing a Directive.

The Treaty of Amsterdam 1999
This Treaty brought changes to the Treaty of Rome thought necessary in order to help prepare the EU and its institutions for further enlargement of membership (particularly countries from the former Soviet bloc), to take account of changing political priorities and the need for stronger EU action in areas such as employment, social policy and the environment. The key provisions of the Treaty are:

• It develops further the principles of democracy and individual rights and for the first time establishes a clear procedure to be followed in the event of 'serious and persistent' breaches by Member States.

• The Council of Ministers is provided with new powers to take more effective action to combat discrimination based on sex, ethnic origin, religion or belief, disability, age or sexual orientation.

• It pledges to remove all remaining restrictions on free movement of labour between Member States by 2004, the only exemptions being the UK and Ireland which will be allowed to retain frontier controls.

• It introduces a new Chapter which relates exclusively to employment.

• The Agreement on Social Policy is incorporated into the Treaty and thus becomes applicable to all Member States.

For the personnel/HR professional, the Treaty was thus significant for three reasons. First, the UK Labour Government agreed to opt into the Agreement on Social Policy annexed to the Treaty of Maastricht. This is what people are referring to when they talk of the Blair Government 'signing up' to the Social Chapter. This agreement was therefore repealed and incorporated into the Social Chapter of the

Treaty of Rome. Secondly, EU institutions were required to encourage 'social dialogue' on issues such as employment, the right to work, working conditions, training, social security and accident prevention.

Third, it contained an Employment Charter committing the EU for the first time to take into account the need to achieve high and sustainable employment opportunities when taking decisions related to its commercial and economic objectives. This was the first time the promotion of a high level of employment had been written down as one of the main objectives of the EU. This is to be achieved by co-ordinating the employment policies of the Member States to develop a common strategy.

The Employment Charter
The Charter is designed to restore balance in the EU by creating a counterweight to its economic and monetary provisions. It asserts that:

• Employment is a matter of common concern.

• The objective of generating high employment is to be taken into consideration when implementing all other common policies.

• The achievement of this objective is closely monitored.

• The EU considers the employment situation in each Member State and in the Union as a whole on an annual basis and conducts a detailed examination of the steps taken by individual governments to promote employment.

• An Employment Committee promotes co-ordination of national measures and encourages dialogue between employers and employees.

The Employment Charter is important because it makes the EU and its institutions for the first time the guardians of an overall employment policy. It is ambitious in the sense that it provides for permanent and regular collaboration within the EU framework.

HOW THE EU WORKS

The Treaty of Rome set up four key institutions to achieve its objectives. These were:

• The European Commission

• The Council of the European Union

• The European Parliament

• The European Court of Justice.

The European Commission
This is the EU's executive body, whose main role is to propose measures and ensure their implementation. There are 20 Commissioners consisting of a President, two Vice Presidents and 17 members. Commissioners, who are usually senior and distinguished politicians, are nominated by the Governments and serve for a period of five years. The President is chosen by agreement between the 15 Heads of State. The President enjoys considerable power and influence

and sets the agenda for the weekly Commission meetings where new initiatives for making European Law are discussed. The larger Member States (UK, France, Germany, Italy and Spain) nominate two Commissioners whilst the others nominate one. The Commissioners think EU-wide and not in national terms. All policy proposals made by a Commissioner must have the support of a simple majority of all Commissioners before they can be launched officially.

The Commission is currently divided into 23 Departments or Directorate Generals (DGs). Each department is responsible for a specific area of activity. The most important one as far as employee relations specialists are concerned is DGV which is responsible for employment, industrial relations and social affairs, throughout the EU. Each Commissioner is supported by a personal 'cabinet' of advisory staff. The Chef de Cabinet is effectively the Commissioner's deputy. The bulk of the Commission's 16,500 civil servants are based in Brussels and, under the direction of the Commissioners, are given a remit to draft proposals for legislation. In the EU, only the Commission can initiate new laws but it is ultimately subservient to the Council of the European Union. The European Commission thus has the monopoly of power to initiate legislation.

The Council of the European Union

The Council comprises 15 members – one representing each member state. The Treaty of Rome gives them the ultimate power to reject or adopt proposals for new laws proposed by the Commission. The Council is made up of several levels.

There is the European Council level which comprises the Heads of State of the EU Member States who hold summit meetings at least twice a year to discuss major issues and decide on broad areas of policy.

There is then the level of the Council of Ministers which comprises a Minister from each Member State according to the subject under discussion. Thus, whilst each country has a permanent seat in the Council, the personalities who fill these seats change in accordance with the subject being considered. For example, if the Council is discussing employee relations matters then the seats are filled by the respective Employment/Labour Ministers from each of the Member States.

There is also the level of Presidency of the Council which is held by each Member State for a period of six months. As President of the Council, the Member State sets Council agendas and can therefore shape, to some extent, which Commission proposals are progressed and given priority. Member States normally run a programme of high profile events during their Presidency. All Council meetings are chaired and negotiations co-ordinated by the representative of the presiding Member State.

The European Parliament

The European Parliament has 626 members, directly elected since 1979, distributed amongst Member States in proportion to their size. Germany is the largest with 99 seats and Luxembourg the smallest with six. The UK has 87 seats. Elections to the Parliament are held at five-yearly intervals. Members of the European Parliament (MEPs) take up their seats according to their transnational political group rather than their nationality. UK MEPs are elected by proportional representation. Labour MEPs sit as part of the European Socialist Group whilst UK Conservatives sit with the European People's Party.

The European Parliament's principal functions are to approve the appointment of the 20 European Commissioners, to determine the EU budget and to propose amendments to measures initiated by the Commission. Initially, the European Parliament had few powers and was regarded as nothing more than a talking shop. However, over the years, it has acquired greater influence and certain powers to influence the legislative process but it still cannot initiate legislation and does not have the final say as to whether proposals for legislation are adopted. The Parliament, however, has limited powers to amend legislation and can reject the annual budget prepared by the Commission although it has only done this on two occasions since 1957.

The Parliament can dismiss the 20 Commissioners but only *en bloc*. They cannot dismiss a single Commissioner. It is 'all of them or no-one'. This power had never been exercised until spring 1999. President Santer and his team of Commissioners resigned *en bloc* – preferring to 'go voluntarily' rather than be 'pushed' by the powers of the Parliament, which on this occasion would most certainly have been used. Santer's Commission collapsed as a result of six cases of mismanagement and petty corruption. The most colourful example was Edith Cresson, a French Commissioner, who had appointed a long-standing friend and personal dentist to an extremely well-paid position where she was responsible for considerable amounts of EU funds.

The demise of the European Commission saw an increase in the credibility and prestige of the Parliament which had for many years been perceived as a group of highly-paid 'second-raters' who had failed to be elected to their own Parliaments. The Treaty on European Union gave the Parliament the right to veto final proposals from the Commission on certain measures, for example free movement of labour and training. Should this happen, then the proposals can only be adopted if a negotiated agreement can be reached between the Council and the Parliament. This 'co-decision' procedure also comes into force in the event of the 'Social Partners' initially commencing negotiations but then finding they are unable to reach a voluntary agreement (see the Framework Procedure below).

The European Court of Justice
This Court is the supreme custodian of the EU enacted laws and its decisions take precedence over any laws or judicial decision taken in the Member States. It comprises qualified nominees (judges appointed for six years) from each Member State and acts as the final arbiter in disputes over the interpretation of the Treaty of Rome and failure to implement EU laws, and can quash any measures introduced by Member States which are incompatible with the Treaty.

The Court has been used by UK individuals, groups and organisations to challenge UK employment legislation on the grounds that it contravenes EU law. For example, the UK Equal Pay Act 1970 was challenged. The Act allowed for equal pay for work of equal value where this was shown to be the case by a job evaluation scheme. Claims by women employees were being rejected after the use of job evaluation. However, a complaint was laid before the European Court of Justice that such claims were failing because the job evaluation schemes being used by UK employers contained gender bias factors. The complaint was upheld and in 1983, the Equal Pay Act 1970 was amended to permit the undertaking of job evaluation by independent job evaluators in the case of claims for equal pay for work of equal value.

Legislative Instruments

Most EU social legislation is based on an Article in the Treaty of Rome and comes in three forms which have important differences:

- Regulations

- Decisions

- Directives.

Regulations are the highest and most rigorous form of EU legislation. They comprise detailed instructions which are immediately applicable throughout the EU once adopted by the Council of Ministers and are 'directly binding' upon all Member States. In other words, regulations have the same direct status as laws passed by the UK Parliament and must be enforced by the UK courts in the same way. Failure to apply Regulations results in the European Commission making a complaint to the European Court of Justice.

Decisions are immediately binding on those to whom they are addressed. Decisions which impose financial obligations are enforceable in national courts. Decisions are used when the EU wants the full force of European law to apply to individuals, to particular firms or enterprises or to specific Member States.

Directives set out specific objectives and each Member State is given time (usually two years) to enact legislation within its own Parliament to ensure the objectives are achieved. Directives, while being less rigid and allowing more flexibility than regulations or decisions, are still binding in all Member States. In itself, a Directive does not have legal force in the Member States but particular provisions may take direct effect if the Directive is not duly implemented. In the UK, Directives are implemented either by being incorporated as they stand into national law or by means of secondary legislation drawn up by the relevant government department or by an Act of Parliament, formulated in the usual way through a Parliamentary Bill.

Softer instruments

In addition to Regulations, Directives and Decisions which are 'hard legislation' enforced by the EU, there are other 'softer instruments' which attempt to regulate behaviour in the EU. These are:

- Recommendations

- Opinion

- Resolutions

- Declarations

- Communications

- Memoranda.

While sounding officious, these are not legally binding. They have a moral rather than a legal force although they can be used as evidence in court. Probably the best known declaration in the employee relations field is the Community Charter on the fundamental rights of workers, commonly known as the Social Charter (see below).

Implementation of the instruments

Of the three categories of European Law with real teeth, the most widely used is the Directive. Out of the hundreds of Directives, Regulations and Decisions that the EU have taken since 1957, only 50 Directives have been adopted in the social field. Over half of these relate to health and safety while the others deal with labour law, equal opportunities, freedom of movement and public health. Of these 50 Directives, 48 have been transposed into UK legislation.

If a Member State fails to transpose directives into domestic law by the target date or if EU law is infringed, complaints may be made to the European Commission. Such complaints can be made by individuals, companies, other Member States, the European Parliament or pressure groups. The Commission investigates the complaint and asks the Member State(s) concerned for an explanation. If this is unsatisfactory, the Commission orders the Member State(s) to put the matter right within one month. If the infringement continues, the matter is referred to the European Court of Justice. If this Court finds against the Member State, it passes a judgement with which the Member State has to comply. If failure to comply results in a denial of individual rights, the European Court of Justice may require the Member State to pay compensation to the individual. The important thing about the European Court of Justice is that it takes precedence over all the Courts within Member States. It has the power to overrule the UK judiciary, including the House of Lords. When issues and disputes reach the European Court of Justice, it is the end of the road. Once it makes its judgement, there is no further appeal.

THE SOCIAL PARTNERS

As shown below, all the above institutions play a role in the EU legislative process. This is also true of the EU-wide representative bodies of employers and employees (referred to as the Social Partners). There are three main Social Partners.

The European Trade Union Confederation

The European Trade Union Confederation (ETUC) has a dual structure. Apart from the Member States' leading national trade union confederations, which are affiliated to the ETUC as full members, it also comprises 14 European sectoral trade unions that until 1995 were called European Industry Committees and are now known as European Industry Federations. These federations represent individual trade unions from a particular sector. They are accepted by the EU institutions as the sectoral (industry) employees' Social Partner.

The Confederation was formed in 1973 and today its full members include 62 national trade union confederations from 28 countries in Western, Central and Eastern Europe and 14 European sectoral trade union organisations. All in all, the ETUC represents the interests of some 57 million trade union affiliates at European level. There are three decision-making bodies which determine ETUC policy – Congress, Executive Committee and the Steering Committee. The Congress, the highest body, is held every four years and decides the organisation's policy priorities. The Executive Committee generally meets every three months and takes the policy decisions required to implement the priorities laid down by the Congress. The Steering Committee normally meets every two months to decide on urgent action required to implement the strategies laid down by the Executive Committee. The ETUC Secretariat is in Brussels and carries out tasks assigned to it by the Congress, the Executive and the Steering Committee.

Union of Industrial and Employers' Confederation of Europe
Union of Industrial and Employers' Confederation of Europe (UNICE) is the official voice of European business and industry in contact with European institutions and was established in 1958. It comprises 33 central industry and employers' federations from 25 European countries with a permanent secretariat based in Brussels. Its aims are: to keep up with issues that interest its members by maintaining permanent contacts with European institutions; to promote a framework which enables industry and employers to secure European policies and proposed legislation and prepare position papers; to promote its policies and position at European and national level and to persuade European legislators to take these into account and represent its members in the dialogue between Social Partners provided for in the European Treaties outlined above. It operates through its Council of Presidents and an Executive Committee which assists in policy formation and suggests actions to be taken.

The European Centre for Enterprises with Public Participation (CEEP) represents the interests of the public sector employers. It was formed in 1961 and has some 200 member organisations.

THE LEGISLATIVE PROCESS

Legislative procedures
Consultation and cooperation procedures
Proposals for EU policy are made by the European Commission. They draft proposals which go through a number of stages, concluding with the Council of Ministers taking a vote as to whether to adopt the proposals into legislation or not. All proposals must be based on an Article in the Treaty of Rome. The Article stipulates whether the proposal is to be processed under the consultation procedure and adoption by the Council of Ministers by a unanimous vote or under

the co-operation procedure and Council adoption by a qualified majority vote. Under the consultation procedure, proposals can be vetoed by one country. The stages in these two procedures are shown in Figures 4 and 5.

Under both procedures, proposals may be blocked at any stage through insufficient support in the Council of Ministers, and the legal basis chosen for a proposal may be challenged. For example, in 1990, the UK government challenged that Article 118a, which, at the time, permitted harmonisation of health and safety issues on the basis of qualified majority voting, was the correct one for the proposed Working Time Directive. The UK opposed the proposed Directive and argued this issue was not a health and safety one and should have been introduced on the basis of Article 100 which required unanimous approval. The UK government took its case to the European Court of Justice but was unsuccessful.

Co-decision procedure
The Treaty on European Union introduced the co-decision procedure. Under this procedure the powers of the European Parliament are increased in the decision-making process (see Figure 6) in the areas for free movement of labour and rights of establishment and training. The Parliament has the right to veto proposals in these areas even though a common position has been reached by the Council of Ministers.

Framework agreement procedure
Under the Social Chapter, a fourth legislative process exists (Article 118b). Under this, the Commission, before submitting proposals in the social field, is required to consult with the Social Partners (ETUC, UNICE and CEEP) and ask for their opinion or recommendation on the proposed initiative. The Social Partners' representatives forward an opinion or recommendation on the proposal to the European Commission. They can suggest that the Commission draft a Directive for eventual approval by the Council of Ministers by either unanimous decision or QMV depending on the issue.

Alternatively the Social Partners can jointly decide to negotiate an EU level Framework Agreement on the issue over a nine-month period, though this may be extended by a joint decision of the Commission and the Social Partners. If agreement is reached it can be implemented in Member States through a collective agreement at national level or it can form the basis for a proposal by the European Commission for approval in the form of Directive by the Council of Ministers by either unanimous vote or a QMV decision depending on the subject and then transposed into national law. The negotiation of an EU-wide Framework Agreement has already happened successfully in the case of parental leave (Parental Leave Directive), part-time work (Part-Time Work Directive) and fixed-term contracts of employment (Fixed Term Contracts Directives). However, on three issues – European Works Councils, burden of proof in sex discrimination cases and information and consultation of workers – the Social Partners were not able to agree to enter into negotiations.

Figure 4 **European employment law made under the Treaty of Rome**

Consultation procedure

for proposals on employment rights (article 100) and some proposals on free movement of workers

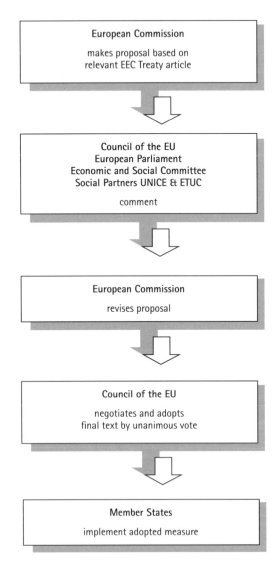

Directives are implemented through national legislation in each member state by an agreed deadline (two or three years)

Regulations and decisions apply in all Member States immediately

Recommendations, Communications and Opinions have no legal force

Proposals may be blocked at any stage due to insufficient support in the Council of the EU. They may change considerably as Council negotiations progress

Figure 5 Co-operation procedure proposals on employment rights under Article 118(a)

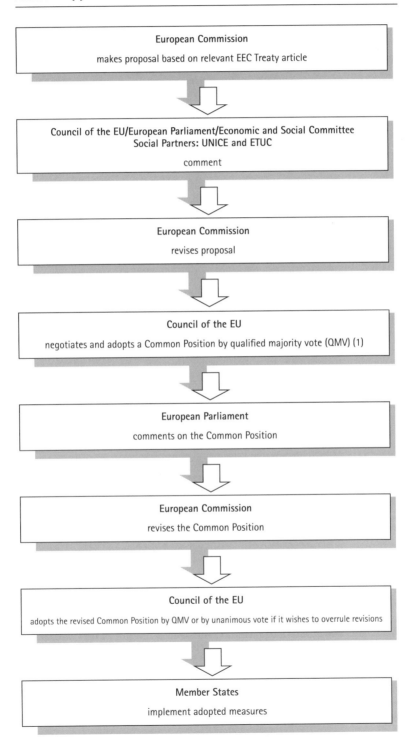

(1) QMV means that 62 of the available 87 votes must be in favour for a proposal to be adopted. Member States have block votes according to their population size. UK, France, Germany, Italy – 10 votes; Spain – 8 votes; Belgium, Greece, Netherlands, Portugal – 5 votes; Austria and Sweden – 4 votes; Denmark, Finland and Ireland – 3 votes; Luxembourg – 2 votes.

Figure 6 **Co-decision procedure**

Introduced by the Treaty on European Union for some proposals on free movement (Art. 49) right of establishment (Arts 54, 56, 57) and training (Art. 126)

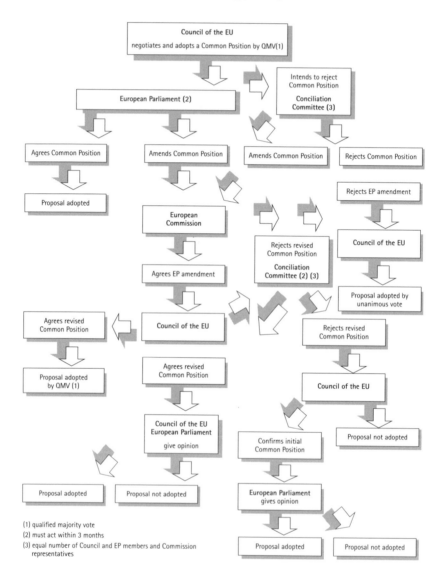

(1) qualified majority vote
(2) must act within 3 months
(3) equal number of Council and EP members and Commission representatives

The actual negotiations are arranged and appropriate venues and interpreters provided by the Commission which also provides a 'Chairperson' to facilitate the negotiations between the Social Partners. All the costs associated with the negotiations, for example, travel, accommodation, etc, are met by the Commission. The negotiations follow the stages described in Chapter 7. The employer and trade union sides usually negotiate against very tight 'mandates' from their respective constituents. Once agreement is reached the Social Partners' affiliated organisations must ratify the agreement.

Figure 7 **The collective agreement procedure**

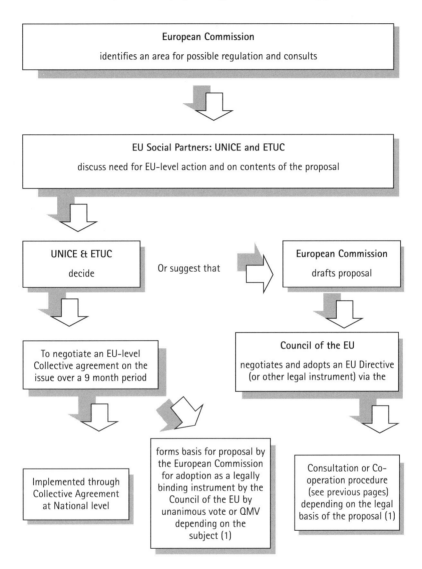

Proposals for Employment Rights Under Article 118(b)

European Commission

identifies an area for possible regulation and consults

EU Social Partners: UNICE and ETUC

discuss need for EU-level action and on contents of the proposal

UNICE & ETUC

decide

Or suggest that

European Commission

drafts proposal

To negotiate an EU-level Collective agreement on the issue over a 9 month period

Council of the EU

negotiates and adopts an EU Directive (or other legal instrument) via the

Implemented through Collective Agreement at National level

forms basis for proposal by the European Commission for adoption as a legally binding instrument by the Council of the EU by unanimous vote or QMV depending on the subject (1)

Consultation or Co-operation procedure (see previous pages) depending on the legal basis of the proposal (1)

(1) Proposals requiring a qualified majority vote (QMV) and involving the Co-operation procedure concern: working conditions, employee involvement, equal opportunity between men and women, integration of those excluded from the labour market, health and safety. Under the Social Protocol QMV requires at least 52 of the available 77 votes to be in favour.

Proposals requiring a unanimous vote and involving the Consultation procedure concern: social protection, termination of employment, terms and conditions of employment, co-determination.

No harmonisation is envisaged on issues related to pay, the right of association, the right to strike or to impose lockouts.

This procedure thus provides for the Social Partners to reach voluntarily collective (framework) agreements on particular issues which are then transformed into 'hard' community legislation. Should the 'Social Partners' refuse to negotiate, or indeed fail to reach voluntary agreements, then a 'fall back' position comes into play. The Commission brings forward its own proposals under the 'co-decision' procedure.

The same social dialogue process is equally available for Social Partners within industrial sectors to use as a means of establishing 'relevant' rules and regulations with regard to social policy issues within specific sectors. The Social Partners at a sectoral level are basically the Industry Federations of the ETUC and the appropriate employers' federations for various sectors, for example transport, engineering, coal mining, agriculture, etc.

Both ETUC and UNICE/CEEP are identifying further issues and areas that might be appropriate for progressing through Article 118(b) procedures in the future. One thing for certain is that this new role in the legislative process of the EU that has been given to employers and trade unions is now a fact of life. Employee relations specialists and practitioners can only ignore the Europeanisation of collective bargaining at their own peril.

THE SOCIAL DIMENSION OF THE EU

The Social Chapter

The founders of the European Union were not just creating a free trade area in which people, goods, services and capital could move freely. They were establishing a political and economic community in which there would be social regulation and protection in its free trade area. Product and service market competition would take place on a 'level playing field' of minimum social conditions. To this end, the Treaty of Rome contained a Social Chapter (Title III Social Policy), subsequently amended by the Single European Act 1987 and the Treaty on European Union 1993 setting out a clear commitment to the harmonisation of social conditions between Member States. The stated objectives of the Social Chapter are:

> ... the promotion of employment, improved living and working conditions, proper social protection, dialogue between management and labour, the development of human resources with a view to lasting employment and the combating of social exclusion ...

It also requires Member States, as a condition of membership, to ensure and maintain the application of the principle that men and women should have equal pay for equal work. The UK became fully covered by the Social Chapter on 1 May 1999 when the Treaty of Amsterdam came into force.

The Social Chapter is not a set of detailed regulations. It is a mechanism which allows the Member States to make new rules and legislation at the EU level on a wide range of social issues. As we have seen, it allows common rules to be introduced by the Council of Ministers by:

• a unanimous vote in the Council of Ministers (Article 100)

- a qualified majority vote (Article 118a)

- a Framework Agreement negotiated by UNICE, CEEP and the ETUC (Article 118b)

which is then issued as a Directive and transposed into national legislation.

Critically, the 118b procedure severely limits the power of the European Parliament or Member States in the Council of Ministers to make any amendments. This power of collective bargaining to shape both the direction and content of legislation is considerable and unique. The CBI and TUC are the UK members of UNICE and ETUC respectively. As a result, they have acquired a new and special significance as organisations in the UK. Both organisations are respectively representing the interests of UK companies and employees in the drafting of legislation that can then become legally binding in the UK and apply equally to unionised and non-unionised companies.

Qualified majority items
Under the Social Chapter (see Table 10) procedures, legislation in any of the following areas can be adopted by qualified majority voting:

- health and safety at work

- working conditions

- information and consultation of workers

- equal treatment and equal opportunities at work for men and women

- the integration of persons excluded from the labour market.

The European Union Works Council Directive 1994 was adopted under this procedure as was the Parental Leave Directive 1996 after the Social Partners had negotiated a framework agreement on the issue.

Table 10 **The Social Chapter: basis on which issues can be decided**

Qualified majority voting

1 Health and safety
2 Working conditions
3 Information and consultation of workers
4 Equal treatment and equal opportunities for men and women
5 Integration of persons excluded from the labour market

Unanimous vote

1 Social security and protection of workers
2 Protection of workers where employment contracts are terminated
3 Representation and collective defence of interests of workers and employers, including co-determination
4 Conditions of employment for third country nationals legally resident in the EU
5 Financial contributions for the promotion of employment and job creation

Excluded issues

1 Pay
2 The right of association
3 Right to strike
4 Right to lock out

Unanimous vote issues

The Social Chapter mechanisms can be used to introduce European Union-wide legislation on the basis of unanimity amongst Member States in the following areas:

• social security and social protection

• protection of workers whose employment contract is terminated

• representation and collective defence of workers' and employers' interests, including co-determination

• conditions of employment for third country nationals legally resident in the EU

• financial contributions for employment promotion and job creation.

Excluded issues

However, certain subjects, namely pay, the right of association, the right to strike and the right to impose lock-outs, are formally excluded from the legislation using the Social Chapter procedures.

However, critics of the EU point out that the fact that some areas are formally subject to unanimity or even excluded altogether is by no means a secure safeguard. They argue that terms such as 'working conditions' and 'health and safety' are open to wide differences in interpretation. They point out, for example, that the European Court of Justice ruled in another context that the British social security benefit, Family Credit, is a working condition. EU critics contend that past experience suggests EU institutions will seek to apply the broadest possible interpretations in order to maximise the scope for adopting measures by qualified majority despite possible objections from individual Member States. The Social Chapter mechanisms are seen as having the risk of costly, far-reaching and unforeseeable legislation being imposed on the UK. It is viewed by its opponents as mirroring the more interventionist approach common in much of the EU and contrary to a deregulated approach to the operation of labour markets.

The Social Chapter in practice

There are four areas of employee relations management in which EU laws have had, and will continue to have, a direct impact on the work of the personnel/HR specialist:

• equality

• employment protection

• employee relations

• health and safety.

HR/personnel professionals need to obtain copies of the actual Directives in these areas rather than depending on summaries. You also need to bear in mind that many Directives are not simply implemented into UK law by one piece of legislation. For example, in areas such as equal opportunities, the requirements of a Directive have been transposed into several separate legal instruments within the UK. (See Table 11.)

Table 11 **Areas of employment where European union-wide legislation impacts on the work of the UK personnel/HR professional**

Equality issues

- Equal pay (1975)
- Parental leave (1996)
- Equal treatment (1976)
- Part-time work (1997)
- Fixed-term contracts (1999)
- Burden of proof in sex discrimination cases (1997)

Employment protection

- Redundancy (1975 and 1992)
- Transfer of undertakings (1977 and 1998)
- Contracts of employment (1991)
- Posting of workers (1996)
- Insolvency (1980)

Employment relations

- Consultation and information (1994 and 1997)

Health and safety

- Organisation of working time (1993)
- Safety and health at work for pregnant employees and new mothers
- Safety and health at work of workers with a fixed duration employment relationship or a temporary employment relationship

Equality

Equal pay

The 1975 Equal Pay Directive sought to improve the effectiveness of equal pay for men and women as laid down in the Treaty of Rome by reducing differences between Member States in the application of this principle through approximation of Member State laws on the subject. The Directive stated the principle of equal pay required the elimination of all discrimination on the grounds of sex with regard to all aspects and conditions of remuneration for the same work or for work to which equal value is attributed. It also provided that any job classification (evaluation) system used for determining pay must be based on the same criteria for both men and women and must be drawn up so as to exclude discrimination on grounds of sex.

In 1983, the Equal Pay (Amendment) Regulations were introduced to comply with the Directive. These Regulations, *inter alia*, introduced provision for 'independent experts' to undertake job evaluation exercises independently of the employer in the case of claims for equal pay based on work of equal value.

Parental leave

In 1996, the Social Partners (UNICE, ETUC and CEEP) concluded a Framework Agreement on Parental Leave which was then issued as the Parental Leave Directive. This provides an individual right for parents to take up to three months' unpaid leave after the birth or adoption of a child before its eighth birthday. Employees are protected from dismissal for asking for the leave and have the right to return to work on the same conditions as before. The Directive also entitles individuals to a certain number of days off work for urgent family reasons in the case of sickness or accident. The UK government transposed this Directive into national legislation via the Employment Relations Act 1999.

Equal treatment

The Equal Treatment Directive 1976 was designed to give effect to the principle of equal treatment for men and women with regard to access to employment, promotion, vocational training and working conditions, including the conditions governing dismissal. As a result of this Directive, the UK had to introduce legislation to equalise the retirement ages for men and women, to remove the difference whereby men could receive statutory redundancy payments up to the age of 65 but women up to 60 and to ensure occupational pensions are equal for men and women. It was under this Directive that Seymour Smith and Perez sought unsuccessfully to persuade the European Court of Justice that the two year continuous service qualification for unfair dismissal rights was discriminatory against women relative to men. The Court ruled the issue should be decided by national courts.

Burden of proof

The Burden of Proof in Cases of Discrimination based on Sex Discrimination Directive 1997 sought to improve the effectiveness of national implementation of the principle of equal treatment by enabling all persons to have their right to equal treatment asserted by judicial process after possible recourse to other competent bodies. The Directive provides that where a complaint to a tribunal establishes 'facts from which it may be presumed that there has been direct or indirect discrimination' then the employer has to prove 'that there has been no breach of the principle of equal treatment'. Thus, the Directive does not provided a reversal of the burden of proof. It places a greater onus on the employer to prove that discrimination did not take place in sex discrimination cases. This Directive must be implemented in the UK by June 2001.

Part-time workers

In 1997, UNICE, ETUC and CEEP negotiated a Framework Agreement on Part-time Work designed to remove discrimination against part-time workers, to improve the quality of part-time work, to facilitate the development of part-time work on a voluntary basis and to contribute to the flexible organisation of working time in a manner which takes into account the needs of employers and workers. A part-time worker is defined as a worker whose normal average weekly hours of work calculated over one year are less than those of a comparable full-time worker. If no comparable full-time worker exists within the same establishment, reference is made to applicable collective agreements or national law.

The Social Partners agreed part-time workers should be treated no less favourably with regard to employment conditions except where justified on objective grounds. Where appropriate, the principle of *pro rata temporis* applies. Employers are to facilitate the transfer between full-time and part-time work by providing information on available work within the establishment and by greater access to vocational training. Member States and national Social Partners were urged to identify and eliminate obstacles to part-time work. The Framework Agreement was transposed into a Directive which at the time of writing has an implementation deadline of 20 January 2000. In April 1998 this Directive was extended to the UK with a deadline for implementation of 7 April 2000.

Fixed-term contracts

In 1999, the EU Social Partners concluded a Framework Agreement on Fixed-Term Contracts. These negotiations had been initiated by UNICE which had proposed in February 1998 that the Social Partners negotiate on fixed-term contracts. This was unique in that it was the first UNICE-proposed, and initiated, legislation in the social and employment field. The agreement generated an EU Directive discouraging the promotion of fixed-term contracts and limiting their use. It states permanent contracts should be the rule and an employer must show objective reasons for using successive fixed-term contracts. It also ensured fixed-term contract employees had the same minimum employment rights as other staff, including the right to join company pension schemes and to receive training.

Employment protection
Redundancy

The Collective Redundancy Directive 1975 introduced the requirement for consultation with employee representatives on mass redundancies in good time, with a view to reaching an agreement. The consultations must cover ways and means of avoiding collective redundancies or limiting the number of workers affected, and of mitigating the consequences through help for redeployment or retraining of workers made redundant. The employer must provide the workers' representatives with certain information, for example, the reason for the redundancies, the number and types of workers to be made redundant and the criteria proposed for the selection of workers to be made redundant.

This Directive was transposed into UK legislation in the Employment Protection Act 1975. The Directive was amended slightly by a further Directive in 1992 which was implemented in June 1994 in the UK in the Trade Union Reform and Employment Rights Act 1993. This ensured consultation takes place at the workplace affected, even if the redundancy decision has been taken by a controlling body in another country.

Transfer of undertakings

The Transfer of Undertakings Directive 1977 sought to protect employees in the event of a change of employer. It introduced the principle that when a business is sold, employees should transfer to the new owner on the same basic terms and conditions of employment and could not be dismissed for reasons connected with the transfer. In implementing the Directive into UK law (the Transfer of Undertakings and Protection of Employment Regulations – TUPE) the government excluded the public sector.

However, in 1992, the European Court of Justice confirmed the Directive applied to employees in both the private and non-profit sectors. The UK law was, therefore, amended by the Trade Union Reform and Employment Rights Act 1993 to include public sector employees. In 1998, an amendment to the 1977 Directive was introduced to clarify and limit existing law by clarifying that transfer of undertaking legislation only applied when an 'economic activity' which retains its identity is transferred, rather than the activity. The deadline for the UK to implement this amendment is July 2001.

Contract of employment

The Proof of an Employment Relationship Directive 1992 imposed an obligation on the employer to inform employees of the conditions applicable to the contract or employment relationship. By doing so, it is hoped to provide employees with improved protection against possible infringements of their rights and to create greater transparency in the labour market. The Directive required all employees working over eight hours per week for more than one month to receive written confirmation of the main terms and conditions of their employment within two months of starting work. Changes to written particulars must be notified in writing within one month. It also required conditions for overseas postings to be provided in writing. Implementation of the Directive in the UK was again via the Trade Union Reform and Employment Rights Act 1993.

Insolvency

The Insolvency Directive 1980 required Member States to set up insolvency funds in order to guarantee reimbursement of outstanding pay to employees if a business collapses. It was implemented in the UK without change to existing law which was already established by the then Employment Protection (Consolidation) Act 1978.

Posting of workers

The Posting of Workers Directive 1996 aimed to ensure minimum protection of workers posted temporarily to another Member State than the one in which they normally work. It was also designed to ensure fair competition and to provide minimum employment conditions for these employees. A posted worker was guaranteed such terms and conditions as laid down in the law and in applicable collective agreements in the Member State to which he/she is posted, in particular, maximum work periods and minimum rest periods; minimum paid annual holidays; minimum rates of pay, including overtime rates; health and safety; the conditions of hiring out workers, particularly temporary employment agencies; protective measures concerning the employment of pregnant women, new mothers, children and young people, and equality of treatment between men and women and other non-discrimination measures.

Member States must establish adequate procedures that allow workers and/or their representatives to enforce the provisions of the Directive. A posted worker can bring a claim under the Directive in the host country, without affecting any right to do so elsewhere. All Member States, including the UK, had implemented the Directive by December 1999.

Employee relations

The European Works Council Directive 1994 provides for a European level information and consultation system to be set up in all organisations with more than 1,000 employees in Member States (except at that time in the UK) and employing more than 150 people in each of two or more of these. A Works Council (or an alternative system) has to be agreed between central management and a Special Negotiating Body of employee representatives. If no agreement is reached within three years, a fall-back system applies. This requires the establishment of a European Works Council of employee representatives with the right to meet central management at least once a year for information and consultation about the progress and prospects of the company and to request extra consultation meetings before certain major decisions are taken affecting more than one Member State.

UK and other foreign companies had to comply with the Directive if their operations in other Member States met the thresholds but were not compelled to include UK operatives in the system. The UK operations of companies headquartered in other Member States could be involved if central management wished to include them. European information and consultation systems already in place before the set deadline implementation date of 22 September 1996 were exempted.

In December 1997, the Directive was extended to include the UK with a set implementation date of 15 December 1999. UK firms that come within the scope of the Directive that establish EU-wide information and consultation machinery before this implementation date will be exempted. The European Works Council Directive is discussed in further detail in Chapter 6 (Employee Involvement and Participation).

Health and safety
Several Directives were adopted in the 1970s and 1980s setting minimum standards for the control of noise, vibration, asbestos and other agents, as well as Directives harmonising safety signs. These have largely been incorporated into UK law via the Control of Substances Hazardous to Health (COSHH) and other national regulations. Since health and safety became a social issue that could be harmonised between Member States on the basis of qualified majority vote, a substantial number of health and safety Directives have been adopted. Health and safety is the most highly EU-regulated area of employment in the UK.

The most controversial EU measure in the area of health and safety is the Working Time Directive 1993 which was eventually transposed into UK law via the Working Time Regulations which became operative on 1 October 1998. The Conservative Government (1992-1997) challenged, before the European Court of Justice, that working time was a health and safety issue. They argued it was an industrial issue and should be considered under the 'Social Chapter' mechanism providing for agreement by the Council of Ministers on the basis of qualified majority voting from which the UK government was, at that time, exempted.

The Regulations (see Chapter 1) introduce a range of significant new rights and entitlements, such as a minimum of four weeks paid annual leave but which can include Bank Holidays. There is significant scope in the Regulations for employers and employees to enter into agreements on how the working time rules will apply in their own particular circumstances. Collective agreements can be made with an independent trade union whilst 'workforce agreements' can be made with workers who are not covered by collective bargaining. Certain activities, or sectors of activities, are excluded from the Regulations. These include those whose working time is under their own control, for example, managing executives, family and religious workers, those in transport industries, domestic servants, trainee doctors and those who work at sea.

Broadly speaking, worker entitlements under the Regulations (eg rest periods and paid annual leave) are enforced by an individual complaint to an employment tribunal. In the case of the mandatory 'limits' on working time (such as the weekly working time and night work limits), employees' rights will be enforced by health and safety authorities (the Health and Safety Executive and local authorities). However, workers have protection against detrimental treatment or unfair dismissals for, amongst other things, refusing to work in breach of an acceptable working time limit. Employers are required to keep adequate records, going back two years, to show the working time limits have been honoured.

The future areas of harmonisation
Working time
In November 1998, the European Commission issued a proposal for a new Working Time Directive that would extend the original Directive (see above) to cover excluded sectors and activities. At the same time, it also proposed a Directive on the working time of mobile workers in road transport and separate measures concerning seafarers. In maritime transport, it is proposed working time be no more than 14 hours in any 24 hour period and 72 hours in any seven days, or rest hours be at least 10 hours in every 24 and 77 hours in every seven days. In road haulage, the Commission has proposed working time be defined more broadly than mere driving, to include activities such as loading and unloading and maintenance work. The maximum working week is proposed at an average of 48 hours calculated over a four-month reference period and it is envisaged the maximum weekly working time does not exceed 60 hours.

It will be several years before these measures are likely to be implemented into UK legislation. Negotiations at the EU level are likely to take at least two years before their final adoption. Following this, the Member States will have two further years to give effect to any agreed Directive.

Information and consultation
Proposed in the autumn of 1997, information and consultation arrangements at the Member State level caused difficulties for both the social dialogue process itself and the Social Partners. After many extensions of time limits, UNICE in March 1998 decided to reject 'negotiated legislation' on the subject. They did so again in October 1998 whereupon the Commission issued a draft Directive on national information and consultation. The proposal, which will apply to public and private sector organisations with at least 50 employees, provides for:

- information to be given on recent and foreseeable developments concerning the enterprise's activities and economic and financial situation

- employees to be informed and consulted on the situation, structure and foreseeable developments relating to employment in the organisation and measures that might be taken in the face of a threat to jobs

- information and consultation on decisions that are likely to lead to substantial changes in work organisation and contractual relations.

The future of this draft Directive, however, remains uncertain. The UK Government has stated its opposition to the proposals, arguing that the proposed Directive breaches the principle of subsidiarity and that the issue is best dealt with by individual Member States. Germany, Ireland, Denmark and Portugal have also expressed opposition to the proposal so there is a real possibility it will be blocked by the Council of Ministers as it falls short of the necessary qualified majority vote. However, if the measure does become adopted, it will be 2001 at the earliest that it will apply to the UK.

European company statute
The draft European Company Statute, which would allow companies operating in two or more Member States to do so under one set of corporate rules, has been blocked by disagreement – primarily on its proposals for employee participation – for over 20 years. European companies, based on EU rather than national law, would be created by the Statute. In May 1997, an expert group set up by the Commission to investigate this matter recommended that worker involvement should be established in each individual case through negotiations. Management would be required to bargain with a special negotiating body, comprising employee representatives. Where no conclusion could be reached within three months, or longer if jointly agreed, a set of 'reference rules' would apply. Management and the special negotiating body would agree on information, consultation and, where applicable, participation at Board level. However, no formal draft Directive has been drawn up and deadlock remains in the Council of Ministers, although some individual states have pledged to have this 20-years-plus issue finally resolved.

The Social Partners have decided not to negotiate on sexual harassment at the workplace but further action can be expected from the Commission either in the form of a non-binding recommendation to Member States or as an amendment to the Equal Treatment Directive 1976. In addition, other forms of flexible working may become the subject of agreement amongst the Social Partners. The preamble to the Framework Agreement on Part-Time Work stated that 'it is the intention of parties to consider the need for similar agreements relating to other forms of flexible work'.

The Social Charter
The Community Charter on the Fundamental Rights of Workers, commonly known as the Social Charter, was adopted by all Member States except the UK in December 1989. It was introduced as a result

of political pressure to provide benefits for employees as a balance to what was seen as the advantages for companies provided by the Single European Act 1987 and the coming into force of the Single Market on 1 January 1993. The Charter is a Declaration and has no legal force in itself. It is in essence a 'wish list' of social objectives.

The Charter proposes a floor of basic common employment rights and objectives which should be established and implemented without discrimination at appropriate levels across all Member States to ensure that:

- The right of free movement in the EU becomes a reality.

- Workers are paid a sufficient wage to ensure a decent standard of living.

- Adequate social security protection is provided by all Member States.

- Basic law on working time, provision of contract, treatment of part-time and temporary workers and collective redundancies is improved and harmonised.

- All workers have the right to join or not to join a union, negotiate collective agreements and take collective action, including strike action.

- All workers have access to continuous vocational training throughout their working life.

- Equal treatment and equal opportunities between men and women are developed, particularly to enable men and women to reconcile family and work responsibilities.

- Information and consultation are developed along appropriate lines taking into account national practices, particularly in European enterprises.

- Health and safety protection is improved.

- Young workers are given access to training and fair treatment.

- The elderly are guaranteed an adequate income.

- Measures are taken to improve the social and professional integration of people with disabilities.

The Charter emphasises that the implementation of these 12 principles would contribute not only towards the improvement of living and working conditions provided in the Treaty of Rome 1957 but would also lead to a more effective use of human resources across the EU and therefore improve economic competitiveness and job creation. Whilst the UK Government at the time did not object to these aims as general principles, it did not sign the Charter because it was concerned it would lead to a moral obligation to accept EU laws which it felt could be costly, restrictive and damaging to competitiveness. However, this, as we have seen, did not restrain the Commission proposing Directives to implement some of the Charter's principles, for example the Working Time Directive, the European Works Council Directive and the Part-Time Work Directive. The Charter highlights the importance the majority of the Member States attach to the social dimension of the Single Market.

SUMMARY

This chapter began by identifying the growing importance of the EU in regulating the UK labour market and how this will continue into the future. It then went on to explain the development of the EU and outlined its aim. We saw that the founding Treaty of the European Union was the Treaty of Rome 1957 which provided for the creation for a common European market (a free trade area) by removing barriers to the free movement of goods, labour, capital and services (the so-called four great freedoms) between Member States. However we also showed how the authors of the Treaty included a social dimension, known as the Social Chapter, to provide for the harmonisation of social conditions between Member States. Product market competition in the free trade area was thus to take place within the constraints of 'a level playing field' of minimum social standards across Member States.

The chapter then pointed out that, recognising legislation would be required to achieve these aims, the Treaty of Rome established legislative institutions. The European Commission was given a monopoly of power to initiate legislation whilst the European Council of Ministers was granted the ultimate power to reject or adopt proposals for new laws made by the Commission. A European Parliament was established to appoint the European Commissioners, determine the EU budget, to be consulted on legislation and to exercise certain power to influence the legislative process. It still cannot initiate legislation and does not have the final say as to whether proposals for legislation are adopted. The fourth institution established was the European Court of Justice which is the supreme custodian of EU-enacted laws and its decisions take precedence over any laws or judicial decisions taken by Member States.

We saw, however, that by the mid-1980s little progress had been made towards the creation of a common market and the harmonisation of social conditions. The lack of progress arose because any Member State could veto proposals to achieve a free movement. It was then explained how the Commission suggested some revolutionary changes to the Treaty of Rome to overcome this problem. We saw the three main changes were: first, the spelling out of a 1992 deadline for the achievement of the four freedoms; second, the introduction of the qualified majority voting (QMV) procedure for any measure aimed at completing the common market by 1992 and, most importantly, for employee relations specialists, it included health and safety as a social issue to be harmonised by QMV; and finally, the formalisation of the EU commitment to involve the Social Partners in the Brussels decision-making machinery. We have seen that these radical changes were key provisions of the Single European Act 1987. These changes meant Europe could never be the same again and its law-making mechanism could actually start to work as envisaged in 1957.

The chapter then moved on to demonstrate how the Maastricht Treaty

1993 brought further changes to the Treaty of Rome. It committed the EU to a single currency by 1999 but more importantly for employee relations specialists made two important changes to the 'social dimension'. First, all States, except the UK, accepted proposed extensions of social and employment issues that could be harmonised by QMV. As the UK objected it was not possible to include new 'social provision' in the Maastricht Treaty. However, a compromise agreement was reached whereby Member States, other than the UK, agreed they could use EU institutions to introduce additional binding legislation within the social field but any such legislation would not apply to the UK. It was explained that the mechanism for doing this was under a separate Social Policy Agreement which listed the specific social issues that the rest of the Member States could legislate on. This agreement, as we saw, was attached to a Social Protocol annexed to the main Treaty spelling out the arrangement described above. This is whence the term 'the UK opt-out from the Social Chapter' came.

Secondly, the chapter explained how Maastricht also saw the introduction of Article 118(b) which provided for compulsory consultation by the Commission with the Social Partners on any social proposals and which permitted the Social Partners the option to agree voluntarily to negotiate a Framework Agreement on the issue and for that Agreement to be made binding on Member States. This unique role for the Social Partners means that in future employee relations specialists will have to become interested in the Europeanisation of collective bargaining since agreements arising from this procedure also apply to non-union workplaces. We have seen that Framework Agreements collectively bargained by the Social Partners were then issued as a Directive and transposed into UK law in three areas – Parental Leave, Part-Time Work and Fixed-Term Contracts.

The chapter then explained how the Treaty of Amsterdam 1998 introduced a new chapter into the Treaty of Rome relating exclusively to employment, and incorporated into the Social Chapter of the Treaty of Rome the Agreement on Social Policy attached to a Social Protocol annexed to the Maastricht Treaty and which in the UK was widely (but incorrectly) referred to as the 'Social Chapter'. It was this 'Social Chapter' that the Blair government took a decision to 'opt into' on taking office in May 1997. The 'Social Protocol' and 'Agreement on Social Policy' therefore no longer exist, as their provisions now comprise part of the EU Treaties as amended at Amsterdam.

We have seen in this chapter that most EU social legislation comes in three forms – Regulations, Decisions and Directives. In addition to these 'hard legislation' instruments it was pointed out there are softer ones of which the chief are Recommendations, Opinions and Declarations. We have also described the different procedures whereby an EU Directive can be issued, namely the Consultation procedure, the Co-operation Procedure, the Co-Decision Procedure and the Collective Agreement Procedure, which enable the Social Partners to reach voluntary framework agreements on particular issues which are then transferred into 'hard' EU legislation. The chapter has explained why employee relations specialists and practitioners can ignore the Europeanisation of collective bargaining at their own peril.

We have also explained the Social Chapter of the EU is not a set of detailed legislation but a mechanism which allows Member States to agree new rules and legislation to harmonise social matters between them. It was noted that all social issues other than health and safety, working conditions, information and consultation of workers, equal treatment and equal opportunities and the integration of persons excluded from the labour market can only be harmonised between Member States on the basis of unanimity. However, we saw that certain issues – pay, the right of association and the right to impose individual sanctions – are formally excluded from EU legislation.

The chapter has also spent time outlining how, and where, EU laws have had, and will continue to have, a direct impact on the work of the HR/personnel specialist. The main areas identified were:

- Equality – equal pay, parental leave, equal treatment, treatment of part-time workers and those employed on fixed contracts

- Employee Protection – redundancies, transfer of undertakings, contract of employment, insolvency and protection of workers posted short-term in another Member State other than the one in which they normally work

- Employee Relations – informing and consulting with employees

- Health and Safety – working time (hours, holidays, rest periods, etc).

REFERENCES AND FURTHER READING

CRESSEY P. 'European monetary union and the impact of UK industrial relations', in Kauppinen T. (ed.) *The Impact of EMU on Industrial Relations in the European Union*, Finnish Labour Relations Association, Publication No 9, 1988.

DEPARTMENT OF TRADE AND INDUSTRY. *The Social Chapter – The British and continental approaches*. London, DTI, 1996.

FERNER A. *and* HYMAN. R. *Changing Industrial Relations in Europe*. Oxford, Blackwell, 1998.

INDUSTRIAL RELATIONS SERVICES. 'Employment law update: what's next from Brussels?' *Employment Trends*. January 1999.

INSTITUTE OF PERSONNEL AND DEVELOPMENT. *Europe: Personnel and development*. London, IPD, October 1998.

INSTITUTE OF PERSONNEL AND DEVELOPMENT. *European Update*. A monthly brief on all the latest EU developments and issues affecting the personnel professional including progress of Directives, new employment case law and copies of relevant EU documents. London, IPD.

INSTITUTE OF PERSONNEL AND DEVELOPMENT. *People Management*. A fortnightly journal covering major developments in the EU.

INCOMES DATA SERVICES. *Industrial Relations and Collective Bargaining*. London, IPD, 1996. (Introduction, pp xviii–xxxvii.)

JENSON C. S., MADSEN J. S. *and* DUE J. 'Phases and dynamics in the development of EU industrial relations regulation'. *Industrial Relations Journal*. Vol. 30 No. 2, June 1999.

KELLER B. *and* SORRIES B. 'The new social dialogue: procedural structuring, first results and perspectives', in Towers B. and Terry M. (eds) *European Annual Review, 1997, Industrial Relations Journal*, 1998.

4 Employee relations institutions

INTRODUCTION

This chapter is concerned with the institutions of employee relations – employers' associations or federations, trade unions and staff associations, umbrella organisations such as the CBI and the TUC, their International and European equivalents (see Chapter 3), and state organisations such as the Advisory Conciliation and Arbitration Service (ACAS), the Central Arbitration Committee (CAC) and the Certification Officer. This list demonstrates that both employers and employees have a range of options open to them in relation to external organisations about which they have to make choices. For example, do employers join their industry association or federation? Do they join umbrella organisations such as the Confederation of British Industry (CBI) or the Institute of Directors (IoD)? If they decide to join their industry or sector organisation do they – assuming that the organisation they are considering joining is one which gets involved in collective bargaining – allow that organisation to bargain on their behalf? Does becoming a member bind them to particular courses of action? Even if the reasons for contemplating membership are nothing to do with collective bargaining, what sort of services are available to employers and how will they be paid for? On the other side of the coin there is a need to examine trade unions and trade union behaviour, including the way trade unions organise themselves. There are also such issues as why people join or do not join trade unions and what opportunities and rights individual members have to influence their union. It is also important to examine the interventionist role of such third party organisations as ACAS and the CAC.

When you have completed this chapter you should be able to:

- explain why some organisations join employers' associations and some do not

- explain how employers' organisations can help personnel professionals in their day-to-day work

- describe the employee relations role of the Confederation of British Industry and the Trades Union Congress

- understand trade union structure

- appreciate the basis of trade union organisation in the UK and other countries

- identify the role of state institutions such as the Advisory Conciliation and Arbitration Service

- understand why some organisations are prepared to use third party intervention.

EMPLOYERS' ORGANISATIONS

Employers' associations are voluntary, private bodies, which exist to provide information and co-ordination in areas of common interest. There are many different associations, covering overlapping areas of geographic spread, industrial sector, and grouping of larger or smaller organisations. The Annual Report of the Certification Officer (1998) lists 107 employers' associations with a total membership of 268,294 organisations. In 1997, the gross income of employers' associations was £235.8 million and gross expenditure was £222 million. Employers' associations vary in size and influence from the very small with no full time staff to large influential organisations like the Engineering Employers Federation (over 5,000 member organisations), the Road Haulage Association (9,700 members) and the Retail Motor Industry Federation Ltd (12,500 members). In both the public and private sector employers' associations are still, despite the views of those who see them as a declining force, significant employee relations players in terms of the help and advice they can provide to the employee relations specialist. The main employers' associations are listed in Table 12.

The origins of employers' associations

Employers' associations primarily came into being as defensive mechanisms against the trade unions in the 18th and 19th centuries and tended to become active only for the duration of an industrial relations problem. 'As with trade unions, early organisation was often informal and ephemeral, or spasmodic' (Clegg 1979 p63) and activities tended to be limited to a geographical basis. By the end of the nineteenth century these local associations were beginning to come together to create national federations of employers whose interests lay in one particular industry. The Engineering Employers Federation, the Building Trades Federation and the Shipbuilding Federation were just some that were formed in this period.

This bias towards a federated approach was, in many respects, a response to the growing power and influence of trade unions and by the early part of this century a move had begun towards a system of industry-wide bargaining. Despite high levels of unemployment in the inter-war years and a relative decline in trade union influence, employers did not try to modify the then prevailing system of industry bargaining. This system continued after the end of the Second World War mainly because Britain's employers had, by the end of the Second World War, 'secured a system of collective bargaining which suited them' (Clegg 1979 p70). Post-1945, the main activity of employers' associations was in the determination of pay and conditions for their particular industry.

However, the pressures of full employment, particularly the resulting skills shortages, made it difficult for industry-wide agreements to regulate pay effectively. As a consequence, a second tier of

Table 12 **Main Employers' Associations**

Engineering Employers Federation
Electrical Contractors Association
Heating and Ventilating Contractors Association
Road Haulage Association
British Printing Industries Federation
Chemical Industries Association
Building Employers Confederation
Newspaper Society
Federation of Master Builders
Paper Federation of Great Britain Ltd
Publishers Association
Dairy Industry Federation Ltd

negotiations emerged as individual companies, competing for the available skills, began to negotiate additional rates of pay at local level. This led to an increasingly complex package of rewards, a huge gap between actual earnings and pay rates as stated in industry-wide agreements and a decline in the authority of employers' associations. As a result, some companies left the employers' associations so that they could determine all conditions locally. Full employment had undermined the regulatory pay function of the employers' association (Donovan, 1968).

Industry-wide agreements also came under pressure in the 1980s and 1990s as increasing competitive pressures and devolving corporate structures led companies, as part of controlling costs, to devolve bargaining down to the business unit level. Expecting managers to manage effectively their business units whilst not at the same time giving them control of labour costs, because of the continuation of industry-wide agreements, was incompatible. As a result, many companies withdrew from national agreements. This further weakened the role of employers' associations in pay matters since they were no longer even determining minimum standards for the industry.

Definition of an employers' association

The current legal definition of employers' association is contained in section 122 of the Trade Union and Labour Relations (Consolidation) Act 1992. The principal part of the definition is that employers' associations are organisations which consist wholly or mainly of employers or individual owners of undertakings of one or more descriptions and whose principal purposes include the regulation of relations between employers of that description or those descriptions and workers or trade unions.

The definition covers those organisations which wish to deal exclusively with employee relations issues and those, like the Building Employers Confederation and the British Printing Industries Federation, which deal with both employee relations and commercial matters. This latter group is by far the most common type of employers' association. Indeed, it is difficult to identify today any employers' association that confines its activities to employee relations. The rapidly changing environment in which they have operated over the last 20 years has caused them to adapt the services they offer to their members.

In common with trade unions, employers' associations who wish to have their legal status confirmed must be registered on a list kept by the Certification Officer (whose role is analysed in more detail later in the chapter). Employers' associations are required to keep proper accounting records, establish and maintain a satisfactory system of control of their accounting records, and to submit an Annual Return to the Certification Officer. An employers' association must submit its Annual Returns and accounts to this Officer before 1 June each year. The Certification Officer can investigate the financial affairs of an employers' association.

The importance of employers' associations
All employers' bodies, whether in the public or private sector, organise themselves in different ways. The priority each gives to employee relations, as opposed to trade matters, will differ according to tradition, the nature of the industry it represents and the degree of unionisation in its particular sector. Generally it remains true that those associations which are most concerned with employee relations are those which comprise companies using semi-skilled and skilled labour in areas where there is a high concentration of a single industry, such as engineering or printing.

There are three types of employers' association: national federations to which local employers' associations are affiliated, eg the Engineering Employers Federation (EEF) which is a federation of 15 autonomous organisations; single national bodies such as the British Printing Industries Federation (BPIF) which is divided into six regions for administrative and representational purposes (until 1982, it had been a federated body like the EEF, but a serious national dispute in 1980 caused it to re-invent itself), and single associations with a national membership like the British Ceramic Confederation.

Employers' associations consist of companies of varying sizes, from the very small to the very large, with the largest sometimes organised into either autonomous local associations (for example, the EEF West Midlands, EEF Lancashire) or non-autonomous district associations, like the British Printing Industries Federation. Some employers' associations have a similar organisational structure to trade unions with the ultimate decision-making authority being a national council or its equivalent. The basis of representation of such a council varies from association to association. Except for those with local autonomy, in most employers' associations local and regional associations are consultative rather than decision-making bodies.

Although organisations of employers have been around for a very long time, there are those who believe that in recent times their prominence and influence over employment issues has declined (Marchington and Wilkinson 1996 p48). While it may be possible to demonstrate a decline in the number of industry-wide collective agreements, there are still many employers' associations which continue to negotiate agreements at national level. In the private sector national agreements still exist, for example, in electrical contracting, paper-making, construction and general printing. In the public sector national pay arrangements still exist for doctors and nurses and the National

Association of Health Authorities and Trusts – an employers' body – provides evidence to the appropriate pay review body. Nevertheless, in many industries national agreements have become, for reasons outlined above, less important. They remain in industries dominated by small companies, which operate in very competitive labour markets. For these companies, who usually do not have the resources to establish a personnel function, the national agreement is still regarded as significant in taking labour out of competition and in providing an infrastructure to the industry via the procedures (eg disputes and grievances) contained in the agreement.

While it has become fashionable for commentators and academics to write off employers' associations, they still exert tremendous influence in respect of employee relations policy and practice. The 1996 annual review of the Engineering Employers Federation (EEF) records how it provides member companies with practical advice about the issues they should consider when reviewing their employee relations policies. The EEF also published, in 1995, a guidance document *Developing Employee Relations*. Given that the EEF has some 5,000 establishments in membership employing in excess of half a million people it would be a mistake to pretend that because the engineering industry has no national agreement then the EEF has no influence on employee relations.

THE ACTIVITIES OF EMPLOYERS' ASSOCIATIONS

Marchington and Wilkinson (1996) identified four major sets of services that employers' organisations have traditionally offered to their members:

* collective bargaining with trade unions

* assisting in the resolution of disputes

* providing general advice to members

* representing members' views.

Collective bargaining

Collective bargaining services to members have clearly declined, even within those industries which maintain some form of national agreement. Although employers' associations continue to have an influence on employee relations it is important to recognise some of the difficulties they face. As the extent of national agreements decreases, there is evidence they are becoming increasingly less attractive to larger employers. Recruitment and retention of such members is becoming more and more difficult. When membership meant buying into a national agreement, persuading employers to join was not so difficult. In today's more competitive business environment, the employers' association membership fee becomes subject to the same scrutiny as any other item of expenditure and it is not easy to persuade a large business to spend 'thousands of pounds' on an intangible product, particularly if it ties them into a collective agreement that they find inappropriate to their business needs.

During the 1980s, a number of companies, particularly large ones, withdrew from those employers' associations whose primary purpose was the negotiation of national terms and conditions. Their preference was to negotiate their own arrangements. They were much more likely to have their own personnel specialists in-house and considered that with these resources they could achieve better results than could be achieved nationally. One reason for them adopting this position was the way in which many national agreements are structured. They can consist of a number of enabling clauses, particularly in the area of productivity improvements, which set out in broad terms that certain things must happen as a consequence of an increase in pay or the provision of other benefit. For example, there may be a clause allowing for full flexibility of labour with no demarcation lines. The difficulty with such clauses is the problem of finding appropriate words to fit the circumstances of every employer and this can lead to a less than favourable endorsement of the principle of national bargaining.

Over the past 20 years, the difficulties posed by national collective bargaining have been considered at one time or another by employers' associations. For example, in 1989, following a review the EEF concluded that as the business policies and practices of its member companies changed during the 1970s and 1980s the relevance of the national agreement declined. By 1989 only minimum rates of pay and working time remained live issues at national level. The EEF, therefore decided to withdraw from national collective bargaining on terms and conditions of employment with the unions representing blue collar employees (EEF Guide 1995). The EEF was reflecting the needs of its members, who continue to enjoy the advantages of strength in numbers, but are not now obliged to follow nationally-agreed terms and conditions. The British Printing Industries Federation tried to introduce a similar concept, but this was not acceptable to its predominantly small membership, who continue to see firm advantages in nationally-agreed wage rates.

Some organisations have left (or resisted joining) employers' associations because of a change in their policy on union recognition. Some may have a policy of non-recognition, or they may have used the 'change in the balance of bargaining power' to opt out of nationally-agreed pay rises and marginalise their union at the same time.

National agreements are also not popular with some employers because the employers' association has few sanctions it can impose against members who don't conform. One of the purposes of a national agreement is to create a level playing-field between competing employers in respect of wages and conditions. The constitution of many associations allows for expulsion for bringing the organisation into disrepute, but there is little or no evidence that this happens. The loss of revenue from expelling a dissenting large company member could have a disastrous effect on the association's finances and thereby its ability to service effectively the remaining members.

Furthermore, if an association becomes involved in a dispute with one or more trade unions, it will tend to have even more problems than the trade unions in retaining solidarity among its members. The pressures of competition between the members of an employers' association may cause the breaking of ranks. A member firm may make a separate deal with the union, resign (or be expelled) from the association and then invade the market of those companies who cannot satisfy the needs of their customers because they are still subject to industrial sanctions.

Dispute resolution

The provision of dispute resolution services has links with national bargaining arrangements in that many national agreements provide access to an established dispute procedure. Such procedures tend to define a number of stages through which a dispute will be processed. Stage one may include the involvement of a local employers' association representative, a union branch secretary, lay union officials from within the organisation in dispute and the organisation's management. If the dispute is not resolved at this stage it may, depending on the employers' association and the union involved, move up to a district or regional level. Some of the players will stay the same as at the first stage, but the full-time officials will probably differ. The third stage will involve national officials of the employers' association and the appropriate trade unions. If there is no resolution of the differences at this stage, some disputes procedures provide for the involvement of an independent third party whose decision will be binding. Such dispute procedures usually contain provisions stating 'no hostile action' is to be taken by either side or that the *status quo* must prevail while the dispute is going through its various stages.

Advisory and information services

During the years when national collective bargaining was in the ascendancy, many employer organisations became bureaucratic and unimaginative. They had a captive audience and paid little attention to membership retention, or to the range of services that they offered members. All this changed as companies began to prefer bargaining at a more local level. This in turn led employers to examine what else they were receiving from their associations, in return for not insignificant subscriptions. Some employers' organisations quickly realised that if they were to continue to have an employee relations influence, they needed to provide a package of benefits and services to their members, which would be seen to add value to businesses. In this context, many employers' associations widened their existing advisory services on best practices and model procedural agreements on issues such as disciplinary, dismissal and redundancy procedures. Their ability to market such services was helped by the growth, particularly in the 1970s and 1980s, of employment legislation that added to employees 'rights at work'. Unfair dismissal, health and safety and equal pay are just three examples.

The recruitment literature of any of the larger employers' associations places greatest emphasis on the employment advice and support services they can offer to members. For example, the Building Employers Confederation (BEF) offers its members advice and support on wage rates and conditions of employment, disciplinary procedures, redundancy procedures, representation at Employment Tribunals and a regular bulletin with articles and relevant developments in employment law. Most employers' organisations also provide employee relations information services. Prominent amongst these are pay and benefits data based on regularly conducted surveys and which are useful for salary and pay comparisons and for use in local negotiations. However, such surveys can be problematic, as the associations have no means of enforcing individual returns. Nevertheless, provided the employee relations professional recognises these limitations, such surveys can be a valuable tool. Other topics on which employers' associations provide information include labour productivity and government and EU behaviour in employee relations.

Does the sector in which you work have any sort of employers' organisation? What benefits could it provide that would assist in the process of employee relations? How would you place a value on their advice?

Representation of members' interests
A major growth area of activity has been the representation of members' views to a range of other organisations, particularly political bodies – government departments, local authorities and political parties. These political lobbying activities can be of particular interest to the large company whose inclination might be to leave an association if its only purpose was the negotiation of a national agreement. With many large organisations now operating in a European and worldwide market they know that their only means of influencing UK Government or European Union policy is through a collective voice (see Chapters 3 and 6). In its 1998 review the EEF reported on its representations to the major political parties to try to ensure the employment policies they develop meet the needs of the engineering industry (EEF Annual Review 1998). UK Governments have found employers' organisations useful in obtaining the collective employer view on a wide range of consultative documents. Examples include reform of the Industrial Tribunal system, possible pension reform, statutory trade union recognition and the removal of any limits to the compensation to be awarded to individuals unfairly dismissed.

NON-MEMBERSHIP OF EMPLOYERS' ASSOCIATIONS

Some companies view employers' associations as too restrictive and see membership as an obstacle to independent action to introduce innovation in employee relations policies and practices. Such companies regard innovation, whether in operational matters or people issues, as an essential managerial activity in today's economic climate. Therefore, they feel the need to be responsible for, to co-ordinate and to control their own negotiations. Nevertheless, it is important to remember that even those companies which negotiate unilaterally, or independently of the appropriate employers' association, must still take into account what is negotiated in their industries at national level. An important part of the employee relations function is to take account of other wage settlements, particularly within the sector in which their organisation operates. Not being aware of such settlements, many of which affect their competitors, could seriously weaken their own bargaining position and impact adversely on their competitiveness.

There are businesses which, despite their feelings, join employers' organisations because of their more traditional trade association activities. A number have arbitration schemes to resolve differences between supplier and customer while others have the ability to remove an organisation from membership if they do not meet agreed standards on, for example, the quality of service or product provided to the customer. This can be an effective sanction for a company which relies on the 'badge' of the trade association to help secure business, such as some of the building trades or electrical contractors.

Finally, there are those businesses which, while finding industry bodies too parochial, value support from external bodies, such as Chambers of Commerce, the Confederation of British Industry (CBI) and the Institute of Directors (IoD).

National and other representative bodies
The best known national employers' organisation is probably the Confederation of British Industry (CBI) whose roots go back to 1915 with the formation of the National Union of Manufacturers, later renamed the National Association of British Manufacturers (NABM). Within five years two further organisations, the Federation of British Industries (FBI) and the British Employers' Confederation (BEC) were formed. The CBI as an organisation was the result of a merger in 1965 between these three bodies. Its membership includes individual companies, national and regional trades and employers' associations. It sees as its overall task the promotion of policies for a more efficient mixed economy. It is estimated around half of the total labour force work in organisations affiliated to the CBI. The CBI is basically a political lobbying organisation whose major function is to provide for British industry the means of formulating, making known and influencing general policy in regard to industrial, economic, fiscal, commercial, labour, social, legal and technical questions.

However, while not specifically engaging in employee relations activities, the CBI does have a human resources programme to promote 'lifetime learning, employee ability and effective employee performance as a source of competitive edge for business' (1995 Annual Report). However, its lobbying activities can have an impact on issues that affect workplace employee relations. In this regard, in recent years the CBI has lobbied successfully on behalf of employers on issues such as the national minimum wage, statutory trade union recognition procedures and a maximum limit on compensation awards in unfair dismissal cases. Although as an organisation the CBI does not engage in negotiations with employee representatives, it does maintain a direct working relationship with the Trades Union Congress (TUC) as well as an indirect one via joint membership of bodies such as ACAS and the Health and Safety Executive.

Another organisation influential with UK Governments in respect of employee relations policy is the Institute of Directors (IoD). This is essentially a professional and business organisation, which plays a key role in representing the views of business to UK Government.

Membership is on an individual rather than company basis, and to that extent its employee relations role is peripheral. In 1998, IoD members were on the boards of 750 of the Times Top 1000 companies, which is a not unimportant reason why it has the ear of government. This has enabled it to contribute to the debate on employee relations issues such as the minimum wage, the working time regulations and trade union recognition.

TRADE UNIONS

Purpose and objectives

Trade unions are organised groups of employees who 'consist wholly or mainly of workers of one or more description and whose principal purposes include the regulation of relations between workers and employers' (Section 1 of the Trade Unions and Labour Relations (Consolidation) Act). The primary purpose of trade unions is to protect the jobs of their members and to seek to enhance their pay and the conditions of employment by the process of collective bargaining and the lobbying of political decision-making bodies. The core business of a trade union is therefore interest representation to employers and to the political decision-makers.

UK trade unions are bodies defending sectional economic interests rather than working class interests as a whole. In Flanders' (1968) analysis, unions are job-conscious, not class-conscious, organisations. He also argued the value of a union to its members is less in its economic activities than in its capacity to protect their dignity at the workplace by establishing worker rights, for example not to be discriminated against, by establishing rights to paid holidays and establishing a standard working week. Unions thus participate in job regulation by establishing a body of jointly agreed rules for jobs. In this sense, for Flanders, trade unions operate primarily as political (with a small 'p') not economic institutions. Trade unions are best seen as economic, social and political agents.

Although trade unions are diverse in character and culture, the TUC has presented a set of generic 'permanent objectives' for them (TUC, 1966). These are:

- improved terms of employment
- improved physical environment at work (eg health and safety, intensity of work, etc)
- security of employment and income
- industrial democracy
- fair shares in national income and wealth
- full employment and national prosperity
- improved social security
- improved public and social services
- a voice to government
- public control and planning of industry.

These 'permanent' objectives reflect the economic, social and political activities of unions. Some are about establishing terms and conditions of employment, some about influencing employer decisions and others about influencing political decisions in that decisions on taxation, welfare and public services and the macroeconomic priorities of national governments bear directly on the living standards of trade union members. In addition to these 'permanent' objectives, trade unions will also have short-term priorities that vary with circumstances.

Union methods

Trade unions attempt to achieve their objectives by a number of different methods. The most common are: collective bargaining (see Chapters 1 and 10), which results in a collective agreement setting out minimum standards to apply to those members covered by the agreement; joint consultation (see Chapters 1 and 6); provision of services to members (representation in grievance and disciplinary matters, sickness, accident and unemployment benefit, employee relations training and development and legal assistance for both work-related and work-unrelated matters); influencing national and local government and by interventional activities influencing inter-governmental political institutions such as the European Union (see Chapter 3) and the United Nations and its agencies to achieve legal regulation of employment conditions.

The former is influenced via the activities of the European Trade Union Confederation and the latter by the International Confederation of Free Trade Unions (ICFTU) which was formed in 1949. ICFTU membership consists of 141 affiliated organisations in some 97 countries on five continents with a membership of 86 million. Its secretariat is in Brussels but it has permanent offices in Geneva and New York. Its objectives include promoting the interests of working people throughout the world, reducing the gap between rich and poor, defending fundamental human and trade union rights and helping workers to organise themselves and secure the recognition of their organisations as free bargaining agents. It also has close relationships with the International Labour Organisation (ILO) which is a UN body made up of government, employer and worker representatives. The ILO has established many international minimum labour standards (known as Conventions) to protect workers' rights and which all governments in membership of the UN are expected to enact in their national parliaments.

Union resources

If unions are to achieve their objectives by the means outlined above, they require resources. The major financial resources of trade unions come from membership subscriptions and interest from investments. Some unions charge their members a flat rate subscription paid either weekly or monthly whilst others, particularly those representing the interests of relatively high paid non-manual employees, charge members a subscription rate on the basis of a percentage rate of their pay. The Certification Officer's Report for 1998 reported that the gross income of trade unions in 1997 was £724.1 million of which £576.6 million was from members' subscriptions. The TUC estimates average size of union subscriptions to be £6–8 per month. Membership

Table 13 Trade union membership, 1978–1996

Year	Membership of TUC	Number of TUC-affiliated unions	Membership of non–TUC unions
1978	11,865,390	112	1,188,206
1979	12,128,078	12	1,084,276
1980	12,172,508	109	463,847
1981	11,601,413	108	709,821
1982	11,005,984	105	738,406
1983	10,510,157	95	789,722
1984	10,082,144	89	691,809
1985	9,855,204	91	963,745
1986	9,580,502	19	1,017,506
1987	9,243,297	87	1,236,853
1988	9,127,278	83	1,259,960
1989	8,652,318	78	1,391,288
1990	8,405,246	78	1,404,773
1991	8,192,662	74	Not Available
1992	7,786,885	72	1,142,017
1993	7,647,443	70	1,018,501
1994	7,117,436	69	1,113,109
1995	6,894,604	67	1,136,722
1996	6,790,339	73	1,147,874
1997	6,756,544	75	1,044,771

Source: *TUC Annual Reports*, Certification Officer, *Annual Reports*

recruitment and retention is essential for trade unions if they are to maintain and gain additional resources. It is for this reason that many trade unions have amongst their objectives the desire to achieve 100 per cent organisation in the workplace where they have members.

Trade unions also require human resources that are competent and effective if they are to represent the interests of their members effectively. This requires competent full-time officials and civil servants to provide research and other back-up. The competency of worker representatives requires the provision of employee relations training and development services and continuing professional development programmes. Without high levels of membership, sound organisation and a competent leadership, a union's ability to perform its interest representation function is seriously weakened. Whilst all unions have broadly similar purposes, and utilise largely the same methods to achieve them, each union has its own unique purpose and uses those methods most appropriate to its particular circumstances.

Trade union membership trends

Table 13 shows trends in trade union membership over the period 1978–1996. Total union membership in the UK peaked at an all-time high of 13.2 million members in 1979, made up of 12.1 million members in TUC affiliated unions and just over 1 million in non-TUC unions. In 1997, the total trade union membership, as reported by the Certification Officer, was 7.8 million. Although trade union membership in the aggregate has declined in many organisations, unions still play an important part in the process of employee relations. In the manufacturing sector, there is still a significant union presence but, as we saw in Chapter 1, the number of people employed in this sector has declined dramatically. Unions still have a large presence in sectors such as the health service, local government and central government. Trade union membership remains low in private sector services (financial, retail), amongst non-manual employees, in small firms and in foreign-owned firms.

This decline in trade union membership can be explained by a number of factors, many of which reflect changes in the economy. The last 20 years have seen changes in the structure of employment (see Chapter 2), which are problematic for trade unions. Employment has switched from manufacturing (a heartland of trade unions) to the service sector where trade union membership has traditionally been low. The size of employing unit has also fallen. It was easier and cheaper for unions to organise in large workplaces than smaller ones. In the past, trade unions have always found it relatively more difficult to organise women than men. The last 20 years have seen an increasing number of women entering the labour force relative to men. Non-manual employees, particularly in the private sector, have always been reluctant to join trade unions. Their share of employment in the last 20 years, relative to manual work employment, has increased significantly and is set to rise further (see Chapter 2). Foreign-owned firms have also been difficult areas of recruitment for trade unions and the share of total employment accounted for by such firms has increased since 1979.

However, structural factors do not tell the whole story. The Conservative Governments between May 1979 and May 1997 inclusive, oversaw the introduction of public policy initiatives in the employee relations field that were unsupportive of trade union behaviour. For example, statutory trade union recognition procedures were repealed in 1980 and legal protection for the closed shops (ie where union membership is a condition of gaining and/or remaining in employment) was progressively removed. Public policy initiatives also weakened trade union bargaining power relative to the employer by restricting severely the circumstances in which a trade union could impose industrial actions on an employer without that employer having the right to resort to the Courts for redress.

As was shown in Chapter 2, with private sector employers facing increasingly competitive product markets and the public sector being privatised or deregulated, there has been an increasing tendency for employers to introduce more flexible employment policies. This has resulted, *inter alia*, in a growth of employment based on a fixed-term contract, on part-time working and on temporary hiring. The last 20 years have witnessed a growth in such so-called 'insecure employment practices' relative to 'secure employment practices'. Employees employed on this basis have always proved more difficult to organise than full-time workers. This is another factor contributing to the decline in trade union membership.

Competitive pressures have also resulted in employers de-recognising trade unions and ending the associated collective bargaining institutions and procedures where the trade union only represented a small proportion of the workforce and therefore was limited in its representative capacity. Other policies introduced by management that have made organising workers difficult have included the introduction of employee empowerment, involvement and participation schemes (see Chapter 6) and the introduction of dual communication channel systems whereby the employer still communicates with the employees indirectly through trade union representatives but more often communicates directly with them.

The likely impact of the Employment Relations Act 1999 statutory trade union recognition procedures is discussed in Chapter 5. The future prospects for trade unions are discussed later in this chapter.

Trade union structure

Union structure in this context refers to the external environment in which particular unions organise themselves and their coverage in terms of industry and occupations. The internal structure of trade unions which covers their decision-making structure is examined below.

The UK trade union structure is characterised by a small number of very large trade unions co-existing with a large number of small trade unions. In 1998, the Annual Report of the Certification Officer reported that the 17 unions with membership of 100,000 or more accounted for 82 per cent of total trade union membership but accounted for only 7 per cent of the 252 trade unions on his list of independent unions. The largest nine unions had a total membership of 5.2 million out of a total of 7.8 million. 127 unions had memberships of less than 1,000 but accounted for 50 per cent of the total number of unions and only ½ per cent of the total membership of trade unions (see Table 14). The largest 17 unions in 1997 are shown in Table 15.

Types of union

The UK trade unions have a complex structure in terms of their recruitment and membership base. This, in part, owes something to

Table 14 Trade unions: distribution by size

Number of members	Number of unions	Membership (000s)	Number of unions		Membership of all unions	
			%	Cumulative %	%	Cumulative %
Under 100	32	1	12.5	12.5	0	0
100–499	71	23	27.8	40.4	0.3	0.3
500–999	21	14	8.2	48.6	0.2	0.5
1,000–2,499	43	72	16.9	65.5	0.9	1.4
2,500–4,999	20	74	7.8	73.3	0.9	2.3
5,000–9,999	14	98	5.5	78.8	1.2	3.5
10,000–14,999	7	92	2.7	81.6	1.2	4.7
15,000–24,999	6	104	2.4	83.9	1.3	6.0
25,000–49,999	19	665	7.5	91.4	8.4	14.4
50,000–99,999	5	314	2.1	93.3	4.0	18.4
100,000–249,999	8	1,210	3.1	96.5	15.2	33.6
250,000 and over	9	5,271	3.5	100	66.4	100
TOTAL	255	7,938	100		100	

Source: Annual report of the Certification Officer, 1997, p18.

Table 15 Trade unions with memberships of 100,000: 1998

Union	Membership
UNISON: The Public Services Union	1,300,451
Transport and General Workers Union (T&GWU)	881,357
Amalgamated Engineering and Electrical Union (AEEU)	720,296
GMB	709,708
Manufacturing Science and Finance Union (MSF)	416,000
Royal College of Nursing (RCN)[1]	312,141
Union of Shop Distributive and Allied Workers (USDAW)	293,470
National Union of Teachers	273,814
Communication Workers Union (CWU)	276,819
National Association of Schoolmasters and Union of Women Teachers (NASAUWT)	245,932
Graphical Paper and Media Union (GPMU)	204,822
Public Services Tax and Commerce Union (PSTCU)	153,343
Association of Teachers and Lecturers (ATL)[1]	154,657
Union of Construction Allied Trades and Technicians (UCATT)	111,657
Civil and Public Services Association (CPSA)	112,972
Banking, Insurance and Finance Union (BIFU)	113,555
British Medical Association (BMA)[1]	104,344

Notes: [1]Non-TUC affiliate

the union movement being the oldest in the world (Clegg, 1979). When unions began to come to prominence in the mid-19th century they developed, principally, as organisations of skilled workers whose main objective was to secure employment for themselves; they did little or nothing for labourers and other unskilled workers. As a result, in the late 19th century, the labourers' union came into being by combining labourers in the craft-dominated industries with workers from previously unorganised industries and services.

From these beginnings, union structure in the UK developed to the point where it has been conventional to divide trade unions into three types – occupational (or craft), industrial and general. However, today few occupational unions exist and those that do are relatively small in size. Examples include British Airline Pilots Association (BALPA), the Associated Society of Locomotive, Engineers and Fireman (ASLEF) and the Professional Footballers Association (PFA). Such unions recruit members selectively, on a job-by-job basis, irrespective of where they work. It is the workers' occupational status, job skills and qualifications or training that determine whether or not individuals qualify for membership, not the industry or the organisation that employs them.

Industrial unions will organise any workers, regardless of their status and skills, employed in a particular industry. They recruit vertically within an industry but will not recruit the same groups working in a different industry. In short, they recruit members vertically from amongst all employment grades, normally including both manual and non-manual workers within a single industry. However, in the UK, because of the constantly changing and evolving structure of industry, it is not a simple matter to define the boundaries between industries. Examples of industry-based unions in the UK are few. The best examples are the National Union of Mineworkers, the Iron and Steel

Trades Confederation and the Ceramic and Allied Trade Union. The Graphical, Paper and Media Union (GPMU) seeks to organise all workers in the general print, newspaper and papermaking industries.

General unions will recruit any workers (both manual and non-manual) horizontally across industries and vertically within industries. Such unions seek to regulate labour markets by trying to establish a monopoly over the supply of all employees. The two best examples of general unions in the UK are the Transport and General Workers Union and the GMB.

Mergers

However, changing product and labour markets and the implementation of technological change have caused unions in the 1990s to change their recruitment and membership base. Loss of membership, employer opposition, financial viability and interunion competition for members have made trade unions attempt to widen their membership base. The net result has been a series of union mergers in the form of amalgamation or a transfer of engagements. The former involves the creation of a new union with a new rule book, which is approved, in a ballot, by both sets of members. The latter involves one union transferring its membership and financial assets into another and so accepting the constitution and industrial policies of the union into which membership is being transferred. To become effective, a merger by the transfer of engagement procedure only requires a majority vote of the members of the transferring union.

Over the last 20 years, as a result of trade union mergers, the number of trade unions affiliated to the TUC has fallen from 112 in 1979 to 75 in 1997. However, many of these mergers have been driven by the political allegiances of union leaderships or the search for a stronger union membership base rather than by the desire to create rational union structures or a more effective industrial organisation. In addition, some unions have sought merger as an easier option than re-establishing viability through membership recruitment. One of the consequences of union mergers has been the creation of a few 'mega' unions, whose membership jurisdictions overlap resulting in competitive membership recruitment and reducing the attraction to employers to manage their enterprises with trade unions. As a result, trade union mergers have not eliminated the problems associated with multi-unionism (see below and Chapter 5) at industry, company and workplace levels and in dealings with employers.

Job-centred unionism

Despite all this merger activity, the job an individual performs still effectively determines the union he or she will join. While legislative changes over the past two decades mean that individuals are free to join any union of their choice, the reality is somewhat different. Where unions exist in a workplace and are recognised by the employer, most individuals who choose to join a union will want to join one that has a significant membership within their work group.

There are downsides to job-centred unions. It has resulted in an unwieldy trade union structure in which multi-union disputes occur.

It can result in unions competing to recruit the same employees (membership jurisdiction), and in unions having different wage policies. Interunion disputes were very much a feature of the 1960s and 1970s employee relations scene and often resulted in strike action, with the employer an unwilling victim of a problem outside its control. Such disputes have decreased over the past two decades – partly as the result of legislative interventions and partly as a consequence of union mergers.

However, interunion disputes do still happen over accusations that one union is trying to poach another's members. An internal dispute at the Ford Motor Company in 1996, relating to alleged discrimination over driving jobs, is a case in point (see TUC General Council Report, 1998). Some driving job-holders were threatening to leave their union (the T&GWU) and join the rival Union of Road Transport Workers (URT) because they felt the T&GWU was not representing their interests. The T&GWU, in turn, accused the URT of encouraging its members to defect. How this particular dispute was resolved is not important. What it demonstrates is that interunion rivalry can still be an issue and the employee relations specialist cannot afford to ignore its impact on employment relationships.

Finally, as we saw in Chapter 1, job-conscious trade unionism has implications for trade union solidarity. There is a tendency to think, especially amongst left-wing political romantics, that unions automatically support each other. In reality, this only happens when the job interests of different trade unions coincide. Only then do they show support and solidarity for each other.

International comparisons
Job-centred trade unionism is also found in the USA, Canada and Australasia. In apartheid South Africa, it was also found amongst those trade unions whose membership was restricted to white employees. Job-centred trade unionism is thus a central feature of trade union recruitment in Anglo-Saxon countries.

In Japan, most trade unions are organised not by occupation, job or industry but by enterprise or establishment. An enterprise union consists solely of regular employees of a single firm, regardless of their occupational status. Since enterprise unions usually include both blue collar and non-manual members, the union density amongst non-manual workers is relatively high. Japanese employees who expect life long employment, make up about a third of all employees and are expected to stay in the same company until their mandatory retirement age, unless they are made redundant or leave voluntarily (Bamber and Lansbury, 1998).

In Germany, trade unions are organised along industrial lines. The German Trade Union Federation (DGB) was established as a non-political grouping based on industrial unionism in 1949. It has 13 affiliated unions with a total membership of 9.7 million. Its affiliates account for some 97 per cent of manual and 75 per cent of non-manual union members. This industrial principle means that one trade union represents all organised employees at a workplace, irrespective of their individual occupation. It is, however, a system based on a sub-division of a company that is being superseded by the growth of a service sector and the blurring of traditional industry boundaries. Employers are also challenging the system by fragmenting their operations into component parts and reassigning them to a variety of industrial branches. On these, and on cost grounds, there has been a series of actual or planned mergers between industry unions but as yet no comprehensive service sector union has emerged.

In France, trade unions are general unions with divisions – not absolutely rigid or consistent ones – along political and religious lines. There are five major, and essentially competing, trade union confederations in the private sector, each with a larger or smaller number of affiliated unions, organised by each sector. Each also has a white-collar affiliate. The CFDT claims 650,000 members and is the largest union confederation of the five recognised by the government at national level. It was established in 1964 and its affiliates have a socialist orientation. The CGT claims 630,000 members and is associated with the Communist Party of France. Its membership is rooted in the manufacturing sector. The CGT-FO was formed in 1948 and has some 400,000 members. It is particularly strong in the public sector, commerce and finance and its affiliates are social democrat in political orientation. The CFTC claims 120,000 members mainly in health, teaching and engineering and is a Christian trade union confederation. The CGC has some 100,000 members and its affiliates organise engineers, executives, supervisors and technicians. Union confederations and their industrial affiliates play a role in collective bargaining at the industry level but their strength at the workplace is patchy. In fact, trade union density in France is only 10 per cent and still falling.

TRADE UNION DECISION-MAKING STRUCTURE

This is the structure in which decisions are made (policy decided), power exercised and the membership serviced (communications channels). This structure is formally set out in the trade union rule book. At the workplace, trade union members elect a representative who is usually called a shop steward. The term used may be different in certain industries, for example in printing and journalism the representative is called the Father or Mother of the Chapel (FOC, MOC), whilst in others they are called the works representative. The 1998 Workplace Employee Relations Survey found that amongst workplaces which recognised trade unions, 74 per cent had a local union representative. A further 8 per cent had recourse to worker representatives from another establishment in the organisation. Only 11 per cent of workplaces without any union members had worker representatives. Amongst workplaces with worker representatives it was most common for there to be several representatives with the median being three representatives per workplace. Overall, the Survey estimated there to be about 218,000 employee representatives, the vast majority being union representatives, across all British workplaces with 25 or more employees.

On average, there were 28 union members per lay union representative. Table 16 shows the issues union representatives deal

Table 16 Issues union representatives at the workplace deal with

Issue	Dealt with (%)	Most important (%)
Maintaining wages and benefits	48	20
Job security	48	23
Treatment of employment by management	63	27
Health and safety	64	21
Resolving disputes	44	6
Improving workplace performance	37	4
None of the above	13	–

Source: 1998 Workplace Employee Relations Survey, p18.

with in a typical year. Of particular note is the relative lack of importance accorded to the most traditional of trade union activities – maintaining wages and benefits – and the high level of activity and importance attached to dealing with problems raised by the treatment of employees by management and resolving disputes. The scope of bargaining was narrow, being mostly confined to negotiations over handling grievances and health and safety. The Workplace Survey also showed that in many workplaces with recognition, management prefers to deal direct with employees than through a union channel. The most significant change that had been introduced at the workplace in the last 10 years was found to be that management was much more likely to have consulted employees than unions.

In most unions, the workplace organisation is usually a branch structure, which is normally geographically based, and above this, depending on union size, there may be a regional or area structure. The primary task of the branch structure is to act as a conduit between members and the union's decision-making body and to elect delegates to the union's conference. At the apex of the union structure is its national executive, which is usually made up of elected delegates and full-time officials. It is the job of the executive to implement the policy of the annual (or in many cases, biennial or triennial) delegate conference. In the Amalgamated Engineering and Electrical Union (AEEU) the process works as follows. Branches elect delegates to a regional conference, which in turn elects delegates to the biennial conference. There is one delegate per 1,000 members. Because of its size and various mergers over the years, the AEEU also has a number of conferences for specific industrial sectors. These are mainly geographical, but some are constituted on a national basis. The industrial conferences also elect delegates to the biennial conference. Indeed, two thirds of the delegates come through this route.

Once conference has decided a union's policy, the implementation of that policy is carried out by the national executive through a number of full-time officers who conduct the affairs of the union on a day-to-day basis. They are normally responsible to the executive, via the general secretary, to whom they report on a regular basis (usually weekly). The general secretary is supported not only by a number of national officers but also a group of regional/area officers (where appropriate) and branch secretaries. Branch, regional/area officers will be involved in the operation at later stages of dispute and other procedures. It is normal for the general secretary and the national officers to be *ex officio* members of the national executive committee, without voting rights (although some do have them). However, because of the influence they can sometimes have, the Trade Union Act 1984 and the Employment Act 1988, provided that all members of union executive committees have to be elected by the membership at least once every five years.

UNIONS AND POLITICS

In order to achieve their objectives, UK trade unions prefer to use industrial rather than political methods. Despite some occasional rhetoric to the contrary, trade unions do not believe in the use of industrial action to thwart proposed legislation of a duly elected government. Trade unions see it as a legitimate right to try to persuade any elected government, regardless of its political colour, to introduce legislation which protects and advances the interests of working people. Should it fail in this, it accepts the right of the elected government to introduce that legislation.

The immunities question

Trade unions, as was seen in Chapter 1, need to be involved in the political process as the government's economic and legal policies can effect the relative balance of bargaining power between employers and employees. However, some trade unions are involved in party politics via affiliation to the Labour Party. This link is an accident of history. In 1901, in the Taff Vale judgement, the Court ruled that employers could sue trade unions for damages for economic loss resulting from strike action. The judgement had severe implications for the trade union movement. If they could be sued by employers for calling out their members on strike, their funds would soon be exhausted and it would be difficult to continue to protect and advance their interests. If this could not be achieved, membership would melt away. The unions decided the best way to overcome the Taff Vale judgement was to persuade a government to pass legislation disallowing employers from suing trade unions for damages when they called out their members on strike.

The major political parties at the turn of the century – the Liberals and the Conservatives – were not prepared to entertain such legislation. The trade unions decided they would have to form their own political party. In 1902, they therefore played the major part in the formation of the Labour Party. This action was not for political ideological reasons but for sound industrial reasons, namely that trade unions required a favourable legal framework surrounding industrial action if they were to protect and advance effectively the interests of their members. The formation of the Labour Party saw a breakdown of the two-party system and the Labour Party quickly gained electoral success. At the start of the 1906 General Election campaign the prediction was there would be a hung Parliament in which the Liberal Party would be the majority party. The Labour Party and the Liberal Party made a pact under which elected Labour MPs would support a minority Liberal government which in return would introduce legislation giving trade union immunity from lawsuits from employers when they called their members to withdraw their labour in 'contemplation or furtherance of a trade dispute'.

The Liberal Party won the 1906 General Election with a large majority but nevertheless decided to deliver the legislation the trade unions desired. It therefore passed the Trades Disputes Act 1906 which gave trade unions legal immunity in the case of industrial disputes. In 1976, this immunity was extended to secondary industrial action (where trade unions call their members out on strike with an employer with whom it has no dispute but where that employer is a major customer of the firm with whom the union does have an industrial dispute). By 1980 then, the trade unions had almost complete legal immunity with respect to industrial action so long as such action was in 'contemplation or furtherance of a trade dispute'.

The 1980s and 1990s saw Conservative Governments considerably narrow this trade union immunity by means of:

• Employment Act 1980

  – Picketing was limited to lawful strikes at their workplace.

  – Secondary industrial action was only lawful if limited to the first supplier or customer of the goods and services of the employer in dispute.

• Employment Act 1982

  – Removed the legal immunity given to trade unions in 1906. This meant trade unions could be sued in the Courts for punitive damages in an unlawful dispute.

  – Introduced a much narrower definition of a trade dispute to exclude solidarity action by workers at home or abroad as well as sympathy strikes or interunion disputes.

• Trade Union Act 1984

  – To retain immunity in a lawful strike, a secret ballot had to be held before a trade union could call its members out on strike.

• Employment Act 1988

  – Legal immunity was withdrawn in the case of industrial disputes designed to enforce compulsory union membership as a condition of gaining or continuing in employment.

• Employment Act 1990

  – Legal immunities were removed from trade unions in any industrial action taken to support people dismissed selectively for taking part in an unofficial strike.

  – Legal immunity was removed from all remaining forms of secondary action.

The 1997 Labour Government has refused to widen the industrial action situations in which trade unions would have legal immunity for civil actions in the Courts (Gennard, 1998). The foreword, written by the Prime Minister himself, of the *Fairness at Work* paper, stated:

> ... There will be no going back. The days of strikes without ballots, mass picketing, closed shops and secondary action are over. Even after the changes we propose, Britain will have the most highly regulated labour market of any leading economy in the world ...

The Employment Relations Act 1999 amended the law on industrial action ballots and notice to make clear that while the union's notice to the employer should still identify as accurately as reasonably practicable the group or category of employees concerned, it need not give names.

Trade union political funds

Trade union expenditure on political activities is regulated by the Trade Union Act 1913. A union can spend money on political activities on certain conditions. It must ballot all its membership to ascertain whether they wish to establish a political fund to cover expenditure on political activities. Second, if such a referendum results in a positive vote then the union must establish a Political Fund financed by a separate contribution from that to the union's Industrial Fund. The two funds must be kept completely separate and there can be no transfer of money from one fund to the other. Third, members who do not wish to pay the Political Fund have the right to do so; they can opt out of payment. A fourth condition is that if members exercise this opt-out right they must not be discriminated against in terms of their receipt of industrial servicing and/or union benefit. The Trade Union Act 1984 added a fifth condition in that a secret ballot of all the union's membership must be held at least every 10 years to ascertain whether they wish to retain political funds.

In 1997, 42 unions had established political funds, which are governed by the Political Fund rule of the union. It is the members contributing to the Political Fund who control where the money will be spent. The decision to affiliate Political Fund payers to the Labour Party is a decision of the subscribers to the Fund. There is nothing that stops money from the Political Fund being paid to other political parties so long as that has the approval of the majority of the Political Fund payers. The majority of trade unions with Political Funds do not affiliate to any political party.

Relationship with the Labour Party

Trade unions that affiliate their Political Fund-paying members to the Labour Party have links other than financial ones with the Labour Party. They have a 33 per cent share of the vote in party leadership elections, 50 per cent of the votes at the Party's Annual Conference, representation on the Party's National Executive Committee and give financial support to Parliamentary constituency parties. The Labour Government elected in 1997 has adopted the stance that it will grant trade unions no preferential treatment but will treat them fairly. There are those in the trade union movement who welcome the changing Labour Party/trade union relationship, arguing that as the political and economic integration of Europe continues regulation of UK labour markets will come more and more from Brussels and therefore trade unions should be diverting political financial resources from lobbying in London to lobbying in Brussels.

THE TRADES UNION CONGRESS

The TUC was established in 1868. In 1997, it had 75 affiliate unions with a total membership of 6.8 million. It performs two broad roles. First, it acts as the collective voice of the UK trade union movement to governments and international trade union bodies. Second, it attempts to influence the behaviour of its affiliated unions. However, the sanctions it possesses to influence its affiliates are limited. When the TUC was established, it was very much the voice of the craft unions which jealously guarded their autonomy. As a result, in devising the TUC constitution, they were not prepared to devolve much power or many resources to it or to allow it to interfere in their activities. This limitation still remains and the autonomy of affiliated unions is still regarded as paramount, particularly in the area of wages and employment conditions. The TUC has limited authority over its affiliates and few resources. It has to persuade its affiliates of the rightness of its decisions. It is not always successful.

Decision-making machinery

The supreme authority in the TUC is its Annual Congress, which is held in September, and to which affiliated organisations send delegates on the basis of one for every 5,000 members or part thereof. Congress Policy is decided on the basis of motions, submitted by affiliated unions, being accepted by a majority vote of delegates.

The implementation of policy decided at Congress is the responsibility of the General Council, which is serviced by the General Secretary who heads a secretariat. The General Council is made up of seven constituencies. Section A is made up from those unions with 200,000 or more members. Those with memberships of 200,000 to 399,999 are entitled to two seats, those with 400,000 to 649,999 to three seats, those with 650,000 to 899,999 to four seats, those with 900,000 to 1,199,999 to five seats and those with 1,200,000 to 1,499,999 to six seats. All this is conditional that where the total number of members of any union in this section is 100,000 or more, that union must nominate at least one woman. Section B consists of members from trade unions with a membership of 100,000 to 199,499. Such unions are entitled to one seat on the Council. In Section C, there are eight seats which are elected by, and from, unions with fewer than 100,000 members. Section D consists of four seats for women members from unions with less than 200,000 members. Section E consists of one black member from a union with a membership in excess of 200,000 whilst Section F consists of one seat for a black member from a union with 199,999 members or less. Section G is a seat for one black woman member from an affiliated union.

Role

Industrial disputes

The TUC has authority from its affiliates to act in three areas – industrial disputes, interunion disputes and the conduct of affiliates. In the case of a dispute between an affiliated union and an employer, the

TUC does not intervene unless requested to do so by the affiliate. If negotiations break down or are likely to break down and the ensuing dispute could result in the members of another affiliated union being laid off, then the TUC general secretary can intervene to try to effect a just settlement to the dispute by giving advice and opinion to the union(s) involved. Should the union refuse assistance or advice from the General Secretary, the General Council can suspend the union concerned from membership until the next Congress, which can then expel the union from TUC membership.

Inter-union disputes

Before 1993 the TUC could intervene in the case of disputes between affiliated unions over membership and job demarcation issues. A complaint by one affiliate against another was investigated by a Disputes Committee which could recommend that a union which had poached members from another affiliate must give those members back. If the union failed to comply with the recommendations of a Disputes Committee, then the General Council could suspend the union from membership until the next Congress, at which it could be expelled from membership.

The Trade Union Reform and Employment Rights Act 1993 required the TUC to revise its procedures in this area as the Act gave individuals the legal right to join a union of their choice. The requiring of unions to hand back members who had been poached was no longer an option and the only effective sanction the TUC can now apply is payment of compensation to the aggrieved union. The first case under this procedure occurred in 1995 when the Amalgamated Electrical and Engineering Union (AEEU) was ordered to pay compensation to the Transport and General Workers Union (T&GWU) and the Union of Construction and Technical Trades Union (UCATT).

Detrimental behaviour

The TUC can also investigate complaints that an affiliated union is engaging in conduct detrimental to the interests of the trade union movement or contrary to the declared principles or declared policy of the Congress. Should such a complaint be upheld, the General Council will recommend to the union concerned what it must do to put the matter right. Should the union fail to do this, the General Council will recommend its suspension from membership until the next Congress, at which it will be expelled unless it complies with the recommendation. The TUC has been reluctant to interfere with the affairs of affiliates.

In 1986/87, in a dispute between the print unions and News International when the latter relocated from Fleet Street to Wapping in London's Docklands, the former complained that another affiliated union (the electricians') had acted in a manner detrimental to the good standing of the trade union movement by openly co-operating with the action of a hostile employer which had put 5,000 members of other affiliated unions out of work. They therefore argued that the electricians' union should be suspended, and then expelled from Congress. The General Council investigated the complaint, censured the electricians and told them what they must do to rectify matters. The threat of suspension, and subsequent expulsion, receded when the electricians' union complied with the rectification recommendations.

The 1994 reforms

Under its new General Secretary, John Monks, the TUC underwent a formal relaunch in March 1994 which involved a thorough overhaul of its decision-making machinery and generation of a new ethos and sense of mission (Heery, 1998). The most visible internal changes within the relaunch were reforms of its representative machinery to secure a more efficient use of TUC staff and to raise the effectiveness of TUC decision-making. The General Council delegated aspects of its business to a 26-person Executive Committee, whilst the joint committees of the General Council such as the Women's and Race Committees and their associated conferences now have more focused aims and objectives. The key new component has been a series of Task Groups, composed of General Council members, other representatives from affiliates and TUC staff which are intended to work towards clearly defined and achievable objectives, report to the Annual Congress via the General Council and then disband. There have been Task Groups to develop policy and campaigns on a range of issues including stakeholding, full employment, representation at work, human resource management, part-time workers and union organisation.

A second characteristic of the relaunch was the re-establishment of the TUC as a body to speak on behalf of a broadly conceived labour interest. This has been expressed by giving priority to 'world of work' issues, such as employment policy, which impinge on the majority of working people but which are also important to non-union members. A third feature of the 1994 reforms was a focus on union organising which became effective in 1996 via the New Unionism Campaign and which in 1998 saw the opening of the TUC Organising Academy to train specialist officers in recruitment and organising techniques and to allocate them to priority recruitment campaigns to be identified jointly by the TUC and affiliated unions.

The reforms have turned the TUC into a more effective representational body in the public policy arena. This has seen increased contact between the TUC and political parties, other than Labour, a greater emphasis on lobbying members of Parliament and seeking to identify cross-party support for TUC policy, strengthening links with the CBI and a greater professionalism in campaigning methods. It has also encouraged the development of contacts with employers on the basis of offering 'social partnership' in terms of union co-operation with improving the competitiveness of British industry and commerce on the basis of flexible working and investment in skills. Heery (1998) considers the 1994 reforms were an attempt both to change the TUC's methods of achieving its objectives and to promote a substantive shift in its strategy.

Future prospects for the unions

Trade unions face an uncertain future. If they are to reverse the decline in their membership then they need to demonstrate to employees they can add greater value to their interests than alternative employee representative systems (works councils, etc). They also need to demonstrate to employers they can add value to the business and it is, therefore, in the best interests of the business that it be managed with a trade union. In these tasks, opportunities can be created by legislation but if the prospects for trade unions are to improve it will depend very much on what steps they can take themselves to improve their position.

The European Union social dialogue (see Chapter 3) and the government's Employment Relations Act 1999 have created an environment in which trade unions have the opportunity to increase the recruitment and retention of members. Statutory trade union recognition, the right for employees in firms of all sizes to be accompanied by a trade union official in disciplinary and grievance hearings about serious issues, the prohibiting of blacklisting of trade union members, protection for those campaigning for union recognition and protection against employers paying more to non-union employees than to unionised employees all potentially create a more favourable environment for trade unions than in the last 20 years. In these circumstances, some employers who have previously kept unions at arm's length, may now grant union recognition voluntarily in order to influence its terms rather than have it imposed by law.

The desire of trade unions to promote co-operative relationships with employers via partnership agreements (see Chapter 10) will provide opportunities for unions to influence the attitude of employers towards managing with unions. Partnership agreements will be helpful in creating a positive attitude on the part of employers towards adopting and retaining a positive relationship with trade unions. The bargained EU legislation process provides trade unions with a competitive advantage over other forms of employee representative bodies since only trade unions can influence such legislation.

Despite these strengths and opportunities, trade unions still have some weaknesses to overcome if they are to reverse their decline in membership. In general, they still lack adequate resources to service their membership and a membership recruitment culture has still to be firmly established. The total resources trade unions in general devote to recruitment and membership retention represent less than 2 per cent of their total resources. The development of a membership culture is vital if trade unions are to gain membership in growing areas of employment, for example, non-manual occupations, private sector services and hotels and tourism. In recent years, even in many areas of relative high union density, total employment has grown but union membership has declined or, at best, remained stable. If unions fail to develop a membership culture then they are unlikely to succeed in growing and expanding through their own efforts.

However, there are a number of threats to trade union attempts to widen, deepen and increase their membership. An increasing number of employers may adopt a 'substitute policy' towards non recognition of trade unions whereby an employer considers it can protect and advance the interests of its employees better than a trade union.

These companies allow employees to join a union but few do because the employer provides them with employment conditions above what an active union can achieve. Such companies compete with the union by extensive investment in people management and development. A second threat is that the number of new start small- and medium-sized companies is increasing. They are generators of new employment. Trade unions have traditionally found it difficult to gain any foothold in such companies.

A further threat to trade unions increasing their membership and influence in the workplace is that employee attitude surveys undertaken by the IPD (1998) and the Workplace Employee Relations Survey (1998) indicate there is a relative absence of a significant 'reservoir of discontent' at the workplace, which is a necessary condition for employees to begin to demand the services of a trade union. In July 1998, the Harris Research Centre interviewed for the IPD 1,000 people in employment, using questions designed by a team from Birkbeck College. Its main findings were:

• 67 per cent reported they were treated fairly by management

• the number of human resources practices (equal opportunities, communications, performance appraisals, interesting and varied work, training and employee involvement in workplace decision-making) in place is a key determinant of whether workers believe they are treated fairly

• unions have little impact on feelings of fairness

• those working long hours are satisfied with working life

• 88 per cent reported they felt very, or fairly, secure in their jobs

• on balance, management was seen as fair, trustworthy and likely to keep its promises

• over half reported they have scope to take decisions affecting how they do their work themselves.

The 1998 Workplace Employee Relations Survey interviewed 25,989 employees in workplaces with 25 employees or more about their views on work. On three of the individual measures – job influence, sense of achievement and respect from managers – around 60 per cent of employees expressed themselves satisfied with these aspects of their job. The proportion of employees expressing positive views increased with age. Part-time workers had higher levels of satisfaction (62 per cent) than full-time workers (51 per cent). The most satisfied were those working less than 10 hours per week (66 per cent). Job satisfaction was highest where employees were consulted about workplace changes.

STAFF ASSOCIATIONS

Staff associations are usually established within a single organisation and for a particular group of employees and their funding and/or office accommodation is often dependent on a particular employer. They are not regarded as trade unions in the traditional sense and stand apart from mainstream trade unionism even if not actually hostile to it. Staff associations included on the Certification Officer's list of independent trade unions have historically been strongest in banking and insurance. However, such staff associations are small in membership size in that more than half have less than 500 members. The main causes of the formation of independent staff associations include employee reaction to:

1. specific events (eg threat of redundancy)

2. the desire for an alternative to a TUC union

3. to replace an existing consultative body by one with negotiating powers

4. wish for collective representation where no representative system previously existed.

They also include employer desires for a management-dominated consultative body or a management-inspired association.

Independent staff associations are characterised by high membership density. For example, the coverage rate within the top 10 building societies typically averages around 70–80 per cent. They typically aim to represent all white-collar employees of a company from managers to clerks and word processor operators. However, a substantial minority limit their membership to specific groups, the two most common being managers or executives and agents, representatives or salesmen. The majority of smaller staff associations have a single tier structure within a governing committee directly responsible to the members. Amongst larger bodies, the structure is more complex, involving additional tiers and committee or sub committee systems. Some associations have at least one full-time official, some have a part-time official whilst others make use of paid advisors or negotiators.

While the largest staff associations may act as independent unions, the effectiveness of the smaller ones is limited by their narrow membership base and weak financial resources. Many operate from a modest, if not precarious, financial base. The majority of the staff associations are recognised by employers for negotiating and representational purposes. Most agreements follow the normal pattern and cover such matters as recognition, provision of facilities, joint negotiating machinery, consultation and grievance and discipline procedure.

However, the ability of independent staff associations to represent truly the interests of their members can be questioned. An organisation whose membership is confined to the employees of a single employer is exposed to pressures, which are much less effective against a broadly based organisation. It will also find it difficult to bargain on equal terms with that employer, particularly if the size of the undertaking places strict limits on its membership and financial resources and means that it must rely for its administration entirely on part-time officers employed by the company. In addition, the fact that senior managers can belong to a staff association, and actually do so, leads some to doubt their genuine independence because of the possibility of management influence being brought to bear on its policies.

In addition to staff associations which have a Certificate of Independence, there are a much larger number of bodies which bear the title of staff association which make no claim to be a trade union even in an informal sense. Such bodies usually have a consultative rather than a negotiating function and little or nothing in the way of independent resources. Membership is usually automatic for all non-manual employees, and there is often no membership subscription since the employer meets any expenses incurred by the Association.

Professional associations such as the British Medical Association or the British Dental Association often represent the interests of their members in negotiation with the relevant employers but also function as organisations responsible for the education and certification of practitioners and the maintenance of professional standards amongst members. The dual role of negotiators and professional standard-bearers can sometimes conflict, as the medical and nursing professions have found. It can be difficult to take legitimate action in support of an industrial dispute without coming into conflict with a professional Code of Conduct.

THE CERTIFICATION OFFICER

This post was established in 1975. The officer is appointed by the Secretary of State for Trade and Industry after consultation with ACAS. The office performs the following functions:

• maintaining a list of trade unions

• determining that a trade union is independent of employer control, domination or interference. The principal criteria used by the Certification Officer for this purpose are history, membership base, organisation and structure, finance, employer-provided facilities and negotiating record

• dealing with complaints by members that a trade union has failed to maintain an accurate register of members; seeing that trade unions keep proper accounting records, have their accounts properly audited and submit annual returns; investigating the financial affairs of trade unions, and ensuring that the statutory requirements concerning the actuarial examination of members' superannuation schemes are observed

• handling complaints by members that a trade union has failed to hold secret ballots for electing members of its executive committee, its president and its general secretary

• ensuring observance of the statutory procedures governing trade unions setting up, operating and reviewing political funds. The Certification Officer also deals with complaints from union members about breaches of political fund rules or about the conduct of political fund ballots

• seeing that the statutory procedures for trade union amalgamations, transfer of agreements and change of name are observed and dealing with complaints by members about the conduct of merger ballots

• maintaining a list of employers' associations, for ensuring that the statutory requirements concerning accounting records, auditors, annual returns, financial affairs, political funds and the statutory procedures for amalgamation and transfer of engagements in respect of employers' associations are observed.

The Employment Relations Act 1999 transferred to the Certification Officer the powers previously performed by the former Commissioner for the Rights of Trade Union members to pay legal costs or obtain legal advice for members bringing cases against their trade union.

STATE AGENCIES

In this section, consideration is given to those organisations which have a statutory role in employee relations, whether that role is in respect of individual or collective issues. In the UK, there are two such organisations, the Advisory Conciliation and Arbitration Service (ACAS) and the Central Arbitration Committee (CAC).

The Advisory Conciliation and Arbitration Service (ACAS)

The state provided third party intervention in industrial disputes long before ACAS was established (Mumford, 1996). They were previously provided by the Department of Employment and its predecessor Ministries (eg Ministry of Labour). The credibility of third party intervention depends on the parties believing that they are independent/impartial from government influence.

In the 1960s and 1970s, the credibility of government-provided third party intervention services became seriously compromised. This arose because Ministers, often as a condition of making the third party services available to the parties, made it clear they expected the independent person to have due regard to the government of the day's income policy. Indeed, on occasions, the Minister refused joint requests from employers and employees for third party intervention on the grounds that the employer's offer was already in excess of the limits of the government's incomes policy. The clash between the government's role as an industrial peacekeeper and its role as an economic manager became most acute in 1968 when the then Department of Employment and Productivity, which was responsible for the provision of third party intervention services, was also given responsibility for ensuring that the government's incomes policy was applied effectively.

The early 1970s, therefore, saw increased demands by unions and employers for a third party intervention service that was formally independent of the state and, in particular, of the whims of different governments' prices and incomes policies. The strength of this feeling was seen in the TUC and CBI establishing their own private third-party arrangements. In September 1974, the then Labour Government established the Advisory, Conciliation and Arbitration Service (ACAS) as a Royal Commission. It was established as a statutory body on 1 January 1976 under the provisions of the Employment Protection Act 1975.

ACAS is formally independent of direct ministerial intervention although its sponsoring Ministry is the Department of Trade and Industry. ACAS is governed by an executive body known as the 'Council' which originally consisted of a chairperson and nine ordinary members – three chosen in consultation with the CBI, three in consultation with the TUC and the remaining three to be independent people with specialist knowledge of employee relations. In 1992, the Council became 11 members with the additional two members representing the interests of small businesses and non-TUC unions.

ACAS seeks to:

• promote good practice

• provide information and advice

• conciliate in complaints to Employment Tribunals

• conciliate in the case of collective disputes

• prevent and resolve employment disputes.

Promote good practice

ACAS organises conferences and seminars on topical employment and industrial relations issues. For small businesses, ACAS also runs self-help workshops where employment policies and procedures are discussed. Unlike the other services provided by ACAS, which are free, there is a charge for conferences, seminars and small-firm workshops. ACAS also sells a range of booklets offering practical guidance and advice on employment and industrial relations topics, for example discipline, job evaluation, recruitment and induction, employee appraisal, hours of work, teamworking and employee communications and consultation. During 1998, ACAS organised 466 conferences, seminars and workshops of which 280 were chargeable events. These make an important contribution to ACAS' objective of disseminating good practice and assisting in the formulation of sound policies for the employment relationship.

ACAS also has issued three Codes of Practice under the Employment Protection Act 1975 which is now Section 199 of the Trade Union and Labour Relations (Consolidation) Act 1992. Its Disciplinary Practice and Procedures in Employment provides practical guidance on how to draw up disciplinary rules procedures and how to operate them effectively. The significance of this Code is discussed fully in Chapter 8. The ACAS Code on the Disclosure of Information to trade unions for collective bargaining purposes sets out best practice in this area whilst its Code on Time Off for Trade Union Duties and Activities provides guidance on time off for trade union duties, time off for training of trade union officials and time off for trade union activities. It also covers the responsibilities which employers and trade unions share in considering reasonable time off and outlines the advantages of reaching formal agreements on time off. These Codes impose no legal obligations on an employer. Failure to observe the Code does not, by itself, render anyone liable to proceedings but their provisions are to be taken into account in proceedings before an Employment Tribunal (Disciplinary Practice) and Central Arbitration Committee (Disclosure on Information and Time Off).

Providing information and advice

ACAS provides information and guidance on a wide range of employment and industrial relations matters. It does this primarily through a network of Public Enquiry Points (PEPs) which can be contacted by anyone. The service is free, confidential and impartial and is designed to assist employers and people at work. PEPs provide a particularly useful and cost effective service for small firms and individuals to help clarify the range and increasing complexity of employment legislation, avoid difficulties at work, or understand the options available for their possible resolution. Most enquiries are dealt with by telephone, but a small number are answered by letter or personal interviews, usually by prior appointment.

In 1998, PEPs received 508,000 calls. Of these, 53 per cent came from individual employees and most of the rest from employers of different types and sizes, trade unions and other organisations. There were high volumes of questions on contract of employment matters, including wages and holiday pay (41 per cent), discipline and dismissal issues (18 per cent), redundancy and transfer of undertakings (16 per cent) and maternity rights (8 per cent). For many, PEPs are often the first point of contact with ACAS. Sometimes an enquiry raises issues which cannot readily be answered by telephone and in such cases the problem is addressed by face-to-face contact with ACAS field staff. In 1997, ACAS held 1,777 face-to-face meetings but not all as a result of PEPs.

Individual employment rights

ACAS provides individual conciliation in cases which are, or could be, the subject of complaints by individuals to Employment Tribunals about alleged infringement of employment rights. Individual conciliation is voluntary, impartial, confidential, free of charge and independent from the Employment Tribunals. ACAS has a duty to conciliate in a wide range of individual employment rights complaints including unfair dismissal, breach of contract (eg non payment of termination payments or commission, discrimination/sex, race and equal pay) guarantee payments, redundancy and disability discrimination. The number of complaints handled by ACAS concerning alleged breach of employment rights is shown in Table 17.

When making a complaint to an Employment Tribunal, a person must first complete form IT1 and send it to the appropriate Employment Tribunal office, which then passes a copy to ACAS. The case is then allocated to a conciliation officer whose responsibility it is to attempt to help the parties settle the complaint without the need for a tribunal hearing if that is their wish. If both parties are willing to accept conciliation, the conciliation officer tries to assist them to reach a settlement of the complaint. The officer's role is to help in a neutral and independent way and involves helping both parties become

Table 17 Individual complaints concerning employment rights (1985–1997)

Date	Unfair dismissal	Total complaints received
1987	34,572	40,817
1988	36,340	44,443
1989	37,324	48,817
1990	37,654	52,071
1991	39,234	60,605
1992	44,034	72,166
1993	46,854	75,181
1994	45,824	79,332
1995	40,815	91,568
1996	46,566	100,399
1997	42,771	106,912
1998	40,153	113,636

Source: ACAS Annual Reports, 1985–1998

aware of the options available to them and thus reach informed decisions on how best to proceed. The conciliation officer explains tribunal procedures as well as relevant law but does not make decisions on the merits of the case or impose or recommend a particular settlement. Any settlement terms are the responsibility of the parties concerned. The conciliation officer conveys the views of one party to the other. If there is information one party wishes to keep from the other then so long as they explain that to the conciliation officer the information will not be made known. Where a case is not settled before the date fixed for the tribunal hearing, an Employment Tribunal resolves the matter.

Conciliation is available also where an individual claims that circumstances exist in which he or she could present a formal complaint to an Employment Tribunal. If both parties agree to ACAS involvement, the conciliation officer can conciliate in the same way as if a formal complaint had been laid to an Employment Tribunal. If conciliation does not result in a settlement then the individual has the right to continue to an Employment Tribunal.

In unfair dismissal cases, the conciliation officers have a statutory duty to explore first the possibility of reinstatement, or of re-engagement on suitable terms, before seeking to promote a monetary or other form of settlement. The Employment Rights (Disputes Resolution) Act 1998, empowers conciliation officers to draw up binding settlements in which both parties opt out of the Employment Tribunal system in favour of resolving the employee's complaint of unfair dismissal through voluntary arbitration. The underlying principle behind the Act is to make the resolving of unfair dismissal claims by this procedure as similar as possible to the arbitrations currently arranged by ACAS in settling trade disputes. In this way, the voluntary arbitration system is a genuine alternative to the Employment Tribunal process rather than an imitation of it (see below).

ACAS's role is to attempt to settle cases without the need for a tribunal hearing whilst recognising that not all cases are capable of a settlement and that some parties may wish to have their cases decided in a legal setting. The proportion of employment rights breaches claims settled by ACAS has remained fairly constant over the years and in 1998 amounted to 39 per cent of the cases cleared. In addition, ACAS conciliation also influences the proportion of cases withdrawn, which comprised 29 per cent in 1998. ACAS involvement is normally welcomed by the parties as it provides a means of settling their differences without the need for what can be expensive, stressful and lengthy legal hearings. An important part of the conciliation officer's job is to diffuse the tension and reduce the acrimony that often exists between the parties so as to enable them to focus realistically on the options open to them.

Conciliation and mediation in collective disputes

Employment disputes are very costly to both the employers and employees so it is sensible to resolve workplace problems before they develop into disputes. ACAS employs two principal methods to help organisations avoid costly disputes:

> workshops in which employer and employee representatives discuss and agree on potential barriers to the achievement of long-term organisational goals. Such workshops are useful for exploring problems where the underlying causes are not clearly known. Once these are identified, courses of action can be agreed to rectify the problems.

> joint working parties in which employer and employee representatives work together to devise and implement practical solutions to specific problems by, for example, collecting and analysing information and evaluating options.

ACAS staff will normally chair the Working Party. However, although prevention is better than cure, employment disputes inevitably occur. When this happens, ACAS can help the parties by offering:

- conciliation

- mediation

- arbitration.

Conciliation

Requests for conciliation normally come from employers, trade unions or employee representatives in organisations where there are no trade unions. Before it agrees to conciliate, ACAS checks that the parties have exhausted any internal dispute resolution procedures they may have. In coming to conciliation, no prior commitment is required from the parties, only a willingness to discuss the problem(s) at issue. Conciliation is an entirely voluntary process and it is open to either party to bring discussion to an end at any time. In the conciliation process, management remains in control, deciding whether to continue with the process or to withdraw from it.

ACAS conciliators help the parties in dispute settle their differences by agreement and, if possible, in a long-term way. The conciliator remains impartial and independent, makes constructive suggestions to facilitate negotiations, provides information at the request of the parties and gains the trust and confidence of both parties so that a sound working relationship is developed. The first step in conciliation is to discover what the dispute is about and this fact-finding process usually requires the conciliator to meet with both sides separately, but occasionally information may be obtained at joint meetings. Almost all conciliations involve a mixture of side meetings, where the conciliator explores issues separately with the parties, and joint meetings, where the parties can explain their position face to face. The exact mix of side and joint meetings is determined by the conciliator in discussion with the parties. Where it is clear a settlement might be achieved, the conciliator seeks to secure a joint agreement, usually in the form of a signed document, which finalises the terms of the settlement. Any agreements reached in conciliation are the responsibility of the parties involved and ACAS has no power to impose or even recommend settlements. There is no time limit to the conciliation process and ACAS continues to assist the parties for as long as they wish and while there appears a chance of reaching an agreed settlement. The role of the conciliator is to keep the two sides talking and to help facilitate an agreement.

Mediation

If a settlement is not reached through conciliation, ACAS can arrange for the issue to be resolved through mediation. In this case, both parties agree an independent person or a Board of Mediation to mediate between them. The process of mediation involves each side setting out its case in writing, followed by a hearing at which the two sides present, in person, their evidence and arguments. Hearings are usually held at ACAS offices or at the premises of the employer or the trade union. The mediator (or the Board of Mediation) makes formal, but not binding, proposals or recommendations to provide a basis for settlement of the dispute. The parties are free to accept or reject the mediator's proposals or recommendations. In mediation, as in conciliation, the employer remains in control of the situation. A settlement cannot be imposed by a third party. The employer remains free to accept or reject.

Arbitration

In arbitration, normally a single arbitrator is appointed to consider a dispute and to make a decision to resolve it. Occasionally, arbitration may be by a Board of Arbitration with an independent chairperson and two side members drawn from employer and trade union representatives. It is the arbitrator who makes the award resolving the dispute and not, as many seem to think, ACAS. Unlike conciliation and mediation, in arbitration the employer loses control because before ACAS will facilitate arbitration both parties must agree to accept the arbitrator's decision as a binding settlement of the dispute. This is a long-established principle and, in practice, arbitration awards are invariably accepted and implemented.

What issues go to the arbitrator?

Table 18 shows the extent to which conciliation, mediation and arbitration has been used in the UK in collective disputes over the last 20 years. It shows a significant fall in the use of the three processes. The types of issues that are the subject of arbitration are

Table 18 The use of third party intervention in industrial disputes

Date	Completed collective conciliation	Mediation	Number of arbitration hearings
1979	2,284	31	394
1980	1,910	31	281
1981	1,716	12	245
1982	1,634	16	235
1983	1,621	20	187
1984	1,448	14	188
1985	1,337	12	150
1986	1,323	10	174
1987	1,147	12	133
1988	1,053	9	129
1989	1,070	17	150
1990	1,140	10	190
1991	1,226	12	144
1992	1,140	7	155
1993	1,118	7	156
1994	1,162	8	148
1995	1,299	5	136
1996	1,197	4	113
1997	1,166	11	60
1998	1,214	10	42

Source: ACAS Annual Reports, 1979–98

what are often referred to as disputes of rights which are issues arising from the parties' rights under collective agreements. Arbitration is very rarely used in what are referred to as disputes of interest, namely issues that arise from the negotiation of new or revised collective agreements.

An analysis of the types of issues under dispute at arbitration in the last 20 years shows a dominance of three – job grading, dismissal and discipline, and other pay and conditions of employment (not annual pay increases). This demonstrates that employers have been prepared to go to arbitration on issues:

• which are important to them, but not to such an extent that they are prepared to impose industrial sanctions on the union

• where the cost of losing is bearable

• where there is unlikely to be adverse publicity from the arbitrator's award.

Why is arbitration so little used?
Arbitration is the accepted instrument of last resort but employers, whether in the private or public sector, continue to be sceptical about the principle of arbitration even over disputes of rights, let alone of interests. Trade unions will essentially remain pragmatic in their approach to accepting arbitration. They are in the bargaining business and are suspicious of anything which impedes their ability to gain by whatever means the best possible deal for their members. Although many trade unions profess to love 'free and unfettered' collective

bargaining, their objections to arbitration are as much pragmatic as principled. However much they might be opposed to it in other circumstances, trade unions whose bargaining power is weak sometimes propose arbitration if and when they sense they could not secure approval for industrial action. As happened in the late 1980s and early 1990s, unions anxious to maintain or expand their membership base (for example, the former EET/PU) showed a willingness to enter into so-called 'new-style' agreement in which pendulum arbitration was provided as the basis of avoiding the need for strike action.

Employers can also be similarly guided by pragmatism. Whatever the principal argument of companies that they should negotiate within their procedure agreements and then, if there is a final 'failure to agree', stand up to the consequences without third party intervention, the fact remains that many companies faced with the prospect or reality of industrial action themselves seek the conciliation and, at times, arbitration route.

However, a major reason for employers' reluctance to resort more readily to arbitration is the reputation of the arbitration process itself, namely that the employer loses control of events and must accept whatever the arbitrator may award, and that the arbitrator will 'split the difference' between the parties. Arbitration is first and foremost a process which transfers the ultimate responsibility for certain key business decisions from management to an independent third party. This is in contrast to collective bargaining, conciliation and mediation, in which each side remains very much in control of events. Either party can exercise the prerogative of walking away at any time. There is little evidence to support the view that in disputes of interests, the arbitrator always splits the difference. However undeserved it is, arbitrators have this reputation. Until ACAS (and the CAC) can effectively nail this misconception, any extension of the arbitration process into disputes of interests is unlikely to be achieved.

In disputes of interest, there is also the criticism that the arbitrator usually improves upon the final offer made by the employer in direct negotiations. In doing this, arbitrators are likely to be acting on two assumptions. First, that the union would not be coming to arbitration unless it felt it could secure more for its members. The second is that in agreeing to arbitration, the employer is anxious to avoid the alternative of industrial action and all its associated costs. The employer would, therefore, be willing to pay a little more if such action could be avoided. An award handed down by an independent arbitrator holds out greater certainty of this than an improved offer by the employer.

Arbitration will remain a vital and indispensable instrument of last resort in dispute resolution. It can never be ignored but it is unlikely to become more extensively used.

The Central Arbitration Committee (CAC)

The Central Arbitration Committee's roots go back to the Industrial Courts Act 1919 which established the Industrial Court as a permanent and independent arbitration body. In 1971, the Industrial Relations Act changed its name to the Industrial Arbitration Board, which in turn became the Central Arbitration Committee under the Employment Protection Act 1975. The CAC now arbitrates on complaints from trade unions about an employer's failure to disclose information for collective bargaining purposes and on disputes arising from the operation of the Employment Relations Act 1999 statutory trade union recognition procedure.

The CAC has a chairperson who has two deputies who are accompanied by an equal number of members (five) with experience as representatives of employers and with experience as representatives of workers. The CAC has had no references under the statutory provision that permits it to undertake voluntary employee relations arbitration. The CAC Annual Report for 1997 reported it had dealt with 463 disclosure of information complaints since its inception in 1976, an annual average of 22.

In the case of the trade union recognition procedure, the CAC has powers to decide on which groups of workers will be included in any recognition agreement and to establish the arrangements for ballots over recognition. The CAC arbitrates on disputes between employers and a trade union over what is the appropriate bargaining unit compatible with effective management. If there is a CAC-imposed bargaining unit and the union still wishes to proceed to obtain recognition, the CAC has to decide on whether the union has majority support. Except where the union has already recruited the majority of employees in the bargaining unit, the CAC will arrange for a secret ballot which can, at the discretion of CAC, be at the workplace, or by post to the employee's home. If the union has a majority and the vote of at least 40 per cent of the whole bargaining unit, the CAC declares the union recognised. If the employer persists in failing to recognise the trade union, the CAC can impose a trade union recognition for collective bargaining purposes agreement which then becomes legally binding on the parties. The CAC also plays a similar role in the trade union derecognition procedure contained in the Employment Relations Act 1999.

INTERNATIONAL COMPARISONS

USA

In the USA, third party intervention is widespread. Although the USA is noted for the very limited role government plays in influencing collective agreements, in the private sector mediators employed by the Federal government, via the Federal Mediation and Conciliation Service (FMCS), are active in the negotiation of new agreements. Their intervention is said to be viewed favourably by the parties. In negotiations involving State government employees, many State laws provide for binding arbitration of unresolved disputes over the terms of the new agreement in employment areas considered to be essential, for example police and fire-fighters. However, as in the UK, arbitration over disputes of 'interests' between the parties is very rarely used in the private sector.

Canada

In the majority of Canadian provinces, there are restrictions on the right to strike for some public sector employees who have access to a system of compulsory arbitration. Whilst the relevant statute requires arbitration, the parties normally can determine the procedures to be followed and select the arbitrator. Arbitration of interest disputes is largely confined to the public sector. In both the USA and Canada, unlike the UK, arbitration when used is highly legalistic. The arbitrators in interest disputes are usually selected on an ad hoc basis from judges, lawyers or academics.

Australia

Australia developed a Federal-wide, compulsory arbitration system via the Conciliation and Arbitration Act 1904 under which a union could force employers to arbitration even if they were unwilling to negotiate and once the Court of Conciliation and Arbitration made an award its provisions were legally enforceable. A similar system of compulsory arbitration developed in the Australian States. In 1956, the Court became the Conciliation and Arbitration Commission. The Federal Commission is empowered to intervene only in disputes extending to more than one State. Either party to the dispute may refer the case to the Commission or it may intervene of its own accord 'in the public interest'. In 1988, the Commission was renamed the Australian Industrial Relations Commission but its functions remained largely the same. Despite the existence of State- and Federal-wide compulsory arbitration systems, unions and employers are free to negotiate additions to the minimum standard established by arbitration. In reality, there has been a considerable amount of direct negotiation between the parties. Directly negotiated agreements co-exist with, or take the place of, arbitration awards. The Australian system of conciliation and arbitration has been based on the assumption that the process of conciliation must be exhausted before arbitration will be brought into play.

SUMMARY

This chapter has been concerned with the institutions of employee relations – employers' associations, trade unions, staff associations and state agencies such as the Certification Officer, ACAS and the CAC.

Although the number of industry-wide collective agreements has declined, there are still some employers' associations which continue to negotiate agreements at national level. They remain, for the most part, in industries dominated by small firms which operate in very competitive labour markets. The main services employers' organisations offer to their members are assistance in the resolution of disputes, advisory and information services (best practice, model agreements, salary data, etc) and the representation of members' views to a range of organisations but particularly political bodies – government bodies, local authorities, political parties and the European Commission.

The primary purpose of trade unions is to protect the jobs of their members and to seek to enhance the pay and conditions of employment and processes such as collective bargaining and political lobbying. UK trade unions defend sectoral economic interests rather than working class interests as a whole. The UK trade union organisation is characterised by a small number of very large unions and a large number of very small unions. Over the last 20 years trade union membership has declined due to structural factors (for example, the switch in employment from manufacturing which was highly unionised to the service sector which has always been traditionally badly unionised, public policy initiatives unsupportive of trade union organisation, the introduction of less stable forms of employment and a growth in the culture of individualism). There are those who believe trade unions are in terminal decline.

In addition to a fall in the number of trade union members there has also been a fall in the number of trade unions. This has resulted from mergers in the light of changing product and labour markets and the implementation of technological change. However, many of these mergers have often been driven by the political allegiances of union leaderships or the search for a strong union membership base, rather than by the desire to create national trade union structures or a more effective industrial organisation.

In order to achieve their objectives UK trade unions prefer to use industrial rather than political methods. Trade unions see it as a legitimate right to try to persuade any elected government, regardless of its political colour, to introduce legislation which protects and advances the interests of working people. Trade unions need to be involved in the political process as the governments and the EU economic and legal policies can affect the relative bargaining power between employers and employees. Although some trade unions are involved in party politics via affiliation to the Labour Party, this is the result of historical accident, namely the Taff Vale judgement of 1901.

Staff associations are usually established within a single organisation. They have traditionally been strongest in banking and insurance. They are characterised by high membership density. Whilst the largest staff associations act in reality as independent unions, the effectiveness of the smaller ones is limited by their narrow membership basis and weak financial resources. The majority of staff associations are recognised by employers for negotiating and representational purposes. Most agreements follow the normal pattern and cover such matters as recognition, provision of facilities, joint negotiating machinery, consultation and grievance and disciplinary procedures. In addition there is a much larger number of bodies which bear the title of staff association but which make no claim to be a 'trade union'. These tend to be employer-dominated, have a consultative rather than a negotiating function and have few resources.

The three main state agencies examined in this chapter were the Certification Officer, ACAS and the CAC. The Certification Officer performs a number of functions including: determining that a trade union is independent of the employer; dealing with complaints by members that a union has failed to hold a secret ballot for electing members of its executives, its president and its general secretary; seeing that unions' mergers procedures are observed, and overseeing the establishment and operation of trade union political funds.

ACAS was established in 1974 and has five main functions. It promotes good practice, provides employee relations information and advice, conciliates in complaints to Employment Tribunals, conciliates in the case of collective disputes and facilitates mediation and arbitration in employment disputes. In promoting good practice it has issued three Codes of Practice – Discipline, Disclosure of Information and Time Off for Trade Union Duties and Activities. The Employment Rights (Disputes Resolution) Act 1998 empowers ACAS conciliation officers to draw up binding settlements in which both parties opt out of the Employment Tribunal system in favour of resolving the employee's complaint of unfair dismissal through voluntary arbitration. The underlying principle behind the Act is to make the resolution of unfair dismissal claims by this procedure as similar as possible to the arbitrations currently undertaken by ACAS in settling trade disputes.

The Central Arbitration Committee arbitrates on complaints from trade unions about an employer's failure to disclose information for collective bargaining purposes. Arbitration in the UK, unlike most other countries, is voluntary and the decisions of arbitrators are not enforceable at law. However, the CAC has an important arbitration role in the trade union recognition procedure of the Employment Relations Act 1999. The arbitration, for example, in disputes over appropriate bargaining units, is compulsory and therefore unique in the UK.

REFERENCES AND FURTHER READING

ADVISORY, CONCILIATION AND ARBITRATION SERVICE. *Annual Reports*.

BAMBER G. J. *and* LANSBURY R. D. (1998) *International and Comparative Employment Relations*. Australia, Allen & Unwin.

CLEGG H. A. (1979) *The Changing System of Industrial Relations in Great Britain*. Oxford, Blackwell.

CERTIFICATION OFFICER. *Annual Reports*.

CENTRAL ARBITRATION COMMITTEE. *Annual Reports*.

FLANDERS A. (1970) 'Collective bargaining: a theoretical analysis' in Flanders A. (1970) *Management and Unions*. London, Faber & Faber.

FLANDERS A. (1970) 'What are unions for?' in Flanders A. (1970) *Management and Unions*. London, Faber & Faber.

GENNARD J. (1998) 'The Labour government: changes in employment law'. *Employee Relations*, Vol 20, No 1.

HERE E. (1998) 'The relaunch of the Trades Union Congress'. *British Journal of Industrial Relations*, Vol 36, No 3.

INSTITUTE OF PERSONNEL AND DEVELOPMENT (1998) *Fairness at Work and the Psychological Contract*. London, IPD.

INDUSTRIAL RELATIONS SERVICE (1995) 'Staff associations: independent unions or employer-led bodies'. No 575, January.

INCOMES DATA SERVICES (1996) *Industrial Relations and Collective*

Bargaining. London, Institute of Personnel and Development. Chapters 3 (Denmark), 4 (France), 5 (Germany), 8 (Italy) and 12 (Sweden).

MILNER S. (1993) *Final Offer Arbitration in the UK: Incidence, processes and outcomes*. Department of Employment, Research Series, No 7.

MUMFORD K. (1996) 'Arbitration and ACAS in Britain: an historical perspective'. *British Journal of Industrial Relations*, Vol 34, No 2.

MCILROY J. (1998) 'The enduring alliance? Trade unions and the making of New Labour, 1994–97'. *British Journal of Industrial Relations*, Vol 36, No 4.

TRADES UNION CONGRESS (1966) *Trades Unionism*. London, TUC.

TRADES UNION CONGRESS (1994) *General Council Reports*. London, TUC.

WORKPLACE EMPLOYEE RELATIONS SURVEY (1998) PSI, ACAS, ESRC and DTI.

5 Employee relations strategies and policies

INTRODUCTION

In the preceding chapters we have identified the main components of employee relations. In Chapter 1 we noted that the balance of bargaining power is affected by the economic, legal and technological environments and that this in turn can influence prevailing management style. In Chapter 2 we developed these issues further as we examined the corporate environment and its importance to employee relations specialists. In this chapter we shall discuss the importance of employee relations strategies and the type and style of employment policies that flow from such strategies.

The management of people is one of the most challenging areas of business management, but it is, in many organisations, the poor relation in terms of importance and profile. This is despite the large amount of research and analysis showing how important it is in differentiating between organisational performance.

One of the most difficult tasks facing the personnel specialist is opening the minds of their management colleagues to adopting different, but proven, approaches to managing people. That is why in this book we lay such stress on gaining commitment from colleagues to employee relations initiatives. However, in order to obtain this commitment, it is important to ensure that a proper business case has been made for the adoption of new techniques or new approaches. It is easy to be critical of managers for not embracing new ideas, but if they are simply invited to buy into them as an article of faith, they will not make available the necessary investment in time and resources.

So, before seeking to change things within the organisation, there has to be a business case made which will demonstrate that such change is necessary. In making this business case it is important to show that there is a link between business performance, human resource management generally, and, in the context of this book, employee relations specifically.

To be successful the business case must flow from the organisation's overall strategy and to understand this connection we need to look at the whole concept of strategy and why, in recent years, it has become the subject of intense discussion and debate. This is because, although organisations have always had strategies, 'only since the 1960s has it been common to address explicitly the question of what their strategy should be' (Kay 1993 p6). One of the reasons for the change in emphasis is, as we noted in Chapter 2, that economic fluctuations and intense competition have forced organisations to face a continuing process of change. This change has to be managed and requires that organisations develop clear business strategies which will then drive functional strategies, one of which is employee relations.

If the last two decades have taught us anything, it is that the pattern of employee relations has been constantly evolving and this is likely to continue. This process of evolution has, quite clearly, been driven by the pace of change to which most businesses have been exposed and has created a need for directors and senior managers to look more carefully at their approach to strategic employee relations management. They have come to accept that there are advantages to be gained in re-shaping employee attitudes. This attitudinal change is of particular importance as organisations, in both the public and private sectors, have sought to maximise efficiency as a means of securing a competitive advantage. Such advantage is now as important an issue for the public sector as it is for the private sector. Public sector organisations have had competition forced upon them as successive governments have insisted on their being more customer and quality focused while private sector organisations have had their own challenges. These are very often linked to new technology or the growth of the global economy. Whatever the challenge, it will impact on and dictate the type of employment policies that the management of an organisation will seek to implement. When you have completed this chapter you should be able to explain:

- what strategy is and the role that overall strategy plays in defining employee relations strategies and policies

- that strategic choices can be driven by the values, preferences and power of those who are the principal decision-makers

- that the choice of particular employment policies will often be a strategic decision

- the concept of management style and its importance to the process of employee relations

- why some organisations continue to embrace collective relationships and others prefer to remain non-union or anti-union.

WHAT IS STRATEGY?

The overall purpose of strategy is to influence and direct an organisation as it conducts its activities. It may be described as the attempt by those who control an organisation to find ways to position their business or organisational objectives so that they can exploit the planning environment and maximise the future use of the organisation's capital and human assets (Tyson 1995). Clearly this is but one definition of strategy and many other writers have attempted to offer their own definition, but out of them all a certain consensus does arise.

Johnson and Scholes (1997) have identified four characteristics of strategy and strategic decision-making and these are:

- strategic decisions are likely to be concerned with or affect the long-term direction of an organisation

- strategic decisions are about trying to achieve some advantage for the organisation

- strategic decisions are likely to be concerned with the scope of an organisation's activities

- strategy can be seen as the matching of the activities of an organisation to the environment in which it operates.

Strategic formulation

To further understand the nature of strategy it may be helpful to gain some understanding of the process of strategy formulation and we can identify a number of different approaches. One of the oldest and most influential portrays strategy as a highly rational and scientific process. This approach is based on one of the characteristics identified by Johnson and Scholes, namely the importance of the fit between an organisation and its environment. Analyses are made of a firm's environment to assess likely opportunities and threats and of its internal resources to identify strengths and weaknesses. This process is often referred to as a SWOT analysis and it is argued that through rigorous planning, senior managers can predict and shape the external environment and thus the organisation itself.

Other approaches to strategy formulation argue that the complexity and volatility of the environment may mean that a SWOT analysis is both difficult and inappropriate. This evolutionary approach believes organisations are at the mercy of the unpredictable and hostile vagaries of the market. The environment in which they operate may be changing so frequently that any data they use, either historical or current, may be worthless.

Some writers argue that it is not possible to apply either a rational or evolutionary label to the process of strategy formulation, but that it is behavioural. That strategic choice results from the various coalitions that are to be found within organisations. The most dominant of these coalitions will be at senior management level and it is they who have to 'create a vision of the organisation's future' (Burnes 1996: 168).

The extent to which managing people is given a high profile within the organisation will be driven by the values, ideologies and personalities of those in positions of power and influence and those individuals who formulate strategy and the long-term direction of the organisation. When we talk about the organisation in strategy terms, we very often mean the directors and senior managers and it is their values and beliefs that will ultimately decide the type and style of employee relations policies that an organisation tries to follow. The senior management team may be very anti-union which, if there are trade unions within the workplace, can have a significant impact on the nature and style of collective relationships. Conversely, if the chief executive of an organisation was personally committed to the implementation of wider communication with the workforce then the organisation might seek to implement initiatives on employee involvement.

Similarly, the values and beliefs of those in power will have a significant impact on the long-term direction of a business. An example of how the personality of an individual or individuals can shape strategy can be seen in the example of British Petroleum (BP). When Robert Horton was appointed Chairman and Chief Executive of BP in 1990 the company was, by most organisations' standards, doing reasonably well. It employed over 117,000 people worldwide and had an annual turnover of $50 billion. By 1995, having survived the recession, BP employed 64,000, of whom 22,000 worked in the UK. When Horton joined the business he recognised that the company was at a crossroads and lacked clear direction. An opinion survey just before his appointment showed that over half of the top 150 managers were unclear about where the company was going and that the internal structure stood in the way of operational efficiency. Against this background Horton commissioned a review, 'Project 1990', to look at what the organisation needed for the 1990s and beyond. One of the main planks of Project 1990 was a massive culture change programme aimed at changing attitudes and behaviour. Without this change programme driven by Horton's personal vision of where the company needed to be, there is some doubt as to whether BP could have survived the recession as well as it did (Blakstad and Cooper 1995).

From this brief description it is clear that there is no one right way of formulating strategy. There are a number of approaches that can be adopted by an organisation, but it is important to understand that whichever one is adopted, it will be constrained by social, environmental, industry-specific and organisational factors, many of which will conflict with each other. If, for example, we take social factors, there can often be significant national differences in the way people approach work and, with the growth in multi-national companies and internationalisation, this can have a major impact on workplace culture.

As we have said, the environment within which any organisation operates will, without doubt, constrain strategic choice. This may be a relatively stable and predictable environment where planning and predicting the future is not a particularly hazardous exercise. Alternatively, it may be a hostile, unpredictable and uncertain environment where planning is almost impossible. Whatever the environment, most organisations have to operate in a constantly changing world and it is this change process that provides the link between business strategy and employee relations strategies. While environmental considerations may provide the stimulus for change, there is a clear consensus that the success or otherwise of individual change programmes is governed by the people in each organisation.

> Consider the environment in which your own organisation has to operate. How would you describe it?

Levels of strategy
Not only is it important to consider the sort of strategic choices that organisations can make, but also the levels of strategic decision-

making. There are three levels with which we need to concern ourselves:

- corporate level strategy which concerns the overall direction and focus of the business

- business unit strategy referring to day-to-day operational matters

- functional level strategy which is concerned with individual areas such as personnel, marketing etc (Burns 1996).

All of these levels are interrelated, but equally, each of them has its own distinctive strategic concerns. We now need to look at each of them in a little more detail.

Corporate level strategy
Corporate level strategy concerns itself with a number of questions and is usually formulated at board level. One of these questions will be about the overall mission of the organisation; what is the game plan? How should the business portfolio be managed? Should you make acquisitions or dispose of parts of the business? What priority should be given to each of the individual parts of the business in terms of resource allocation? How is the business to be structured and financed?

Whatever the mission, it needs to fulfil a number of criteria if it is going to be achieved. Firstly, it needs to be expressed in language that is understandable to the bulk of employees. This means paying attention to the communication process (see Chapter 6). Secondly, it needs to be attainable. That is, employees must recognise that the organisation has some chance of achieving the objectives that it has set itself. Thirdly, the mission needs to be challenging. For example, Ford Motor Co once declared, as part of its Corporate Strategy, that by the year 2000 it would be the best car manufacturer in the world. One of the challenges within that mission was directed at the HR function. Their challenge was to provide the expert advice and counselling that would allow operational management to do its job. Operational management is seen as the means whereby the overall mission can be accomplished.

If the organisation in which you work has a declared mission, how does it fit with the criteria we describe? If it does not fit, how would you express it so that it meets the need to be understandable, attainable and challenging? Alternatively, if no mission has been articulated, what do you think it should be (again, making it fit with our declared criteria)?

Business unit level strategy
Competitive or business unit level strategy is concerned with the way a firm or business operates in the short- to medium-term. Which markets should it attempt to compete in and how does it position itself to achieve its objectives? How does it achieve some form of 'distinctive capability' (Kay 1993)? What should its product range or mix be? Which customers should it aim for?

As far as products, markets and customers are concerned Porter (1985) argued that there are only three basic strategies:

- cost leadership which aims to achieve lower costs than competitors without reducing quality

- product differentiation based on achieving industry-wide recognition of different and superior products and services compared to those of other suppliers

- specialisation by focus, in effect seeking out a niche market.

All of these decisions have an effect on employee relations in that they impact on the way that the organisation structures itself internally and on the way that relationships are managed.

Functional level strategy

Functional level strategy is, in a sense, fairly straightforward. At this level strategy is concerned with how the different functions of the business (marketing, personnel, finance, manufacturing etc) translate corporate and business level strategies into operational aims. As Johnson and Scholes describe it, 'how the component parts of the organisation in terms of resources, processes, people and their skills are pulled together to form a strategic architecture which will effectively deliver the overall strategic direction'. But at this level it is important that the various functions pay attention to how they organise themselves, not only in order to achieve their aims, but to ensure synergy with the rest of the business. We can now turn specifically to the strategic issues concerning the management of people.

People strategy

One aspect of strategy concerns the match between an organisation's activities and its resources. These resources can be physical (equipment, building) or they can be people. Strategies in respect of physical resources may require decisions about investment or even about the ability to invest. Strategies about people also require decisions to be made about investment, but it is a different type of investment decision, not the type that fits easily into the process usually reserved for capital expenditure.

We said at the beginning of this chapter that if personnel professionals want their organisation to make an investment in people management issues and practices then a business case has to be made that such investment will show dividends in terms of performance improvements.

Research carried out by the Institute of Work Psychology and the Centre for Economic Performance, and published by the IPD (1997) and by Deloitte & Touche (1998) shows a clear link between the adoption of human resource management practices and business performance. This demonstrates how much of the variation between companies in change in productivity and profitability is attributable to focusing on key people management issues. Table 19 shows that significant improvement in both productivity and profitability can be achieved by focusing on:

- ensuring people are satisfied with their jobs, rewards, working conditions and career prospects

Table 19 Impact of people management on productivity and profitability

Factor	Productivity %	Profitability %
Job/work satisfaction	12	25
Organisational commitment	13	17
Organisational culture	10	29
HRM practices	18	19

- developing commitment by encouraging people to move beyond the contractual commitment to emotional commitment, where they develop a strong sense of loyalty to the organisation, its customers and clients and will not only see what needs to be done for the benefit of the organisation, but will initiate action and urge action from colleagues

- managing organisational culture through focusing on all the key cultural dimensions

- adopting an integrated approach to Human Resource Management programmes and processes which will develop satisfaction and commitment.

The research then goes on to show (see Table 20) that the use of Human Resource Management practices and effective job design can have more impact on productivity and profitability than other fundamental business activities.

This research is of some significance and, while it talks about HRM practices rather than personnel practices, it is not the purpose of this book to debate the distinctions between the two terms. What is important is that the research provides very clear evidence that concentrating on people is one of the keys to success and therefore an effective strategy for their management is a key requirement for any business.

But what makes an effective strategy for managing people?

The Deloitte & Touche survey in 1998 identified twelve key factors in five main areas of management activity that differentiate between high-growth businesses and low/no-growth businesses. The five main areas of management activity are:

- taking a strategic view of managing people

- involving people in the business

Table 20 Relative importance of core business functions on productivity/productivity

	Productivity %	Profitability %
Business strategy	3	2
Emphasis on quality	1	1
Use of advanced technology	1	1
Research and development	6	8
Use of HRM practices and job design	17	17

- investing in communication

- managing people's performance

- focusing on employees as individuals.

Some of these activities will be covered in much greater detail in Chapter 6, 'Employee Involvement', but as they are key features in the development of strategy we will summarise them here.

In taking a 'strategic view of managing people' it is imperative that people are at the centre of strategic planning for the organisation. Key questions about the organisation's people need to be addressed in planning business strategy. Are the right knowledge, skills and competencies available within the organisation and if not can they be acquired? Are people capable of taking forward new directions in business strategy? Can the knowledge, skills and competency available be deployed in a way that opens up new business opportunities?

It is also important in developing strategy to take account of company culture. This is a complex area, says the Deloitte & Touche survey, and requires a focus on:

- the artefacts and symbols of the organisation, such as the layout of the working environment, the technology used, the use of information and reporting

- the stories and myths that are commonly shared in the organisation and that indicate success and failure

- the rites and rituals that reinforce behaviour patterns and demonstrate the organisation's values

- the rules systems and procedures that set the parameters for behaviour and action

- the organisational heroes and heroines that act as role models for people

- the beliefs, values and attitudes that are expressed and displayed in everyday activity

- the ethical standards that guide the boundaries of what is acceptable and not acceptable

- the basic assumptions that are made about human behaviour, human nature, relationships, reality and truth.

'Involving people in the business' requires careful job design with a particular emphasis on team working whereby teams have a high degree of autonomy and freedom for self-management. To be effective teams need clear objectives and targets and the autonomy to plan and undertake work, acquire resources, and improve processes, products and services. Parameters need to be specified so that integration with the organisation as a whole is not compromised, but these need to be as wide as possible.

There are very few managers who would disagree with the third main activity, 'investing in communication'. Successful businesses invest heavily in communications and there are three aspects of communication that distinguish high growth businesses from the less successful. These are:

- communicating business strategy to all employees
- regularly giving feedback on performance measures to all employees
- using a wide range of communication methods.

The fourth activity, 'managing people's performance', is also self-evident, but failing to pay sufficient attention to this area can cause significant employee relations problems. People perform best if they know what they have to do, how well they are doing it, what they have to improve and how the improvement is going to be achieved. Setting clear, individual objectives for employees is a critical element in any successful organisation. However, where people do not know what is expected of them, it can lead to dissatisfaction, low morale, high labour turnover and high levels of absenteeism; these are all classic employee relations problems.

The final activity is to 'focus on individuals' and while the use of terms such as 'human resources' and 'human capital' encourages a view of an organisation's employees as a homogenous group, they can diminish the view of employees as individuals. However, high-performing organisations do focus on people as individuals and use techniques of involvement that are designed to encourage satisfaction and commitment (see Chapter 6).

All of the activities identified by Deloitte & Touche are important in formulating strategy, but they must not be viewed in isolation. They have to ensure that the whole range of people management activities – recruitment and selection, reward and recognition, training and development and employee relations – are integrated into the strategic planning process. This is important for any manager concerned with business performance because the research and evidence from companies that are achieving the best results in productivity, profitability and growth show that good people management strategies make the real difference.

Strategy and employment policies

Having discussed the process of strategy formulation we now need to look at how this links into employee relations in particular, but not forgetting that there must be a link with other aspects of the employment relationship: employee resourcing, employee reward and employee development.

Whatever means organisations choose for formulating their strategy, at either corporate or business level, maximising the organisation's competitive advantage has to be a major issue. This inevitably means an organisation constantly needs to re-evaluate itself in order that it can sustain any necessary improvements. Organisations therefore are concerned with the design and management of employment policies and processes that will deliver and sustain business improvement. The process of change and its impact on the development of strategy present many challenges for the employee relations specialist. For example, as we discuss later, there is the whole issue of trade unions and the new provisions on recognition. Where trade unions already exist and are recognised within an organisation, the current trends towards individualism, as opposed to collectivism, mean that strategic choices need to be made about whether those unions are encouraged or marginalised. Where they do not exist and requests for recognition are received, are these resisted or accepted voluntarily?

Overall, strategies and policies on employee relations need to have a direct relationship with the business strategy and need to be imaginative, innovative, clear and action-orientated. They need to be formulated by a continuing process of analysis to identify what is happening to the business and where it is going. In this context, the relevance of clear business objectives, as expressed through the medium of a mission statement, cannot be overstated. The key is to develop an employee relations strategy which is responsive to the needs of the organisation, which can provide an overall sense of purpose to the employee relations specialist and assist employees in understanding where they are going, how they are going to get there, why certain things are happening and, most importantly, the contribution they are expected to make towards achieving the organisational goals.

If we examine some of the challenges facing the personnel specialist both now and in the future, we can identify some of the important links between the various personnel disciplines. In the area of employee resourcing, organisations face continuing challenges in developing policies on recruitment and selection. In employee reward there are continuing and continuous challenges to the personnel practitioner. Stimulating employee commitment, motivation and enhancing job performance are matters which will be discussed in Chapter 6, but among the issues that need to be considered is the balance between pay and non-pay rewards and individual versus collective bargaining. But reward policies need to be 'developed and managed as a coherent whole ... they need to be integrated with one another and, importantly, with the key business and personnel processes of the organisation' (Armstrong 1996 p53).

As far as employee development is concerned, the personnel practitioner faces three challenges, all of which impact on employee relations. Firstly, is it in the company's interests to buy in or develop its own staff? Where do the long-term interests of the business lie? If they get the balance wrong and buy in too much labour, then there is a risk that existing employees will become disillusioned and assume that the organisation is not interested in investing in their future.

Secondly, what sort of employees are required? Generalists or specialists? Personnel professionals have a significant role to play in helping to identify what value there is to the organisation in particular types of employee. Although it is popular to support the idea of multiskilling, this concept does not always serve the organisation's best interests. Too many people may want to be trained in specific skills, some of which may never be fully utilised, and this can lead to resentment or resistance to further training interventions.

Finally, if investment is to be made in employee development, is it simply a question of training people to carry out the current tasks that they are required to fulfil, or is it strategically valuable to create a learning environment as many organisations have done?

All of these challenges are strategic issues that are interlinked and have an impact on employee relations. In each case they will be conditioned in their scope and their impact by the type and size of the organisation.

What external factors over the next five years are likely to impact on corporate strategy, both in the wider business context and in the specific challenges that your own organisation is likely to face? How, if at all, will these impact on your employee relations strategy?

You should have looked at any trends in your organisation's business strategy that might have an impact, such as:

• plans for expansion

• proposals for new investment

• the need to improve profitability or productivity.

You need to consider the impact of changes to your employee relations strategies on the other policy areas, for example resourcing, reward, health and safety, and development. Finally, you need to consider the impact of external influences such as political (a change of UK Government), economic (interest rates, inflation, unemployment), social (demographic trends), new technology and any possible changes in legislation, particularly European influences.

EMPLOYEE RELATIONS POLICY

Once it is clear what the overall philosophy of an organisation is, the employee relations specialist can use this knowledge to put together an employee relations policy for the business. This can then be used as the guiding principle on which individual policies are drawn up. The needs of an organisation in terms of its employee relations policy are potentially infinite, but could emanate from two specific areas. One, the 'management of change', could encompass issues as diverse as improving productivity, greater employee involvement, changing reward systems or introducing team working. The second is the organisation's attitude towards trade unions.

Let us look at the last of these for a moment. We have already discussed the impact that the values and preferences of an organisation's dominant management decision-makers have on strategy formulation. These values and perceptions will in part be determined by whether the organisation adopts a unitary or pluralist approach to its employee relations. The unitary approach emphasises organisations as harmonious and integrated, with all employees sharing the organisational goals and working as members of one team. The pluralist approach recognises that different groups exist within an organisation and that conflict can and does exist between employer and employees.

These are broad definitions and it must be noted that simply because an organisation is described as unitarist, it does not mean that management and employees share the same agenda. Unitarist organisations can be either authoritarian or paternalistic in their attitudes and this, as we will examine later in the chapter, can have a major impact on management style. Pluralism, while generally used to describe an organisation that embraces collective relationships, can emphasise co-operation between interest groups, not just conflict. It is this distinction in approach to the management of people that leads to variations in employee relations policies, ranging from the paternalistic, no-union approach of Marks and Spencer through the single-union, no-strike philosophy of Japanese firms like Nissan, to the multi-union sites of companies like Ford.

The influence of external and internal factors needs to be taken into account in drafting employee relations policies and then implementing them. We identified what some of the external factors were in Chapter 2, in particular existing and future legislative constraints, but there are other influences. It is important to be aware of the type of policies other employers in your sector or industry are pursuing. These may have an impact in your own organisation if, for example, they have taken a particular stance on employee involvement as a means of retaining key employees. This could impact on your own ability to retain staff. What is considered to be prevailing 'good practice'? In this context 'good practice' means identifying those acts or omissions that distinguish the good employer from the perceived 'bad' employer. For example, if you fail to operate your disciplinary procedure in line with natural justice you may find that your ex-employees constantly file complaints against you with tribunals, and not only that, but they win compensation as well. Many employers when drafting policies and procedures only 'scratch the surface'. They either do not consider how the policy might operate in practice and whether it will meet the needs of their employees, or they are careless in its operation with the result that it fails to meet the criteria of 'best practice', which is a standard that we pursue throughout this book. Whatever the policy, therefore, it is important to incorporate monitoring mechanisms within it so that checks can be made on its effectiveness.

Management style
While external constraints on employee relations policy formulation are an important factor, the internal constraints are probably of greater significance. Factors which often determine management style are organisational size, ownership and location. Style can be an important determinant in defining an employee relations policy and is as much influenced by an organisation's leaders as is business strategy. Since Fox first categorised management and employee relations as unitarist or pluralist others have sought to define the topic in greater detail. In particular Purcell and Sissons identified five typical styles:

- authoritarian

- paternalistic

- consultative

- constitutional

- opportunist.

The authoritarian approach sees employee relations as relatively unimportant. There is no attempt to put policies and procedures in place and as a consequence people issues are not given any priority until something goes wrong. Typically, firms with an authoritarian approach are small owner-managed businesses and it is not unusual to find that the things that go wrong revolve around disciplinary issues. In many of the small firms that we have contact with, complaints against them of unfair dismissal are a common problem. An employer who has paid little attention to setting standards of performance dismisses an employee who makes a mistake and then finds that the dismissed employee wins a tribunal claim for compensation. This is usually because no previous warnings were issued and no disciplinary procedure is followed. An analysis of the size and ownership of organisations appearing in tribunal cases would seem to support the view.

Paternalistic organisations share many of the size and ownership characteristics of the authoritarian type. They tend to have a much more positive attitude towards their employees.

A consultative or problem-solving organisation welcomes trade unions as partners in the enterprise and employee consultation is a high priority. Staff retention and reward are seen as key issues.

The type of constitutional organisation described by Purcell and Sissons assumes a trade union presence. Although sharing some of the characteristics of the previous types of organisation, management style in employee relations is more adversarial than consultative.

In the opportunist organisation management style is determined by local circumstances. This would determine whether it was appropriate to recognise trade unions or not, or the extent to which employee involvement was encouraged.

Purcell (1987: 535) moved his analysis of 'management style' forward and redefined it as 'the existence of a distinctive set of guiding principles, written or otherwise, which set parameters to and signposts for management action in the way employees are treated and particular events handled'. This principle of setting parameters is of vital importance in the management of people. Hilary Walmsley (*People Management* April 1999 page 48) argued that 'to get the most out of people, managers need to adapt their styles to fit different situations'. However, she went on to say that 'managers typically use the same personal style to handle a range of situations. Usually they do this out of habit. Some are not clear about the array of potential styles available to them. Even those who are aware that there are, for example, different ways of developing and motivating people, or of approaching problem solving, often fail to apply this knowledge to their day to day activities. Those who do want to apply new styles can feel confused about where and when they should try them'.

Individual and collective dimension
Purcell suggests that management style has two dimensions, individualism and collectivism, with each dimension having three stages. Individualism is concerned with how much policies are directed at individual workers and whether the organisation takes into account

the feelings of all its employees and 'seeks to develop and encourage each employee's capacity and role at work'. The three stages in the individual dimension are commodity status, paternalism and resource status. In the first the employee is not well regarded and has low job security; in the second, the employer accepts some responsibility for the employee; in the third, the employee is regarded as a valuable resource.

The collectivist dimension is, in a sense, self-explanatory. It is about whether or not management policy encourages or discourages employees to have a collective voice and collective representation. The three stages in this dimension are:

- unitary

- adversarial

- co-operative.

At the unitary stage management opposes collective relationships either openly or by covert means. The adversarial stage represents a management focus that is on a stable workplace, where conflict is institutionalised and collective relationships limited. The final, co-operative stage has its focus on constructive relationships and greater openness in the decision-making process.

> Can you identify the management style that operates within your organisation? Do you think that it changes to meet different needs or is it static?

Remember, identifying a particular management style is not simply a question of labelling an organisation 'individualist' or 'collectivist'. Purcell points out that the interrelationship between the two is complex and that simply because an organisation is seen to encourage the rights and capabilities of individuals, this should not necessarily mean that it is seeking to marginalise any representative group.

Selecting employee relations policies
The ability to identify which policies are suitable and which are unsuitable for particular types of organisation is an important skill for the employee relations specialist to develop.

All organisations need to have policies on grievance, discipline, health and safety, pay and benefits and sickness absence, and these should always be written down and consistently applied. It is also important to acknowledge that while each of the policies mentioned above might differ in scope and depth from one organisation to another, no one, irrespective of the type of organisation that they work in, would seriously question their selection in the range of employment policies adopted.

However, where we do need to examine seriously questions of selection, is in respect of those policies that have a clear impact on corporate and business strategies and can seriously affect relationships at work. As we enter the new millennium, an organisation's approach to strategy formulation and thus its approach to employee relations will continue to be influenced by UK Government actions and consumer preferences. This will impact on their decisions about the way that they manage people and the policies that underpin these management processes.

In Chapter 2 we explained that for well over a decade the main thrust of industrial, economic and legislative policy has been to create a market driven economy and that 'from an industrial relations perspective, the most telling feature of this policy has been the successive pieces of legislation designed to limit the role and rights of trade unions' (Guest 1995: 110). Because the question of why some firms recognise trade unions and others do not is so important to employee relations, it is dealt with separately within this chapter. For the moment we will concentrate on policy choices in other areas. For many organisations who try to link policy choices in employee relations to their business strategies, the real question is not about trade unions, but how to ensure that their workforce is committed to the organisation. Obtaining employee commitment is one of the ways organisations can position themselves in order to achieve a competitive advantage, one of the necessary prerequisites of a successful business. However, employees will only give their commitment if they feel secure, valued and properly motivated; a sense of well-being that will, in part, be derived from the type of employment policies that are adopted. Such policies need to be capable of 'adding value' to the business and, for the employee relations specialist who may be trying to decide on the advice they give in respect of a particular policy, this is of some importance.

In respect of trade unionism, the question is not about pro- or anti-union stances, it is about whether entering into a relationship with an appropriate trade union can add value to the business. It would be wrong to assume that the answer to this question will always be no. The search for competitive advantage and employee commitment are key issues and are linked to the management of change in an organisation.

Managing change may require variations in organisational culture, the introduction of flexible working practices, empowerment or some form of team-working. If any of these routes, or a combination of them all, are followed, the devising and implementation of policies to support them will be required. This is where the involvement of the employee relations specialist can be of crucial importance and before we examine the subject of change, it is important to recognise that the process of designing and implementing policies to support change requires the employee relations specialist to develop certain skills. In this context one of these is evaluation (see Chapter 1). It may be that you have been asked by the Board to establish whether a particular initiative will be suitable for your organisation and proper evaluation is of critical importance because there is a danger that organisations will invest in new ideas that are not suitable for them.

Managing change

The management of change is something that most organisations have to undertake at some time or other, and during the change process employee relations can be under tremendous stress. In most change programmes it is safe to assume that no more than 25 to 30 per cent of people will be in favour, that up to 50 per cent will probably sit on the fence to see what happens and up to a quarter of people will actively resist any changes. That is why, as Machiavelli said,

> There is nothing more difficult to plan, more doubtful of success, nor more dangerous to manage than the creation of a new system. For the initiator has the enmity of all who profit by the preservation of the old institutions, and merely lukewarm defenders in those who would gain by the new ones.

Given the importance of people to the change process it is important that management is able to articulate a clear vision of the objectives of its change programme. To gain commitment to change that vision has to be expressed clearly and unambiguously and, as the following case study illustrates, that commitment can be obtained if management takes the right steps in managing the process.

CASE STUDY

British Telecom

Eight years ago BT employed 250,000 people – 1 per cent of the country's working population. Today it employs around 110,000 people, who now achieve higher standards than ever before. Consequently, the company's overall business performance is good. But orchestrating this change has been tough. Despite the fact that all redundancies were voluntary and that the downsizing took place without industrial action, it was still a destabilising and, at times, morale-sapping experience.

It was against this background that BT launched a new way of working called '... for a better life'. In 1993 BT formed a 20,000-strong consumer division covering all the front-line staff. The new divisional managing director, Stafford Taylor, realised they could not survive in the newly liberalised telecommunications market without a customer-focused and motivated workforce. Sympathetic people with a strong desire to put customers first are the essential ingredient of any service provider, and that defined the BT approach.

The new way of working was designed to help bridge that gap, not only by making clear what was expected of staff, but by changing the way they worked at the same time as instilling a sense of excitement and belonging. Taylor insisted that all employees should be encouraged to develop four attributes:

- to know instinctively how to contribute to the success of BT

- to take personal accountability for customers' requirements

- to take decisive action on behalf of the customer

- to take considered risks to delight the customer.

Now referred to as 'own, decide, do', this underpinning behaviour had far-reaching consequences for the relationship between employee and manager. If this new way of working were to take root, managers

Table 21 Employee attitudes in BT's consumer division

| | % of staff agreeing | | | |
	Mar 95	Sep 95	Sep 96	Jan 98
Are you satisfied with your line manager?	61	74	83	84
Do you have a sense of ownership of your job?	73	86	90	89
Are you confident about making decisions?	84	91	95	94
Do you feel able to take a considered risk?	64	83	89	86
Have you received enough coaching to be completely helpful to customers?		54	81	82

would need to take on more of a coaching role to help people make decisions. Staff were in turn expected to be more assertive and creative.

And it worked. Staff attitude surveys (see Table 21) have shown a huge increase in the number of people who feel able to take important decisions and even risks. Employees are also becoming more satisfied with the way they are being managed – 84 per cent of staff in the consumer division reported that they were either satisfied or very satisfied with their relationship with their line manager, compared with 61 per cent three years ago.

BT's new way of working has been based on a two-pronged approach. First, they had to convince staff that they were serious about what they were saying, that they were free to approach their jobs more flexibly and that they could expect their managers to behave differently. Second, they had to encourage their managers to change their behaviour.

Bob Mason, the HR Director, says,

> Crucially, we have not called '... for a better life' a programme or initiative. How many management-led initiatives are forgotten after six months? We always knew that this would be a long-term investment and could take years to embed into the company culture. We therefore tend to refer to it as a crusade, and I am pleased to say that it is alive and well four and a half years after its inception. More that three-quarters of our staff now say they perceive improvements as a direct result, and the model has inspired similar moves in other parts of the company.
>
> [Source: *People Management* October 1998 Page 46]

The BT experience demonstrates that the introduction of most new initiatives will be an evolutionary process and that there is unlikely to be a 'big bang'. Any sort of organisational change can mean that responsibilities have to be altered, which means that the boundaries of jobs need to be clarified and people given time to prepare. This may mean that it may be important to examine organisational structure because some change programmes will challenge traditional hierarchies, a change that can give rise to considerable resentment and individual resistance. It is important to ensure that other policies which might be required to underpin a new initiative are themselves in place, for example, equal opportunities, single status workforce ... With any new policy there will always be those who oppose it, sometimes openly and sometimes covertly, and the employee relations specialist will recognise this. They will not assume that the process is complete just because an initiative has been properly evaluated and then properly communicated to all employees. They will monitor implementation and seek ways to reinforce the initial communication about the policy change.

MANAGEMENT AND TRADE UNIONS

Although the influence of trade unions has been declining steadily since 1978, the question of trade unionism *per se* is very important to the employee relations specialist in trying to determine policies and procedures for their own organisation. As we have acknowledged elsewhere in this chapter, management style and philosophy will cause different managers to have different approaches to the role and involvement of unions. This will range from encouragement to active resistance and refusal, but the Employment Relations Act 1999 will make it more difficult, if not impossible, for them to say no.

However, before making the assumption that all existing non-union firms will become unionised, we need to understand what we mean by the term 'non-unionism'. Salamon (1998) explains that the term can be used to explain two different types of organisation:

- Type A: where an organisation has a policy not to recognise unions for any employees or for particular groups of employees (such as managers) and, therefore, it is a distinct aim or element of management's employee relations strategy to avoid any collective relationship (i.e. non-unionism results from management decision)

- Type B: where union membership within the organisation or group of employees is low or non-existent and, therefore, unions are not recognised because of the absence of employee pressure for representation (i.e. non-unionism results from the employees' decision not to join unions).

Clearly, type B organisations have little to fear from the new legislation unless something happens in the working environment that fundamentally alters the status quo. Unless the company has a history of treating its employees badly and those employees have now succumbed to the blandishments of a union recruiting drive, in which something will have changed for the worse in the employment relationship. If it is possible to identify some causal act, can something other than union recognition remedy it? If in a type B organisation there were a sudden rush to join a trade union, the organisation would have to ask itself some very searching questions. Have recent redundancies created a climate of uncertainty? Has there been a change in management style? Have grievances been ignored or badly handled? Any of these could trigger a change in employee attitudes to collective representation and, therefore, if management wants to remain non-union, it needs to consider how such issues are managed (Judge 1997). But, before we examine the new recognition procedures in detail, we need to understand a little more about non-unionism.

Non-union organisations
One of the unsubstantiated myths in employee relations has been the

idea that non-unionism is the panacea for business success, with organisations such as Marks and Spencer and IBM put forward as prime examples of the concept. There will always be a debate between those who see trade unions as a negative influence and those, like most of our European partners, who see rights at work (including trade union membership and collective bargaining) as part of an important social dimension to working relationships. It is this polarisation which results in many politicians and business leaders being antagonistic towards the social dimension of the European Union. Post-war industrial relations has allowed some commentators the opportunity to promote non-unionism as the ideal state to which all businesses should aspire and believe that to allow interventions from Europe would be a massive step backwards.

While the debate about unionism versus non-unionism continues, the real question tends to be ignored. That is, is it easier to manage with unions or without unions? Personal prejudice ought not to come into the process of effective management, but many managers' attitudes towards trade unions have been conditioned by their negative experiences during the 1970s and 1980s, a period when the unions contributed to their negative image with some self-inflicted wounds. In too many organisations union representatives were allowed to take the initiative because managers were unsure of how to respond. There were two reasons for this:

- poor training in core skills like negotiation, communication and interviewing

- a lack of clear policy guidance.

It is because of this lack of skills that the second part of this book concentrates on issues like bargaining, negotiating, managing grievances and handling discipline.

As personnel practitioners ourselves we have received many requests for help from organisations which are having difficulty in managing their employee relations. In almost all cases, blame is laid at the door of the union and there is no recognition that poor management might also bear some responsibility. When appropriate training interventions have been agreed and implemented we find that there is a complete turnaround. Not only do managers seize responsibility, but they find that they are able to do so with little or no union resistance. In truth, union representatives were merely filling a vacuum that nobody else was interested in. These experiences have caused many managers to become very biased against unions, and many of those that we speak to genuinely believe that without the unions business success would be guaranteed.

This faith in managing without unions has meant that some of the larger non-union firms within the UK have become the focus of attention for developments in employee relations. Companies like Marks and Spencer and IBM, as we have said, have always been held up as exemplar non-union employers, but now others, such as Hewlett Packard, Texas Instruments, Gillette and Mars, have joined the list. 'At the risk of over-generalisation, the generic characteristics of these non-union companies tend to be a sense of caring, carefully chosen plant locations and working environments, market leadership, high growth and healthy profits, employment security, single status, promotion from within, an influential personnel department, competitive pay and benefit packages, profit sharing, open communications, and the careful selection and training of management, particularly at the supervisory level.' (Blyton and Turnbull 1994: 234). How many of the companies who yearn for non-union status would be prepared to make the investment in people management that the organisations which they envy have done? Because, as we have said, the real issue is how well a business is managed. That is what determines success.

Notwithstanding the influence of large organisations, data from the 1990 Workplace Industrial Relations Survey (WIRS) found that non-union establishments are more likely to be small, single plant establishments located in the private services sector. This result is not surprising, given the great encouragement that the small firms sector has received and continues to receive. The number of business start-ups has risen and many of the new organisations have not been able to see the relevance of trade unions. Many of their employees may have been the victims of redundancy in older, traditionally unionised industries, and a reluctance to embrace the supposed cause of industrial decline (trade unions) may be understandable.

However, one must also question how active trade unions have been in trying to recruit from new industries and the new workforce. In Chapter 4, we suggested that trade unions needed to do more to market themselves if they wanted to attract members from previously untapped sources. Have the unions been so busy defending the interests of their existing members that they have not been able to devote sufficient resources to recruitment? Another question that needs to be asked is how will people's feelings of insecurity about their long-term job prospects act as a feeding ground for trade union recruiters?

These and other questions link back to the issue of policy choice. If a business wishes to be, or remain, non-union, then it needs to be clear about the relationship it will have with its employees. To be a Marks and Spencer, a company needs to be very people-orientated, with great importance placed on respect for employees. This means highly developed and effective leadership skills and this requires an investment in people. Gaining commitment and becoming a harmonious and integrated unitary workplace requires more than words; it can mean changing the established order.

Alternatively, a business can be a type A organisation as identified by Salamon. These organisations need to be prepared to deal with a request for recognition. While the idea might be anathema to an anti-union organisation, having an identifiable policy relating to trade unionism and trade union recognition could be very helpful. We are certainly aware of organisations that have been traditionally non-union, which are taking steps to prepare for a recognition claim by, for example, training their managers in bargaining skills.

UNION RECOGNITION

The 1998 Workforce Employee Relations Survey (WERS) found that in 47 per cent of workplaces there are no union members at all – 'a substantial change from 36 per cent of workplaces in 1990'. The survey found that there are 'strong associations between the type of union presence and workplace employment size', but as we have noted elsewhere, 'even stronger associations with management attitudes towards union membership', as can be seen in Table 22.

During the past decade trade union recognition has continued to fall, to the point where only 45 per cent of workplaces now recognise trade unions, compared to 66 per cent in 1984 and 53 per cent in 1990. If this trend of a decline in union-recognised workplaces is going to be reversed by the Employment Relations Act, where are the recognition requests going to come from? WERS found that there are 8 per cent of workplaces with union members but no recognition agreement, and in 1 per cent of these workplaces union members account for a majority of the workforce. Logic indicates that these workplaces will be the starting point for any new recognition claims.

Obtaining union recognition

The Employment Relations Act 1999 sets out the basis on which employees can obtain recognition. In summary, those provisions are as set out below:

• One or more independent trade unions seeking recognition must apply to the employer in writing requesting recognition. The employer has 10 days in which to respond. If, by the end of the 10-day period, the employer has not responded or has rejected the request, the union

Table 22 Indicators of union presence, by workplace size and management attitudes

	Union density	Any union members	Union recognition
	% of employees who are members	% of workplaces	% of workplaces
Workplace size			
25 to 49 employees	23	46	39
50 to 99	27	52	41
100 to 199	32	66	57
200 to 499	38	77	67
500 or more employees	48	86	78
Management views on union membership			
In favour	62	98	94
Neutral/not an issue	23	40	29
Not in favour	7	16	9
All workplaces	36	53	45

Base: all workplaces with 25 or more employees
Figures are weighted and based on responses from 1,889 managers

may apply to the Central Arbitration Committee (CAC) for a decision on the 'appropriate bargaining unit' and/or whether a majority of the workers support recognition for collective bargaining.

- If however, the employer indicates during the 10-day period that, while not accepting the request, he is prepared to negotiate to agree the bargaining unit and recognition for it, a negotiation period of 28 days (or longer, if mutually agreed) is available. If these negotiations fail, the union may apply to the CAC as above, but it may not apply if it has rejected or not responded within 10 days to an employer proposal for ACAS to assist.

- Once a recognition claim is referred to the CAC, it must try to help the parties reach agreement within 28 days (or such longer appropriate period as it may determine). If agreement is not reached within that period, the CAC then has 10 days (or a longer period where it specifies the reasons for extension) to decide the appropriate bargaining unit.

- In respect of an application to decide the appropriate bargaining unit and whether the union has the support of the majority of the workers in it, the CAC must not proceed unless it decides that:

  - members of the union (or unions) constitute at least 10 per cent of the workers constituting the proposed bargaining unit, and

  - there is prima facie evidence that a majority of the workers constituting the proposed bargaining unit would be likely to favour recognition of the union (or unions) as entitled to conduct collective bargaining on behalf of the bargaining unit.

- In deciding the appropriate bargaining unit, the CAC must take these matters into account:

  - the need for the unit to be compatible with effective management

  - the matters listed in sub-paragraph (4), so far as they do not conflict with that need.

The matters are:

- the views of the employer and of the union (or unions)

- existing national and local bargaining arrangements

- the desirability of avoiding small fragmented bargaining units within an undertaking

- the characteristics of workers falling within the proposed bargaining unit and of any other employees of the employer whom the CAC considers relevant

- the location of workers.

If the union shows that a majority of the workers in the bargaining unit are members of the union the CAC must declare the union recognised, *unless* one of the following three conditions applies:

- The CAC is satisfied that a ballot should be held in the interests of good industrial relations.

- A significant number of the union members within the bargaining unit inform the CAC that they do not want the union (or unions) to conduct collective bargaining on their behalf.

- Membership evidence is produced which leads the CAC to conclude that there are doubts whether a significant number of the union members within the bargaining unit want the union (or unions) to conduct collective bargaining on their behalf.

If the union cannot show majority membership, or if it can but one of the three conditions above applies, the CAC must arrange (through a qualified independent person) a secret ballot of the workers in the bargaining unit, asking whether they wish the union to conduct collective bargaining on their behalf.

- If the ballot result shows that the union is supported by a majority of those voting and at least 40% of those in the bargaining unit, the CAC will declare the union recognised.

Note that the CAC must not proceed with a recognition application from more that one union unless:

- the unions show that they will co-operate with each other in a manner likely to secure and maintain stable and effective collective bargaining arrangements, and

- the unions show that, if the employer wishes, they will enter into arrangements under which collective bargaining is conducted by the unions acting together on behalf of the workers constituting the proposed bargaining unit.

Where the CAC declares a union recognised, the parties have a negotiating period of 42 days (or longer if mutually agreed) to agree a method for conducting collective bargaining. If they have not reached agreement then, they can seek CAC assistance during a further period of 28 days (or longer if mutually agreed with CAC). If they still cannot agree, the CAC must specify the method by which the parties must conduct collective bargaining (which they can vary by written agreement) and which will be a contract legally enforceable through the courts, by orders for specific performance, with which failure to comply will constitute contempt of court.

Employer concerns
Writing in *People Management* (January 1999 page 54), Mike Emmott, IPD Policy Adviser on Employee Relations, stated that 'one thing is clear beyond any doubt: most employers are opposed to the idea of a law on trade union recognition'. Many of these concerns are centred around the timescales within the recognition procedure. Throughout the process, the time allowed for each stage is very short. If the CAC is hard pressed, there is the possibility that it will make hurried and ill-considered decisions rather than exercise the discretion to extend that is available to it. There is also the possibility that employers and trade unions will not have the necessary resources to deal with a large number of recognition claims.

One scenario that has been put to us by a number of employers is the inability of an organisation to respond to or reject a union recognition request within 10 days. What if the senior management or the principal of the business is away, perhaps for a fortnight's holiday? It is therefore likely that employers will continue to lobby for an extension of the timescale.

A further concern that has been expressed by employers is the membership of the CAC. There is a real fear that there will not be sufficient people with the necessary qualifications and experience to make the critical decisions it will be called upon to make.

The government, for its part, takes a much more benign view of its new legislation. It sees unions, 'where they are run efficiently along modern lines, as important partners for employers in promoting competitiveness and good practice' (Ian McCartney – *People Management*, 17 September 1998, page 38). In May 1999 the Prime Minister, Tony Blair, announced that the Government would be putting up to £5 million of public money into programmes aimed at encouraging more employer/union partnerships. And, while this is a laudable attempt to improve management and trade union relationships, the unions' attempts to present a vision of themselves as modern are not always borne out by the experience of employers. In his article, Mike Emmott recorded that 'for every employer prepared to testify to more positive union attitudes, there are two or three who see little or no change'.

This negative view will not necessarily diminish and the 1999 dispute over bargaining rights at the Western Mail & Echo in Cardiff, if repeated, could seriously undermine the Government's position.

At the Western Mail & Echo, management invited three unions to make an approach for bargaining rights – the GMB, the boilermakers' union; the MSF, the manufacturing, science and finance union; and the AEEU – all low profile in comparison with the traditional publishing industry unions, the Graphical Paper & Media Union (GPMU) and the National Union of Journalists (NUJ). After some negotiations the GMB and MSF withdrew, leaving the company to draw up a no-strike agreement with the AEEU. This agreement was then disputed by the GPMU and the NUJ.

If, once the recognition procedures in the 1999 legislation are more widely used, such disputes over bargaining rights become commonplace, it may herald the start of a greater use of the law in employee relations. This is likely if unions try to protect their position within a particular industry.

Employers and their use of the law
The laws that are now on the statute book impact on employee relations in a number of ways and, as we explained in Chapter 2, changes in legislation have meant that trade unions are much more responsible for the actions of their members than they used to be. This means that it is potentially much easier for employers to seek a legal remedy when industrial action is taken against them. There is a much stricter definition of what constitutes strike action and this can only be lawful if it follows a properly conducted ballot, relates wholly or mainly to matters such as pay and conditions and can only take place

between an employee and his direct employer. This is intended to rule out sympathy or secondary action by those not involved in the main dispute.

Other provisions in the legislative package include restrictions on the numbers of people that can mount a picket outside a workplace and compulsory ballots to test union members' support for contributions to a political fund. The law has also outlawed the closed shop, which is not to say that *de facto* closed shops do not still exist, because they do, most notably in the printing industry.

Against this background we need to consider the employers' use of such laws. Why do some employers seek legal assistance in the resolution of disputes and not others? Much has been made of the rights that employers now have to take legal action against their employees, either to sue for damages caused by industrial action or to seek injunctions prohibiting action taking place.

While the occasional high profile case hits the headlines, there is no evidence to suggest that employers seek to exercise their legal rights every time they are faced with disruptive action. Indeed, there is probably more evidence to suggest that most employers resist the temptation to use the law. This is because they enjoy reasonably good employee relations and are more interested in maintaining those relationships in the long term than they are in short term victories. This is not to say that some organisations, in industries such as transport, set out deliberately to alienate their workforce. It is simply that there are often other considerations. If they were not seen to challenge 'unnecessary' strikes, they would run the risk of losing, perhaps permanently, many of their customers. For this reason, any employer faced with the threat of industrial action has to take seriously concerns voiced by its customers and seek to balance these against the long-term relationship with its workforce.

The circumstances in which an employer might have to consider using the law will usually follow a breakdown in negotiations with a recognised union. Such a breakdown could lead the union to seek a formal mandate from its members supporting industrial action or there could be some form of unofficial industrial action encouraged by lay officials. The response that an employer makes in such circumstances is extremely important and can have a critical effect on employee relations.

> Consider how you would respond to a ballot for industrial action in your organisation and what factors you would take into account.

Industrial action ballots

If, for whatever reason, negotiations with a recognised union have broken down, there is every possibility that they will seek to organise a ballot of their members. They may do this not just because they have a desire to take industrial action, but because a positive vote can be a very useful means of forcing the employer back to the bargaining table. If you are faced with a ballot for industrial action there are a number of steps to be taken to check that it complies with all the legal requirements. Firstly, was the ballot conducted by post? Before any form of industrial action can commence all those employees who it is reasonable to believe will be called upon to take part in the action must have been given a chance to vote. Secondly, were you as the employer given seven days' notice before the ballot took place? Thirdly, has the union appointed independent scrutineers to oversee the ballot? Finally, did you receive notice of the result, and was this at least seven days before any proposed action?

Let us assume that all the legal requirements have been complied with. What are the legal options? Can any action be taken against the union? Not really, unless it can be demonstrated that the proposed action would not be a lawful trade dispute within the meaning of the legislation. There used to be a right to take sanctions against individuals, but this has been changed by the Employment Relations Act 1999. The legislation makes it automatically unfair to dismiss workers taking part in protected (lawful) action within eight weeks of the action beginning. Furthermore, after eight weeks it will still be unfair to dismiss if the employer has not followed an appropriate procedure for the resolution of the dispute. An appropriate procedure is one established in a collective agreement.

What happens when the union or its members are in breach of an agreed procedure, for example, if the ballot for industrial action was not conducted properly? In these circumstances, and before seeking a legal remedy, it is important to consider all the options. Decisions on using legal intervention should never be taken without a full and extensive evaluation. Firstly, it might be appropriate to sit down with those who organised the ballot to discuss concerns about its validity. It is possible that they are already aware of its flaws, but are merely seeking to demonstrate the depth of feeling about a particular issue in order to get a resumption of negotiations. Alternatively, it might be appropriate to talk to those who might have been excluded from a ballot. They may be prepared to back the company in any dispute and it is possible their votes, in a rerun ballot, might overturn the original result. The third option is to seek an injunction against the union restraining it from taking any action until a proper ballot is conducted. Again, this can be a high-risk strategy because in a rerun ballot those who previously voted against the union might vote with them on the basis of solidarity.

Ultimately, as with many aspects of employee relations, whether particular employers choose to seek a legal remedy to constrain the actions of their workforce will depend on management style and whether there is a desire to maintain good working relationships.

SUMMARY

In this chapter we have looked at the link between corporate and business strategies and functional activities such as personnel. This has allowed us to see the relationship between the decisions of the board and the role of line managers in translating those decisions into actionable policies. We have looked at the process of strategy formulation and have seen that a number of different approaches are available. The methodology employed will, inevitably, differ, but as we saw in the discussion on types of environment, the markets that you operate in will have a clear impact on strategic choice. We have also tried to identify the link between business strategy and employee relations strategies and employment relations policies, but we also pointed out that employee relations, like every other function within the business, does not operate in a vacuum. This means that there has to be a relationship with employee development, reward and resourcing.

The chapter has also examined some of the issues that need to be taken into account when drawing up an employee relations policy and managing change. We have highlighted the need to incorporate monitoring mechanisms into policies so that checks can be made on effectiveness. We looked at the skills required in selecting and applying particular policies to the organisation and the skills needed to manage change effectively. Two key issues were identified. One was the need to evaluate new initiatives and ideas and the second was the need to gain overall commitment to particular policies. In the context of gaining commitment we highlighted a number of core skills which we feel are an absolute necessity for the professional personnel practitioner.

In this chapter we have also looked at management style and noted its role in the determination of an employee relations policy in respect of trade unionism, union recognition, non-unionism and an employer's use of the law. We noted that different organisations have different approaches to the role and involvement of unions and we examined the causes of non-unionism. We looked at some examples of non-union firms and whether their success was due to good management or the fact that they kept unions at arm's length. We concluded that good management was the most important factor. We identified the role that the law can play in management/union relationships and what factors employers needed to consider before they used the legal processes against trade unions or trade union members, but noted that decisions on whether, and when, to use the law can be quite complex and should not be taken lightly.

REFERENCES AND FURTHER READING

ARMSTRONG M. *Employee Reward*. London, Institute of Personnel and Development, 1996.

BLAKSTAD M. *and* COOPER A. *The Communicating Organisation*. London, Institute of Personnel and Development, 1997.

BLYTON P. *and* TURNBULL P. *The Dynamics of Employee Relations*. London, Macmillan, 1994.

BURNES B. *Managing Change: A strategic approach to organisational dynamics*. London, Pitman, 1996.

DELOITTE & TOUCHE. *Business Success and Human Resources*. Management Survey, 1998.

EMMOT M. 'Collectively cool'. *People Management*, Vol 5, No 2, January 1999.

GUEST D. 'Human resource management, trade unions and industrial relations', in Storey J. (ed.) *Human Resource Management: A critical text*. London, Routledge, 1995.

INSTITUTE OF PERSONNEL AND DEVELOPMENT. *The Impact of People Management Practices on Business Performance*. London, IPD, 1997.

JOHNSON G. *and* SCHOLES K. *Exploring Corporate Strategy*. 4th edn. Hemel Hempstead, Prentice-Hall, 1997.

JUDGE G. 'United firms stand, but divided they fail'. The *Guardian*. 29 April 1997.

KAY J. *Foundations of Corporate Success*. Oxford, OUP, 1993.

MARCHINGTON M. *and* WILKINSON A. *Core Personnel and Development*. London, Institute of Personnel and Development, 1996.

MASON R. 'Switchboard'. *People Management*. Vol 4, No 21, October 1998.

MCCARTNEY I. 'In all fairness'. *People Management*. Vol 4, No 18, September 1998.

MILLWARD N., STEVENS M., SMART D., *and* HAWES W. R. *Workplace Industrial Relations in Transition: The ED/ESRC/PSI/ACAS surveys*. London, Gower, 1992.

PORTER M. *Competitive Advantage: Creating and sustaining superior performance*. New York, Free Press, 1985.

PURCELL J. 'Mapping management styles in employee relations'. *Journal of Management Studies*, Vol 24, No 5, 1987. 535.

SALAMON M. *Industrial Relations Theory and Practice*. 3rd edn. Hemel Hempstead, Prentice-Hall, 1998.

TYSON S. *Human Resource Strategy: Towards a general theory of human resource management*. London, Pitman, 1995.

WALMSLEY H. 'A suitable ploy'. *People Management*. Vol 5, No 7, April 1997.

6 Employee involvement

Employee involvement covers a wide range of actions. It comprises any means of informing and consulting employees about, or associating them with, one or more aspects of running an organisation. As well as traditional forms of information and consultation it includes subjects such as financial participation, involving employees in problem-solving and quality management, including development and training. It concentrates on individual employees and the degree to which they associate with the aims and needs of the organisation. By the use of employee involvement and commitment, management seeks to gain consent from the employees for its proposed actions on the basis of commitment rather than control (Walton).

Employee participation, on the other hand, concerns the extent to which employees, often via their representative, are involved with management in the decision-making machinery of the organisation. This includes joint consultation, collective bargaining and worker representation on the board.

After reading this chapter you will be able to:

- explain the advantages of involving employees in the affairs of the business

- assess the strengths and weaknesses of the various involvement schemes available to management

- understand the importance of communicating with employees and participation schemes

- assess the situations in which involvement and participation schemes, in whatever form, are appropriate.

WHY INVOLVE EMPLOYEES?

The control-orientated approach to workforce management associated with FW Taylor took shape in the early part of the twentieth century in response to the growth in the division of labour into jobs for which individuals were considered accountable. To monitor and control effectiveness in these jobs, management organised itself into a hierarchy of specialised roles supported by a top-down allocation of authority and status symbols to their position in the hierarchy. At the centre of this workforce control method was the desire to establish order and efficiency from the employee who was expected to obey and not challenge management instructions.

However, increasing international competition and technological change in the last 20 years mean that higher skills and far greater flexibility are required of the employee. According to Walton (1985) in this environment a commitment strategy towards the workforce is required. In this strategic approach to managing the workforce jobs are designed more broadly than before (job enlargement) to combine planning and implementation and to include efforts to upgrade operations, not just to maintain them. Individual employee responsibilities are expected to change as conditions change (functional flexibility) and teams, not individuals, are accountable for employee performance. The teams will control how they will deliver their output objectives. Employees are thus empowered. A commitment strategy therefore involves dispensing with whole layers of management and minimising status differentials, with control depending on shared goals, and expertise rather than formal position determining influence.

According to Walton, under an employee commitment strategy performance expectations are high and serve not to establish minimum standards but to emphasise continuous improvement and reflect the requirements of the marketplace. As a result, pay and reward strategies reflect not the principles of job evaluation but the importance of group achievement and concerns for gain-sharing and profit-sharing. Equally important, claims Walton, is the challenge of giving employees some assurance of security by offering them priority in training and retraining as old jobs are destroyed and new ones created, and providing them with the means to be heard on issues such as production methods, problem-solving and human resource policies.

Underlying all these policies is a management philosophy that accepts the interests of a company's multiple stakeholders – owners, employees, customers and public. At the heart of this approach is an acceptance that growing employee commitment will lead to improved performance. No organisation in today's modern world can perform at peak levels unless each employee is committed to the corporate objectives and works as an effective team member. Employees want to use and develop their skills, enhance their careers and take pride in their work. The commitment strategy involves employees contributing their own ideas as to how their performance and the quality of product or service they provide can be improved. There is clear

Table 23 **The aims of employee involvement and participation**

The involvement of and the participation by employees in any organisation should aim to

- generate commitment of all employees to the success of the organisation
- enable the organisation better to meet the needs of its customers and adopt to changing market requirements
- help the organisation to improve performance and productivity, adopt new methods of working to match new technology
- improve the satisfaction employees get from their work
- provide all employees with the opportunity to influence and be involved in decisions which are likely to affect their interests.

evidence that employees want to be part of a successful organisation which provides a good income and opportunity for development and secure employment.

Harnessing this potential enthusiasm requires an investment of time and resources to build up mutual trust and understanding. The potential rewards are great. Many organisations have discussed the benefits employee commitment can bring. The Department of Employment publication, *The Competitive Edge*, quotes the following examples:

- Improved performance and productivity. One case study company reported a 33 per cent drop in production costs as a result of implementing new employee involvement initiatives.

- Improved quality and customer care – a 55 per cent reduction in customer complaints was achieved by a large manufacturer

- A more co-operative atmosphere in the workplace – reduced costs and increased profits enabling many companies to make resources available to improve employees' terms and conditions of employment

- Reduced staff turnover – most companies reported an increase in employee job satisfaction

- Reduced lost time through absenteeism and disputes – one company reported absenteeism halved

- Added value through drawing on the skills and knowledge of employees – operating profit per full time employee increased by 58 per cent over a five-year period.

Employee involvement by giving employees greater influence and control over their own work and involving them in workplace decisions is designed to increase their commitment to the organisation and thereby, to mutual advantage, to improve the economic performance of the enterprise. However, commitment is a two-way process. Management also needs to demonstrate a commitment to its employees in terms of:

- job security

- pay and other employment conditions (single status)

- access to training and retraining

- provision of a safe working environment

- a balance between work and employees' commitments outside the workplace (for example, families).

THE OBJECTIVES OF EMPLOYEE INVOLVEMENT METHODS

Ramsay (1996) points out that the means of achieving the aims of employee involvement lie in acting on five areas – changing attitudes, increasing business awareness, improving employee motivation, enhancing employee influence/ownership and the involvement of trade unions (see Table 24). This is not an exhaustive list but

Table 24 **Possible management objectives for employee involvement**

Attitudes

> Improved morale
> Increased loyalty and commitment
> Enhance sense of involvement
> Increased support for management

Business awareness

> Better, more accurately informed
> Greater interest
> Better understanding of reason for management action
> Support for/reduced resistance to management action

Incentive/motivation

Passive	Accept changes in working practices
	Accept mobility across jobs
	Accept new technology
	Accept management authority
Active	Improve quality/reliability
	Increased productivity/effort
	Reduced costs
	Enhanced co-operation and team spirit
Personal	Greater job interest
	Greater job satisfaction
	Employee development

Employee influence/ownership

> Increased job control
> Employee suggestions
> Increase employee ownership in the company
> Increase employee ties to company performance and profitability

Trade unions

Anti-union	Keeps union out of company
	Representative needs outside union channels
	Win hearts and minds of employee from union
With union	Gain union co-operation
	Draw on union advice
	Restrain union demands

Source: Ramsay in BJ Towers (ed) *The Handbook of Human Resource Management*, 2nd edn, Oxford, Blackwell, 1996

nevertheless demonstrates the need for careful definition of objectives. Vague and general terms like 'changed attitudes' or 'greater incentive' are inadequate for evaluating whether employee involvement schemes are operating as management intends. The list also illustrates the potential conflict, or at least strain, between employee involvement schemes. As Ramsay remarks:

> ... To exemplify this last point, a general sense of unity and belonging may sit poorly with the need to sharpen individual competition and incentive and it may be advisable to use distinct kinds of scheme to achieve each if both require enhancement.

Trade unions

In organisations where trade unions are recognised and membership is high, it is important management involves trade union representatives and their officials in developing participation arrangements and procedures. In some cases, especially where trade union density is high, their co-operation, support and advice are likely to be important factors in establishing employee involvement methods. Some employers, however, see employee involvement schemes as a means of restricting the scope of union influence. Evidence from WIRS (1990) published in the TUC Report, *Human Resource Management* (1994) showed that over the period 1987–90 inclusive, 54 per cent of establishments that derecognised unions introduced forms of employee involvement. However, caution is required before drawing the conclusion that employee involvement is a route to union avoidance. The same study also showed that 43 per cent of establishments who derecognised had made no attempt to develop wider employee involvement. Equally, 38 per cent of those employers without unions claimed to have implemented an employee involvement initiative during the same period.

If the management already recognises unions, then to use employee involvement methods to reduce its influence over its employees is a high-risk strategy. If the union has a high level of membership, controls its members, has bargaining power and delivers on agreements, then only an unprofessional manager would attempt to introduce employee involvement schemes as an alternative to dealing with a trade union. If the union has a low level of membership, cannot control its members, has little bargaining power and cannot keep to agreements, then management will have little difficulty in using employee involvement and participation schemes as a means of by-passing what is a weak trade union.

Increased business awareness
If the business's awareness of employees can be improved then they are more likely to be better and more accurately informed, the rumour 'grapevine' will be reduced and there is a higher probability they will have greater job interest, improved knowledge and understanding of the reasons for management decisions and greater support for (or resistance to) management action. Table 24 suggests that by using employee involvement schemes to increase employee influence/ownership, management is more likely to provide its employees with greater job control and at the same time, via financial participation schemes, create increased employee ownership in the company and enhanced employee ties to company performance and profitability.

Ramsay (1996) claims that if management can change employee incentive and motivation in a positive direction, it may have passive, active and personal effects. The employees may benefit from greater job interest, enhanced job satisfaction and increased opportunities to develop themselves. Active advantages may arise for the organisation stemming from improved quality/reliability of the product or service, increased labour productivity and effort, reduced costs and enhanced co-operation and team spirit. Amongst the passive advantages accruing to the organisation Ramsay notes these are likely to stem from a greater willingness on the part of employees to accept changes in working practices, flexibility across jobs, the implementation of new technology and enhanced first line management authority.

Increased commitment

As we have seen, if management can achieve a positive change in employee attitudes, this is likely to improve not only the morale of employees but also their loyalty and commitment to the organisation. Their sense of belonging and involvement is also likely to be enhanced. In addition, there will be a greater probability that employees will give greater support to management's position. Employee involvement mechanisms are thus an important means whereby management can bring about organisational cultural change. However, such cultural change can only be achieved in any organisation on an incremental basis. The full benefits to the organisation from cultural change arising from the successful implementation of involvement methods will not accrue immediately. The attitudes of every employee, or manager, will not change in a positive direction at the same moment in time. Some will take longer than others to develop a positive change in attitude towards the actions of management. Management needs to be aware of this phenomenon of incremental cultural change when reviewing and monitoring the impact of the introduction of employee involvement and participation schemes.

INVOLVEMENT MECHANISMS

General principles

So far we have examined the aims of employee involvement. We now turn to look at the various employee involvement and participation mechanisms available to management. In choosing the appropriate schemes, the guiding principle for management is the extent to which they will assist the organisation to achieve its corporate objectives. Management cannot select schemes at random. They must be relevant to the purposes which they are designed to achieve.

> Do you have employee involvement and participation schemes in your organisation? What do your managers expect to achieve from these schemes? If there are no involvement and participation schemes, why is this the case?

In implementing employee involvement schemes there are a number of basic principles to bear in mind. Amongst the most important are:

- The arrangements and procedures should be appropriate to the needs of the organisation.

- Agreement on arrangements should be arrived at jointly with the employees.

- The arrangements should involve trade unions where they are recognised by the organisation.

- The lead in establishing, operating and reviewing arrangements should be taken by management.

Table 25 **Principles underlying employee involvement schemes**

- General application to all organisations in which people are employed.
- Arrangements and procedures appropriate to the organisation. There is no one best scheme.
- Joint agreement on agreement for participation.
- Involvement of trade unions.
- Leadership by management.
- Inclusive of all employees
- Education and training to enable participants to fulfil their role in a constructive manner.
- Management retains the responsibility for business decisions.
- To employees' rights and trade unions' responsibilities not prejudiced.

- All employees in the organisation should be covered by the arrangements.

- Education and training should be provided to enable the participants in the arrangements to perform effectively.

- Management should retain full responsibility for business decisions.

- Employees' rights and trade unions' responsibilities should not prejudiced.

Needs of the organisation

Employee involvement and participation can be achieved through a wide range of schemes. However, those selected by management must be appropriate to the characteristics of the organisation including the nature of its activities, structure, technology and history. Processes and structures appropriate to older industries will not necessarily match the needs of newer organisations formed in a different social, industrial and commercial context. There is no one way of managing employee involvement and participation and the guiding principle must be that the arrangements are compatible with the organisation's circumstances. It is not essential, for example, to establish employee involvement mechanisms to help improve product and service delivery quality if the organisation operates in a product market where competitive advantages rests with price and not the quality and reliability of the product.

Joint agreement

Employee involvement and participation arrangements in organisations are best developed by joint agreement between management and the employees and/or their representatives. If arrangements are introduced on a jointly agreed basis then employees will have some ownership of them and will have a greater commitment to ensuring the success of schemes. If management imposes the arrangements, the employees have no ownership of them and therefore no stake in ensuring their success. Joint agreement by management and employees means joint commitment to operate the arrangements in good faith and as intended. Both parties have an interest in ensuring they succeed. It is something they have jointly created. In addition, employees see advantages in their representatives being involved in the management decision-making processes, if for no other reason than to act as the custodians of their interests and to ensure management accountability.

Employees are desirous that all levels of management should take notice of their views and concerns.

It thus makes sense on the basis of the joint agreement/joint commitment argument that best practice in introducing employee involvement and participation schemes into organisations where trade unions are recognised is that union representatives and their officials should be involved in deciding the appropriate arrangements and their operation. This helps reassure the trade unions that management's real agenda is not to undermine their influence. In initiating the necessary action to implement effective schemes the lead must come from management. Employee involvement and participation will not occur or develop of their own accord.

Training and development
Two other key principles are that there should be the opportunity for all employees, including managers, to participate in employee involvement participation schemes and that appropriate training and education should be provided for the participants in the schemes. The former principle involves all employees having the confidence that their views, which are being actively sought, will be taken into account by management before it makes a final decision and not after it has made a decision. An important consideration in this regard is the quality of relationships between individual employees and their immediate superiors and managers. If the quality of decisions made by management is to be improved, then they must gain information by listening to what their employees have to say and by asking them appropriate questions. By the same token, employees require information from employers. Both employees and employers require training in communication skills, presentational skills and chairing meeting skills.

Employee involvement and participation arrangements do not relieve management of its responsibility for making business decisions falling within the area of its own accountability and for communicating such decisions, with relevant background information, to the employees. The quality of management business decisions is likely to be improved if it takes into account, before making a final decision, the views of the workforce and/or their representatives. However, the employees do not have a veto on management decisions. The prerogative to make business decisions continues to lie with management.

Employee involvement forms
Although it can take a multiplicity of different forms, effective employee involvement is likely to comprise most if not all of the following elements:

• effective and continuous two-way communication between management and employee, especially about the organisation's objectives and its progress towards reaching them

• encouragement of employees to contribute their knowledge and experience to operational decisions

• promoting employees' commitment to achieving the organisation's goals; this is most directly achieved through profit- or target-related pay or employee share ownership schemes

• training all employees to ensure that they are able to perform their jobs efficiently and effectively

• doing things in the way best suited to the particular culture and needs of the organisation.

There is no single model for successful employee involvement. Many considerations have to be taken into account by management in deciding which techniques to select (see Table 26). Individual organisations have to develop and adapt arrangements to fit their own needs. These can vary over time as the organisation's size, structure and activities change. There is no single blueprint for success. Consideration has to be given to the context in which the arrangements will be introduced and operated. If they are to be introduced as part of a coherent and consistent strategy to improve the performance of the enterprise, then the proposed arrangements to be introduced will be the result of a full evaluation of all the possible techniques. On the other hand, if they are being introduced to deal with a crisis situation then it is likely the arrangements selected will have been ill-thought out and possibly rationalised on the flimsy basis that the employee involvement arrangements have been successfully introduced in other organisations. Without any detailed assessment and evaluation, the management will be assuming the arrangements can be transplanted successfully into their own organisation. Arrangements introduced without proper analysis and evaluation are unlikely to be successful, or to provide management with the expected advantages that might

Table 26 Factors to be considered in the selection of appropriate employee involvement and participation schemes

Context

• as part of a coherent and consistent strategy
• as part of 'crisis' management

Single v multiplicity of arrangements

• the mix can vary
• a greater mix does not necessarily mean a greater quality of arrangements

Integration

• between the mix of arrangements (horizontal integration)
• with the strategic objectives of the organisation as a whole (vertical integration)

Success elsewhere

• why successful elsewhere?
• could they be transplanted successfully elsewhere?

Legal

The Companies Act (1989)
• statement in Directors' Report describing action taken to introduce, maintain or develop information/communication consultation, financial participation and economic awareness

European Works Council Directive (1994) extended to UK (1997)
• European Union wide information and consultation systems in pan-European companies

accrue from the implementation of employee involvement and participation schemes.

Multiplicity of arrangements

Research by Marchington (1993) into the operation of involvement and participation arrangements revealed that single measures designed to enhance employee commitment to the organisation are much less likely to succeed than a multiplicity of arrangements. Nevertheless, the mix of employee involvement and participation techniques adopted must be appropriate to the organisation's needs as revealed by a thorough assessment and evaluation. Marchington (1993) found, for example, that in some companies the mix of employee involvement arrangements was no more than one or two practices, whereas in some larger manufacturing organisations there were as many as eight or nine different schemes for developing employee involvement and participation. However, he points out it is dangerous to assume that the greater the number of employee involvement and participation arrangements an organisation introduces, the greater will be their overall quality. He warns that multiple techniques can lead to potentially conflicting pressures and confusions or communication overload for the staff subject to these arrangements.

If a multiplicity of different employee involvement and participation schemes is appropriate, then not only must they integrate with each other (horizontal integration) but they must be integrated with the strategic objectives of the organisation as a whole (vertical integration). This may require schemes to be customised so that they are relevant and appropriate for the organisation's needs and practices (see below). Since a wide range of employee involvement and participation schemes are available to organisations, giving careful consideration to all of them before attempting to implement them is common sense. If employee involvement and participation arrangements are to make an impact they need to be integrated with the business objectives and be consistent with other management practices. Just because schemes have proved to be successful in one organisation there is no guarantee they will work as successfully in another organisation operating in a quite different context. Copying those arrangements that have been perceived to be successful elsewhere is a poor basis for selection. A full analysis and investigation of their appropriateness to another organisation is essential. Information is required on what factors made them successful in that organisation. Do these factors exist in other organisations? Are there factors at one organisation that would prevent the practice from being successfully transplanted in another organisation?

Legal requirements

There are also legal considerations influencing management's choice of which involvement and participation arrangements to introduce. The Companies Act 1989 requires any organisation employing more than 250 employees to include a statement in its Directors' report describing the action taken in the previous financial year to introduce, maintain or develop arrangements in the following areas:

- Information/communication – providing employees systematically with information on matters of concern to them as employees.

- Consultation – consulting employees or their representatives on a regular basis so that the views of employees can be taken into account in making decisions which are likely to affect their interests.

- Financial participation – encouraging the employees in the company's performance through an employee share scheme or some other means.

- Economic awareness – achieveing a common awareness on the part of all employees of the financial and economic factors affecting the performance of the company.

The European Works Council Directive 1994 provides for a European Union-wide information and consultation system to be set up in all organisations with more than 1,000 employees in European Union member states and employing more than 150 people in each of two or more of these. As the Directive was issued under the Agreement on Social Policy in the Social Protocol of the Maastricht Treaty 1993 and not the Social Chapter (see Chapter 3) at the time the UK was exempt from giving effect to the Directive. However in September 1997 the directive was extended to the UK (see Chapter 3). A Pan-European Works Council (or alternative system) must be agreed between the central management of the company and a Special Negotiating Body of employees elected from the various EU countries in which the company has productive capacity.

The Directive requires the establishment of a European Works Council of employee representatives with the right to meet central management at least once a year for information and consultation about the progress and prospects of the company on a pan-european basis. At this annual meeting, the employees' representative will receive information and be consulted about the enterprise's structure, economic and financial situation, probable developments in the business and in production and sales, the employment situation and probably trends, investments and substantial change concerning the organisation, new working methods of production processes, transfers of production, mergers, cutbacks or closures of undertakings, establishments or important parts thereof or collective redundancy. Employees also have the right in exceptional circumstances to trigger an additional meeting with management to be informed and consulted on 'measures significantly affecting employees' interests'.

COMMUNICATIONS AND BRIEFING SYSTEMS

Communication systems
Employee communications means the provision and exchange of information and instructions which enable an organisation to function effectively and employees to be properly informed about developments. It covers the information to be provided, the channels along which it passes and the way it is communicated. Communication is concerned with the interchange of information and ideas within an organisation.

Whatever the size of an organisation and regardless of whether it is unionised or non-unionised, employees only perform at their best if they know their duties, obligations and rights and have an opportunity of making their views known to management on issues that affect them. With the trend towards flatter management structures and the devolution of responsibilities to individuals, it is increasingly important that individuals have an understanding not only of what they are required to do but why they need to do it.

Good communication and consultation are central to the management process. All managers need to exchange information with other managers which necessitates lateral or interdepartmental communications. Failure to recognise this need is likely to result in inconsistency of approach or application. The ACAS Advisory booklet on Employee Communications and Consultation lists the advantages of good employee communications as follows:

- improved organisational performance – time spent communicating at the outset of a new project or development can minimise subsequent rumour and misunderstanding

- improved management performance and decision-making – allowing employees to express their views can help managers arrive at sound decisions which are more likely to be accepted by the employees as a whole

- improved employee performance and commitment – employees will perform better if they are given regular, accurate information about their jobs such as updated technical instructions, targets, deadlines and feedback. Their commitment is also likely to be enhanced if they know what the organisation is trying to achieve and how they as individuals can influence decisions

- greater trust – discussing issues of common interest and allowing employees an opportunity to express their views can engender improved management-employee relations

- increased job satisfaction – employees are more likely to be motivated if they have a good understanding of their job and how it fits into the organisation as a whole and are actively encouraged to express their views and ideas.

Employee communications strategy
When devising an employee communications strategy, the following questions have to be addressed:

- Why should the company communicate?

- What is to be communicated?

- Who are the audience(s)?

- How is communication to be handled?

- Who is responsible?

- How will success be measured?

In the IDS/IPD publication, *The Merit Factor – Rewarding Individual Performance*, 12 rules for internal communications were produced, and these are worth listing here as a background to any communications plan or strategy:

Table 27 **Information to be communicated**

Information about conditions of employment

- Written statements specifying the main contractual details within two months of the commencement of employment.
- Written statement must cover pay, hours of work, holidays, length of notice of termination and, where there are more than 20 employees, any disciplinary rules.
- Itemised pay statement.

Information about the job

- Work objectives and performance.
- General information (administrative procedures, social and welfare facilities).
- Arrangements for trade union representation.
- Operating and technical instructions (work to be carried out, use of equipment, standards to be met, reporting procedures).
- Health and safety matters.

Information about the organisation

- The organisation's objectives and policy.
- The organisation's past and present performance and progress.
- Future plans and prospects.
- Financial performance, state of the market, order book.
- Developments in technology and methods.
- Investment.
- Changes in product or services.
- Financial data – sales, turnover, income and expenditure, profit and loss, assets and liabilities, cash flow, return on investment and added value.

Source: ACAS Advisory Booklet *Employee Communications and Consultation.*

- If a board cannot or will not clearly spell out its business strategy, employees are entitled to assume it does not have one.

- Assume that in an information vacuum, people will believe the worst.

- Never take it for granted that people know what you are talking about.

- Always take if for granted that people doing a job know more about it than you do.

- Telling people something once is not much better than not telling them at all.

- Never assume that people will tell you anything that reflects unfavourably upon themselves.

- Remember that employees read newspapers, magazines and books, listen to radio and watch television.

- Do not be afraid to admit you were wrong; it gives people confidence that you know what you are doing.

- Asking for help, taking advice, consulting and listening to others are signs of great strength.

- Communicating good news is easy but even this is not often done by management; bad news is all too often left to rumours and the grapevine.

Figure 8 Conditions for successful implementation of employee
involvement and participation schemes

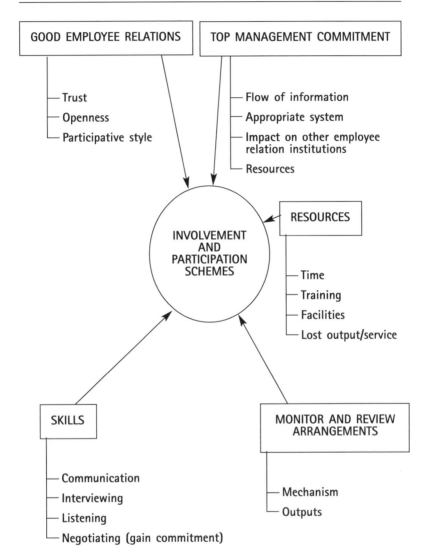

- Changing attitudes in order to change behaviour takes years;
  changing behaviour changes attitudes in weeks.

- There is no such thing as stone-cold certainty in business decisions.

Implementing an employee communications strategy
A variety of communication methods (both spoken and written, direct
and indirect) are available for use by management. The mix of
methods selected will be determined by the size and structure of the
organisation. Two main methods of communication can be
distinguished. First, there are face-to-face methods which are direct

and swift and enable discussion, questioning and feedback to take place. However, it is often advantageous to supplement these methods by written materials, especially if the information being conveyed is detailed or complex. The main formal face-to-face methods of communications are:

- group meetings – meetings between managers and the employees for whom they are responsible

- cascade networks – a well-defined procedure for passing information quickly and used mainly in large or widespread organisations

- large-scale meetings – meetings involving all employees in an organisation or at an establishment, with presentations by a director or senior managers; these are a good channel for presenting the organisation's performance or long-term objectives

- inter-departmental briefings – meetings between managers in different departments encourage a unified approach and reduce the scope for inconsistent decision-making, particularly in larger organisations.

Second, there are written methods. These are most effective where the need for the information is important or permanent, the topic requires detailed explanation, the audience is widespread or large and there is a need for a permanent record. The chief methods of written communications include company handbooks, employee information notes, house journals and newsletters, departmental bulletins, notices and individual letters to employees. Electronic mail is useful for communicating with employees in scattered or isolated locations whilst audio visual aids are particularly useful for explaining technical developments or financial performance.

Communications strategies, policies and techniques need senior management support and they require discipline to follow them through. Industry and commerce are littered with communications schemes which were introduced with the best of intentions but other matters became priorities and briefing sessions or newsletters were missed. The outcome is the development of cynicism amongst employees. It is also true that strategies, policies and tools tend not to be effective without the support and interest of staff. As it is put in the publication *Profit with People*:

> ... think of it this way. If I am not a big enthusiast, preferring to laze around the house at weekends, the existence of a tool box in the house is unlikely to persuade me to put in a couple of shelves. However, if I am very enthusiastic about DIY and very keen to put up the couple of shelves, the fact that I have no tool box will not deter me. I will simply borrow or buy a tool box. It is my enthusiasm that is the driver, not the toolbox ...

Monitoring
It cannot be taken for granted that communications systems are operating effectively nor can it be assumed that because information is sent it is also received. The communications policy and its associated procedures need regular monitoring and review to ensure practice matches policy, the desired benefits are accruing, the information is

accepted, received and understood, and the management communicators know their roles. Monitoring is largely dependent on feedback from employees through both formal and informal channels although other indicators will include the quality of decision-making by management, the involvement of senior management and the extent of employee co-operation. In monitoring and reviewing an organisation's communication policy, the criteria for assessing its effectiveness will therefore be related to the outputs from the operation of the policy. For example, has employee morale improved? Has productivity increased? Is there a greater willingness to accept change on the part of employees and managers? Do the employees have an improved understanding of the company and business generally? Review and monitoring should take place on a regular periodic basis, for example quarterly or annually, depending on the size of the organisation.

Briefing groups

Dangers of the use of such groups, from a management perspective, are that as the information 'cascades' down, it becomes watered down, hedged around with rumour, becomes out of date and imprecise. As we noted above, many communications policies are less effective than they might be because a lot of information passed down from the top to the bottom of the organisation concentrates on the wider perspective with the result that the local receivers of the information do not take note of it as it relates to issues which to them are remote and marginal to their interests and concerns.

Of all the communication methods in use, team briefing is perhaps the most systematic in the provision of top-down information to employees. Information is disseminated or 'cascades' through various management tiers, being conveyed by the immediate supervisor or team leader to a small group of employees, the optimum number being between four and 20. In this way, too, employee queries are answered. This takes place throughout all levels of the organisation, the information eventually being conveyed by supervisors and/or team leaders to shopfloor employees. On each occasion the information received is supplemented by 'local' news of more immediate relevance to those being briefed. Meetings tend to be short but designed to help develop the 'togetherness' of a workgroup, especially where there are different grades of employee involved in the team.

Each manager will be a member of a briefing group and will also be responsible for briefing a team. The system is designed to ensure all employees from the managing director to the shopfloor are fully informed of matters affecting their work. Leaders of each briefing session prepare their own brief, consisting of information which is relevant and task-related to the employees in the group. The brief is then supplemented with information which has been passed down from higher levels of management. Any employee questions raised which cannot be answered at the time are answered in written form within a few days. Briefers from senior management levels are usually encouraged to sit in at briefings being given by more junior managers whilst line managers are encouraged to be available to brief the shopfloor employees. While team briefing is not a consultative process and is basically one-way, question and answer sessions do take place to clarify understanding. Feedback from employees is very important and professional managers will explain management's view to the employees in a regular and open way, using examples appropriate to each workgroup.

There are, however, practical problems to be borne in mind in introducing team briefing. First, if the organisation operates on a continuous shift working basis, is it technically feasible for team briefings to take place since the employees are working all the time except for their rest breaks? Second, management has to be confident it can sustain a flow of relevant and detailed information. Third, if the organisation recognises unions the management cannot act in such a manner that the union(s) believes management is attempting to undermine its influence. Team briefing cannot possibly succeed if the relationships between management and the representatives of its employees are distrustful.

TASK AND WORK GROUP INVOLVEMENT

The objective of these employee involvement and participation techniques is to tap into employees' knowledge of their jobs, either at the individual level or through the mechanism of small groups. These techniques are designed to increase the stock of ideas within the organisation to encourage co-operative relations at work and to justify change. Task-based involvement encourages employees to extend the range and type of tasks they undertake at work. It is probably the most innovative method of employee involvement given that it focuses on the whole job rather than comprising a relatively small part of an employee's time at work. Such techniques include job redesign, job enrichment, team working and job enlargement. Job enrichment centres on increasing the number and diversity of tasks carried out by an individual employee, thereby increasing their work experience and skill.

Team working is seen by its advocates as a vehicle for greater task flexibility and co-operation as well as for extending the desire for quality improvement. Geary (1994) remarks:

> In its most advanced form team working refers to the granting of autonomy to workers by management to design and prepare work scheduled, to monitor and control their own work tasks and methods to be more or less self-managing. There can be considerable flexibility between different skills categories, such that skilled employees do unskilled tasks when required and formerly unskilled employees would receive additional training to be able to undertake the more skilled tasks. At the other end of the spectrum, management may merely wish employees of comparable skill to rotate between different tasks on a production line or the integration of maintenance personnel to service a particular group of machines. It may not result in production workers undertaking tasks which were formerly the preserve of craft people or vice versa. Thus, flexibility may be confined within comparable skills groupings. In between, there is likely to be a diversity of practice.

The team size is usually seven to ten people, although some are much larger. Task flexibility and job rotation can, however, be limited, partly by the sheer range of tasks and partly by the nature of the skills involved. Organisations operating team working programmes see major training programmes as a necessary accompaniment. Team working provides management with the opportunity to remove and/or amend the role of the supervisor and to appoint team leaders. However, research by Grapper (1990) indicates management time saved in traditional supervision and control may be more than offset by the need to give support to individuals and groups.

Quality circles

A quality circle aims to identify, in a section of the workplace, work-related problems causing low quality of service or productivity and to recommend solutions to the problems. They provide opportunities for employees to meet on a regular basis (once a month, fortnightly) for an hour or so to suggest ways of improving productivity and quality and reducing costs. They typically involve a small group of employees (usually six to eight) in discussions seeking to resolve problems which are work-related under the guidance of their supervisor. Their members select the issues or problem they wish to address, collect the necessary information and suggest to management ways of overcoming the problem.

In some cases, the group itself is given authority to put its proposed solutions into effect but more often it presents formal recommendations for action, which management considers whether or not to implement. Quality circles encourage employees not only to identify with the quality of their own work but also with the management objectives of better quality and increased efficiency throughout the organisation. Members of a quality circle are not usually employee representatives, but are members of the circle by virtue of their knowledge of the tasks involved in their jobs. They are under no obligation to report back to their colleagues who are not members of the circle.

If quality circles are to be effective, a strong commitment from management is necessary. Management does not supply members to a quality circle but allows time and money for its members to meet and provides them with basic training in problem-solving and presentational skills. A professional management treats all recommendations from a quality circle with an open mind and if it rejects a proposal will explain reasons for the decision to the circle. If the organisation recognises trade unions then it is advisable to consult them on the establishment of quality circles and to encourage their support for a device which, if operated properly, will contribute to constructive employee relations.

After a dramatic increase in their number such that by the mid-1980s over 400 such circles were known to be in existence, the popularity of quality circles declined rapidly. Quality circles fail either at their introduction or after a short period of operation, mainly because of a lack of top management commitment, a lack of an effective facilitator to promote and sustain the programme, a management unwillingness to bear the costs of operating circles in terms of time, including training time for participants, employees being off the job and through an absence of the suggestions from circles being followed up and acted upon by management.

Total Quality Management (TQM)

Total quality management programmes derive from a belief that competitive advantage comes not simply from low cost competitiveness but from high and reliable quality, achieved from the associated welding of more stable and mutual relationships between suppliers and customers. The total quality ethic is a philosophy of business management, the aim of which is to ensure complete customer satisfaction at every stage of production or service provision. Although TQM was initially driven by the demands of external customers, the concept has evolved into a more wide-ranging principle to encompass internal operations. TQM programmes are designed to ensure that each level and aspect of the organisation is involved in continuously improving the effectiveness and quality of the work to meet the requirements of both internal and external customers.

While quality issues were traditionally assigned to specific departments, TQM requires that the quality of products and services is the concern of every employee. Quality management offers service management an effective way of organising and increasing employees' responsibility while meeting the interests of employees at every level offering them an opportunity to become more involved in the decision-making process. The Prudential Assurance Company claimed in the mid-1990s that TQM had produced many benefits for them, including a reduction of 45 per cent in the average time spent in dealing with a life assurance claim.

Geary (1994) points out that TQM places considerable emphasis on enlarging employees' responsibilities, reorganising work and increasing employee involvement in problem-solving activities and that this search for continuous improvement is a central thrust. He further notes:

> ... The manufacture of quality products, the provision of a quality service and the quest for continuous improvement are the responsibility of all employees, managed and manager alike, and all functions. TQM requires quality to be built into the product and not inspected by a separate quality department. Where employees are not in direct contact with the organisation's customers, they are encouraged to see their colleagues at successive stages of the production process as internal customers. Thus, a central feature of TQM is the internalisation of the rigours of the marketplace within the enterprise.

A second feature of TQM follows on from the first. As each employee and department is an internal customer to the other, problem-solving necessitates the formation of organisational structures designed to facilitate interdepartmental and interfunctional co-operation. A consequence of this is that problems are best solved by those people to which they are most immediate. Employees are to be encouraged and given the resources to solve problems for themselves. Employees, it is contended, will embrace such job enlargement and undertake activities conducive to an improvement in the organisation's efficiency.

Ramsay (1996) argues that total quality management subsumes quality circles or team work arrangements into a more integrated approach and concentrates on stressing change throughout the entire organisational system. It is essentially a top-down management-driven process. If total quality management is to succeed, again top management commitment is essential. Departments have to be persuaded that resistance to integration is self-defeating whilst the employees need to have demonstrated to them that total quality management is not a cover for job rationalisation and redundancies. In short, the employees require evidence there is a 'stake' for them in the total quality management 'world' that is superior to their present world.

FINANCIAL PARTICIPATION

Offering employees a direct stake in the ownership and prosperity of the business for which they work is one of the most direct and tangible forms of employee involvement. By giving employees the chance to participate in financial success, employees can stimulate a greater sense of identity with the business and an appreciation of the business needs; employers also benefit. A financial stake gives them increased enthusiasm for the success of the organisation and often a voice in its operation. In its most developed form, employee share ownership means that employees become significant shareholders in the business, or even their own employer.

Financial employee involvement and participation schemes link specific elements of pay and reward to the performance of the unit or the enterprise as a whole. They provide an opportunity for employees to share in the financial success of their employing organisation. The main forms of financial participation are:

- profit-related pay
- employee share schemes
- profit-sharing schemes
- discretionary share option schemes
- employee share ownership plans.

Profit sharing
These schemes aim to increase employee motivation and commitment by giving employees an interest in the overall performance of the enterprise. In this way management hopes to raise employee awareness of the importance of profit to their organisation and that rewards which accrue from co-operative effort, rather than individual effort, encourage teamwork. Profit-sharing schemes ensure employees benefit from the organisation making profits.

However, there are practical problems which must be addressed if profit-sharing schemes are to have the desired effect. Any scheme has to contain clearly identifiable links between effort and reward. Individuals must not feel that no matter how hard they work in any year that effort is not reflected in their share of the company's profits. There is also the issue of whether there is a clearly understood formula for the sharing of any profits so that employees can calculate their share. Profits cannot be assessed quickly enough to secure early movements in pay in response to rapidly changing market conditions. Due account has to be taken of employee feelings of equity and fairness or there is a risk of intergroup dissatisfaction in that some employees might perceive other groups have received the same profit-share payment but have made less effort.

Profit-related pay

Profit-related pay is a mechanism through which employers can reward employees for their contribution to the business. It works by linking a proportion of employees' pay to the profits of the business for which they work. Employees are encouraged in this way to strive for commercial success. Employers who have introduced such schemes tell us that, as well as helping to create a more motivated and committed workforce, profit-related pay provides greater flexibility in the negotiation of pay settlements. Registered schemes provide employers with significant tax benefits. Profit-related pay is tax free up to a limit of 20 per cent of pay or £4,000, whichever is the lower. There are estimated currently to be 7,000 live registered schemes covering some two million employees.

Share ownership

Share ownership takes financial involvement a step further by giving employees a stake in the ownership of the enterprise. It grants them shareholder rights to participate in decisions confined to shareholders voting at the annual general meeting. Employee share ownership schemes seek to give individual employees a long-term commitment to the organisation and not just to a short-term financial gain from a sharing of profit. Such schemes are usually linked to profit but the employees' portion is distributed in the form of shares, either directly to each individual or indirectly into a trust which holds the shares on behalf of all employees. Distributing shares to employees involves them in a tax liability and has restricted the development of employee share ownership schemes. A means of avoiding this tax liability are employee share ownership plans (known as ESOP) which were given a boost when the UK Government in the late 1980s provided important tax concessions for investment in such schemes.

In employee share ownership plans the company shares are initially bought, using borrowed money, by a trust representing the employees. They may not be required to put down a cash stake. The transfer of a portion of the company profits to the trust over subsequent years, as laid down in the initial agreement, enables the trust to pay off the loan and to allocate shares to individual employees.

Employee share ownership plans are clearly a means of promoting employee involvement in ownership. They give individual employees democratic control over significant holdings of company shares. They also have limitations. Employees may view the shares as simply a source of income, thereby undermining the 'shared ownership' concept. Financial participation shares money and on its own is unlikely to give rise to a greater commitment on the part of the individual employee to the interests of the organisation.

Do you have any employee involvement schemes in your organisation? If yes, why those particular schemes? To what extent and why are they effective?

REPRESENTATIVE PARTICIPATION

The main form of representative participation is joint consultation, which is a process by which management and employees or their representatives jointly examine and discuss issues of mutual concern. It involves seeking acceptable solutions to problems through a genuine exchange of views and information. Consultation does not remove the right of management to manage – they must still make the final decision – but it does impose an obligation that the views of employees will be sought and considered before final decisions are taken. We saw that employee communication is concerned with the interchange of information and ideas within an organisation. Consultation goes beyond this and involves managers actively seeking and then taking account of the views of employees before making a decision. It affects the process through which decisions are made in so far as it commits management first to the disclosure of information at an early stage in the decision-making process and second to take into account the collective views of the employees.

Consultation does not mean that employees' views always have to be acted on since there may be good practical or financial reasons for not doing so. However, whenever employees' views are rejected the reasons for doing so should be carefully explained. Equally, where the views and ideas of employees help to improve a decision, due credit and recognition should be given. Making a practice of consulting on issues that management has already decided is unproductive and engenders suspicion and mistrust about the process amongst employees.

Consultation requires a free exchange of ideas and views affecting the interests of employees. As such, almost any subject is appropriate for discussion. However, both management and trade unions may wish to place some limits on the range of subjects open to consultation, for example because of trade confidences or because they are considered more appropriate for a negotiation forum. However, whatever issues are agreed upon as being appropriate for discussion, it is important that they are relevant to the group of employees that will be discussing them. If consultation arrangements are to be effective it is important to avoid them discussing trivialities. This is not to say that minor issues should be ignored. Although the subject of consultation are a matter for agreement between employer and employees, there are a number of issues upon which employers are legally required to consult with recognised trade unions. These are:

- The Health and Safety at Work Act 1974 places a duty on employers to consult with safety representatives appointed by an independent recognised trade union.

- The Transfer of Undertakings (Protection of Employment) Regulations 1981 provide for trade unions to be consulted where there is a transfer of a business to which the regulations apply. This consultation must take place with a view to reaching agreement on the measures taken.

- The Trade Union and Labour Relations (Consolidation) Act 1992 requires employers to consult with trade unions when redundancies are proposed. Such consultation must be undertaken by the employer with a view to reaching agreement and must be about ways of avoiding the dismissals, reducing the numbers to be dismissed and mitigating the consequences of any redundancies.

- The Social Security Pensions Act 1975 requires employers to consult with trade unions on certain matters in relation to the contracting out of the state scheme of an occupational pension scheme.

Joint Consultative Committees

Joint Consultative Committees (JCC) or Works Councils as they are sometimes known, have long been used as a method of employee consultation. They are composed of managers and employee representatives who come together on a regular basis to discuss issues of mutual concern. They usually have a formal constitution which governs their operations. The number of members of a JCC will vary depending on the size of the organisation. However, as a general rule the size of the committee should be as small as possible consistent with ensuring that all significant employee groups are represented. It is necessary, in order to demonstrate management's commitment to consultation, that the management representatives on the committee include senior managers with authority and standing in the organisation and who regularly attend its meetings.

Every meeting of the JCC should have as its focus a well-prepared agenda and all members should be given the opportunity of contributing to the agenda before it is circulated. The agenda should be sent out in advance of the meeting so that representatives have the opportunity of consulting with their constituents prior to the committee meeting. The JCC needs to be well chaired if it is to be run effectively. It is important that employee representatives know exactly how much time they will be allowed away from their normal work to undertake their duties as committee members and what facilities they are entitled to use. Employee representatives need to be reassured that they will not lose pay as a result of attending committee meetings. If joint consultation is to be effective, the deliberations of the committee should be reported back to employees as soon as possible. This can be done via briefing groups, news sheets, noticeboards and the circulation of committee minutes.

Do JCCs exist in your organisation? If so, what forms do they take and are they successful? How could they be improved? If there are no JCCs, what mechanisms are in place to consult with the workforce? Would a JCC be useful? Why/why not?

INTRODUCTION OF EMPLOYEE INVOLVEMENT SCHEMES

In implementing employee involvement schemes, employee relations managers will be mindful that different organisations operate under very different environmental circumstances and what is good for one may not necessarily be appropriate for another. There are a number of necessary conditions to be met if employee involvement and participation arrangements are to be successfully implemented and operated.

First, a good employee relations climate is essential. Second, if a strong commitment to the introduction and operation of the schemes is not forthcoming from top management there is little likelihood they will have much chance of survival beyond their initial establishment. If such commitment is forthcoming, there is a greater likelihood that there will be a free flow of information up, down and across the organisation, that employee involvement mechanisms appropriate to the organisation's needs will be selected and that the impact of the operation of the schemes on the value and credibility of other employee relations institutions and procedures will be protected. A management prepared to commit resources in terms of time, lost wages, training, facilities and lost output/service to support the operation of employee involvement schemes is increasing the probability that they will be successful. Appropriate mechanisms to review and monitor the operation of employee involvement and participation arrangements to ensure they are achieving their objectives are also a necessary condition. However, they are not sufficient on their own to improve their chances of success. Management requires the skills of oral and written communication, interviewing, listening and team building. It also needs negotiating skills to gain the commitment of managerial colleagues and the workforce to the implementation of selected employee involvement and participation schemes. Without management and employee commitment, employee involvement and participation schemes will not survive very long. Let us now look at these conditions in more detail.

Good employee relations

Employee involvement schemes are more likely to be effective if there is a willingness on the part of both management and employees/the union to be open in their attitude and behaviour. Employee involvement and commitment will not be gained in an atmosphere of lack of trust and motivation. Effective schemes require 'openness' and trust of each other on the part of employees. They cannot operate effectively in a background of disputes and confrontation. If there is insufficient motivation on the part of management and employees to make involvement and participation techniques work, or there is insufficient mutual trust to allow them to work, this is more likely to be the cause of their failure than the substance of the arrangements. If management introduces employee involvement and participation schemes but shortly afterwards changes its management style to one that is less open and participative, the employees are likely to regard this behaviour as management attempting deliberately to sabotage the schemes. Employee scepticism towards employee involvement and participation schemes will arise and the schemes will be less effective.

Good employee relations is thus a necessary precondition for effective employee involvement and participation schemes. An open style of management in which employee support for proposed action is gained by consent, and not coercion, is essential. However, by itself a good employee relations environment is not a sufficient condition for the successful implementation and operation of involvement and participation schemes. This also requires unquestioning commitment from top management.

Commitment by top management

This is a key condition but again is not sufficient on its own to deliver effective involvement and participation schemes. They are unlikely, however, to be effective unless top management, by its own behaviour, demonstrates a belief in such schemes. Top management's commitment requires not only to be felt positively but also to be seen to be so by employees. All managers should accept the value of employee involvement and participation schemes and not give the impression they are supporting a 'fad' in management practice or are speaking rhetoric behind which there is no substance. While a good committee structure may be important for some participation schemes, it is totally irrelevant if individual managers are not committed to their success. Support for introducing employee involvement and participation schemes needs to be secured throughout the whole management structure. If management are not committed to their success, employees will view the arrangements as 'tokenism' and not genuine attempts to gain their commitment, loyalty and support.

If managers wish employee involvement schemes to succeed then they must ensure there is no loss of momentum following the initial enthusiasm of their introduction. Management commitment has to last longer than just the introduction of schemes, since many are costly in management time if they are not run properly. Nothing destroys employee participation schemes more quickly than management action that is inconsistent with the philosophy of worker involvement. This is particularly so when management's behaviour conveys to the employees that it really considers employment involvement and participation of little significance and something which is quickly dropped when there is short-term production/service provision pressure to meet customer needs. Care needs to be exercised by management in deciding the timing of meetings. If they are scheduled late on a Friday afternoon and there is little opportunity to explore issues in sufficient depth, then employees will question management's commitment to employee involvement as a means of improving management decision-making. The same applies if employees feel their views do not really count since their contributions are dismissed without serious examination.

Two important causes of failure of employee involvement and participation schemes are the attitudes of middle and lower managers to such schemes, and what Marchington (1993) calls the 'lack of continuity caused by the dynamic career patterns of managers who are the driving force behind the schemes'. Middle and supervisory management often lack commitment to, and support for, the development of employee involvement and participation schemes. Some regarded them as mechanisms by which senior/top managers 'pamper' the employees and their representatives and at the same time undermine supervisory authority over employees. They perceive top management in supporting employee involvement and participation as being 'soft' on employees who they perceive as only too pleased to be paid whilst not working and who, as a result, will always have issues they want to discuss with employers.

Frequently in large multi-firms, senior managers only expect to stay at an establishment for a short period of time and the time there is regarded as part of their development package en route to senior management positions. Marchington (1993) refers to this phenomena as the 'Mobile Champion', reflecting a picture of the manager who introduces a scheme then moves on to other duties, frequently at another site, or to employment elsewhere. The successor often has different priorities and the employee involvement schemes which were the 'baby' of the predecessor lapse because of operational difficulties or because the successor expects no praise from his/her senior managers for administering another individual's creation.

The introduction of employee involvement and participation arrangements on the basis of fashion and 'fad' will quickly create feelings of disillusionment amongst employees and a suspicion that management has no real focus to its current and future activities. However, a management committed to employee involvement is highly unlikely to select arrangements on the basis of 'fad' rather than what is appropriate to the organisation's commercial and business needs. Proper analysis of the objectives desired from any participation arrangements before their introduction should prevent any possible confusion or conflict between the arrangements introduced. This is particularly important when the organisation is introducing a multiplicity of schemes. Rather than just select any scheme, it can be helpful to management to give extremely careful consideration as to how it will apply and modify any schemes introduced to the needs of the workplace. Schemes which are 'customised' (see above) offer better prospects for success than those that are lifted down from the shelf and which may clash with production or service provision considerations.

An all too common mistake by management in introducing involvement and participation schemes is that they become seduced by the prevalence of public relations accounts into believing that any scheme introduced is a panacea to solve their product market problems. The impact of employee involvement and participation in securing a positive change in employee attitudes and behaviour is less profound and permanent than is often claimed if schemes selected turn out to be inappropriate to an organisation's needs. The inappropriate choice of systems is most noticeable, Marchington (1993) claims, amongst companies which bring in consultants to advise them on how to implement a new scheme without establishing its relevance or purpose. A company might decide to introduce a system of monthly team briefings. However, it is a waste of time to do so without having assessed whether there will be sufficient information to sustain it on that basis or whether the supervisor has the necessary skills or motivation to make it work. This difficult problem becomes further complicated when different management functions or levels in the management structure have a responsibility for introducing employee involvement, often at the same time and with conflicting objectives. This is especially the situation with service sector companies where the issue of customer care often falls within the province of both the personnel and the marketing departments.

A management fully committed to employee involvement and participation will ensure those participating in such schemes have access to a free flow of information to enable them to operate effectively. This flow of information is most effective if it is up, down and across the organisation. A willingness to listen, evaluate and act on views expressed by employees is a sensible approach. There are many pitfalls into which management can fall with respect to the information it makes available to participants in the employee involvement schemes. Management needs to strike a balance between providing too little information and providing too much information, otherwise employees can become confused. Managers have to avoid too much 'tell and sell' since this triggers employee mistrust of involvement and participation schemes, especially if most information is bad news and is accompanied by rallying calls for belt-tightening and restraint.

Effective employment involvement and participation involve two-way communication. To focus on downwards communication carries the risk that employees and/or their representatives might feel they are only being informed of changes or decisions after the event rather than before. This may seem an obvious statement but, unfortunately for many managers, common sense is not common practice. A further problem management faces is the tendency for employee involvement and participation schemes to regress, rather than grow and develop, from their original position with respect to their expected objectives. Several involvement and participation schemes that are successful in one organisation have come apart in another because in the latter their scope collapsed to the level of 'canteen tea discussions'. When the subjects discussed become non-controversial or less interesting, employee indifference, if not scepticism, develops. Given that employees are the principal objects and recipients of many employee involvement and participation schemes, this is perhaps potentially the most common cause of failure. A management fully committed to involvement and participation, introducing it for the right reasons and having selected the schemes appropriate for its business objectives, will provide no opportunities for employee scepticism to arise.

A professional management will also ensure participation schemes do not become ineffective because their operation produces adverse impacts on the workings of other employee relations institutions in the organisation. Some of the most successful involvement and participation programmes have been established in unionised companies with the joint involvement of management and unions. In contrast, arrangements set up independently of trade unions, where they are recognised and are fully representative of their members views, have often led to difficulties. This can happen because unions, especially those which are weakly organised, regard the introduction of an independent system of employee involvement as an attempt to bypass it and undermine its relationship with its members. In strongly unionised organisations, involvement and participation schemes are unlikely to be used to undermine the normal bargaining process with the trade unions. Attempts to bypass or undermine established trade unions channels are likely to backfire and founder on union opposition taken to the point of withdrawal, for example, a refusal to sit at the same table as non-unionists. In non-union companies, the danger that employee involvement schemes may adversely effect other employee relations institutions is less likely to be a potential hazard for management.

A management committed to employee involvement and participation will adopt an open and participative style of management, will select appropriate schemes tailored to the organisation's needs, will ensure there is a full flow of information up, down and across the organisation and will commit the necessary resources in terms of time, finances, paid time off for employees, people and physical assets to support the operation of participation schemes.

Resources
If employee involvement and participation schemes are to be effective, then resources are required to meet the direct and indirect costs (time lost, production/service foregone, meetings, training, paid leave, etc) associated with introducing, operating and maintaining them. An uncommitted management is likely to regard them as a cost without any benefit and seek to ensure there is insufficient business to be discussed by those participating in the schemes. The employee relations manager has an obligation to persuade his/her colleagues to view employee involvement and participation schemes in a positive light and to educate them as to the value they can add to the business if they are embraced by all levels of management.

The impact of employee involvement schemes is often diminished by a lack of skills or knowledge on the part of the participants. It is important, therefore, to provide both managers and employees with training in the skills required to operate involvement and participation schemes in an effective way. This involves acquiring and developing skills of chairing meetings so that people keep to the agenda, bring out suggestions and ensure that employee's contributions are appropriate to the subject matter under discussion. Managers also need training in presentational skills to present information by word of mouth or in writing and by the use of visual aids. In addition, they require interviewing skills to question employees to gain information and to seek clarification of employee views. Listening skills are essential since consultation involves management listening to what the employees have to say. In participating in involvement schemes managers therefore need to limit their contributions and allow the employees to do most of the talking. By listening, employers acquire additional information. Managers also require the skills of negotiation to gain the commitment of their managerial colleagues at all levels and in all functions, and of the workforce to the effective operation of employee involvement and participation mechanisms. If the organisation's management does provide training for its managers and employees to prepare them to participate in employee involvement schemes it is best practice to evaluate periodically the effectiveness of any training undertaken.

Spending resources on training for all involved in the operation of employee involvement and participation schemes is an investment by management. It demonstrates openly to all concerned its commitment to the schemes. To do otherwise invites employee disillusionment with the schemes. A serious and continuing commitment to employee involvement is not easy to achieve and requires significant support from the highest levels of management. The gaining of employee commitment, via employee participation and involvement, is a time-consuming process. It is much easier to undermine the operation of the schemes than to continue them. Financial resources are necessary to ensure training is executed effectively and efficiently and that sufficient time, balanced against production and customer service needs, is set aside for joint consultation meetings, briefing groups and regular management walkabouts.

Management needs to be aware of the potential problems that face employees and/or their representatives operating in participative arrangements. For example, employees may lack knowledge of the subjects under discussion and may have problems of coping with the social situation of 'rubbing shoulders' with top management. They may also experience undue pressure from their constituents who have an unreal expectation as to what employee involvement and participation schemes can achieve in protecting and advancing the interests of the employees. A professional management will assist employee representatives and individual employees overcome these problems by providing them with the necessary facilities to keep communication channels open between themselves and their constituents. It is of little value to an organisation which is committed to employee involvement schemes to have employee representatives who are unable to represent their members or to report back to them or to have union representatives that suspect management is really opposed to their activities.

Monitoring and reviewing arrangements

The establishment of mechanisms for the regular monitoring and reviewing of the operation of employee involvement and participation schemes is essential. Monitoring takes place to assess whether the schemes are producing the desired outputs of improved efficiency, productivity, quality of service, a greater willingness on the part of employees to accept change, etc. The effectiveness of employee involvement and participation mechanisms is measured against the outputs of their operation in terms of contributing to the achievement of the overall objectives of the organisation. The outcomes of the operation of the schemes are the important criteria against which their effectiveness must be judged.

Assessing effectiveness in this way avoids management and employees being sucked into accepting a public relations image of the alleged success of the operation of employee involvement. Nevertheless, it is not easy to quantify the contribution of employee involvement and participation schemes to the achievement of corporate objectives. There are problems of identifying appropriate benchmarks and isolating the influence of other factors.

The results of any monitoring exercise are best discussed with employee representatives and, where appropriate, recognised trade unions. Where the monitoring process exposes weaknesses, remedial action should be taken as soon as possible. Regular monitoring and review also enable an organisation to assess the cost-effectiveness of its employee involvement and participation schemes.

REFERENCES AND FURTHER READING

ADVISORY, CONCILIATION AND ARBITRATION SERVICE (1995) *Employee Communications and Consultation*. London, ACAS.

DEPARTMENT OF EMPLOYMENT. *The Competitive Edge: Employee involvement in Britain*, undated.

GAPPER J. (1990) 'At the end of the honeymoon'. *Financial Times*, 10 January.

GEARY J. F. (1994) 'Task participation: employees' participation enabled or constrained' in K. Sissons (ed) *Personnel Management*, 2nd edn. Oxford, Blackwell.

INSTITUTE OF PERSONNEL AND DEVELOPMENT (1995) *Code of Practice on Employee Involvement and Participation in the UK*. London, IPD.

MARCHINGTON M. (1994) 'The dynamics of joint consultation' in K. Sisson (ed), *Personnel Management*, 2nd edn, Oxford, Blackwell.

MARCHINGTON M., WILKINSON A. and ACKERS P. (1993) 'Waving or drowning in participation'. *Personnel Management*, March 30–33.

RAMSAY H. (1996) 'Involvement, empowerment and commitment' in B. Towers (ed) *The Handbook of Human Resource Management*, 2nd edn. Oxford, Blackwell.

TOWNLEY B. (1994) 'Communicating with employees' in K. Sisson (ed), *Personnel Management*, 2nd edn, Oxford, Blackwell.

TRADES UNION CONGRESS (1994) *Human Resource Management: A Trade Union Response*. London, TUC.

WALTERS M. (1996) *Employee Attitude and Opinion Surveys*. London, IPD.

WALTON R. E. (1985) 'From control to commitment in the workplace', *Harvard Business Review*, March–April.

Part 4

PRACTICE AND SKILLS IN EMPLOYEE RELATIONS

7 Negotiating

THE PURPOSE OF NEGOTIATIONS

Negotiation involves two parties (such as individuals, companies, employers, trade unions, employee representatives) coming together to confer with a view to concluding a jointly acceptable agreement. It is a process whereby interest groups resolve differences between and within themselves. It can, therefore, apply to a number of situations, from resolving an argument between two managers to meeting with the trade union to determine this year's annual pay increase.

If both parties to the agreement do not have the same understanding as to what they have agreed, then they run the risk of having to spend time that could be used for more fruitful purposes, resolving disputes between themselves over whether one party is behaving in accordance with what was agreed. Making an agreement commits the parties to operate within its parameters until they agree jointly to change the terms of the agreement. So what has been agreed must be capable of standing the test of time.

Common Elements
Negotiation involves two main elements:

• purposeful persuasion

• constructive compromise.

Each party attempts to persuade the other to accept its case by marshalling arguments backed by factual information and analysis. However, the probability one party can persuade the other to accept its case completely is extremely low. If an agreement is to be reached then both parties must move closer towards each other's position. To do so they must identify the parameters of common ground within and between their positions. Constructive compromises can then be made within these parameters. Compromise is only possible if sufficient common ground exists between the two parties. The overriding objective of any negotiation is for the parties to reach an agreement and not to score debating points or save the face of one or both parties. Negotiation is a problem-solving technique.

So we can define negotiations as:

> Two parties coming together to confer with a view to making a jointly acceptable agreement by the use of purposeful persuasion and constructive compromise (see Figure 9).

This does not confine negotiation to set-piece bargaining situations. It also covers any employee relations occasions where any two parties have a difference but need to co-operate and so have a requirement to sit down together and, through discussion and give and take, come up with a solution.

After you have read this chapter, you will be able to:

• appreciate the different negotiating situations in which a management may find itself

• explain how employee relations negotiations differ from commercial negotiations

• identify the different stages in the negotiating process

Figure 9

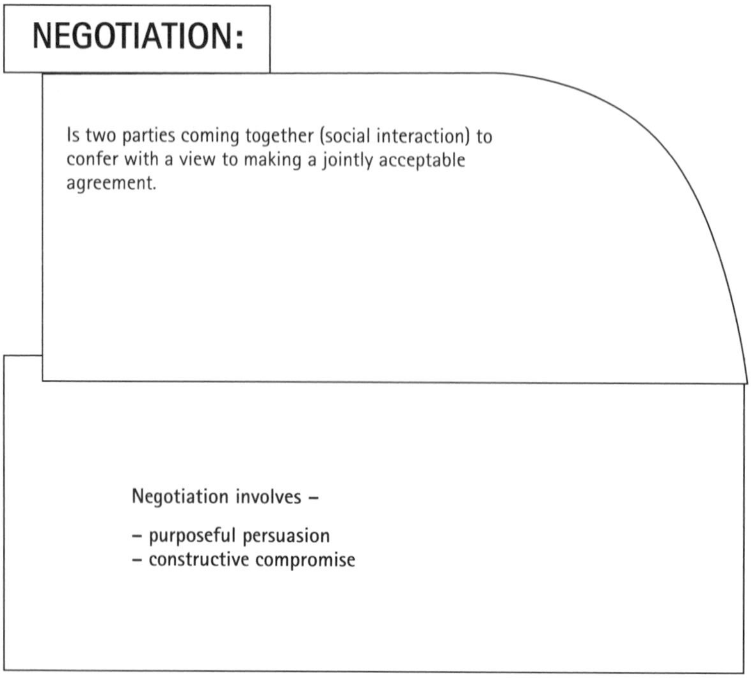

NEGOTIATION:

Is two parties coming together (social interaction) to confer with a view to making a jointly acceptable agreement.

Negotiation involves –

– purposeful persuasion
– constructive compromise

- understand the steps involved in preparing for negotiations
- describe the activities involved in conducting and concluding negotiations
- define the importance of the skills required by an employee relations manager involved in the negotiation process.

This chapter provides an overview to the negotiation process. Chapter 9 deals in more detail with managing employee grievances and Chapter 10 with bargaining.

DIFFERENT TYPES OF NEGOTIATING SITUATIONS

Figure 10 identifies four main types of negotiating situations in which managers may find themselves:

- between managers – involves a negotiated settlement to an issue(s) usually confined to an individual (for example, establishing an employee's objectives for the coming year at an appraisal interview) and resolving a difference between two managers
- grievance handling to resolve complaints by employees about the behaviour of management. Grievances normally relate to individual employees but if they are not handled with care, they can develop into a concern to a group of employees
- bargaining results in a negotiated agreement to resolve issues of collective concern to employers and employees, for example, pay, hours of work, holidays. However, bargaining can, and does, take place between management and individual employees resulting in a personal contract
- group problem-solving results in a negotiated agreement to resolve issue(s) such as the conditions on which one party will co-operate with the other with regard to action initiated by the other party.

Figure 10 **Different types of negotiating situations**

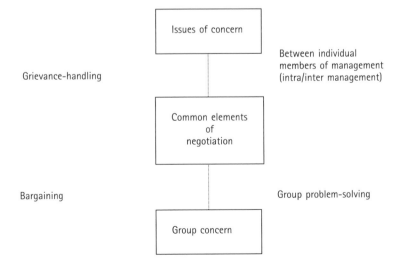

Between individual managers

The most common negotiating situation in which employee relations specialists are likely to find themselves is the one shown in the top right hand quadrant of Figure 10, namely negotiation with their management colleagues. Each day managers find themselves negotiating with their colleagues, either in the same management function or in another management function (for example, marketing, finance, sales, operations management). These managers can be of the same, higher or lower status than themselves. Negotiations between individual members of management are likely to be over issues such as:

- suggested courses of action (for example, how to deal with an employee complaint against management behaviour)

- the introduction of new employment practices and procedures (for example, the introduction of a new incentive scheme)

- securing the allocation of additional financial, staffing and equipment resources to support the people function

- gaining the commitment of managerial colleagues to a course of action.

Courses of action

Two or more managers may disagree as to how a problem should/might be resolved. In such situations, each manager will seek purposefully to persuade the other of the merits of their proposed solution to the problem. If one is able to persuade the other that their proposed solution (or some compromise) is acceptable then that is what will be implemented. However, if managers with different views as to how a problem might be resolved cannot persuade each other to accept either their desired approach or some compromise solution, then a senior manager will intervene and decide how the problem will be resolved.

Gaining resources

Employee relations managers also frequently negotiate with senior managers to gain resources to enable them to implement new policies, procedures and practices which they have devised on their own initiative or which a more senior manager has asked them to do. Negotiations between individual managers involve 'parties' protecting the same economic and political interest, and the style of negotiations in such situations will be friendly and constructive and certainly not adversarial.

Gaining commitment

Managers in any management function and at any level of seniority cannot assume their proposed actions, policies and arrangements will be accepted without question by their management colleagues. There is likely to be some opposition from those management colleagues who have different interests and priorities. Financial pressures may mean one manager's progress is another's hold-up whilst inter departmental rivalries can be a problem in organisations. So, if unanimous management commitment and support to proposed changes to policy and/or strategy (for example, a major change in reward strategy or a new training and development strategy) are to be gained then some manager has to make a persuasive case that carries their colleagues along with them. The agreed management position thus emerges via the process of intra- or inter-management negotiation.

So negotiation is not, as is popularly thought, an activity confined to relationships between managers and trade unions or other representative bodies. It is a daily activity in which all managers, inside and outside the employee relations function, are involved. Negotiations take place day in and day out between managers of different and similar levels of executive authority and between the different managers from the different management functions. Nevertheless, some managers have difficulty viewing such circumstances as negotiating situations, preferring to regard them as a process of 'influencing others' and/or gaining the support/commitment of others.

> When were you last involved in a negotiating situation where the other party was a management colleague? What arguments did you use to persuade them your view of handling the problem might be the right one? What counter-arguments did they put forward? How were your differences of approach to solving the problem overcome?

Grievance handling
What is a grievance?
A grievance is a complaint, real or ill-founded, by an employee against the behaviour of management. If management believes the employee has no genuine complaint, perhaps because the employee has simply misunderstood the situation, then it must be explained to them why this is the case. Not to do so carries the danger of adding another complaint to the original one as well as sending a message to the employee that management considers it is not worth listening to their complaint.

Grievance issues
Complaints about management's behaviour tend to come from individual employees and can range over a wide number of issues such as:

- a bonus payment has been calculated incorrectly

- a disciplinary penalty is too harsh

- promotion has been unreasonably denied

- access to a training opportunity has been disallowed

- the job is currently undergraded

- the employee has been sexually harassed by another employee or manager

- there are insufficient car parking spaces in the company car park.

Although complaints about management behaviour usually come from individual employees, if they are not handled sensitively they can (and do) develop into collective employee complaints. The resolution of employee grievances involves negotiation in that both management and the complaining employee seek to persuade each other that their suggestions to resolve the grievances are the correct ones. However, this is unlikely to happen and a mutually acceptable solution will involve the parties making concessions towards each other's positions.

Most Grievances do not go to procedure

Most organisations have a grievance procedure. Employee relations managers need to be knowledgeable about the procedure. However, when an employee raises a grievance against management behaviour, it does not automatically go into procedure. The vast majority of employee grievances are settled either informally or by a voluntary negotiated, agreed settlement before the procedure is triggered. Informal settlements can include an employer apology or the employer merely admitting and then rectifying the mistake that is the cause of the employee's complaints, and explaining why the employee's grievance is ill-founded.

Bargaining

Bargaining is a situation where the parties involved have a 'shopping list' of demands of each other. One party (usually the employees collectively) proposes a list of improvements to employment conditions – a pay rise, a shorter working week, longer holidays – whilst the other (usually the employer or an organisation of employers) responds with counter-proposals such as changes in working practices, changes in the pattern of working hours, etc.

In a bargaining situation a constructive compromise is achieved by 'trading' taking place over the items that each party has flagged up to the other for negotiation. Identifying which items in their shopping list the parties are prepared to trade is a key activity in preparing for bargaining. The parties come to an agreement in bargaining situations by trading items in their respective 'shopping lists'. The aim of the parties is to use 'trading' to advance, or protect, their own interests and thus create new 'prices' (new rules) at which labour services will be bought and sold. So bargaining is about trading with the other party and not about conceding to the other party.

Group/joint problem-solving

This is a situation where two or more parties negotiate the details whereby one party will co-operate with the other, which is usually management initiating some action to resolve a problem which is of common interest to both parties. Let us consider such an example.

The organisation is currently performing comfortably in terms of sales, profitability, etc but recognises that in the near future product market competition will become more intense. The top management has started to consider suitable policy initiatives that might be introduced to minimise any adverse consequences in terms of sales, etc when the greater product market competition becomes a reality.

As a first step, the organisation has decided to invite a team of consultants to examine its work organisation and systems and to produce a feasibility study as to what action/policies it might introduce and what their effect might be on improving its future product market competitiveness. The management has committed itself to implement none of the report's recommendations until the workforce has been consulted and involved in thorough discussions on the report.

However, if the consultants are to gain a full picture for their report, they will need to speak to and have the co-operation of the workforce. The company believes the best way is to achieve this is for the consultants to go into the departments and speak to the employees on an individual basis. However, they will inform the supervisor/team leader and the representative of the employees of what they intend to do in the department. Supervisors/team leaders have been told to release employees from their workstation so that they can speak to the consultants.

The workforce has an interest in seeing the organisation's efficiency improve as this will enhance their job security. They are therefore prepared to co-operate with the work of the consultants but they have some concerns. First, they know that in other firms where this firm of consultants has done work, redundancies have been declared shortly afterwards. Secondly, the employee representatives are worried that management wishes them to have no role when the consultants are speaking to their constituents. They would prefer to be present at any interviews the consultants carry out with their constituents in the various departments.

The workforce is not against the use of consultants as a matter of principle. Its representatives have decided to approach the management about its concerns. So the ensuing negotiations between the parties would be over:

- whether the firm of consultants preferred by management to produce the feasibility report will be used or whether another firm of consultants will be commissioned

- the procedure to be adopted by the consultants when in the departments. Will they have direct access to employees? Will employee representatives be present at interviews?

The example illustrates the manner in which a group problem negotiating situation operates. Management is normally seeking the co-operation of its workforce to some proposed action to gain information which can then be used to solve, jointly with the employees, a problem to mutual gain. As a result, the management negotiating style will not be adversarial. Management wants something from its employees so it will start by demonstrating to them that there is advantage in co-operating. For management to bang the table and be insulting in the negotiations toward the employee representatives would be inappropriate to the context and unlikely to secure management's primary objective, which is to gain employee co-operation with the work of the consultants.

INDUSTRIAL NEGOTIATIONS v COMMERCIAL NEGOTIATIONS

Industrial negotiating situations are very different from commercial contract negotiations. Many managers outside the employee relations function find it difficult to understand why industrial negotiations involve so much quasi-theatrical behaviour and take so long to conclude. It is, therefore, important employee relations managers understand how employee relations negotiations are different from commercial contract. The main differences are summarised in Table 28.

Choice of negotiating partner

Commercial negotiations tend to be conducted on a more polite basis than those normally witnessed in grievance handling or bargaining situations. In commercial negotiations, purchasers tend to buy from individuals or organisations they prefer whilst sellers can give preferential deals to those they like. In industrial negotiations, the parties cannot deal with those they prefer. Each party selects its own representatives and management selects its best team to conduct the negotiations. In addition, the parties have to develop a professional relationship regardless of their feelings towards each other. Industrial negotiations are always conducted by representatives of the parties who report back to constituents. Commercial contract negotiators are not accountable to constituents but usually to a line manager.

Face-to-face/adjournments

Many negotiations in the commercial field do not take place on a face-to-face basis. They may be done by telephone (for example, telephone sales from call centres) or even letter. Industrial negotiations, however, always take place on a face-to-face basis. The use of adjournments is less common in commercial negotiations than in industrial ones. In this latter case management (union) negotiators may adjourn several times in bargaining situations, but usually on fewer occasions in grievance handling to consider a union (management) proposal. Adjournments enable the parties to obtain and analyse more, and new, information, to reassess their objectives, aims, strategy and tactics, to regroup as a team where the negotiations are conducted via working parties and, on occasions, to allow emotions to calm down.

Status of agreements

An important difference between industrial and commercial negotiation is the legal status of the agreement that emerges. In the commercial world the contract outlining the conditions of the sale is legally binding and its contents can be enforced via the courts. The agreement that emerges from industrial negotiations, as we saw in Chapter 1, is not legally binding. It is binding in honour only.

Table 28 Main differences between industrial and commercial negotiations

Unlike commercial negotiations, industrial negotiations:

- involve an ongoing relationship
- are carried out by representatives
- are always conducted on a face-to-face basis.
- do not result in legally enforceable contracts
- make more frequent use of adjournments
- always result in an agreement

Neither party can enforce its rights, contained in the agreement, via the courts.

'No agreement'

In commercial negotiations, an outcome of 'no agreement' is quite acceptable and quite common. Buyers and sellers may have every reason to conclude, after some negotiating, that a deal would not be in their interests and so amicably part and seek other suppliers or purchasers whose needs and terms are more acceptable. In employee relations negotiations, the aim, not just the possibility, is to reach an agreement and the outcome is always a new, or revised agreement, even if on occasions that agreement is a unilateral imposed one.

Quality of future relationships

Grievance handling, bargaining, group problem-solving and intra- and inter-management negotiations all take place against an assumption that the parties have to have an ongoing and permanent relationship. When the negotiations are over, the parties who have met on a basis of equality have to meet again the next day and continue their employer-employee relationship in which the latter is in a subordinate role. Industrial negotiators, unlike their commercial contractor counterparts, cannot simply walk away from the party with which they are currently dealing and make a more favourable agreement with another party. For the motor car seller negotiating with a buyer, the relationship will be probably confined to that one negotiation. Whether a sale is concluded or not the parties are unlikely to meet again in a buyer/seller relationship so one party can insult the other with impunity. By the same token, a cash buyer can use his or her bargaining power to obtain a discount on the product or service he or she wishes to purchase.

The continuous relationship between industrial negotiators at the workplace acts as a restraining influence on their behaviour during and after the negotiations. Each party must retain their dignity, preserve their professional self-respect and bear in mind the importance of preserving the quality of their future relationship. This involves management avoiding any implications that the negotiation outcome indicates the employee and/or their trade union has 'lost' but management have 'won'. Both parties must be able to leave the negotiations (whatever the negotiating situation) without losing face. Once the negotiations have been concluded, regardless of the outcome, the parties have to return to a constructive working relationship as soon as possible. For management to use its 'victory' over its employees to humiliate them is not professional behaviour. To do so will result in decreased employee morale, increased absenteeism and reduced quality of product or service to the customer.

In industrial negotiations, the negotiators have always to bear in mind the importance of preserving the quality of their future relationships. Whatever the outcome of the negotiations and whatever the atmosphere in which they are conducted, the two parties have to be able to co-operate and work together many hours a day, five or more days a week, indefinitely at the end of the negotiations. However, if the union official with which management has to deal is a national or regional one rather than an employee workplace representative, and therefore not someone who works on the premises and with whom a day-to-day working relationship has to be maintained, then clearly the need to maintain amicable relationships is less imperative because local management may not meet face-to-face with full-time officials again.

List at least four ways in which industrial negotiations are different from commercial contract negotiations.

STAGES IN THE NEGOTIATION PROCESS

All negotiating situations involve the stages shown in Table 29 although the length of time each stage will last and the degree of formality in the stages will vary. For example, in a 'between management' negotiating situation, the 'agreement' as to how to deal with a problem is unlikely to be written down except perhaps in the form of a letter and/or an internal memorandum to management colleagues. In all negotiating situations, the preparation stage lasts the longest in time terms. The amount of time the two parties spend in a face-to-face situation across the table is small relative to the total time spent by both sides in the whole negotiating process.

The preparation stage
There are three stages in preparing for negotiation. These are:

• analysis

• establishment of aims to be achieved in the forthcoming negotiations

• planning the strategy and tactics to be used in those negotiations.

The analysis stage
The analysis stage involves management collecting and analysing the relevant information to substantiate the proposals it will put to its employees or their representatives. In grievance handling, for example, the necessary information is normally collected by word of mouth from those (including other employees and managers) who witnessed the incident or behaviour alleged by the employee. So in managing an employee grievance, the employee relations specialists requires competency in interviewing skills in order to gather and then analyse all the facts surrounding the employee's complaint.

On the other hand, in bargaining situations, management is likely to have to analyse information coming from its own records. For example:

• labour productivity trends

Table 29 **The stages in the negotiation process**

• Preparation
• Presentation
• Search/Identify common ground
• Concluding the agreement
• Writing the agreement

Table 30 **Preparing for negotiations**

There are 3 stages in preparing for negotiations:

1 Analysis
2 Establishment of aims
3 Strategy and tactics

Analysis

- The facts/sources of information of the incident, claim, etc
- Any relevant rules (company) agreements or 'custom and practice'
- Any relevant precedents or comparisons
- Attitude of management on the issue(s)
- What issues are tradable? Which issues will the other party trade?
- Significance of the issues for the employees, their representatives and their trade union.

Aims

- Ideal (like to achieve)
- Realistic (hoped for)
- Fall back (must have)
- Consider feasibility of aims against relative bargaining power.

Strategy and tactics

- Size of team
- Who is to speak? In what order? On what subject?
- Anticipation of most likely of the other side's arguments and counter to them
- Be familiar with the meaning and intent of the agreements, procedures and rules of your organisation.

Preparation is vital

Wrong analysis = Incorrect aims = Failure to achieve objectives

Golden Rule

Failure to Prepare
is
Preparing to Fail

- profitability

- labour turnover

- sales.

It is also likely management will have to consider information from external sources, such as employers' associations (see Chapter 4), employee relations professionals, press and government departments. Such information will include:

- inflation rate

- pay and salary surveys

- trends in earnings by occupation, industry, region, gender, etc.

The analysis stage also involves management checking on existing arrangements relevant to the forthcoming negotiations such as:

- company rules

- collective or individual agreements

- other arrangements or custom and practice

• procedural arrangements.

The employee relations manager should be familiar with the meaning and intent of those policies giving effect to such rules, agreements and custom and practice.

Identification of key issues

However, the most important activity in the analysis stage is the identification of the key issues involved in the forthcoming negotiations and which of these issues management is prepared to trade and which it is not prepared to trade. In making this decision, management must weigh up the significance of the issues at stake for the protection and advancements of its economic interests.

In bargaining at any given time some of the issues are tradable and others are not. Let us give an example. Management has just received a list of demands from its employees of a 2.5 per cent increase in basic rates, the introduction of a productivity bonus, an increase in holidays, changes to paternity leave arrangements and removal of non-strike arrangements. Management may decide, because of market conditions, that any increase in basic rates and any removal of 'no strike' arrangements are simply not tradable options. However, it may decide to trade the introduction of a productivity bonus as this can be self-financing, an improvement in holiday entitlement and changes in existing paternity arrangements.

Having decided which items it is prepared to trade, management now anticipates which issues it believes its employees' representatives will be willing to trade. In doing this, management has to assess how strongly the employees feel about each of the items on their bargaining agenda, including whether their feelings are so strong that they would be prepared to undertake industrial action in support of their demands. Let us say, for example, that management anticipates that the employees and their representatives feel most strongly about the introduction of a productivity bonus and gaining an increase in holiday entitlement (ie these are their non-tradable items). So in this case management anticipates its employees are willing to trade basic rate increases, the no-strike clause and paternity arrangements (that is, their tradable items) to obtain improvements in holiday entitlement and the introduction of a productivity bonus. Management thus sees a basis for agreement around a productivity bonus, an increase in holidays and paternity leave changes in return for retention of a 'no-strike' clause and no change in basic rates.

In grievance

In grievance handling an acceptable solution is usually found by trading the details of the complaint without breaching the substance of the issue. Let us consider a situation where employees, for example, believe the disciplinary penalty of suspending one of their colleagues for one week without pay for swearing at a manager is too harsh. The workforce has shown its concern by instructing its representatives to approach management for a reduction in the terms of the sentence.

Management has decided it would be unacceptable for the employee not to be disciplined. The imposition of a disciplinary penalty is absolutely crucial for management (that is, not a tradable issue). However, after completing its analysis of the situation, management considers the workforce feels very strongly about the severity of the penalty, although it accepts a disciplinary penalty should be imposed on their colleague. The management calculates that industrial action would be imposed and this would give rise to difficulties since the volume of business is increasing steeply. Management therefore might decide it is prepared to see some reduction in the length of the suspension. Management would therefore establish the limits of this reduction to, say, a maximum of five days and a minimum of three.

Establishing negotiating aims

The second phase of the preparation stage is the establishment by management of the objectives it wishes to achieve in the forthcoming negotiations. It also requires management to consider the negotiating aims and objectives of its employees and/or representatives. Again, this task can be done more competently if the management knows and understands what motivates the representatives of the workforce with which it has to deal. Getting to know them does not mean agreeing with their position. However, it is only by knowing what 'makes them tick' (for example, their attitudes, pressures upon them, personalities) that management can predict/anticipate with any reasonable degree of certainty:

- how the employees' representatives might react to management proposals

- the issues they are prepared to trade in negotiations

- the negotiating style they are likely to adopt

- the strategy and tactics they might develop.

By setting objectives, the negotiators know what they are trying to achieve. Negotiation is about compromise and flexibility so it is normally unrealistic to set inflexible objectives as this usually gives only two options – win or lose. Negotiators have to arrive at some sort of prioritised approach. It is standard practice for negotiators to establish three positions for each item involved in the negotiations. These positions are:

- What would management ideally like to achieve?

- What does management realistically believe it can achieve?

- What is the least for which management will settle (the fall-back or sticking position)?

The 'fall-back' position represents the lowest package at which management will settle. It is the minimum that can be accepted without failing to meet the negotiators' objectives. If this position cannot be achieved, then management prefers to enter into a dispute situation with its employees. It means management is prepared to withstand industrial sanctions that the employees may take against them rather than settle for less than their 'fall-back' position. Management, therefore, as part of preparing for negotiations, needs also to draw up plans to minimise/offset any costs that may accrue to

Table 31 **An Aspiration Grid**

- sets parameters for the expected outcome of the negotiations
- shows the issues management is prepared to trade
- shows management's anticipation of the issues its employees or their representatives will trade
- gives a picture as to how the forthcoming negotiations are expected to develop
- helps management identify the information it requires from the other party
- helps management identify the information it needs to convey to the other party.

the organisation should a failure to agree result in industrial action by employees.

The aspiration grid

Having established its negotiating objectives, the next step for management is to anticipate the negotiating aims/objectives of the other party along the same lines: what are likely to be their ideal, realistic and fall-back positions on each issue involved in the negotiations? Having considered which items it is prepared to trade, having anticipated the tradable items of the other party, having established its own negotiation objectives and having anticipated those of the other party, management can now construct an Aspiration Grid which sets out the parameters for the expected outcome of the negotiations. Such a grid shows the issues management is prepared to trade as well as management's anticipation of the issues its employees will trade. It gives a picture as to how the forthcoming negotiations are expected to develop. It helps management identify the information it requires from the other party and that which it requires to convey to the other party (see Table 31).

An example of how the grid can be used is given below. An X indicates a party is not prepared to trade that item. An O indicates the party is prepared to trade that item. It has been based on the example outlined previously. If both parties have an X against the same item in their fall-back column, then it indicates there will be no accommodation on that issue and the expectation would be that the negotiations will break down. There would be no basis for an agreement.

AN ASPIRATION GRID

Possible solutions	Management			Employees/Union		
	Ideal	Real	Fall–Back	Fall–Back	Real	Ideal
Basic rate increase of 2.5 per cent	X	X	X	O	O	X
Introduce productivity bonus	X	X	O	X	X	X
Increased holiday entitlement	X	O	O	X	X	X
Changes to paternity leave	X	O	O	O	O	X
No strike clause	X	X	X	O	X	X

The grid shows there is a basis for agreement in that there is no X against any item for both parties on their fall-back position. Each of the three positions shows a greater degree of trading as demonstrated by the higher number of Os. It also shows management is not prepared to trade a basic rate increase, nor the ending of the 'no strike' clause. These are, however, tradable items for the employees, who are themselves not prepared to trade the introduction of a productivity bonus nor an increase in holiday entitlement, though these are tradable issues for management. An X for an item in all three positions indicates the issue/item is non-tradable.

The use of the Aspiration Grid is explained in more detail in Chapters 9 and 10. Its basic principle is that it enables the negotiating party to structure its own position systematically and to record the outcomes of empathising with the other party's position. It sets out each side's objectives, known or anticipated, and their three positions. The grid gives an expected structure to the negotiations prior to their beginning. It indicates to the parties information they need to gain, and give to each other, during the forthcoming negotiations to ascertain whether their expectations of the position of the other party are as anticipated. If information received during negotiations indicates that expectations about the position of the other side are incorrect, then the Aspiration Grid has to be revised and amended.

The Aspiration Grid gives management a picture of how the bargaining sessions will develop. In the actual negotiating sessions, they will test out whether their anticipation of the employees' objectives is correct or needs to be reassessed by ensuring the employees and their representatives receive a clear message from them as to management's negotiation objectives.

If management enters negotiations without having established objectives, then the probability of reaching an unsatisfactory outcome or entering into a dispute situation is increased. It is essential in establishing its 'realistic' and 'fall-back' negotiating objectives that management takes proper and due account of the relative balance of bargaining power between itself and the employees (see Chapters 1 and 2). The balance of bargaining power influences the shape of both parties' Aspiration Grid and their objectives. Even in intra- and inter-management negotiating situations the balance of bargaining power operates. The employee relations manager negotiating with a financial manager to secure resources for training and development courses and seminars will hold the balance of bargaining power if the chief executive backs such courses or legislation requires such courses (for example, health and safety) to be run. On the other hand, if financial resources are severely limited and accountancy managers dominate, then the balance of power in the allocation of resources will lie against the employee relations manager.

Planning strategy and tactics
Size of negotiating team
The third phase of the preparation stage is the planning of strategy and tactics to deliver the negotiation objectives. Management works out a plan by which it hopes to achieve its negotiating objectives. This

involves deciding first the size of the negotiating team. Not every negotiating situation requires a team. Grievance handling is often dealt with by an individual manager. Intra-management negotiations usually consist of those involved – one from each party. However, in bargaining and group problem situations, a team approach is the norm. There are no set ground rules for deciding the size of the negotiating team. Quality of presentation and arguments to support the case are more important than whether the negotiating teams have parity of size in terms of numbers. However, as a minimum, most negotiating teams will have:

• a leader who is respected by the rest of the team

• a note-taker who records what is happening in the negotiating meetings and then in adjournments can advise the team on whether the negotiations are going according to plan, and from whose notes the terms of the negotiated agreement will be drafted

• an observer who listens and watches but does not speak

• a strategist whose role is to check whether the expected common ground and anticipated trading of items have been identified correctly and, if not, to suggest how management's negotiating objectives might be amended. The strategist also assesses and monitors proposals from the other party as they are made

It is also advisable to have an odd number in the negotiating team. Odd numbers mean there will be a majority if the negotiating team has to decide its position on the basis of a vote.

It is important that a management negotiating team, before meeting with the other party, decides who is to speak, in what order and on what issues or items. Only one individual should speak at a time. It is not advisable for the members of the negotiating team to disagree as a team in the presence of the other side.

Anticipation of arguments and counter-arguments
An important part of planning the strategy and the tactics to achieve the negotiation objectives is the anticipation of the arguments mostly likely to be used by the other party against your case and how they might be countered. In this regard, it is helpful if a member of management team can 'play the devil's advocate' to probe management's case for its weak points and how the employees' and/or their representatives' arguments against management's case can be exposed and answered. Plans can then be made as to how they might be answered.

Communication with the team
During the negotiations the team may find it necessary to communicate without the need to call for an adjournment (see below). Any agreed method of communication will have to be non-verbal. Research shows the most common method used in negotiating teams is the passing of notes.

Common front
Whether it be a grievance handling, bargaining or a group problem-solving negotiating situation, by the time management has completed

its preparation for the forthcoming negotiations, all members of the negotiating team (including the note-taker) should understand and have agreed the negotiation analysis, aims, strategy and tactics. The leader of the team should ensure that this is actually the case.

In any of the four negotiating situations identified in this chapter, the preparation stage is the most important. If management's analysis of the information it has gathered, whether by interview techniques, or from statistical data, is incorrect then it will establish inappropriate negotiating objectives and develop an unrealistic strategy and tactics with the result that the chances of achieving its negotiating objectives will be significantly reduced. If it does achieve its objectives, despite inadequate preparation, it is likely to be because management holds the upper hand in the relative balance of bargaining power stakes or by good fortune. Good luck, however, is not a management skill. A 'seat of pants' approach to a negotiating situation is understandable but any competent negotiator will tell you there is no substitute for preparation. The golden rule to remember when preparing for negotiations is:

> Failure to prepare
> is Preparing to fail

If management fails to prepare adequately, it is not a disaster. The situation can be rescued by management reassessing its negotiation analysis, objectives, strategy and tactics in the light of new information it gains and which was not available at the preparation stage. Indeed, it is essential management reassess its negotiating objectives and the analysis upon which they are based every time it gains information it did not have, or did not take into account, when preparing for the negotiations. During any negotiations – whether grievance handling, bargaining, joint problem-solving or intermanagement – management should frequently monitor and review its negotiating objectives (including the Aspiration Grid) in the light of how the negotiations are developing and progressing.

Justify the actions a manager needs to take in preparing to resolve a grievance raised by an employee against the behaviour of the organisation.

The presentation stage
At the first meeting with the other side, if the negotiators are unknown to each other, it may be necessary to break the ice by the respective negotiating teams introducing themselves to each other. If the negotiators are well known to each other this is unnecessary. It may be appropriate at the initial meeting in grievance-handling situations for management to suggest to the complainant and/or their representative a procedure whereby the negotiations will proceed and to suggest a schedule for their completion.

Management initiates the meeting
If management is making the initial presentation, then it gives a general

summary of its case. After informing the employee(s), or their representatives, of the issues it is going to raise, management then substantiates its case supported by facts and figures but emphasises the rationale behind the proposals and its strength of feeling towards each of them. So the first part of the presentation stage of negotiations involves both parties telling each other what they want from each other.

Although it is perhaps not *common* practice, it is *good* practice for each party to put on the table all the issues it wishes to see subject to the negotiations, and not just to present its views on selected issues. This avoids the possibility of a set of long negotiations over many issues ending in apparent agreement only for one party then to say 'Oh, by the way, we need to talk about X [a new issue] as well'. Some negotiators believe there can be advantages in 'keeping something up your sleeve to hit them with later'. Bearing in mind that the purpose of negotiations is to make an agreement, this is a dangerous tactic because:

- the hidden issue might be a non-negotiable issue for the other side, or one on which it is only prepared to trade if the alternative is no agreement at all. If this turns out to be the case, then there is high probability the negotiations will break down, taking with them a loss of issues on which an accommodation has been made.

- it can destroy the mutual trust between the leaders of the respective negotiating teams. Negotiators do not like to have negotiated in good faith and to have honestly and openly raised all the issues to secure an agreement, only to find the other party has behaved differently.

- if one party consistently behaves in this way then the other party will regard it as part of that party's negotiating ritual and will discount it in future negotiations. The alleged surprise, and with it hopefully further improvements in the offer/claim of the other side, is trumped.

At best, management will get away with the 'keep something up your sleeve' tactic, once. The employee relations specialist should be an open, and not a devious, negotiator who puts all the cards to be considered in the negotiations on the table from the outset.

Management receives proposal(s)
If management is receiving a proposal(s) from its employees' representatives then it listens carefully to what they are saying and does not interrupt their presentation. When the employee side has completed its presentation, management should avoid an unconsidered (ie knee-jerk) response. By the same token, it is unwise for management to respond with immediate counter-proposals unless they have been agreed beforehand. If management is receiving proposals, or listening to an employee complaint, for the first time, it should confine its response to asking questions to seek clarification of the proposals. For example, typical questions might be:

- What does the actual proposal really mean? Could you please give us more details?

- What is the source of information of the statistic on wage rates/inflation rate, etc you have quoted?

- When you make reference to average earnings, what kind of average do you mean? – mode, median, unweighted arithmetic etc?

- Could you just remind us of the individuals you have interviewed in connection with the alleged management behaviour of which you are complaining?

It is essential at the end of the employees' proposals that management is 100 per cent certain as to what has been proposed and what it is the employees' proposals actually mean. It is, therefore, good practice, before the employees' presentation session concludes, for management to summarise back in a neutral manner what it understands has been proposed on behalf of the employees. At the end of the employees' presentation, management should arrange to meet with the employees at a future date so that management can give a full and measured response to employees' proposal(s).

By the end of the presentation stage, both parties will have put to each other their ideal positions. There is unlikely to be much common ground between them. However, the issues to be resolved during the negotiation are now known to both parties who now begin the task of seeking confirmation of their expected common ground.

Identifying common ground
The emphasis of the negotiations now switches from concentrating on differences to identifying points of common ground that can form the basis of a possible agreement. The point has now been reached at which both parties must seek to confirm the expected common ground. Each needs to obtain, in future negotiation sessions with the other party, information which will enable it to confirm whether these expectations and aspirations are correct.

Each subsequent negotiating session is to be used constructively to gain the necessary information. At the same time, management needs to supply information to the other party so that the employees can assess the correctness of their expectations as to management's position on the issues which are the subject of the negotiations. Negotiation sessions which do not provide the information needed by the two parties to evaluate their anticipated areas of common ground are not a constructive use of time. However, negotiation sessions do happen in which neither party gains relevant information. This happens when either party tries to:

- score points

- lay blame

- issue threats

- shout down the other side or be sarcastic

- interrupt

- talk too much

- attack personalities on the other side.

Management can seek to confirm its expectations as to where the common ground with the other side lies by a number of techniques (see Table 32). The most important of these are:

Table 32 Techniques available to management to test the common ground with the other side

- The if and then technique
- Discussion
- Questioning
- Watching
- Listening
- Summarising
- Linking of issues

- The 'if and then' technique, which involves using language such as 'if you move closer to our position on issue y then we shall move closer to your position on x'. If the response is positive, then x and y are tradable items. The technique deliberately emphasises the requirement of the other side to move. It is a conditional offer.

- Open discussion within broad parameters. For example, management may indicate an issue can be considered but only in return for something, say, a different set of employee representative agreements. Management would then outline these arrangements so that they form the basis of discussion and negotiation.

- Questioning (interviewing)

- Watching the body language of other party (frowns, glances, nods, etc) when reacting to proposals

- Listening carefully to what is being said, including any conditions placed on any offers/proposals. If one party says to the other 'we are not prepared to discuss that at this stage', what it is saying is that it is prepared to trade that issue but does not feel it necessary to do so at this moment.

- Periodic summarising of the other party's position on an issue. This is particularly helpful where the issue concerned is complex and an example of the kind of statement that might be made would be '... so what you are saying is that you understand that our offer on issue x means that ... [at this point there is a complex example given of how the party believes what the other party has proposed will operate] ... and that gives us no problem'. Each separate negotiating meeting begins with one party summarising the stage the negotiations have reached. Such a summary outlines the areas upon which agreement has been reached and the issues upon which an agreement has still to be reached.

- Linking issues, which is crucial if the exact details of the issues the parties are prepared to trade are to be identified. Linking issues also ensures the negotiations have a momentum.

- Seeking agreement in principle before discussing details. It is pointless discussing the details of how flexibility of labour between different tasks will operate if one party is totally opposed to labour flexibility.

If the use of the techniques outlined above leads to new information, an adjournment can be called, if thought necessary, to consider the implications of the new information, including whether there is a need to reassess negotiating aims (amend the Aspiration Grid), analysis and strategy and tactics.

The confirmation of the common ground enables the negotiations to have a momentum. If the negotiations become 'bogged down' on a particular issue their momentum can be sustained by switching to a new issue. This reinforces the importance of the negotiators' putting all issues on the table from the outset. The difficult issue can be returned to later and if it is then the only outstanding issue to an agreement being secured the parties are likely to readjust their attitude towards that issue to a more accommodating one. Both are now faced with a stark choice. Either an accommodation is reached on the one outstanding issue or no agreement is made and the agreement on issues which has been made falls by the wayside. The party feeling strongest on the remaining, but difficult, issue is thus faced with a 'do we throw the baby out with the bath water?' type of choice.

> Outline the various techniques whereby a management negotiating team can search for the common ground and thereby the basis of an agreement with representatives of the workforce. Which of these techniques, and why, do you consider to be the most important?

Adjournments
Frequently, negotiations adjourn because a natural break has been reached. Presentations have been made, information has to be checked, proposals from the other party have to be assessed and other parties (such as a more senior level of management) may need to be consulted. In other circumstances, adjournments have a tactical purpose and some skill is required in deciding when (or when not) to call for an adjournment. The number and frequency of adjournments will depend upon the normal practice of negotiations in the environment in which they are operating. The use of the adjournment is discussed more fully in Chapter 10.

Concluding the agreement
After completing the identification of the common ground stage, the negotiations move to their concluding stages. Entering this stage, particularly in bargaining situations, is a matter of timing and judgement. The ability to recognise that the best deal in the circumstances has been reached and will be acceptable to the constituents represented in the negotiations is an important skill for the employee relations specialist to acquire.

Factors to consider in concluding the agreement
There are a number of considerations management should bear in mind in closing the negotiations. First, they need to be satisfied all the issues have been discussed and agreed and that both parties fully understand what they have accepted. If there is a misunderstanding over what has been agreed the negotiations must recommence. It is crucial that both sides have the same understanding of what they have agreed.

Second, management has to convince the other party its final offer is final. A series of 'final offers' from management will destroy its credibility with the other party and undermine its ability to convince the workforce the 'bottom line' has been reached. Management gains little by telling the employees they have made their 'full and final' offer, only to make an improved offer in the light of the threat of industrial action. If management says its offer is final then that must be the case.

Third, management should avoid being rushed into concluding a final agreement, no matter how tempting the offer/proposal sounds. It makes sure it has all the information it requires from the employees (or their representatives) and then seeks an adjournment. This enables management to examine the final offer and identify any potential problems that may have gone unnoticed before.

Writing the agreement
After the agreement is reached it is written up. In the case of an employee grievance this may be no more than an internal memorandum and/or a letter to the individual employee concerned stating clearly what has been agreed to settle the agreement. However, in the case of a written agreement arising from a bargaining or group problem-solving negotiation it will contain clauses covering:

• who are the parties to the agreement

• the date it was agreed

• the date upon which it will be implemented

• its content (clauses)

• how disputes over its interpretation and applications will be resolved

• its duration

together with the signatures of representatives of the parties covered by the agreement.

The agreement is usually drafted by management and then sent to the other party which will usually initial the clauses the wording of which it accepts. Only when both sides are happy with the wording of the agreement will it be printed and formally signed.

Agreement means commitment to operate until it is changed so it is important the wording of the agreement is checked carefully. There is a big difference between a clause which states 'employees may be dismissed if they report for work with the smell of alcohol on their breath' and a clause which states 'employees will be dismissed if they report for work with the smell of alcohol on their breath'. The first clause implies there may be circumstances in which dismissal may not take place. The second leaves no room for doubt. Every employee knows what will happen to them if they behave in this way.

Management needs to keep an accurate record of what was agreed in the negotiations. This is the only protection it may have from the other party trying to get into the agreement something that was not agreed during the negotiations. Fortunately, such attempts to 'pull a fast one' when writing up the agreement are extremely rare amongst

Figure 11 The Reconciliation of Differences Over Time

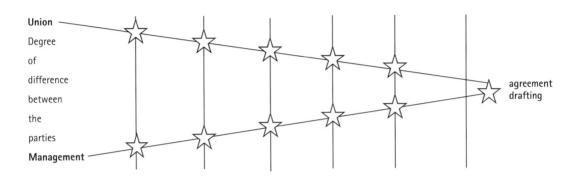

management, employees and employee representatives. The importance of the role of the note-taker in negotiations cannot be stressed enough (see Chapter 10).

So we have completed our analysis of the stages through which a set of negotiations go. It has been shown that throughout the process there is a gradual movement towards common points of agreement. At the end of the presentation stage, there is little common ground between the parties but at each subsequent meeting there should emerge, via an exchange of information, an increasing degree of common ground. Each meeting of the two parties should make progress towards a constructive compromise (see Figure 11).

THE OUTCOME OF NEGOTIATIONS

The best outcome of the negotiating process is where both parties make some gains – the so-called win/win situation. This is normally achieved by professional negotiation which concentrates on achieving well-prepared objectives, on maintaining long-term relationships between the parties, on emphasising a pragmatic approach, and on making an agreement which meets the needs of both parties. However, the relative balance of bargaining power between the two parties still influences heavily the outcome of the negotiations regardless of the professionalism management displays.

The opposite outcome is the lose/lose situation which arises from a lack of professionalism on the part of the negotiators. This results in:

• neither party achieving its objectives

• no agreement being secured

• long-term relationships being soured

- the constituents of the negotiating parties no longer respecting/ trusting their negotiators

- both parties becoming disillusioned with the negotiating process.

A third possible outcome is the so-called win/lose situation where one party dominates the other and secures something from the other party without giving anything in return. This outcome is often the result of unprofessional negotiations on the part of one or both parties. Such negotiating situations are characterised by an 'us and them' distinction between the parties. The negotiation teams' energies are directed towards victory ('I win you lose'), a strong emphasis on immediate solutions regardless of their long-term consequences, personalised conflicts rather than assessing facts, information and arguments, and no consideration of the quality of future relations between the parties after the negotiations are over.

SKILLS REQUIRED IN THE NEGOTIATING PROCESS

So far we have examined what negotiators do. These tasks have included the establishment of aims to be achieved from the negotiation, the planning of strategy and tactics to achieve the objectives, anticipation of the other side's reactions and arguments, reassessment of objectives in the light of previously unknown information becoming available, and the need to have regard to the quality of relationship with the other party after the negotiations have finished. Describing these tasks does not identify the skills required of a negotiator. Table 33 outlines the major skills required of a negotiating team in each stage of the negotiation process. Some skills are common to all stages but others are specific to particular stages. The key skills are interviewing, note-taking, presentational, listening, watching, analytical and judgmental.

Interviewing skills
Why interviewing skills?
Much of an employee relations manager's job is dealing with employee problems and/or complaints. This activity requires the collection of information, on the basis of which a manager analyses the complaint, decides whether it is genuine or ill-founded, establishes how the employee grievance might be solved and then plans a strategy and tactics to achieve this end. Most of the information required to undertake these tasks is collected from individuals (both employees and managers) by word of mouth. Competence in interviewing skills is therefore crucial to employee relations managers.

In resolving employee grievances the employee relations specialists needs to collect information from interviews with all individuals concerned. Interviewing skills are also necessary in the preparation, presentation, confirmation of common ground and conclusion of the agreement stages of the other negotiations. In addition, they are important in helping the parties clarify each other's proposals and test their understanding of what they have agreed with each other.

Table 33 Skills required by an individual or a negotiating team

Preparation stage	Presentation stage	Common ground stage	Concluding the agreement stage	Writing the agreement stage
Team building Interviewing Balance of bargaining power	Interviewing	Interviewing	Interviewing	
Assessment. Note-taking Analysis of data/ information	Note-taking	Note-taking Analysis of Data/Information	Note-taking	Note-taking
Anticipating other party's reaction Oral communication	Oral communication Listening Watching	Oral communication Listening Watching Summarising neutrally	Oral communication Listening Watching Summarising Judgement	Language

Purpose of an interview

The purpose of an interview is to gain complete and consistent information. All the facts, including those that weaken the case as well as those that strengthen it, must be obtained. Incomplete information will mean inadequate preparation for negotiations. It is important during an interview to strike the right balance between showing sympathy towards the interviewee and adopting a businesslike approach to obtain all the information required. In an interview, the interviewee does the talking since they have the facts the interviewer requires. The interviewer, therefore, limits their oral contribution, concentrating on listening to the interviewee. If the interviewer talks too much they become preoccupied with formulating the next question and can miss vital information, or limit the opportunity for the interviewee to supply relevant information. Research suggests that the effective interviewer spends some 85 per cent of an interview listening to what the interviewee is saying.

There are a number of things an interviewer can do to get the interviewee talking:

- conduct the interview in a quiet place where there is little possibility of interruption

- put the interviewee at ease by, before starting the interview proper, asking questions about his or her interests outside work, for example, family, hobbies, sport

- avoid cross-examining the interviewee as this does not create an environment which supports the exchange of quality information

- calm down the interviewee if he or she is angry. In grievance-handling situations, the individual is often angry and only too willing to talk. However, this should put the interviewer on their guard.

When individuals are angry they are likely to give partial rather than full information. It is the other half of the story which is likely to be the vital one for management.

What do interviewing skills entail?

During an interview it is not only a case of obtaining all the facts but also of being sure they make a complete and consistent story. A useful guideline for collecting the basic facts in a grievance-handling situation is the 5Ws technique:

What   =   what is the employee complaint or proposal about?

When =   when did the cause of the complaint take place? Note the specific dates and times

Where =   where did what is being complained about happen? From where did the information come?

Who   =   who was involved?

Why   =   why does what happened create a problem for the employee? Why is a particular remedy being sought? It is important to understand what it is the employee is asking the organisation to do on his or her behalf.

The 'why' question is the most difficult. Individuals always like to give a favourable view of their behaviour but employee relations managers need also to know the downside of the interviewee's behaviour. In addition, they need to know background information about the interviewee, for example, length of service, domestic situation, to help gain a full picture. Interviewers are likely to have to probe behind the answers they receive from interviewees by asking for more information and evidence to support what has been said.

The information received from the interviewee must be complete and consistent. If the facts are inconsistent, then it is usually a sign some information is missing and the interviewee needs to be probed further. Naturally, people give a favourable account of their case, preferring to withhold information which makes it look less favourable. They may also withhold information because they do not realise its importance in supporting their case. So if the facts do not add up, the interviewee needs to be told why it is necessary to have any missing information.

Another technique available to help obtain missing, but vital, information is the 'play back', whereby what the interviewee has said is recounted back to them. The technique has a number of advantages. It demonstrates the interviewer has been listening, thereby increasing the interviewee's confidence in the interviewer and increasing the probability of the former volunteering information on their case which they would prefer not to reveal. It enables any misunderstandings by the interviewer concerning the information received to be corrected by the interviewee. The 'play-back' also enables the interviewer to see whether the story given by the interviewee is consistent and adds up and, if it does not, to formulate the appropriate questions to obtain the missing information.

Checking whether the facts from the interviewee are consistent and complete can also be done by corroborating their account during an interview with another individual who has an interest in the outcome of the issue which is the subject of the original interview, or who witnessed the incident which is subject to the management investigation. A further clue that the interviewee is or might be 'withholding' important information is given by their facial and body movements in response to open-ended questions such as 'What else would you like to tell me?' If eye contact changes (the head goes down) or the individual significantly changes posture, then these are outward signs the interviewee is likely to be withholding information which might put the problem or alleged incident in a different perspective.

At the conclusion of an interview, it is good practice to summarise what has been agreed. This helps avoid misunderstandings. It is also good practice to write up the notes of the interview while it is fresh in your mind. There is no general rule for taking notes during an interview except that if notes are taken they should be brief and not break the flow of the interview. In some situations, the making of brief notes indicates to the interviewee that what they are saying is regarded as sufficiently important for notes to be taken. However, in other situations, note-taking can create an inhibiting environment. In such circumstances, shorter notes should be taken and then written up in more detail as soon as possible after the interview.

Interviewing skills are crucial to the employee relations manager. Defective interviewing skills will mean gaining imperfect information and then undertaking a partial analysis of the situation. This, in turn, will result in management establishing inappropriate negotiating aims and planning misguided strategy and tactics.

Explain why competent interviewing skills are crucial to a manager.

Note-taking skills

Note-taking is another vital skill for employee relations managers and is required at every stage in the negotiating process. It is important to take accurate and clear notes. First, if the manager does not make notes he or she may promise to do something but forget. Second, he or she may agree something with a managerial colleague, an employee or a representative of the employees and forget what was agreed. Third, accurate and clear notes are essential for producing a report to management. Fourth, an employee relations manager needs to be able to make accurate notes from documents and articles they read.

Notes reduce the probability of missing something. Without notes it may be difficult to demonstrate that colleagues and/or employees have been informed of something or that they have agreed to something. To avoid these problems, it is helpful to carry a notebook and take regular notes whenever you meet with a management colleague or an employee or their representative. Note-taking skills are needed at every stage in the negotiating process.

The problem with note-taking is deciding how much detail to record. However, it is good practice always to note background details such as:

- subject

- date

- time

- place

- people involved.

It is also good practice to make a note of conclusions agreed at meetings and any follow-up action to be taken. It is bad practice to try to produce a word-for-word account of a meeting or interview. Attention centres on recording the essential information. This may seem obvious but it is surprising how many people do attempt to produce a word-for-word record of a meeting, speech, etc.

However, there are occasions when employee relations managers do need a verbatim record of a meeting. This would be the case, for example, if they were taking a statement from a management colleague (or employee) who witnessed an incident in the workplace. It would also be appropriate when agreeing the wording of an agreement concluded with the workforce. Accurate notes are particularly important at the writing-up stage of an agreement. There is a big difference between workers being granted an increase in basic pay and an increase in earnings (ie basic pay plus overtime plus shift premiums, etc). As was explained previously, a clause in an agreement which states that management (employees) *may* do something, for example, grant employees an additional day's paid holiday after five years' continuous service, is different from one which says management *will* do something, for example, granting employees an additional day's paid holiday after five years' continuous service. The former example gives management discretion. The latter imposes an obligation.

There are three main styles of laying out notes. These are:

- the 'brain-pattern' or bubble style

- the 'chronological' style

- the 'presentational' style.

Brain pattern
The 'brain-pattern' technique can be used to structure rambling speeches, long and complex statements, arguments or discussions. It is particularly useful in grievance handling and operates on the basis that an individual's brain thinks in pictures of associated ideas and themes and not in lines of typewritten script. The mind is chaotic but within this chaos a pattern can be identified.

The 'brain-pattern' or 'bubble' technique moves away from the traditional note-taking style of a layout in a vertical lines to produce a record in a pattern that replicates the working of the mind. The note produced in this layout is directly related to the individual producing the patterns (bubbles) and can be unintelligible to another individual. The most important aspect, however, is the construction of a note which is an identification and summary of the key elements of the subject under discussion but which uses words that are meaningful to the note-taker. The 'bubbles' are the key words which, along with their associated words, trigger the individual's memory.

An example of the 'brain-pattern' or 'bubble' technique format of note-taking is shown in Figure 12 which represents notes taken at a management meeting to discuss the introduction of a new shift system. The meeting was chaotic in that those present kept switching from one aspect of the proposed new system to another and to topics unrelated to the subject. The meeting started by discussing when the new system would be introduced and then some attendees began to talk about the size of the likely shift premium. Attention then returned to the proposed implementation date, after which a discussion started about a birthday party some of those present had attended the previous night. The meeting then returned to discuss the period of notice that would be given to introduce the new shift. The meeting subsequently, again, returned to the implementation date but next started to talk about the performance of the company's sports team the previous weekend before returning again to the size of any likely shift premium. The

Figure 12 'Brain pattern' or 'bubble' technique

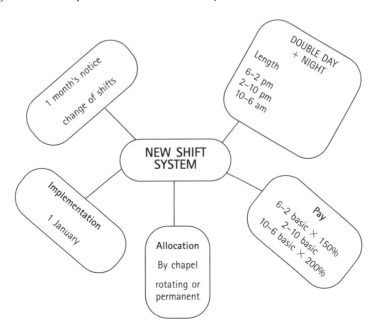

meeting carried on in this unstructured way until it ended three hours after it had started.

Figure 12 demonstrates that the meeting discussed five key elements (period of notice, implementation date, allocation of shifts to employees, shift premium rates and the times of the shift) although they were not discussed in any logical sequence. Each of the key elements is shown as a 'bubble' around the topic of the subject under discussion – the new shift system. Within each 'bubble' are words which trigger the memory as to what was agreed in each key element connected with the introduction of the new shift system. For example, the shift premium key element shows the meeting decided the 6.00am to 2.00pm shift would carry a 150 per cent premium, the 2.00pm to 10.00pm shift no premium and the 10.00pm to 6.00am shift a 200 per cent premium. A highly structured and logically sequenced report of what was a very chaotic meeting can now be given. From the notes, an oral presentation would be something like the following:

> Yesterday, I attended a meeting of senior management which discussed the introduction of a new shift system. It discussed, and made decisions, in five aspects of its introduction, namely the length of notice to be given to workforce as to its introduction, the date of implementation, the allocation of the shifts to employees, shift premium and the timing of the three shifts to be introduced. Turning to the date of implementation of the new system, it was decided this would be 1st January. On the question of the allocation of shifts to employees, it was decided this would be done by the supervisor. Turning to shift premium it was decided as follows: 6.00am–2.00pm a 150 per cent premium, 2.00pm-10.00pm no premium and 10.00pm–6.00am a 200 per cent premium. Turning to the timing of the shift, it was decided there would be three and their hours would be 6.00am–2.00pm, 2.00pm–10.00pm and 10.00pm-6.00am. Finally, it was decided the employees should be given one month's notice as to the implementation of the new system.

The 'bubble' style can be used in negotiations to take notes from long-winded and disjointed oral presentations from the other party covering their proposals and/or their arguments in favour of those proposals. It can also be used to take notes during formal and informal interview situations in grievance handling. In addition, it is a useful technique to use when taking notes during committee meetings or meetings at which management is preparing for a grievance handling, or a bargaining or group problem-solving negotiation situation.

The chronological style

The 'chronological' style is a technique which can be used when it is important to record how an interview, discussion or negotiating session evolves in terms of who 'responded' to whom, what with and when. The notepaper is divided into two with management's comments recorded on one half and those of the employee or their representatives on the other. Table 34 records the verbatim exchange between a managing director (MD) and a shop steward over the disciplining of an employee. The whole negotiating session is not recorded but Table 34 contains sufficient information to understand the general principle of the chronological style of note-taking.

Table 34 'Chronological' style of note-taking

Management	Union
2.30 pm	
MD To discuss the grievance of Ms Jones. Thank you for coming to this meeting. Management believes it is correct in the action it has taken to discipline Ms Jones for swearing at her supervisor.	SS We understand what your position is, however, the union believes the disciplinary penalty is too harsh given that the alleged swearing was only in the presence of and not at the supervisor.
PM Management cannot accept that a disciplinary penalty should not be imposed. The loss of pay is a matter of fundamental principle to us.	
3.00 pm	
MD The need for a disciplinary penalty remains. We might give consideration to the reduction of the length of suspension but the issue of pay lost is not for negotiation.	SS That may be the case but we believe the length of her suspension and the loss of pay for that period are too harsh. We believe they should be reduced to one day.

MD = Managing director
SS = Shop steward
PM = Personnel manager

In using the 'chronological' style the note-taker to the negotiation team is recording what is said by whom and when and what was actually agreed. So, when it comes to drafting the negotiated agreement, the record of the note-taker becomes invaluable. It is from their record that the clauses of the agreement are drafted. The note-taker of the negotiating team is a key player as well as being a full member of the team. Their role far exceeds that of being the 'secretary' to one side of the negotiations.

Presentation style

The 'presentation' style is a technique for converting into detail notes that have been taken in a summarised form. This style is thus a form of notes similar to those emerging from a normal meeting (ie what was covered, who agreed what). It is particularly useful in inter-management and joint problem-solving negotiating situations. It is a valuable note-taking style for recording decisions taken and subsequent actions required, for entry into an official record and for informing management of decisions taken at particular meetings, etc. An example of the 'presentation' style is shown in Figure 13.

When taking notes, employee relations managers are best advised to choose the style best suited to the situation in which they find themselves. They need to develop competence in all three styles if they are to become effective negotiators. However, in practice, they may find it easier to develop a note-taking style which is a combination of all three styles.

Presentation skills

Employee relations managers rely heavily upon the spoken word

Figure 13 'Presentation' style of note-taking

Management Committee Meeting
22 March 1999 at 4.00 pm

Present: J Wade, A N Other, B Jones, L Dixon, J Jones, T White

1 Sick pay

Complaints from employees about sick pay not being paid on time have increased. It was decided the matter be investigated and a report containing recommendations be given at next meeting.

Action: B Jones and T White to undertake investigation and production of report for next meeting.

2 Overtime working

It was discussed that overtime working should be reduced by half.

Action: J Wade to brief all supervisors of this and report on progress to next meeting.

3 Fumes in machine room

Complaints have been made about fumes from solvent and new inks in machine room.

Action: Safety representative to investigate immediately

and although some have natural gifts as presenters, most need to acquire and develop such skills. The best advice is to develop a style which suits their own personality and the situation in which the presentation is to take place. It has a well-defined structure which contains:

a) An introduction outlining what the audience will be told in broad-brush terms. For example, in starting a presentation, management might say, 'We want to talk about the need for redundancies, the measures to be introduced to reduce their possibility and the basis upon which individuals will be selected for redundancy.'

b) A main section outlining management's position in detail backed by facts, arguments and illustrative examples. In this stage of their presentation, management would, taking the example in (a) above, detail the causes of the intended redundancy (for example, fall in demand) and explain the personnel and production/provision of service measures to be introduced to minimise the number of redundancies (for example, bans on recruitment, lay-off of contract workers, etc).

c) A conclusion in which management summarises the proposals it has put forward. The language used in this stage of a presentation is typified by the following statement:

So, what we have been explaining to you is why we need redundancies, how we intend to minimise the number required, what compensation we propose to give to employees made redundant and the ways in which we intend to select employees for redundancy.

A concluding section should inform the audience what they have been told in the presentation.

In an oral presentation, preparation is just as vital as preparing for negotiations. There are a number of key tools an employee relations manager can use to make oral presentations a success. These are the:

• voice

• body

• eyes

• enthusiasm of the speaker.

The volume, speed and pitch of the voice should alter during the presentation. Effectiveness is improved by emphasising and repeating particular words and phrases, introducing effective pauses and employing gestures and conveying meanings by expression. However, if to do this will complicate what is already for you a nerve-wracking experience, then you are better off concentrating on delivering your presentation in as interesting a way as possible.

The attention of the audience can also be held by the use of information technology-based aids. Amongst these is the use of PowerPoint. However, care needs to be taken because if the presentation is too concentrated in its use of technology then the audience will stop listening to the message you are trying to convey and will focus on the 'firework display' of technology instead.

Body language is important in conveying a message to an audience but mannerisms can distract the audience to the point where they 'turn off' from the message being relayed and concentrate on the presenter's performance. Presenters are best advised to behave naturally and not to attempt to put on an act. Eye contact involves looking directly at the audience. Although many people find this difficult, if eye contact with the audience can be developed, advantages flow. For example, individuals (or groups of individuals) are more likely to listen if spoken to directly. Effective communicators are enthusiastic about their subject. If they want their audience to understand, and hopefully accept, their case then they have to believe in it themselves.

Listening skills

Employee relations mangers cannot operate merely by issuing instructions. They also require information and intelligence. An important source of information is interviews with colleagues and employees. Interviewing involves the important skill of listening which the employee relations manager needs to acquire and develop. However, the ability to listen is too often taken for granted. Too frequently it is not regarded as a skill.

There are three main problems associated with acquiring and developing listening skills:

• there is only one chance to hear the spoken word

• interpretation

• the brain thinks faster than people can talk.

There is normally no chance to hear the spoken word repeated. There can be no action replays. The spoken word must be absorbed immediately.

What one person means by a particular word or phrase may not necessarily be what another person means by that particular word or phrase, so confusion can arise when listening to what people are saying. What, for example, does 'coke' mean to you? Individuals can think more quickly than a person can talk, so once a speaker outlines an issue the listener may start to think ahead as to how to deal with the particular problem. If this happens before the person has finished telling all the facts, the listener may miss vital information through lack of concentration.

To acquire and develop effective listening techniques, the employee relations manager must concentrate on developing competencies in attention, comprehension and absorption. Among the measures a listener can take to increase their concentration is to sit where they can see the speaker. They can then watch the speaker at all times, observing their facial expressions and other gestures which the speaker uses to emphasise different parts of their presentation. Research shows individuals can accommodate at least 500 words per minute in thinking and 150 in listening, so we only use something like one third of our mental capacity. The remaining two thirds of the mind will wander if not otherwise used. The best uses of this spare capacity are thinking ahead and taking notes of what the speaker has said. Note-taking while listening also helps comprehension and absorption.

Comprehension will be easier if you do some 'homework' and anticipate what the speaker might say. By preparing, you increase your capacity to understand. Similarly, if, while the speaker is talking you mentally summarise their argument so far and think ahead about its consequences, your understanding will be enhanced. An effective listener sets aside any preconceived personal bias and listens to the message of the speaker. If you disagree with what the speaker is saying you should think of reasons why they might think differently to you. It is also sensible to take notes as this helps formulate your thoughts and aid your comprehension.

Individuals' memories differ. Immediately after they have read a sentence some people are capable of recalling it word for word. A few minutes later they can probably recall the concept but not the actual words. By the next day they will probably barely recall reading the sentence. Understanding a talk is fundamental to the process of transferring relevant information to the long-term memory. After a few hours, few people retain more than half of what they hear. This absorption rate can be improved if the listener takes notes of what they are hearing. Note-taking helps to fix information in the memory. A review of the note, perhaps a day later, fixes a little more information for a little longer. A further review in a week or so will fix the information even more permanently. A written note preserves the gist of the transitory spoken word.

In negotiations it is important to acquire listening skills. As we have seen, the note-taker has to record the exact words of management proposals and the counter-proposals made by the employees and their representatives. Effective listening also enables managers to hear the real meaning and to decide the hidden language of signals in negotiations.

Let us look at some examples of hidden language frequently used in negotiations:

1. 'At this stage, we are not prepared to consider that.'

2. 'We would find it extremely difficult to meet that demand.'

3. 'I am not empowered to negotiate on that.'

4. 'We can discuss that point.'

5. 'There are company standard terms.'

6. 'It is not our policy to make incentive payments and even if we did, they would not be 10 per cent.'

These are coded messages. You have to listen to (or read) the words very carefully to decipher what they mean. Well, what do the six statements listed above really mean? They mean:

1. 'This is a tradable item but at this stage we don't need to trade it.'

2. 'Difficult but not impossible.'

3. 'Either you or I need to see my line manager.'

4. 'It is negotiable.'

5. 'It is possible to create something specific from standard terms, so these are negotiable.'

6. 'We could negotiate on this.'

Other skills
Information is exchanged not only by word of mouth but also by people's expressions, eyes, hands and postures. The physical distance people keep from other individuals and the way they orientate their bodies are all signals and signs. Individuals' bodies regularly indicate how they feel. Employee relations managers need to acquire and develop the skills of obtaining information by 'watching' people (or as it is more commonly referred to, 'body language' or 'non-verbal communication'). For example, if in an interview the interviewee does not look at the interviewer, avoids eye contact, crosses their arms, leans away and fidgets in their chair, it is likely that they are hiding some vital information which, if revealed, would make their case look less convincing. Watching for these signs is a skill for the negotiator to develop for all the four negotiating situations that have been outlined in this chapter.

However, watching is not a simple skill to acquire and develop. It is easy to misinterpret the position or pick up the wrong information. This is particularly so if the individual being questioned is good at hiding their inner feelings, or if one signal doubles up in a number of contexts. For example, it is commonly said that the pupils of someone's eyes are dilated when they are attracted to you. However, it would be inadvisable to make any advance based on this signal as they could be drunk, on drugs, not feeling well or sitting in the dark.

In negotiating situations, employee relations managers require the skills of anticipating the likely positions and reactions of the other party to their behaviour. This can only be acquired by getting to know and understand the workforce and/or its representatives. Think about their normal behaviour when they are working since personalities do not change. Are they calm, logical and confident? What motivates them? If a manager understands those with whom he or she has to deal then it becomes easier to anticipate, in any negotiation situation, their objectives, strategy and tactics and the common ground that will exist between them and management. An employee relations manager needs to understand the people they manage and their points of view. Understanding, however, does not necessarily mean agreeing.

Having identified the different negotiating situations in which a management may find itself, the stages involved in the negotiation process and the skills (including their definition and significance to management) required of competent negotiators, we next turn to look in more detail at the managing of employee discipline.

SUMMARY

This chapter has defined negotiations, distinguished the different stages in the negotiating process, and examined the generic skills needed by the employee relations negotiator. Negotiation was defined as two or more parties coming together to make an agreement by purposeful persuasion and by making constructive compromises.

Four different negotiating situations were identified – between managers, grievance handling, bargaining and group problem solving. It was pointed out that the most common negotiating situation in which employee relations specialists are likely to find themselves is negotiating with their managerial colleagues over issues such as the appropriate course of action to solve a problem, to gain resources to implement new policies, procedures and practices and to gain the commitment of their managerial colleagues to support, for example, a major change in the organisation's pay and reward strategy. Grievance handling is negotiating a settlement to an individual employee's complaint about management's behaviour whilst bargaining is a negotiating situation where the parties involved reach an agreement by trading items in the lists of demands they have of each other. Group problem solving was identified as a situation where two or more parties negotiate the details whereby one party will co-operate with the other, which is initiating some action to resolve a problem which is of common interest to both parties. It was shown how each of these four situations has the common elements of persuasion and constructive compromise.

The chapter then explained the main differences between employee relations negotiations and commercial negotiations. These differences were seen to lie in the choice of negotiating partner, face-to-face relationships, adjournments, the status of agreements reached, and the quality of future relationships.

It was then noted that there were five stages to the negotiation process – preparation, presentation, searching for the common ground, concluding the agreement and writing up the agreement. Of these stages the most important is the preparation and the chapter stressed the importance of preparation using the phrase – 'Failure to Prepare is Preparing to Fail'. In analysing the preparation stage you were introduced to the Aspiration Grid which sets the parameters for the expected outcome of the negotiations, shows the issues management is prepared to trade, reveals management's expectations as to the tradable issues of the other party, gives a picture as to how the forthcoming negotiations are expected to develop, helps management identify the information it requires from the other party and helps identify the information management needs to convey to the other party. The chapter then identified and explained a number of techniques management can use to seek to confirm its expectations as to where the basis for an agreement lies. The most important of these were the 'if and then' technique, intelligent questioning, body watching, listening, periodic summarising and the use of the adjournment.

In concluding the agreement stage of negotiations it was noted that management needs to assure itself that it and the other party both fully understand what they have agreed and that management's offer is its final one and will not be increased in the light of employee pressure. In writing up the agreement, the importance of having clear and strong wording was stressed so as to avoid future disputes over whether one of the parties is interpreting and operating the agreement properly.

The chapter concluded by examining the skills required in the negotiating process. Competency in interviewing, note-taking and listening skills was stressed by explaining not only what these skills involved, but why possessing or not having them is significant to employee relations specialists if they are to be effective negotiators.

REFERENCES AND FURTHER READING

CAIRNS L. (1996) *Negotiation Skills in the Workplace: A practical handbook*. London, Pluto Press.

HONEY P. (1997) *Improve Your People Skills*. 2nd edn. London, Institute of Personnel and Development.

FOWLER A. (1996) *Negotiation Skills and Strategies*. 2nd edn. London, Institute of Personnel and Development.

FOWLER A. (1995) *Negotiating, Persuading and Influencing*. London, Institute of Personnel and Development.

FOWLER A. (1998) *The Disciplinary Interview*. London, Institute of Personnel and Development.

KENNEDY G., BENSON J. *and* McMILLAN J. (1987) *Managing Negotiations*. 3rd edn. London, Hutchinson.

MacKay I. (1995) *Listening Skills*. London, Institute of Personnel and Development.

Walton R. E. *and* McKersie R. B. (1991) *A Behavioural Theory of Labor Negotiations*. 2nd edn. New York, Ithaca.

Walton R. E., Cutcher-Hershenfeld J. E. *and* McKersie R. B. (1994) *Strategic Negotiations*. Cambridge, Mass., Harvard Business School Press.

8 Managing discipline

INTRODUCTION

This chapter and the one that follows cover two related topics, discipline and grievance. Although they are to be dealt with separately, it is important to recognise both are a two-way process and concern complaints, real or imagined, by one party against another. A second factor is the way in which the two subjects are treated by the law. Disciplinary procedures and practices are covered by a specific Code of Practice, which we examine in detail later in the chapter. This tends to give the disciplinary process a much higher profile within organisations than grievance procedures which are not as legally regulated.

NB grievance procedure not regulated by law [handwritten margin note]

What is discipline?

Discipline is an emotive word in the context of employment. The dictionary offers several definitions of the word discipline, ranging from 'punishment or chastisement' to 'systematic training in obedience'. There is no doubt that discipline at work can be one of the most difficult issues with which a manager has to deal. It brings to the forefront matters relating to an individual's performance, capability and conduct and, in the context of employment, the most appropriate definition to adopt is:

> to improve or attempt to improve the behaviour, orderliness, etc., of by training, conditions or rules
>
> (Collins Concise Dictionary)

In this chapter we examine the principles of discipline handling, the characteristics of a fair and effective disciplinary procedure, the legal aspects of discipline and dismissal and the monitoring and evaluation of disciplinary procedures. A fair and effective disciplinary procedure is one that concentrates on improving or changing behaviour and not one that relies on the principle of punishment.

Management problems with the discipline process

Many managers have a problem with the disciplinary process because they believe it is cumbersome and ineffective or that the law on employment rights is heavily biased against them. This can often result in problems being ignored because it is felt effective action against individual employees either takes too long, or is liable to mean an appearance before an Employment Tribunal. Many managers share this basic misconception, and it is the responsibility of the employee relations specialist to advise and guide their managerial colleagues through what, to many, is a minefield.

Best practice

It is important managers, at all levels, appreciate that the effectiveness of the business can be undermined if issues relating to conduct, capability and performance are not handled professionally and consistently, or if such matters are ignored altogether. This chapter looks at the concept of 'best practice' in relation to discipline at work, with the steps that need to be taken when managers are trying to alter behavior and how to ensure that all employees are treated fairly. 'Best practice' is a concept that many managers have difficulty with because it is a term that is difficult to define. In the context of managing discipline, it is about acting with just cause, using procedures correctly, acting consistently, following the rules of natural justice – it is all four of those things – and more. But overall, it is about developing those good management habits which ensure you do follow procedure, you do act consistently and that you do take account of the rules of natural justice when taking disciplinary action. Best practice is, therefore, an important principle. Not only does it help to ensure fairness and consistency, but it makes good business sense and can add value.

When you have completed this chapter you should be able to explain:

• the development of disciplinary procedures

• how the law supports the use of disciplinary procedures and protects individuals from unfair treatment

• the importance of clear rules about conduct

• the importance of counselling to the disciplinary process

• how to use the disciplinary process to manage different disciplinary problems

• the basic composition and procedure of an Employment Tribunal.

THE ORIGINS OF DISCIPLINARY PROCEDURES

Until the beginning of the 1970s employers had almost unlimited power to discipline and dismiss individual employees and in many instances they were not slow to exercise this power. While it was possible for a dismissed employee to sue for 'wrongful dismissal' under the common law, this was rarely a practical option because of the time and heavy costs involved. The only time that this employer power was likely to be restricted was where trade unions were present in the workplace and dismissal procedures were established through the collective bargaining process.

This changed with the Industrial Relations Act 1971. This Act gave individual employees the right, for the first time, to complain to an Industrial Tribunal that they had been unfairly dismissed. Industrial Tribunals themselves had only been established in 1964 so in 1971 were a relatively new feature of business life. They were renamed Employment Tribunals with effect from 1 August 1998 by the

Employment Rights (Dispute Resolution) Act 1998 and this change has been carried through to all pre-existing enactments. As well as introducing the right not to be unfairly dismissed, the 1971 Act also introduced, in 1972, the Industrial Relations Code of Practice. This introduced the idea that there was a right and a wrong way to deal with issues of discipline. It was subsequently superseded by the ACAS Code of Practice 'Disciplinary Practice and Procedures in Employment' which is dealt with in more detail later in the chapter.

The 1971 Act was a turning point in the relationship between employer and employee. The relative informality of the then Industrial Tribunals and the fact that access to them did not depend on lawyers or money meant that for many employees the threat of dismissal without good reason disappeared or diminished. This does not mean that employees cannot be unfairly dismissed. They can. The law has never removed from management the ability to dismiss who it likes, when it likes and for whatever reason it likes. All that has happened since 1971 is that where employees are deemed to have acted unreasonably and unfairly in dismissing employees they can be forced to compensate an individual for the consequences of those actions. Most employers have accepted this legal intervention without serious complaint and seek to manage disciplinary issues in as fair a way as possible. Some clearly do not and take a cavalier attitude to individual employment rights. Others, as was mentioned previously, suffer from a misconception as to what they can do and how the law impacts upon their actions.

THE CURRENT LEGAL POSITION

Until 1996, the law relating to discipline and dismissal was contained in the Employment Protection (Consolidation) Act 1978. In August of that year the Employment Rights Act 1996 came into force, consolidating provisions contained in the 1978 Act together with provisions of the Wages Act 1986, the Sunday Trading Act 1994 and the Trade Union Reform and Employment Rights Act 1993 (TURERA).

The starting point for the disciplinary process is to be found in section 1 of the 1996 Act which deals with an employee's right to a statement of employment particulars. Section 3 states that any statement of particulars shall include a note:

> specifying any disciplinary rules applicable to the employee or referring the employee to the provisions of a document specifying such rules which is reasonably accessible to the employee.

The section goes on to state that the statement of particulars must also specify who an employee can appeal to if they are dissatisfied with any disciplinary decision that is made. Given that this has been the law in one form or another since 1971 it is surprising that many employers still have no effective disciplinary code or appeals procedure.

Sections 94 to 134 of the Act deal specifically with unfair dismissal and these set out the:

• legal definition of dismissal

- specific reasons for which it is fair to dismiss an employee
- position of shop workers who refuse to work on a Sunday
- position of trade union officials
- position of health and safety representatives
- position of pension trustees.

Fair dismissals
There are three ways in which an individual can be legally dismissed: their employment is terminated with or without notice; they are employed under a fixed term contract and that contract comes to an end without being renewed, or they resign (with or without notice) because of the employer's conduct. This book is not intended as a legal text and more detail on the meaning and applicability of these three definitions can be found in *Essentials of Employment Law* by David Lewis (IPD 1997), Legal Essentials: *Dismissal,* or in the IPD *Employment Law Service* which has been specifically designed to aid all practitioners with the legal aspects of their work.

The Act defines a number of reasons for which it can be fair to dismiss an employee and these are:

- conduct
- capability or qualifications
- redundancy
- breach of statutory provision
- some other substantial reason.

Dismissals relating to capability, conduct or some other substantial reason are probably the most common and have the most links with the disciplinary process. However, they all have one thing in common. To be considered fair reasons for dismissal they have to pass the test of reasonableness set out in section 98 of the Employment Rights Act. This states that:

> the determination of the question whether the dismissal was fair or unfair, having regard to the reason shown by the employer shall depend on whether, in the circumstances (including the size and administrative resources of the employer's undertaking), the employer acted reasonably or unreasonably in treating it as a sufficient reason for dismissing the employee; and that the question shall be determined in accordance with equity and the substantial merits of the case. (s.98(4)ERA)

It is this requirement that makes it even more important to follow the principles of 'best practice' as it is the most effective way of demonstrating reasonableness.

Although the Act sets out minimum qualifying periods of employment for the acquisition of employment rights, these limits can be, and have been, changed. For example, on 1 June 1999 the minimum period of continuous service with an employer to qualify for unfair dismissal was reduced from two years to one year. It is always disturbing when we hear, as we do, managers talk of having a free hand to take whatever actions they like during an individual's first months of employment. Making distinctions about how to deal with discipline based on an individual's length of service is to invite the possibility of inconsistency to creep into the process and to lay the organisation open to legal challenge. To avoid this possibility it is prudent for all managers and employee relations specialists to treat disciplinary issues in exactly the same way, regardless of an individual's length of service.

DISCIPLINARY PROCEDURE

ACAS Code

The ACAS Code of Practice 'Disciplinary Practices and Procedures in Employment' is of significant importance in the management and resolution of disciplinary issues. While breach of the Code of Practice is, in itself, not unlawful, its provisions and impact are central to the understanding of the disciplinary process. The legislation makes it very clear just how central this is:

> A failure on the part of any person to observe any provision of a Code of Practice shall not of itself render him liable to any proceedings; but in any proceedings before an [employment] tribunal or the Central Arbitration Committee any Code of Practice .... shall be admissible in evidence, and if any provision of such a Code appears to the tribunal or Committee to be relevant to any question arising in the proceedings it shall be taken into account in determining that question
>
> Employment Protection Act 1975 section 6(11).

Given such a very clear statement of the Code's status it is a foolish organisation that does not take it seriously and is not prepared to invest time in devising its own disciplinary procedure based on its provisions. Since the 1960s, when very few establishments had formal procedures, the intervening years have seen significant growth in their use and now only a small proportion of establishments do not have some form of mechanism for dealing with discipline and dismissal (Edwards 1994). Our own research indicates that it is usually establishments with less than 25 employees who do not have formal procedures.

Because of the importance that ACAS places on drawing up disciplinary procedures and company rules, they have produced an example procedure which is set out in their advisory booklet *Discipline at Work*. This sets out:

- the purpose of a disciplinary procedure

- the scope of a disciplinary procedure

- the principle of a procedure

- the procedure itself

- the appeals process.

The disciplinary procedure

If you examine your own organisation's disciplinary code against the ACAS template you are likely to identify, if not a mirror image, remarkable similarities. The starting point for the actual procedure should be:

- an oral warning

- a subsequent written warning if the required improvement is not forthcoming

- a final written warning if conduct or performance is still unsatisfactory

- finally, dismissal.

There are a number of important points to note about this staged procedure. Firstly, it is important that a record be kept of every disciplinary warning issued, even an oral warning. Secondly, it is important to advise individuals how long a warning will be 'live'. 'Live' in this context indicates the length of time that a particular disciplinary sanction will stay on the record. Warnings can be taken into account if further disciplinary issues arise but warnings that have expired cannot. Many organisations will have different timescales for different levels of warning, for example, an oral warning might only be 'live' for six months, whereas a written warning might be 'live' for twelve months. Finally it is important that employees are advised of what will happen next if no improvements are made.

The purpose and scope of a disciplinary procedure should be very clear. It should allow all employees to understand what is expected of them in respect of conduct, attendance and job performance and set out the rules by which such matters will be governed. The aim is to ensure consistent and fair treatment for all.

> To what extent does your organisation's disciplinary procedure meet the criteria of clarity? Does it set out the time that individual warnings will be 'live' and is it capable of ensuring consistent and fair treatment for all employees? You may consider it worth reviewing your procedure against these benchmarks.

Principles underlying disciplinary procedure

When we look later in the chapter at handling discipline you will note that the only way to ensure consistency is by taking a 'best practice' approach and recognising that a disciplinary procedure is more than just a series of stages. There are a number of principles that underlie the procedure which are extremely important and help to ensure good personnel management practice. As with the mechanics of the procedure itself, ACAS offers guidance on these principles, which are set out below:

- No disciplinary action will be taken against an employee until the case has been fully investigated.

- At every stage in the procedure the employee will be advised of the nature of the complaint against him or her and will be given the opportunity to state his or her case before any decision is made.

- At all stages the employee will have the right to be accompanied by a shop steward, employee representative or work colleague during the disciplinary interview.

- No employee will be dismissed for a first breach of discipline except in the case of gross misconduct when the penalty will be dismissal without notice or payment in lieu of notice.

- An employee will have the right to appeal against any disciplinary penalty imposed.

- The procedure may be implemented at any stage if the employee's alleged misconduct warrants such action.

The right to be accompanied by a steward used to apply only to workplaces where there was a recognised union. However the Employment Relations Act 1999 provides all workers with the right 'when required or invited by [their] employer to attend a disciplinary or grievance hearing ... to be accompanied by a single companion'. This individual can be a trade union official or representative and it makes no difference whether the employer recognises a union or not. Many employers view this change as unhelpful because it introduces an external element into what they have always understood to be an internal procedure.

After 'live' warnings expire

Although it is to be hoped that any disciplinary problems within an organisation can be resolved at the earliest opportunity, and without recourse to all levels of the procedure, the world of work is not so simple. Many managers complain that having given an individual an oral warning or, in some cases, having got all the way through to final written warning stage, the problem to which the disciplinary action related resurfaces once the warning ceases to be 'live'. It is then assumed, mistakenly, that the whole process must begin again.

This is not so and three points need to be considered. Firstly, for what length of time do warnings stay 'live'? If it is for too short a time then you run the risk of only achieving short-term changes in behaviour, but on the other hand you do not want it to be too long. A sanction that remains on an employee's record for an excessive period of time relative to the original breach of discipline, can act as a demotivating influence. Secondly, has the warning been too narrow? Very often, it makes more sense to issue a warning in such a way that an employee is left in no doubt that 'any further breaches of the company rules will result in further disciplinary action'. As the ACAS principles set out above identify, the procedure may be implemented at any stage. If you have an employee against whom you constantly have to invoke the disciplinary procedure, or the offence is serious, but does not amount to gross misconduct, then it may be appropriate to begin with a written rather than an oral warning. In extreme cases, a final written warning could be appropriate.

Gross misconduct

Before leaving procedural requirements it is necessary to examine what the concept of gross misconduct means. You will have noted above that according to the ACAS principles it is permissible to dismiss an individual without notice if they have committed an act of gross misconduct. Gross misconduct can be notoriously difficult to define and often difficult to prove and ACAS very helpfully provides a list of actions which would normally fall into this category. These are:

- theft
- fraud
- deliberate falsification of records
- fighting
- assault on another person
- deliberate damage to company property
- serious incapability through alcohol or under the influence of illegal drugs
- serious negligence
- injury or damage
- serious acts of insubordination.

While that is quite an extensive list, it is also notable for its lack of clarity. For example, what is an act of serious insubordination? Would it cover the refusal to carry out instructions received from a supervisor? What is serious negligence or serious incapability through alcohol?

The potential difficulties caused by this lack of clarity mean that whatever procedure you establish, it reflects the organisation's structure and culture – the norms and beliefs within which an organisation functions. This is where the writing of clear company rules is so important. Not only do they help to distinguish between ordinary and gross misconduct, but they provide employees with clear guidelines on what is acceptable in the workplace, in terms of both behaviour and performance.

> How sure are you, that your organisation's procedure is working as it should? What criteria would you use to assess whether it is or is not?

RULES IN EMPLOYMENT

Rules should be written for the benefit of both employer and employee. Their purpose should be to define and make clear exactly what standards of behaviour are expected in the workplace. Typically, rules will cover the following areas:

- time-keeping
- absence
- health and safety
- misconduct
- use of company facilities
- confidentiality
- discrimination.

There are some (including ACAS) who would argue that rules about poor performance should also be included, but there are some practical difficulties about writing rules in respect of poor performance. Individuals need to know what is expected of them in respect of performance, but this ought to be done through a clearly written job description that sets out their prime tasks and responsibilities and how their performance will be measured. Clearly, if rules relating to behaviour are broken and, as a consequence, performance is impaired, for example through drunkenness, then it is easy to see a link between poor performance and rule breaking, with the disciplinary procedure being used to correct the problem.

But if someone is simply not competent to carry out the tasks for which they have been employed, then it is hard to identify what sort of rule has been broken, notwithstanding the fact that the disciplinary procedure may be used as a means of correcting the problem. This, however, is a minor point. The important point is to ensure that the following principles are followed, whatever rules are established:

- they are clear

- they cannot be misinterpreted

- they are capable of distinguishing between ordinary misconduct and gross misconduct.

The importance of clear rules

Failure to be clear and failing to make a proper distinction between types of misconduct have caused many organisations to suffer losses at Employment Tribunals. It is no good having a very clear procedure, laying down the type and number of warnings that an individual should receive, if the rules which are being applied are imprecise or do not reflect the attitudes and requirements of the particular business. 'How people expect to behave depends as much on day-to-day understanding as on formal rules. Workplaces may have identical rule-books, but in one it may be accepted practice to leave early near holidays; in another, on Fridays; in a third, when a relatively lenient supervisor is in charge, and so on' (Edwards 1994 p563).

There is also a need to ensure that rules reflect current industrial practice as is illustrated by the following case. The applicant, who was a union representative, had been dismissed for gross misconduct for gaining unauthorised access to his employer's computer system. He had gained access to a part of the system that would normally be inaccessible to him by using another employee's password. In his defence it was argued that 'he had only been playing around' with the system and that there had been no intent to obtain information to which he was not entitled. Furthermore, that while he may have been doing something wrong it was not 'gross misconduct' and could have been covered by a disciplinary warning. In upholding the dismissal for gross misconduct the Employment Appeal Tribunal (EAT) stated as follows:

> the industrial members are clear in their view that in this modern industrial world if an employee deliberately uses an unauthorised password in order to enter or to attempt to enter a computer known to

contain information to which he is not entitled, then that of itself is gross misconduct which prima facie will attract summary dismissal, although there may be some exceptional circumstances in which such a response might be held unreasonable.

Denco v Joinson (1991) IRLR 63

In essence the EAT were making the same point that had been made some years earlier in C A Parsons & Co Ltd v McLaughlin (1978) IRLR 65, that some things should be so obvious that it ought not to be necessary to have a rule forbidding it. However, for the avoidance of doubt, the EAT went on to say in the Denco case that

it is desirable, however, that management should make it abundantly clear to the workforce that interfering with computers will carry severe penalties. Rules concerning access to and use of computers should be reduced to writing and left near the computers for reference

While the comments of the Employment Appeal Tribunal about certain things being obvious may seem perfectly reasonable, it should be remembered that employers have an absolute duty to demonstrate that they have acted reasonably when they dismiss somebody. In Denco, even the EAT acknowledged that there might be circumstances in which an employer's particular response might be 'unreasonable', even about something which is supposedly obvious. The message is very clear. If something is not allowed then say so, and spell out the consequences of breaching the rule. Because technology, or the ownership of businesses, can change, what may have been acceptable once may now be frowned on. The prudent employee relations specialist will ensure that the organisation's rules are the subject of regular monitoring to ensure that they properly reflect the organisation's current values and requirements.

The need to be clear about the behavioural standards that are expected in any workplace, and the sanctions that will be applied for non-compliance, is particularly important in distinguishing between gross and ordinary misconduct. Frequently organisations commit the error of making vague statements in their company rules to the effect that certain actions '*may*' be treated as gross misconduct or that the failure to do something '*could*' leave an individual liable to disciplinary action. For example, many rules on theft which we have seen simply state that 'theft may be considered to be gross misconduct'.

This sort of wording can only leave room for doubt and confusion. If an employee stole a large sum of money from the company there is little doubt that they would be charged with gross misconduct and, if the allegation was proved, dismissed without notice. What, though, would happen if the alleged theft were of items of company stationery or spare parts for machinery? Would every manager treat the matter as one of gross misconduct and dismiss, or would the value of the items taken be a consideration? Employee relations specialists need to be aware of these potential contradictions when helping to frame rules that govern the employment relationship. If it is normal practice to turn a blind eye to the misappropriation of items like stationery, then this can cause problems when someone is accused of a more serious theft. We have already highlighted the importance of discipline being applied fairly and consistently. Is this happening if different managers are given the opportunity to apply different standards to the same actions? Allowing different managers to take a different view about the seriousness of certain acts of theft brings inconsistency into the process. This could prove very costly at an Employment Tribunal. One way to avoid this problem is to make positive statements, for example, that theft *will* be treated as gross misconduct.

A better rule on theft might be:

> Theft: stealing from the company, its suppliers or fellow employees is unacceptable, whatever the value or amount involved, and will be treated as gross misconduct.

Using this style of wording should help to ensure that every employee in the organisation knows the consequences of any dishonest action on their part. Ensuring managers apply the sanction consistently is another problem and one we will deal with later in the chapter.

How often are the rules in your organisation reviewed and when were they last updated? Do you know whether different standards apply to the application of the rules?

Theft, whatever standards different organisations might apply, is usually associated in the public mind with gross misconduct, notwithstanding the problems of definition that we have just discussed. The distinction between gross misconduct and other serious infractions of the rules can often be harder to identify. The first thing to acknowledge is that no clear distinction exists, but it is possible to apply common sense to the issue. For example it is easy to understand that a serious assault on another person ought to be treated as gross misconduct, whilst that of poor time-keeping would not. While a consistent failure to observe time-keeping standards might ultimately lead to dismissal, clearly the two offences initially provoke different outcomes, namely immediate dismissal in the first case and normally a verbal warning in the second. Therefore, perhaps one way in which a distinction might be drawn is by a reference to the expected outcome of the disciplinary process and to the relationship of trust that needs to exist between employer and employee.

While not wishing to explore the wider issues relating to the contract of employment, it is implied in every contract that for an employment relationship to be maintained there has to be mutual trust and confidence between employer and employee. When issues of discipline arise, that relationship is damaged. One of the purposes of disciplinary action is to bring about a change in behaviour. If the offence is one of poor time-keeping there is usually no question of a total breakdown of trust and the expected outcome of disciplinary action is of improved time-keeping and a rebuilding of the relationship. If the cause of the disciplinary action is a serious assault on another employee, perhaps a manager, a disciplinary sanction might bring about a change in behaviour or ensure that the offence is not repeated, but there is a high probability that the relationship of mutual trust and confidence will be damaged beyond repair and it might be impossible for the employment relationship to be maintained.

HANDLING DISCIPLINARY ISSUES

The way in which managers and employee relations specialists approach disciplinary issues will be subtly different depending on the nature of the problem. Most organisations will have some form of disciplinary procedure, and probably some company rules, but the use and application of the procedure may vary from company to company and from manager to manager. In some organisations disciplinary action is very rarely taken either because standards are clear and accepted by employees or because standards are vague and applied haphazardly. In others, standards are maintained by an overreliance on mechanistic procedures, which usually acts as a demotivating influence on the workforce.

The purpose of any disciplinary procedure should be 'to help and encourage all employees to achieve and maintain standards of conduct, attendance and job performance' (ACAS Code). This is what 'best practice' means and the aim of all managers should be to handle disciplinary issues in as fair and equitable a way as is possible. They should do this because it represents 'best practice' in terms of management skill, but also because of the influence of the law. The law on unfair dismissal is now so ingrained into the fabric of the workplace that only by maintaining standards of 'best practice' does it cease to become an issue. Good managers have nothing to fear from the laws relating to individual employment rights. That is not to say the law should be ignored, but neither should it be feared. In an ideal world managers would act in such a way that they avoided accusations of unfair treatment. But this is not an ideal world and even the best managers can find themselves defending their actions before an Employment Tribunal and this is why it is important for the concept of 'best practice' to become part of the organisation's ethos.

Not only does this allow them to demonstrate 'consistent and fair treatment for all' (ACAS Code), but it ensures that they meet their absolute duty to act reasonably as set out in section 98(4)(a) of the Employment Rights Act 1996. Furthermore, such an approach not only makes good business sense, it fits the concept of 'natural justice' that is so important in handling disciplinary issues.

The 1996 Act identifies reasons for fairly dismissing an employee as conduct, capability and 'some other substantial reason'. A good manager will consider whether some other route will be more appropriate before becoming embroiled in the disciplinary process. Maintaining good standards of discipline within an organisation is not just about applying the rules or operating the procedure. It is about the ability to achieve standards of performance and behaviour without using the 'big stick'. One way to avoid becoming embroiled in the disciplinary process is counselling, which might provide the required change in behaviour without making the individual concerned feel they are some kind of dissident.

Counselling

Counselling is more than simply offering help and advice. It is helping, in a non-threatening way, an individual to come to terms with a particular problem. The problem may be about performance, about time-keeping, about drug or alcohol abuse or about another employee, for example an accusation of sexual harassment. Counselling an employee, whatever the nature of the problem, needs careful preparation. With a drug or alcohol problem most managers lack the necessary skills to carry out such a sensitive task, but even if they conclude that specialist help is required they can still help to bring the problem out into the open. In other cases, provided the problem is approached in a systematic way, this type of intervention may avoid disciplinary action.

One example of where counselling might be an appropriate first step would be in respect of an allegation of sexual harassment or bullying. Provided the complainant has not suffered any physical assault and, most importantly, that the complainant is happy for the matter to be handled in an informal way, then counselling can be very helpful not only to the alleged harasser, but also to the victim. Without wishing to minimise or condone what can be a very serious problem in some workplaces, it can often be the case that the alleged harasser or bully does not realise that their behaviour or actions are causing offence or fear. Sitting down with an individual and explaining to them that some of their words or actions are causing distress to another employee can often be very effective. However, it is important not to leave it there, but to monitor the situation and ensure that the behavioural change is permanent, and that the complainant is satisfied with the action taken and the eventual outcome. If not, you may find yourself dealing with a formal grievance or even a claim for 'constructive dismissal'.

> Does your organisation's Disciplinary Code say anything about equal opportunities or discrimination? Is there, for example, a clear rule that says sexual harassment or racial discrimination will not be tolerated? Do you have a Code of Practice that gives guidance on how to manage these sorts of problems?

Similarly, if the problem concerns poor performance, 'best practice' would be to discuss the problem with the employee concerned rather than go straight into the disciplinary procedure. The first step would be to speak to the employee, in private, explaining what aspects of performance were falling short of the desired standard and most importantly, what actions were required by the employee to put matters right. The 'golden rule' to remember is to set clear standards. If the employee does not know what is expected of them, how can they deliver the performance that is required? Another step in this process might be to consider whether some additional training might be an option. All of this might be best dealt with under a formal appraisal scheme if one exists within the organisation.

The formal approach

However, if after following the counselling route there are still complaints of harassment, or the quality of work being carried out still falls below standard then it may be necessary to begin disciplinary proceedings. Again it is important to remember the principle of 'best practice'. The operation of the disciplinary procedure can often lead to managerial disenchantment because of the claim that 'it takes too long'. This is where the employee relations specialist has a clear duty to advise and guide management colleagues. Since starting down the disciplinary path can, ultimately, lead to a dismissal it is important to remember the requirement that in taking a decision to dismiss somebody you should act reasonably and in accordance with natural justice.

It is easy to understand the frustration a line manager might feel if the disciplinary process takes too long, but it is the employer who is in control of the process and can determine the timings. The question of fairness relates not to how long the process takes, but to the quality of the procedures followed. For example, say you had an experienced employee who was responsible for carrying out a very important task within the organisation and which had serious cost implications if it were not carried out efficiently. If the task was not being performed satisfactorily, the amount of time you could allow the employee to improve their performance would be limited. Alternatively, if the employee was inexperienced and performing a task that was less cost-sensitive and important, then the time allowed for improvement should be longer.

It is also necessary to consider how long the sub-standard performance has been allowed to continue unchallenged, because it may be the case that a previous manager was prepared to accept a lower standard of performance. What is important in either of these scenarios is that the employee is made aware of the standard that is required and understands the importance of achieving that standard in whatever timescale is agreed. Under the ACAS Code it is acceptable to miss out stages in the procedure and this may be the more obvious solution if the consequences of the poor performance are so serious.

USING THE DISCIPLINARY PROCEDURE

Whatever the nature of the problem, once the decision has been taken to invoke the formal disciplinary procedures it is important to ensure that its application cannot be challenged. The following guidelines, which are broken down into two stages, help to ensure a consistent and fair approach:

Preparing for the disciplinary interview
There are steps that need to be taken in preparing to conduct a disciplinary interview. There are twelve points to consider:

1. Prepare carefully and ensure that the person conducting the disciplinary hearing has all the facts. This sounds straightforward, but it is not always possible to obtain all the facts. Frequently the evidence of alleged misconduct is no more that circumstantial, particularly in cases involving theft. However, the guiding principle is to ensure that a thorough investigation takes place and that whatever facts are available are presented.

2. Ensure that the employee knows what the nature of the complaint is. This again sounds straightforward, but is often the point at which things begin to go wrong. For example, it would not be sufficient to tell an employee that they are to attend a disciplinary hearing in respect of their poor performance. They need to be provided with sufficient detail so they can prepare an adequate defence.

3. Ensure the employee knows the procedure to be followed. Simply because an individual was provided with a copy of the Disciplinary Code when they commenced employment, does not imply they know the procedure to be followed. It is always wise to provide them with a new copy of the disciplinary procedure, not least because there may have been amendments since they received their original version.

4. Advise employees of their right to be accompanied. Where individuals work in a unionised environment this tends to be automatic, with an invitation to attend the meeting sent directly to the appropriate union official. However, in non-unionised environments, people are not always sure who would be an appropriate person to accompany them or whether they want to be accompanied at all. As a matter of best practice it is wise to encourage somebody to be accompanied, but if they refuse their decision has to be respected. When that does happen the fact of an employee wishing to attend a disciplinary interview alone should be recorded.

5. Enquire whether there are any mitigating circumstances. What is or is not a mitigating circumstance will be dictated by each case. It is not for the employer to identify matters of mitigation, but it is important to ask the employee who is facing a disciplinary sanction whether there are any particular circumstances that might account for their actions. Whether an individual manager accepts what may seem to be no more than excuses is a question of fact determined by individual circumstances. For example, an employee with a bad time-keeping record might be excused if they were having to care for a sick relative before attending work, whereas another employee might put forward a less acceptable excuse, such as a broken alarm clock.

6. Are you being consistent? This is where the employee relations specialist can provide invaluable assistance to the line manager. Most line managers deal very rarely with disciplinary issues and may not be aware of previous actions or approaches that have been taken in respect of disciplinary issues. The employee relations specialist can provide the advice and information that ensure a consistent approach.

7. Consider explanations. This is not the same as mitigating circumstances or excuses. This is the opportunity that you must give to an employee to explain their acts or omissions. For example, if the hearing was about poor performance, the employee might want to point out factors that have inhibited performance, but which might not be immediately apparent to the line manager

conducting the hearing. There may be issues around the quality of training received or the quality of instructions given.

8. Allow employees time to prepare their case. The question here is, how much time? It is important that issues of discipline are dealt with speedily once an employee has been advised of the complaint against them, but it is important for the employee not to feel unfairly pressured in putting together any defence that they have.

9. Arrange a suitable place for the interview. This would seem to be obvious, but as with so many things in employee relations, what may seem obvious to the specialist is not always apparent to the busy line manager. There is a tendency for managers to arrange meetings within their own offices where the potential for being interrupted is more pronounced or privacy less easily guaranteed.

10. Ensure that personnel records etc are available. This covers more than basic information about the individual, but also records relating to any previous disciplinary warnings, attendance, performance appraisals etc.

11. Where possible, be accompanied. It is very unwise for a manager to conduct a disciplinary interview alone because of the possible need to corroborate what was said at some future time. It also helps to rebut any allegations of bullying or intimidation that may be made by a disgruntled employee.

12. Try to ensure attendance of witnesses. This should not be a problem if the witnesses concerned are in your employ, but can prove difficult when they are outsiders.

It cannot be stressed, too strongly, the importance of careful preparation as it is at this stage that things often go wrong.

The disciplinary interview
Good preparation helps the second part of the process, conducting the actual disciplinary interview. There are six points to remember at this stage:

1. Introduce those present. Not just on grounds of courtesy, but because an employee facing a possible sanction is entitled to know who is going to be involved in any decision. In a small workplace this may be unnecessary, but it can be important in larger establishments.

2. Explain the purpose of the interview and how it will be conducted. This builds on the need to ensure the employee fully understands the nature of the complaint against them and the procedure to be followed. As with any hearing, however informal, what it is for, what are the possible outcomes and the method by which it is to be conducted are important prerequisites for demonstrating that natural justice has been adhered to.

3. Set out precisely the nature of the complaint and outline the case by briefly going through the evidence. This may seem like overkill, but it is important to ensure that there are no misunderstandings.

4. Give the employee the right to reply. Put simply, if there is no right of reply, there is no natural justice.

5. Allow time for general questioning, cross-examination of witnesses etc. If this does not happen, it will be difficult to persuade a tribunal that the test of reasonableness has been achieved.

6. Sum up. There is a need to be clear about what conclusions have been reached and what decisions are to be made and for this reason it is better to adjourn, if only briefly, so that a properly-considered decision can be made.

Careful preparation and a well-conducted interview are not guarantees that individuals will not complain of unfairness, but they are essential if the test of reasonableness is to be satisfied.

MISCONDUCT DURING EMPLOYMENT

There are two distinct types of misconduct. The persistent rule-breaker and the individual who commits an act of gross misconduct. In most instances, dealing with the persistent rule-breaker is be relatively straight forward, provided that the Disciplinary Code is applied in a sensible and equitable manner. Assuming that it has been possible to go through some form of counselling with the employee, but the required change in behavior has not been forthcoming, then it is likely that the only alternative is to begin the disciplinary process. The likely first step would be a verbal or written warning followed, if necessary, by the subsequent stages in the procedure, leading ultimately to dismissal.

While the dismissal of an employee is never an easy task for a manager, it can, if the steps outlined above are followed, be a relatively straightforward process. Furthermore, individuals who are dismissed for persistent infringements of the rules, for which they have had a series of warnings and the opportunity to appeal, rarely go to Employment Tribunals. It is difficult for an individual to claim that the employer acted unreasonably when they have been given a number of opportunities to modify their actions. The only complaint that an individual might have in such circumstances is that the procedure itself is unfair or has been applied contrary to the rules of natural justice. This could happen if some people are disciplined for breaches of the rules and others are not.

> Imagine that your organisation has dismissed somebody for bad time-keeping and unauthorised absences and the employee has challenged this in an employment industrial tribunal. What evidence would you need to present in support of your organisation's action?

Gross misconduct

Gross misconduct, on the other hand, presents totally different problems for the manager. Earlier, some of the issues surrounding the concept of gross misconduct were examined, as was the need to be absolutely clear what breaches of the rules 'will' mean as opposed to 'might' mean. For the manager who is called upon to deal with a case of alleged gross misconduct it is vitally important that all procedural steps are strictly adhered to as mistakes can be costly. For obvious reasons managers are often under extreme pressure to resolve matters quickly. This is not just because it is much fairer to the accused individual that the matter is resolved, but because other colleagues may have already prejudged the outcome. Pressure cannot always be avoided, but it is necessary that in such circumstances the requirement to prepare properly and conduct a fair hearing is not forgotten.

Some cases of gross misconduct are very clear cut and the employee concerned either admits the offence or there are sufficient witnesses to confirm that the alleged offence was committed by the employee. In such cases the first decision for the employer is to decide whether to treat the matter as gross misconduct, for which the penalty is summary dismissal without notice or pay in lieu of notice, or to take a more lenient line. Such decisions are made easier if the company rules are clear and unambiguous about what constitutes gross misconduct. But, in our experience, many cases of gross misconduct are not clear cut and managers are very unsure about how to deal with them. Some of the cases in which we have been asked to assist include suspected theft of goods or money, suspicion of tampering with time-recording devices, suspected false expense claims or seeking payment of sick pay while fit for work. One reason why managers can be unsure about these type of offences is that some of them could lead to criminal charges being laid against the employee or employees concerned.

One way to approach this very sensitive issue is by ensuring that the Burchell Rules are applied. These rules relate to a case dating back to 1978 involving an incident of alleged theft (British Home Stores v Burchell 1978 IRLR 379). The specific facts of the case are not particularly important, but it is significant because of the test of reasonableness that flowed from it. The Burchell test states that where an employee is suspected of a dismissable offence, an employer needs to show:

- the dismissal was *bona fide* for that reason and not for a pretext

- the belief that the employee committed the offence was based on reasonable grounds – that is, that on the evidence before them, the employer was entitled to say that it was more probable that the employee did, in fact, commit the offence than that they did not

- the belief was based on a reasonable investigation in the circumstances – that the employer's investigation took place before the employee was dismissed and included an opportunity for the employee to offer an explanation.

Implications of Burchell test
Let us look at this test in a little more detail and try and relate it to events as they might take place in the working environment. Take the example of a suspected fraudulent expense claim. The first part of Burchell says that the dismissal must be *bona fide* and not for a pretext. This means not using the alleged offence as a convenient means of dismissing an employee whose face no longer fits, or who has a history of misconduct for which no previous action has been taken. The second and third parts of Burchell relate to the employer's belief

in the employee's guilt and to the standard of the investigation carried out. As Lewis states (1997 p171) 'the question to be determined is not whether, by an objective standard, the employer's belief that the employee was guilty of the misconduct was well-founded, but whether the employer believed that the employee was guilty and was entitled so to believe having regard to the investigation conducted'.

Using the Burchell test in the case of a suspected fraudulent expense claim, the employer would need to be very diligent in assembling the evidence. What guidelines were laid down for the benefit of those allowed to claim expenses? What expenses had been accepted in the past? Were the same standards applied consistently to all staff? Had any other employee made a similar claim in the past without challenge? Assembling such an array of evidence is only likely to happen if there is a thorough investigation, but this is only the first part of the process; the employee is also entitled to offer an explanation. What do you do if the explanation is linked to the lack of guidelines about what is and is not claimable?

While the finding in the Parsons case (see above) that some things are so obvious that they do not need a rule is relevant, the seniority of the employee concerned might also be relevant. A 'reasonable' belief that a senior employee, who regularly claimed expenses, was acting dishonestly might be easier to demonstrate than a situation in which a junior employee was claiming expenses for the first time. We acknowledged above the uncertainties that sometimes can be encountered when the possibility of criminal proceedings is on the agenda. The question we are asked is, can we dismiss somebody if we have asked the police to investigate with a view to prosecution? The short answer is yes, providing that the Burchell test is followed. Quite properly, the burden of proof placed on an employer in such circumstances is totally different from the burden of proof imposed by the criminal justice system. In a criminal trial the prosecution must prove 'beyond all reasonable doubt' that an offence was committed. This is entirely reasonable when an individual's liberty is at risk and it is why, under the Burchell test, you can dismiss somebody 'fairly' for dishonesty, who may be found 'not guilty' in a criminal trial.

LACK OF CAPABILITY

This is the second of the fair reasons for dismissing an employee and we need to consider this under two subcategories. Firstly, capability that is linked to an employee's ability to do their job because of poor performance and secondly, capability that relates to an individual's ability to do their job because of poor health or sickness.

Performance

Advising a line manager who has a member of their team delivering less than adequate performance is very common for the employee relations specialist. Very often the initial step in this advisory role is persuading the line manager not to take precipitant action. It is not unusual for the personnel professional to be told by a manager that a particular employee is 'useless' and that they need help to 'get rid of them'. Persuading a line manager not to launch into a formal disciplinary process without considering what other options are open to them is very important. Earlier we looked at the question of counselling and in the event of an ultimate dismissal, an Employment Tribunal would want to satisfy itself that such a step had, at the very least, been considered before formal disciplinary procedures had begun. Another option might be the provision of alternative work for the employee concerned if they had demonstrated an incapability for their present tasks.

Whatever options are taken, the employee is entitled, on grounds of fairness, to be told exactly what is required of them, what standards are being set and the timescale in which they are expected to achieve them. During the period of time that an individual is being given to reach the desired standards, a good manager ensures they are kept informed of their progress; this again is the operation of the principle of 'best practice' or good management habits.

One important point to remember in looking at capability is the obligations placed on employers by the Disability Discrimination Act 1995, the principal purpose of which is to protect disabled people from discrimination in the field of employment.

Managing absence

This can be one of the most emotive issues that any manager has to face and has always to be handled with sensitivity by managers. Now that the Employment Rights Act has been amended to provide 'time off for domestic incidents' there is even more scope for disputes to arise in this difficult area. Under the amended legislation the government will have the power to make regulations specifying what is 'reasonable' time off, requirements for notice etc, but at the time of writing these had not been published. It is important, however, that employee relations specialists make themselves aware of all such regulations.

Absence from work can occur for a number of reasons; some, like holiday or paternity leave, will normally be arranged in advance and cause minimum disruption to the employing organisation. The absences that cause disruption within any organisation are those that are unplanned, either because the employee concerned is sick or has simply failed to turn up for work. It would be normal to treat the second reason as a breach of the rules on unauthorised absence and deal with it as a case of misconduct.

One reason for unauthorised absence could be that an employee has failed to return from an authorised absence, say a holiday, at the due time. Individuals returning late from holiday has become a much more widespread problem in recent years due to the increase in overseas travel and for most individuals who return to work late in such circumstances the fault lies with delayed air flights or other travel problems. For some employers the disruption caused by a late return from holiday will be minimal and they may treat it as no more than an irritation, but for others, particularly at a time of the year when large numbers of people are on holiday, the disruption caused can be very serious. Notwithstanding the fact that the cause of the problem (a late flight) is outside the employee's control, the employer might take the view that steps could have been taken to minimise the disruption, for example, by telephoning. Whether disciplinary action is taken in such circumstances will clearly rest on the facts of each individual case, but in any event action should follow the guidance given above for preparing and conducting a disciplinary interview, particularly in respect of mitigating circumstances and other explanations.

However, in most establishments, the most widespread cause of absence from work is sickness or alleged sickness and, while it would be wholly unreasonable to treat a case of genuine sickness as a disciplinary matter, incapacity for work on health grounds can be a fair reason for dismissing an employee. For this reason the way in which an employer deals with health-related absences is very important.

Sickness absence

Dealing with sickness absence can be a minefield for any manager, but for the employee relation specialist who is expected to give clear and timely advice, it is even more so. Estimates of the cost to the UK economy of sickness absence currently hover around the £10 billion level and absence therefore needs to be managed effectively. Unauthorised absence is usually a disciplinary matter, but most absences do not fall into this category. They will be recorded as sickness. Without wishing to suggest that any employee deliberately seeks to be untruthful, notifying the employer of 'sickness' remains the most common reason for absence from work and most organisations have staff who consistently accumulate 25–30 sick days per annum, through a mix of 'flu', 'migraine' and 'stomach upsets'.

The starting point is adequate record-keeping and ACAS advise that 'records showing lateness and the duration of and reason for all spells of absence should be kept to help monitor absence levels'. Such records enable the manager to substantiate whether a problem of persistent absence is real or imagined. All too often the employee relations specialist who is asked for advice is expected to work with insufficient data. Managing absence is not just about applying rules or following procedure; it is about addressing problems of persistent absence quickly and acting consistently. This sends out a clear and unambiguous message to all employees that absence is regarded as a serious matter.

But, how do you act rigorously and at the same time retain fairness and consistency? The most effective way is through the 'return to work' interview. This has been shown to be the most effective method of controlling sickness absence. The employer demonstrates that absence matters, that it has noticed the employee's absence and that it cares.

In their booklet 'Discipline at Work', ACAS set out the following guidelines for handling frequent and persistent short-term absences which support the principle of the return to work interview and help to ensure a consistency of approach:

• Absences should be investigated promptly and the employee asked to give an explanation.

- Where there is no medical advice to support frequent self-certified absences, the employee should be asked to consult a doctor to establish whether medical treatment is necessary and whether the underlying reason for absence is work related.

- If, after investigation, it appears that there were no good reasons for the absences, the matter should be dealt with under the disciplinary procedure.

- Where absences arise from temporary domestic problems, the employer in deciding appropriate action should consider whether an improvement in attendance is likely.

- In all cases the employee should be told what improvement is expected and warned of the likely consequences if this does not happen.

- If there is no improvement, the employee's age, length of service, performance, the likelihood of a change in attendance, the availability of suitable alternative work and the effect of past and future absences on the business should all be taken into account on deciding appropriate action.

Disabilities and absence

The above is very helpful and useful advice in respect of absences that are deemed not to be genuine or sickness-related, but what happens if the reason for the absences is illness or injury supported by medical certificates? Or if it is in respect of a disability covered by the Disability Discrimination Act (DDA)?

As part of this protection provided by the DDA employers may have to make 'reasonable adjustments' to employment arrangements and in the context of managing absence, section 4 (2)(d) of the Act states that 'it is unlawful for an employer to discriminate against a disabled person by dismissing them or subjecting them to any other detriment'. Because the Act applies equally to existing employees as well as to new recruits employers should be careful of initiating action in respect of employees with a permanent health problem without paying due regard to the legislation. Section 6(1) of the Act states that an employer has a duty to make 'reasonable adjustments' if any employee is disadvantaged by either the physical features of the workplace or by the arrangements for the work itself. The Code of Practice which accompanies the Act lists a number of 'reasonable adjustments' that an employer might have to consider. These could include:

- making adjustments to premises

- allocating some of the disabled person's duties to another person

- transferring the person to fill an existing vacancy

- altering the person's working hours

- assigning the person to a different place of work

- allowing the person to be absent during working hours for rehabilitation, assessment or treatment

- giving the person, or arranging for them to be given, training

- acquiring or modifying equipment

- modifying instructions or reference manuals

- modifying procedures for testing or assessment

- providing a reader or interpreter

- providing supervision.

Clearly, employers will not have to make 'reasonable adjustments' in respect of all 'sick' employees, but only those who fit the Act's definition of disability. A disabled person is a person with 'a physical or mental impairment which has a substantial and long term adverse effect on [their] ability to carry out normal day-to-day activities' (Section 1). This chapter is about discipline and not disability, but employee relations specialists must be aware that the disability legislation imposes challenges which must be taken into account when managing absence. Most importantly, it must be remembered that dismissal of a disabled employee is automatically unfair and on that basis will almost certainly be impossible to defend.

Persistent absence
If doubt still remains about the nature of the illness, injury or disability the employee can be asked if they are prepared to be examined by an independent doctor to be appointed by the company. Normally, unless there is some form of contractual provision which allows for this, an employee cannot normally be compelled to attend. However, with the growth of occupational sick pay schemes, many organisations have overcome this problem by building compulsion into their scheme rules. Very often, advising an employee that such an examination will be required if attendance does not improve, will be sufficient to resolve the problem. Complications can arise when the injury or illness which necessitates persistent short-term absences is genuine, because it could never be reasonable to discipline in such circumstances. It can be fair to dismiss the employee concerned, but only after a careful process of assessment and examination has been carried out. A similar problem arises in respect of employees whose absence is long term and again ACAS provide guidance in recommending a procedure to be followed. They say that:

- The employee should be contacted periodically and they (the employee) should maintain regular contact with the employer.

- The employee should be advised if employment is at risk.

- The employee should be asked if they will consent to their own doctor being contacted. The employee's right to refuse consent, to see the report and to request amendments to it, must be clearly spelt out to them.

- The employee's doctor should be asked if the employee will be able to return to work and the nature of the work they will be capable of carrying out.

- On the basis of the report received, the employer should consider whether alternative work is available.

- Employers are not expected to create special jobs, nor are they expected to be medical experts. They should simply take action on the basis of the medical evidence.

- As with other absences, the possibility of an independent medical examination should be considered.

- Where an employee refuses to co-operate in providing medical evidence they should be told, in writing, that a decision will have to be taken on the basis of what information is available and that the decision may result in dismissal.

- Where the employee's job can no longer be kept open and no suitable alternative is available the employee should be informed of the likelihood of dismissal.

All of the above makes good sense and is consistent with the principle of managing absence with a 'best practice' ethos. However, employee relations managers need to consider what other methods they can use for managing absence. This could be the introduction of flexitime and annual hours schemes so that employees can manage domestic commitments without resorting to 'taking a day off sick'.

Some other substantial reason
The final fair reason for dismissal set out in the Employment Rights Act 1996 is 'some other substantial reason'. This concept was introduced into the legislation 'so as to give tribunals the discretion to accept as a fair reason for dismissal something that would not conveniently fit into any of the other categories' (Lewis 1997 p177). Dismissals for 'some other substantial reason' have, as Lewis points out, been upheld in respect of employees who have been sentenced to a term of imprisonment, employees who cannot get on with each other, or where there are problems between an individual and one of the organisation's customers. Interestingly, the cases which Lewis quotes all relate to the 1970s and 1980s which might indicate that businesses are now less reliant on this rather vague concept. It is certainly the case that the more professional employee relations specialists, recognising that such issues and conflicts do arise, have amended their disciplinary procedures accordingly and many organisations will have a rule relating to general conduct which may be worded in the following way:

> Any conduct detrimental to the interests of the company, its relations with the public, its customers and suppliers, damaging to its public image or offensive to other employees in the company, shall be a disciplinary offence.

It is easy to see how such a rule could be used to deal with any of the examples cited by Lewis and, in the context of managing discipline, it is a much more systematic route. Some other substantial reason can, to the non-lawyer, be a rather vague concept and being able to proceed against an individual for a breach of a specific rule is much clearer to everybody involved.

APPEALS

Every disciplinary procedure must contain an appeals process otherwise it is almost impossible to demonstrate the organisation has acted reasonably within the law. In common with every other aspect of the disciplinary process, it is important to ensure fairness and consistency within an appeals procedure which should provide for appeals to be dealt with as quickly as possible. An employee should be able to appeal at every stage of the disciplinary process and common sense dictates that any appeal should be heard by someone who is senior to the person imposing the disciplinary sanction. This will not always be possible, particularly in smaller organisations, but if the person hearing the appeal is the same as the person who imposed the original sanction, then ACAS advise that the person should hear the appeal and act as impartially as possible. In essence, an appeal in these circumstances is going to be no more than a review of the original decision, but perhaps in a calmer and more objective manner.

As with the original disciplinary hearing, an appeal falls into two parts: action prior to the appeal and the actual hearing itself. Before any appeal hearing the employee should be told what the arrangements are and what their rights under the procedure are. At the same time it is important the employer obtains, and reads, any relevant documentation and at the appeal hearing the appellant should be told its purpose, how it will be conducted and what decisions the person or persons hearing the appeal are able to make. Any new evidence must be considered and all relevant issues properly examined. While appeals are not seen as the opportunity to seek a more sympathetic assessment of the issue in question, it is equally true that appeals are not routinely dismissed. Overturning a bad or unjust decision is just as important as confirming a fair decision. It is an effective way of signalling to employees that all disciplinary issues will be dealt with consistently and objectively.

Many organisations fall into the trap of using their grievance procedure in place of a proper appeals process. This is to be avoided wherever possible. The grievance procedure should be reserved for resolving problems arising from employment and is covered in the next chapter. Finally, not only should appeals be dealt with in a timely fashion but the procedure should specify time-limits within which appeals should be lodged.

EMPLOYMENT TRIBUNALS

While it is not appropriate to make this chapter too legalistic it would be remiss not to take a brief look at the composition and procedure of Employment Tribunals. No matter how well you manage the discipline process, no matter how much attention you pay to 'best practice', there is no guarantee that a former employee will not ask a Tribunal to rule on the fairness or otherwise of their dismissal.

The composition of a Tribunal
Employment Tribunals are independent judicial bodies whose composition is governed by the Employment Tribunals Act 1996 (ETA). Tribunals will usually comprise three members:

• a legally qualified chairman (a solicitor or a barrister of seven years standing)

- an employer representative

- an employee representative (usually a trade union representative).

At each hearing the lay members are selected at random according to their availability, except in sex discrimination cases, where one member of each sex is chosen, or in race or disability discrimination cases, where at least one member will have particular experience of race or disability discrimination.

Although an Employment Tribunal should usually comprise three members, provided the parties agree, it is permissible for a Tribunal to comprise a chairman and one lay member.

It is also possible for a Tribunal chairman to sit alone in cases involving pension scheme trustees, unlawful deductions from wages, breach of contract issues and the dismissal of health and safety representatives. These are set out fully in the ETA section 4(3).

Tribunal procedure

Proceedings are commenced by an employee (the applicant) presenting an 'originating application' commonly known as an IT1. When the application is received by the Tribunal office it is registered and a copy sent to the former employer (the respondent) and to ACAS. It is then for the respondent to enter a notice of appearance (IT3) which has to be sent to the Tribunal office within 21 days of receiving an IT1. In essence the IT3 is the respondent's defence which they have to return if they wish to contest the case. A copy of the notice of appearance is sent by the Tribunal office to the applicant and to ACAS. Once all the necessary forms have been completed the Tribunal office will set a date for a hearing and notify the parties.

In the interim period ACAS, through one of its conciliation officers, will ask the parties if they require any assistance in reaching an out-of-court settlement. This is an entirely voluntary process and the parties do not have to participate if they do not want to.

If it is not possible to resolve matters through the existing ACAS conciliation route, then the matter will go forward for a full hearing before the Tribunal.

At the hearing the Tribunal will normally hear evidence from the respondent followed by the applicant. Both parties have the right to cross-examine each other's witnesses and are entitled to know what documents the other party are going to rely on. The Tribunal members will also have the opportunity to question witnesses. Because it is never possible to say whether a disciplinary matter will ultimately finish with a Tribunal hearing, it is vital that the employee relations specialist ensures that during any disciplinary meetings clear and comprehensive notes are made and retained. These will form the basis of the employer's defence and, as a Tribunal is a judicial body that can award compensation or an individual their job back, lack of clear evidence can be very expensive.

The Employment Rights (Disputes Resolution) Act 1998 enabled ACAS to draw up the ACAS Arbitration Scheme to provide voluntary arbitration in the case of alleged unfair dismissal by individual employees. The scheme allows applicants and respondents to agree for the case, if not settled or withdrawn, to be heard by an independent arbitrator appointed by ACAS. In order to do this, the parties have to agree voluntarily to give up the right for the claim to be heard by an Employment Tribunal. The ACAS scheme provides voluntary arbitration as an alternative to an Employment Tribunal hearing which is speedy, informal, private and less legalistic. It also provides greater certainty as to outcome and cost as there is no appeal on a point of law or fact against the arbitrator's decision.

Once ACAS has been informed by the parties themselves, or by the Employment Tribunal office, that a former employee has alleged unfair dismissal against an employer, an ACAS conciliator is allocated to deal with the case. The conciliator contacts the parties to try and help them

Table 35 **Employment Tribunals and ACAS arbitration: a comparison**

Unfair dismissal – key process areas	Employment tribunal	Arbitration
Decision (fair or unfair dismissal) based on:	Statute and case law/'Test of Reasonableness'	ACAS Code of Practice and Handbook
Those hearing the case:	Legally qualified Chairman and side members from panel of employer and trade union nominees	ACAS arbitrator with knowledge/experience of employment relations, sitting along
Location of hearing:	ET office	By agreement at a hotel/ACAS office/the workplace/representatives' premises
Length of hearing:	Normally at least one day	Normally 2/3 hours
Presentation of evidence:	Cross-examination of 'witnesses' on oath	Informal presentation, no oaths or direct cross-examination
Availability of 'witnesses' and documents:	Witnesses orders, orders for discovery/inspection or production of witnesses of documents	No powers in Scheme to make orders, but failure of parties to co-operate can count against them when decisions is made
Expenses to attend hearing/loss of earnings:	Tribunal can reimburse expenses and losses for parties, witnesses and some representatives	No expenses paid by ACAS, but compensation for unfair dismissals may include a sum for cost of attending hearing
Remedies/Awards:	Statutory provisions Interim relief available	ACAS Scheme Interim relief not available
Publicity:	Public hearing and award	Private hearing and award
Appeal/Challenge:	Can be made to EAT and Appellate courts	No appeal on point of law or fact – challenge only for serious irregularity

reach their own settlement of the matter in dispute and without passing judgement on the issues involved. If the parties are unable to reach a settlement and the former employee does not withdraw the case, the conciliator will remind the parties they can choose whether to have the case heard by an Employment Tribunal or an independent arbitrator. The conciliator explains the details of both methods of hearing the case. The differences between the two systems are outlined in Table 35.

If both parties agree in writing, either through the conciliator or by means of a compromise agreement, that they wish to opt for binding arbitration under the Scheme, ACAS appoints an arbitrator to hear the case and a date for the hearing is arranged. ACAS has established a panel of arbitrators selected through a transparent, accountable and non-discriminatory process. The arbitrators have been selected for their knowledge, skills and employment relations experience. They are not employed by ACAS but are appointed by it on a case by case basis. Once the parties agree to go to arbitration under the Scheme, an Employment Tribunal can no longer hear the unfair dismissal claim.

SUMMARY

In this chapter we have explained discipline in a systematic way, starting with the origins of disciplinary procedures and then explaining the current legal position. We have discussed the importance of procedures and the need to follow as closely as possible the guidelines set out by ACAS. We put great stress on the need for clear and unambiguous rules within the workplace and recommended that both procedures and rules be regularly monitored.

In the final part of the chapter we concentrated on the handling of disciplinary issues, looking at counselling, preparing for and conducting a disciplinary interview, misconduct and capability. We explained the need for a fair appeals procedure and, finally, we looked at the composition and procedure of Employment Tribunals and the ACAS arbitration scheme which provides for voluntary arbitration to settle unfair dismissal claims as an alternative to the tribunal system.

It is because poor management of discipline can create employee relations problems that we make no apology for the stress placed on the importance of best practice and the need to act professionally. We have tried to reflect the realities of managing discipline within an organisational context, because discussions that we have had with managers from a whole range of organisations show that disciplinary issues can cause major employee relations problems due to breaches of rules being ignored, treated with differing degrees of seriousness by different managers, or simply used as a control tool.

There is also an overwhelming business case for the effective management of discipline. More and more organisations are actively seeking to gain employee commitment by involving them in the business (Marchington 1995). Assuming that this is a trend that most organisations would wish to see continuing, then an employee relations climate that recognises the rights and responsibilities of both parties to the employment relationship is absolutely vital. One factor in establishing this climate is the need to manage discipline fairly and consistently. This will not happen unless certain principles are adhered to. There must always be a just cause for disciplinary action whether this be misconduct, inability to perform the job in a satisfactory manner or some other reason. Employers have to act reasonably as demonstrated by the operation of a procedure that conforms to principles of 'natural justice'. Finally, employees are entitled to know the cause of the complaint against them, entitled to representation, entitled to challenge evidence, and entitled to a right of appeal.

None of this guarantees success in the handling of a disciplinary issue, but it is more likely to ensure good personnel management practice and that in itself aids the establishment of a positive climate for employee relations.

REFERENCES AND FURTHER READING

ADVISORY CONCILIATION AND ARBITRATION SERVICE. *Discipline at Work: The ACAS Advisory Handbook.* London, ACAS, 1997.

EDWARDS P. 'Discipline and the creation of order', in K. Sisson (ed.), *Personnel Management: A comprehensive guide to theory and practice in Britain.* Oxford, Blackwell, 1994.

HAMMOND SUDDARDS. *Dismissal.* London, Institute of Personnel and Development, 1999.

IPD Employment Law Service.

LEWIS D. *Essentials of Employment Law.* 5th edn. London, Institute of Personnel and Development, 1997.

MARCHINGTON M., 'Involvement and Participation'. In J. Storey (ed.), *Human Resource Management: A critical text,* London, Routledge, 1995.

EMPLOYMENT RIGHTS ACT 1996.

EMPLOYMENT RIGHTS (Dispute Resolution) Act 1998.

9 Managing employee grievances

INTRODUCTION

Grievance is a complaint by an employee about management behaviour. It may be real or it may be the result of a misconception or a misunderstanding. In either case, settling it quickly and effectively is important. To the individuals concerned, their grievance is important. In addition, they cannot be ignored by the organisation as an individual grievance mishandled can escalate into a serious collective dispute. The purpose of managing grievances is to rectify matters that have been and are going wrong, by:

- investigating the situation

- identifying what has caused the employee complaint

- taking the appropriate action to resolve the complaint to the mutual satisfaction of the employee and the management.

The grievance needs to be resolved at the earliest possible stage. A key aspect of fairness at work is the opportunity of the individual employee to complain about, and receive redress for, unfair treatment. So, in this chapter, the fundamentals of grievance handling as an important element in the employee relations specialist's work are discussed.

Grievance handling is primarily a line manager responsibility. In this regard they require help, advice, support and expertise from the employee relations specialist. This assistance includes devising effective grievance procedures and training line managers to operate these procedures in a fair and reasonable manner. The employee relations specialist is also responsible for monitoring and reviewing the effectiveness, especially in terms of outcomes, of grievance procedures.

After you have read this chapter, you will be able to:

- appreciate the business case for resolving grievances

- explain why grievances are or are not taken up by employees

- understand the principles that underpin grievance procedures

- describe the steps involved in managing employee grievances

- be aware why some grievances are dealt with by a specific procedure separate from the standard grievance procedure

- demonstrate the importance of reviewing and monitoring the operation of grievance procedures

- illustrate the skills required to manage employee grievances effectively.

THE BUSINESS CASE FOR RESOLVING GRIEVANCES

Grievances may arise even in the best-run organisations on a wide variety of issues including discrimination, harassment and bullying. If grievances are not dealt with or handled quickly, they are likely to fester and harm relationships. A grievance may also be felt by a group, as well as an individual, and, if left unresolved, may develop into a major collective dispute involving a trade union. However, whether individual or collective, all employee grievances have the potential to damage the quality of an organisation's employee relations and thereby its competitive position. As was shown in Chapter 7, the golden rule in managing employee grievances is that they are important to those who express them and must be treated seriously by management.

Employee grievances are an outward expression of worker dissatisfaction which, if not resolved, can result in unsatisfactory work behaviour which has adverse consequences for the organisation's competitive position. Unresolved dissatisfaction gives rise to:

- employee frustration

- deteriorating interpersonal relationships

- low morale

- poor performance seen in lower productivity and a poorer quality of output or service

- disciplinary problems including poor performance by employees

- resignation and loss of good staff (increased labour turnover)

- increased employee absenteeism.

In addition, if unresolved grievances lead to complaints by employees who feel their employment rights have not been respected, they may resign their employment and claim a fundamental breach of contract amounting to 'constructive dismissal'.

If an organisation has a reputation for having a high level of employee dissatisfaction, then this will be a disincentive for individuals or organisations to purchase goods and/or services from the organisation, fearing they are likely to be of poor quality. A reputation for employee dissatisfaction also gives an organisation a 'poor employer' image in the labour market. Such an image accentuates an organisation's problems of recruiting and retaining the appropriate quantity and quality of labour services necessary to achieve its corporate objectives.

Organisations in which the presence of employee feelings of unfairness exist will have relatively higher cost structures than in a competitor organisation with absolute and lower levels of employee dissatisfaction.

The former organisation has a competitive disadvantage relative to the latter which will be expressed in sales, revenue and profitability.

If grievances are not addressed, they can adversely affect an organisation and the quality of life of its employees. It is therefore essential to the continued prosperity and wellbeing of the company and its employees that employee complaints about management behaviour are addressed as quickly as possible and as near to their source as can be. There is a clear business case for the effective and professional management of employee grievances.

It is important employees know to whom they can take a grievance, and that new employees are informed of the grievance procedure, which should be readily accessible, for example, set out in the company handbook, and written in simple straightforward language. Training for team leaders, supervisors and other line managers in dealing with employee grievances effectively has to be a business priority.

WHAT IS A GRIEVANCE?

A grievance usually arises because an aggrieved individual regards some management decision (or act of indecision) as 'unfair'. However, not all employee complaints are justified in that the management action complained of may be legitimate behaviour within the terms and spirit of a collective agreement between the employees and the management, or within a company rule contained in the company's staff handbook. In managing employee grievances, management acquires and develops an ability to distinguish real from unfounded grievances and then to explain clearly to the employee why their complaint merits no action by management.

However, all grievances, whether real or unfounded, are important to the individual concerned and have to be treated on their merits. If management receives a complaint which appears somewhat frivolous, then it is not good practice to reject it without at least an investigation into how it has arisen. If such an inquiry reveals the employee's complaint to be ill-founded, then why this is the case must be explained to the individual. By acting on just cause after investigation in a fair, reasonable and consistent manner, management demonstrates to its employees that both unfounded and genuine complaints are treated seriously and in a businesslike and effective manner.

Non-trading of grievances

In negotiating a settlement of grievances, management treats each on its merits thereby demonstrating to the individual that management accepts the complaint as a serious issue for that individual. An employee's grievance has to be dealt with independently of that (those) of another employee(s). In resolving employee grievances, management proceeds on the basis of one at a time. It negotiates an agreement to resolve the individual's grievance of a particular issue and then moves on to negotiate an agreement to settle another employee's grievance over a different issue.

The effective negotiation of grievances, unlike bargaining, excludes a trade-off between employee complaints about employer behaviour.

Table 36 Most Common Employee Grievances (IRS Survey, 1997)

Issue	Number of organisations
Introduction of new working practices	36
Disciplinary matters	18
Interpretation of terms and conditions	8
Staffing levels	7
Personal issues	6
Discrimination	6
Grading	6
Bullying	4
Health and safety	4
Pay	4
Sexual harassment	2

Management does not offer to settle one person's grievance in exchange for getting another employee to agree to drop their grievance. In grievance handling neither management, nor employee representatives, take part in 'trading' (namely 'if you drop that grievance then we shall accept another employee's grievance'). The employee relations specialist does not fall into the trap of being forced to deal simultaneously with a whole list of different grievances over different issues from a number of different employees.

MOST COMMON EMPLOYEE GRIEVANCES

Complaints from individual employees can centre on many aspects of management behaviour. An employee complaint may be that the employer has acted in breach of a collective agreement (ie management is not applying it as the parties intended), the canteen facilities are poor and inadequate, the workplace is unsafe and/or unhealthy, and the disciplinary penalty imposed upon them is too harsh. Other areas of individual employee complaint against management can include that they have been passed over for promotion; they have been denied access to a training and development opportunity; their holiday allocation does not meet their family circumstances, and their job is graded at an inappropriate level.

Industrial Relations Service published in 1997 the results of its survey into the handling of individual grievances (see IRS, No 635, July 1997). It had sent a questionnaire to 600 companies and received 72 usable returns representing 277,500 employees in firms varying in size from 39,000 employees to 75 people. The most common employee grievances are shown in Table 36.

The dominance of grievances over the introduction of new working practices reflects organisational change in the companies concerned with its resulting revisions to working practices greatly affecting employees and how they feel about their working life.

Of the 1,000 people interviewed in 1998 for the IPD Study of the psychological contract (see Chapter 1) 17 per cent reported they had been treated unfairly in the last 12 months on grounds of age, race, gender, disability, experience, qualifications or other grounds. The highest proportion of complaints was amongst employees in the health sector and amongst young workers. The main stated reasons for unfair treatment were:

- personality clashes   (19 per cent)
- lack of experience   (11 per cent)
- gender   (10 per cent)
- age   (8 per cent)
- lack of qualifications   (6 per cent)
- race   (4 per cent)

Increasingly then, many employee complaints are falling into what can broadly be described as 'equality' issues. Women employees are increasingly laying complaints to management that their jobs are inappropriately graded and paid. An increasing number of employee complaints are based on claims of injustice in that the behaviour complained of is motivated by a dislike of the employee on the grounds of their gender, race, creed, colour or disability. Sexual harassment also constitutes an employee grievance. Such complaints can be difficult in that in some cases the behaviour complained of is by another individual who is also the manager of the complaint.

Employee grievances can be collective in that a group of employees have a common complaint relating to their employment or an individual has a grievance which has collective implications. All employees in an office, for example, may complain the temperature is too high or too low, whilst employees collectively in the workroom may complain their level of pay or bonuses seem unfair compared with other groups of employees in other sections of the organisation. The IRS Survey mentioned above found that the main causes of grievances raised by a group of employees were:

- interpretation and application of an existing agreement
- pay and bonus arrangements
- organisational change
- new working practices
- grading issues.

It also revealed that 52 organisations out of the 72 who replied had a policy for dealing with collective disputes. Of these, 16 had a distinct procedure for dealing with collective grievances whilst 36 used the same procedure as for dealing with individual grievances. In some of the organisations, the procedure for dealing with problems shared by groups of employees was referred to as a Disputes Procedure or an Avoidance of Disputes Procedures whilst in others it was referred to as the Collective Grievance Procedure.

THE TAKE-UP OF GRIEVANCES

Employees unable to resolve grievances informally should follow the formal grievance procedure (see below) that covers all employees. The aim of the procedure is to encourage employees who believe they have been treated unfairly to raise the matter and have it discussed and resolved as quickly as possible. Management needs a knowledge and understanding of how to operate these procedures and most organisations provide training for team leaders and other frontline managers in managing employee grievances effectively. Organisations have the appropriate mechanisms to ensure employee dissatisfaction is identified quickly and dealt with to mutual satisfaction before the individual's complaint is put formally into their grievance procedure. Activating the grievance procedure is costly in terms of management time.

Most employees' complaints against management behaviour do not reach the formal grievance procedure. There are many reasons for this. First, something happens to make it unnecessary. As Torrington and Hall (1998) point out, the employee's dissatisfaction can disappear after a good night's sleep or a cup of tea with a colleague.

Second, the employee merely wants to get their dissatisfaction off their chest. The grievance is resolved simply by an appropriate manager listening to the employee. 'A shoulder to cry on' provides sufficient satisfaction for the employee to withdraw their disapproval of management's behaviour.

Third, in times of high levels of unemployment, individuals are reluctant to raise formally their grievance with the company because of a fear that management may hold this against them and react by denying them promotion, access to training and development programmes and merit award payments. Fourth, employees may see little point in raising their grievance, having no confidence that their management will do anything about it. Finally, some individuals are unwilling to express their dissatisfaction with management for fear of offending their immediate superior who may regard the complaint as a criticism of their competency.

The IPD publication *The Psychological Contract and Fairness at Work* (1998) interviewed 1,000 people, of whom only 10 per cent had made a formal complaint about the way they had been treated in their organisation in the last year. Indeed, only 28 per cent said they had ever made a complaint against their organisation. They either did not regard their unfair treatment as really serious or they had no faith in or knowledge of any complaints procedure.

Of the 10 per cent who had laid a complaint, 21 per cent reported the procedure in their organisation was fair in dealing with their complaint whilst 27 per cent considered it very unfair. 28 per cent claimed it was quite fair and 18 per cent argued it was not fair. This is a very uneven distribution but suggests that many of those who formally complained were unhappy with the operation of the grievance procedures. While this level of dissatisfaction is perhaps an inevitable consequence of the failure to uphold some complaints, it is, at the same time, disturbingly high. The results may also help to explain why many of those who felt they had been unfairly treated did not follow up their grievance.

The lack of individual grievances being put formally into the grievance procedure does not necessarily mean employee relations in the organisation are in good shape. However, employee dissatisfaction identified at an early stage can be settled quickly through informal discussions. Behaving in this way reduces considerably the probability of the employees' level of dissatisfaction reaching the point where they are prepared to make a formal complaint against management behaviour.

A situation where employee complaints are being suppressed because they feel senior management will not act against a team leader/supervisor whose style of management is the cause of the grievance cannot be allowed to continue. Senior management might, for example, counsel the team leader/frontline manager as to why their management style needs to change or provide them with formal training after which their style should change for the better. If such action fails to produce a more constructive management style then management either redeploys the team leader/frontline manager elsewhere or considers dispensing with their services. If employee complaints are shown, following thorough investigation, to be the result of a personality clash between the team leader/front line manager and the individual employee then the grievance is best resolved by redeploying the individual to another area of employment.

> What are the sources of employee dissatisfaction in your organisation? Are these well-founded? If yes, why is this the case? If no, why is this the case? How many formal grievance complaints have been raised in the last three years?

GRIEVANCE PROCEDURES

The grievance procedure provides the means whereby individual employees process their complaint against management behaviour. A procedure for dealing with grievances is found in organisations which operate without trade unions as well as those that operate with them. In the former case, the procedure informs the individual of the action they need to take to raise a grievance and the steps management will take in giving it consideration.

A grievance procedure benefits employees as they know where they stand and know what to expect. The purpose of the procedure is to:

- ensure consistency in managing grievances
- reduce the risk of 'unpredictable' action
- clarify how grievances will be dealt with
- support a positive employee relations environment.

Underlying principles

In managing employee complaints, management is guided by a number of principles – fairness, consistency, representation and promptness. Fairness is ensured in that the procedure prevents management from dismissing employee grievances out of hand on the grounds that they are trivial, too time-consuming or too costly, provides the employee with adequate time to prepare their case and to question management witnesses, allows for the case to be heard by individuals not directly involved in the complaint and provides for the right of appeal to a higher level of management and, in some cases, to an independent external body. A grievance procedure with a clearly demarcated number of stages and standards of behaviour at each stage provides consistency of treatment and reduces the influence of subjectivity.

In raising a complaint, the procedure provides an individual with the right to be represented by another individual independent of the employer. Such a representative is usually internal to the organisation (for example, an employee representative, a shop steward, a work colleague) rather than external (for example, a full-time trade union official, a solicitor). The promptness principle is achieved by the procedure having a small number of stages, each of which has time limits for its completion. This enables the grievance to be resolved as quickly and as simply as possible.

The grievance procedure ensures the rights of employees to complain if they feel aggrieved and if they exercise this right to be treated in a fair and reasonable manner by acting in accordance with procedural rules which conform with the principles of natural justice. The individual employee is treated with dignity and respect. Thus, a grievance procedure provides 'order and stability' in the workplace by establishing standards of behaviour and due processes to resolve employee grievances in a peaceful and constructive manner.

Form of procedure
The forms of grievance procedure vary immensely. In a small non-union establishment, the procedure will be found in the employee's contract of employment and expressed in a statement, of which the following would be typical:

> If you have a grievance relating to your employment, you should raise it with your immediate supervisor.

In a larger and unionised organisation, a grievance procedure is likely to be a clause in a collective agreement. However, in such organisations, the grievance is likely to be reproduced in the further particulars of the employment contract where a typical wording would be:

> If you have any grievance relating to your employment, you should raise it with your immediate supervisor. If the matter is not settled at this level you may pursue it through the grievance procedure agreed between the company and the trade union representatives. Further details of such procedural agreements are maintained separately in writing and may be consulted on request to management.

Typical procedure
A typical grievance procedure follows a standard format which:

• opens with a Policy Statement followed by General Principles and sometimes by what constitutes a grievance

• consists of a number of stages. At each stage, the aim is to identify

Table 37 **Managing employee grievances**

- Employee makes complaint.

- Manager carries out grievance interview.

- Outcomes of grievance interview:
  - grievance is unfounded – management behaviour complained of is legitimate
  - employee decides to drop grievance
  - management decides the grievance is genuine. Management can deal with the problem immediately (miscalculated pay is corrected, holiday allocation changed)
  - management needs to consider its response

- Preparation for meeting with employee and representative:
  - analysis   – what are the issues?
    - on what will management be prepared to compromise?
    - on what will employee and their representative be prepared to compromise?
  - aims   – ideal, realistic, fallback
  - strategy and tactics

- Resolution of grievance:
  - common ground
  - write up resolution

action that stops the problem recurring or continuing. There are usually three to four stages in a procedure.

- defines time limits for the completion of each stage, designed to ensure a speedy resolution of the grievance

- provides a right to representation for the employee laying the complaint against management by an individual independent of the employer.

In most organisations, procedures for managing employee complaints relating to health and safety provision, job grading (job evaluation scheme), sexual harassment and discrimination are distinct from the general grievance/disputes procedure. Grievances about job grading, sexual harassment, etc are thus normally dealt with by means of a purpose-built procedure. Their degree of differentiation from the general grievance procedure depends on the volume of business and on the speed, efficacy and acceptability required by the parties. These specific procedures are discussed in greater detail later in the chapter.

Stages
There are a number of stages in a typical grievance procedure. Common factors to all the stages are:

- they spell out the details of who hears the case (eg the departmental manager, managing directors) and the individuals to be present (eg the personnel manager, the line manager and the employee concerned) including who can represent the employee (eg a shop steward, a colleague or a friend)

- they explain the appeal mechanisms available to employees

- they define the time limits by which the stage must be complete

- they explain what will happen if the grievance is not resolved or remains unsettled.

The aim of grievance procedures is to reach a resolution of the employee complaint as quickly as possible but without undue haste. As we have seen, a grievance procedure usually specifies how, and to whom, employees can raise a grievance and spells out the stages through which the complaint will be processed. To ensure a speedy settlement, time limits are specified by which each stage of the procedure must be completed (see above). The first stage invariably states that any employee who feels they have a complaint against management will, in the first instance, raise it with his/her immediate manager. If that manager is unable to resolve the matter the parties move to the second stage of the procedure which usually involves the employee consulting with their representative who then accompanies them in taking up the complaint with the appropriate level of management. If the complaint remains unresolved, the third stage is entered in which the employee and their representative take their case to higher levels of management (for example, the departmental manager).

If there is no resolution to the grievance at this stage the complaint is normally next considered by the employee's representative and the general manager. In unionised establishments at this fourth stage the local union branch secretary usually becomes involved. If a resolution still eludes the parties, this usually is the end of the matter. However, some procedures (especially those designed to deal with collective grievances) contain a fifth stage which involves external parties such as an independent arbitrator or conciliator, a representative of an employers' association and a district/regional trade union official.

In managing grievances, management's objective is to settle the complaint as near as possible to the point of its source. If employee complaints are allowed to progress to a higher level than necessary this principle is undermined. A professional employee relations manager ensures that managerial colleagues, particularly line managers, understand the limits of their authority when acting within the constraints of the grievance procedure. The problem-solving objective of the procedure is achieved and the significance of the different procedural stages maintained when grievances are settled as near as possible to the point of origin.

Although defined stages through which a grievance can be processed are essential there is no ideal number of stages. The number is a function of many factors, including the size of the organisation. However, natural justice principles would point to a minimum of two stages as this at least ensures one level of appeal from the immediate decision. Neither should the procedure contain too many stages since this makes the process unduly long and is in conflict with the principle of resolving grievances as quickly as possible and as close as can be to their origin.

Do you have a grievance procedure in your organisation? If not, why not? If yes, how many stages does it have? Why does it have that number?

Time limits

An employee with a complaint wants his or her grievance settled as soon as possible, and is likely to regard it as the highest priority for the manager to whom the complaint is made. That manager, on the other hand, needs time to gather the facts, consult with other managers and consider what action to take, all of which has to be fitted around all the other tasks for which that manager is responsible. The idea behind a time limit is that it provides a manager with an opportunity to consider the problem whilst also committing them to provide an answer within a fixed period of time. This relaxes the pressures on the employee, or their representative, both of whom now know that if a satisfactory answer has not been provided at the end of the time limit, the grievance will be processed to the next stage in the procedure.

The usual practice is to allow longer time limits for the completion for each successive stage. Internal stages' time limits can vary from a low of 24 hours to a maximum of five days but such limits are longer for external stages. Time limits alone do not ensure the expeditious handling of grievances but they are useful in establishing standards of reasonable behaviour by the parties. When the external stages of a grievance procedure are triggered, time limits for their completion again provide reassurance for the employee that inordinate lengthy delays in dealing with their complaint are not possible. Most of the doubts and criticisms against time limits (for example, loss of flexibility, undermining mutual trust, the issue not being dealt with properly at the lower levels) are to be overcome if there is a proviso in the procedure to permit, by mutual agreement, the extension of the time limits by which each stage of the process must be completed. The guiding principle is that the employee's complaint progresses quickly to the level needed to find a solution to the problem and that managers do not 'sit on' grievances.

Employee representation

Fair and reasonable behaviour by an employer in managing employee grievances requires the employee, as in disciplinary cases, to have representation by an individual who advocates their case. Representation assists the individual employee who lacks confidence and experience to negotiate with their line manager or senior manager, especially those operating at the executive level (for example the managing director). This individual is independent of the interests of the employer and is not present merely to witness what management says to the individual. The employee's representative, as we have already seen, is internal to the organisation.

The IRS Survey (1997) reported that of the 72 organisations surveyed, 54 had grievance procedures which allowed employees to have a representative accompany them in a grievance hearing at every stage, whilst 15 allowed the employee to be represented at each stage but the first. However, as we noted in Chapter 8, the Employment Relations Act 1999 gives individual employees the statutory right to be represented in grievance, as well as disciplinary, hearings by a representative of their choice including a full-time trade union official regardless of whether the employer concerned recognises a trade union.

What stage representation?

In many procedures, representation starts at the second stage after the individual has raised their complaint with their immediate manager. Representation then only becomes necessary if the employee is dissatisfied with the response from their immediate manager and wishes to take the matter to a higher level of management. The assumption behind this is that a grievance is not a grievance if the individual employee's immediate manager resolves the problem.

However, there are employee relations managers who consider the employee should have representation from the very start of their complaint. In these circumstances the employee's first step is to take the grievance to their workplace union representative, rather than their immediate superior, and persuade them they have a genuine grievance and to represent them in processing their complaint. The union representative has an important responsibility to act as a useful 'filter' sifting the genuine grievance from the unfounded.

Equality of representatives

In the internal stages of the procedure, the individual employee's representative is also an employee of the organisation. Such a representative wears two hats – one as an employee and the other as an employee representative. Their relationship with management in status terms is very different depending upon which hat they are wearing. As employees they are in a subordinate position to management whose representatives can give them instructions, empower them, verify the quality of their work, monitor their time keeping and initiate disciplinary action against them. Employees' workplace representatives are contracted to supply work to the employer.

However, when they wear an employee representative hat they interact with management as partners of equal status. This equality is expressed in the grievance procedure in that it sets out the 'players' to be involved in each stage of processing the grievance. When management and the employee's representative meet at different stages they do so on the basis of equality. So if, for example, the third stage of the procedure states the employee's representative and the chief executive/managing director will meet to try to resolve the grievance and the meeting is held in the managing director's office, they meet there as employee relations players of equal status. The managing director thus treats the employee's representative as such and ensures they have the proper facilities (seating, appropriate space for their documents, etc) to represent their 'client' in a professional manner.

The procedure also protects the employee representative from the front line manager/team leader refusing to allow them to leave their job to represent their 'client's' interests. The procedure is management's acceptance that in certain circumstances the individual employee's role as an employee relations player takes preference over their role as an employee. If in managing grievances management and employee representatives are equal partners then they have a joint responsibility for settling grievances.

This equality relationship in grievance handling is difficult for some line managers to accept. Many find it difficult to recognise employee representatives other than as employees of the company and therefore subject to their control and direction. Some managers never come to terms with the status distinction relative to management between the individual as an employee representative and the individual as an employee under their supervision and direction. Such managers feel their authority is undermined by more senior managers treating employees, when wearing their representative hat, as equal. They find it difficult to understand why their senior managers show so much consideration and grant such facilities towards individuals who they perceive as merely employees of the organisation.

Operation of the procedure
Role of the employee relations professional
Grievance procedures are an integral part of the whole way in which an organisation is managed. They affect directly line management at all levels. Line managers have always had the main responsibility for operating the procedure, assisted and advised by the employee relations professional. It is important the employee relations professional does not take on board line managers' problems and take responsibility for them. It is becoming standard practice in modern organisations for team leaders/frontline managers to manage people in partnership with human resource managers (Kelly and Gennard, 1996). The role of the employee relations professional, therefore, in managing grievance is to:

- identify and meet line management training and development needs with regard to managing grievances

- ensure line managers have a clear understanding of the way in which grievance procedures are intended to operate

- devise a grievance procedure which conforms with 'best practice' and spells out not only what has to happen at each stage but why

- promote awareness of 'best practice' in managing grievances amongst line managers

- make sure employees are aware of their rights under the procedure

- promote a constructive grievance policy at board level.

The employee relations manager also has an important role to play in monitoring and reviewing the operation of the grievance procedure and for recommending revisions to its design or operation or both. This involves reviewing what have been the outcomes of the grievances taken through the procedure and whether these outcomes have been the desired ones for management. This review and monitor function also requires the employee relations manager to analyse the subject matter of individual employee grievances, why the outcomes have been what they have and to check the procedure has been applied in all cases fairly and consistently (ie management has behaved reasonably in processing employee grievances).

Role of line manager
The first line manager remains a key player in the operation of the grievance procedure. An employee filing a grievance may be seen by

first line managers as reflecting badly on their managerial competency. If grievance procedures are to operate effectively, then senior management must reassure first line managers they do not see this as being the case. On the contrary, line managers should be encouraged to hear grievances. It is important they are aware of employee dissatisfaction as early as possible. It is usually easier to resolve grievances informally in a satisfactory manner for the individual and management if they are handled as quickly and as close to the source of the complaint as possible.

The first line manager has the least executive authority and this limits their ability to make decisions without reference to a more senior manager. If a frontline manager/team leader has continually to refer a grievance to a superior, then the employee will realise the best way to have their problem resolved is to short circuit the first line manager and go directly to their superior. When this happens, the legitimate authority of the frontline manager is undermined. It, in turn, threatens the credibility of the procedure by in reality reducing its number of actual stages. The ultimate impact is to remove the grievance from its source of origin, to slow down the process by having to go back through the correct stages and to cause confusion and bad feeling. To avoid this happening, the employee relations professional needs to ensure three things:

- everyone knows, within the procedure, the limits of their own and others' authority

- the procedures are adhered to consistently by line managers

- first line managers have the authority to settle grievances.

In situations where union workplace representatives believe line managers are unable to take a decision at the appropriate level, good practice requires management to insist the protocol of the procedures is followed. By doing this, management demonstrates it will apply the procedure consistently and that its operation is understood by those managers who have a part to play in its operation. It is important that first line managers have authority to deal with as many types of grievance as possible. The frontline manager/team leader must be able to say 'yes' as well as 'no'.

It is equally important first line management continues to be involved in the settling of grievances even if they pass beyond them, either by being at subsequent meetings or at the very least by being informed of the outcome of the grievance process. It is bad management practice if a first line manager is first to hear the outcome of an employee's complaint from the employee themselves and/or their representative.

Grievance Records
When a grievance passes to a higher stage in the procedure documentation of what happened at the previous stage is necessary for the benefit of those managers who are not familiar with the complaint of the individual employee and their supporting arguments and evidence. In practice, the extent to which records of grievances are kept varies widely. In some organisations the completion of grievance records is a required activity for line management. In others, only the

personnel/HR department keeps records. In yet others no documentation of any kind is kept except when an employee complaint progresses to the external stage of the procedure.

Grievance records serve several useful purposes for management. If there is a failure to agree at any stage, a written record clarifies the complaint, and the arguments in favour of it presented by the individual employee. This is also helpful to those managers involved in the next stage of the procedure. If the record is agreed by both parties – commonly completed by the manager concerned and counter signed by the employee and/or their representative – it is even more valuable. Grievance record forms assist the personnel/HR function to keep in touch with the progress of unresolved grievances.

Grievance records are also useful because the resolution of the grievance may provide a significant interpretation or perhaps an important precedent. Records are particularly useful for analysing trends in the use of the grievance procedure. Analysis of the record will show where, and why, delays in the procedure occurred. When a resolution to the individual's grievance has been reached, a written and agreed statement helps to ensure there are no misunderstandings as to what has been agreed. In the absence of an agreed statement, the parties may find they have different versions as to what they thought they had agreed. A written statement is also useful for communicating the outcome of the employee's complaint.

However, systems which require line management to keep records of grievances are not easy to keep going unless management keeps a watchful eye on matters. Some first line managers who handle grievances complain that having to keep grievance records is an extra, irksome administrative chore. Without a watchful eye from more senior management, grievance record systems at the first line level may not operate effectively.

The law

The basic statutory requirement covering employees' grievances is that the employer has to specify, by description or otherwise, a person to whom the employee can apply if they are dissatisfied with a disciplinary decision or have a grievance under the Employment Rights Act 1996. This information is to be given to the individual employee in the statement of particulars of terms of employment. A formal grievance procedure is not legally required but almost every organisation finds it useful to adopt one. When they do, the statement of particulars specifies any further steps available to the employee beyond the first point of contact. This, as we have seen, is often in a separate document setting out the organisation's full grievance procedure.

Goold v McConnell (1995)

However, employers who do not have a formal grievance procedure can fall foul of the law. In *W A Goold (Pearmack) Ltd* v *McConnell* (1995) an industrial tribunal held that the employer's failure to supply a grievance procedure to its employees amounted to a breach of the employment contract which entitled the employees to resign and therefore claim constructive dismissal. The two employees concerned were also held to be unfairly dismissed. The facts of the case were simple. Mr McConnell and Mr Richmond were jewellery salesmen paid a basic salary and commission. In 1992 their employer changed sales methods and, as a result, commission suffered. The employees wished to complain about this issue but there was no established grievance procedure and the employer had not issued them with a written statement of main terms and conditions of employment.

In July 1992 a new managing director joined the firm and the employees tried to complain to him. He told them he was unable to deal with their complaint immediately. The two employees then decided to seek an interview with the chairman but were prevented by his secretary. The employees resigned and claimed constructive dismissal. The Employment Appeals Tribunal agreed with the Industrial Tribunal's view that it was an implied term in any employment contract that employers should reasonably and promptly give employees an opportunity to obtain redress of any grievance.

Reed and Another v Stedman (1999)

In this case the EAT gave Employment Tribunals general guidance as to how they should approach complaints to sexual harassment at work. Ms Stedman was employed by Bull Information Systems Ltd from 1 June 1995, initially as a temporary secretary and then in a permanent position to Mr Reed, the marketing manager. She found working with him intolerable and resigned on 28 June 1996.

He had behaved in an unwelcome sexual manner towards her and her health had begun to deteriorate, which she put down to his behaviour. Although she had complained to him only once about that, she had complained about it to her mother and to colleagues at work. Members of the company's personnel department were aware of those complaints and of her deteriorating health. Ms Stedman thus had a grievance which had failed to be investigated. In finding that Ms Stedman had been constructively dismissed by the company and sexually harassed by Mr Reed EAT ruled the company had breached the contract of employment by failing to investigate the cause of Ms Stedman's ill health and complaints she had made to colleagues. This case demonstrates the importance of management investigating an employee grievance. Indeed it is incumbent on a company to do so as a failure to do so may justify a legal ruling that such behaviour breaches trust and confidence.

Metcalf Ltd v Maddocks (1995)

The benefits of having procedures for handling employee grievances, even though the law does not require them, are also clear from the case of *Chris Metcalf Ltd* v *Maddocks* (1985). The crux of the matter was that an employee had refused a particular instruction and had been dismissed. In this case the company had no formal grievance procedure for its 90 employees and had failed to issue statements of particulars to its employees. In the Tribunal hearing the argument was that these omissions by management had caused a breakdown in communications between management and the employee, to the point where the employee's reasons for refusing the instruction had no means of being expressed or heard properly. The Industrial Tribunal ruled a grievance procedure would have enabled employees to articulate their worries and anxieties and thus have prevented the problem occurring. An appeal by the firm against the decision failed.

Organisations are fairly tightly constrained by the law with regard to discipline matters (see Chapter 8). Employee grievance, on the other hand, is subject to much less case and statute law. Some argue that it is the strength of the legal framework for discipline relative to grievance that is the central reason why in organisations discipline rates a higher priority than grievance handling.

MANAGING GRIEVANCES

Much of an employee relations manager's work can be occupied in dealing with individual employees' problems or complaints. However, most employee grievances are dealt with satisfactorily before they reach the formal grievance procedure. For example, take the case of an employee claiming they have received an incorrect amount of pay.

There are a number of possibilities:

1 On checking, management accepts the amount of pay due has been miscalculated and rectifies the matter immediately. In that case, the grievance will end there and has been resolved at the individual level to everyone's satisfaction.

OR

2 The payment is correct although the employee believes they have been underpaid; there is no real grievance and there are two things that might happen:

(a) the situation is discussed and explained adequately and the matter is resolved

(b) the employer fails to explain the details to the satisfaction of the employee who still believes they have been treated unfairly even though they have not. Now there is a danger that a collective dispute might develop taking an simple problem to an appropriate level.

OR

3 The details of the complaint are accepted by the employer who nevertheless fails to take corrective action quickly. Another grievance arises which takes the place of the original. The employee was relying on a correct payment to meet commitments but now cannot do so because the company is 'holding on' to their money.

The first possibility is obviously the preferred one as it puts right a genuine error promptly and efficiently. Possibilities 2b and 3 carry the risk of generating feelings of mistrust and suspicion.

However, not all grievances are of as simple a nature and resolved quickly. Management deals with all grievances in a competent and systematic manner which involves a number of stages:

• hearing the grievance

• preparing for meeting with the employee and/or their representative

- meeting with the employee and/or their representative

- confirming the common ground between the employee and the management

- resolving the grievance

- reporting the outcome.

The Grievance Interview

The purpose of the grievance interview is to enable an individual to state their complaint and for management to discover and remove the cause of the employee's dissatisfaction. From the interview, management obtains the facts of the situation, analyses the problem and, if appropriate, decides action to resolve the grievance. Good management practice in preparation for a grievance interview is to check the employee's employment record with the organisation; although circumstances and time pressures may make this impossible, it is worth bearing in mind that an employee with a grievance against management may be angry and possibly adopt an aggressive attitude. If this turns out to be the case, management helps calm down the individual. When dealing with an individual who has lost their temper, management needs to guard against responding in a similar way or being provoked into such a reaction. This can easily happen when faced with an aggressive employee critical of management's behaviour. Few people can think rationally when they are angry.

As we saw in Chapter 7, gathering information about an employee's grievance is extremely important. If incorrect, or insufficient, information is collected, then it is likely to lead to wrong analysis and an incorrect decision. Competent interviewing, watching and listening skills are crucial in this regard. Why this is so was explained in Chapter 7 and before continuing you should now re-read pages 232–44 which outline some do's and don'ts when gathering information by verbal and non-verbal techniques. Remember the 5Ws, the recall technique, to take notes, get the interviewee talking, and keep a balance between being sympathetic to the individual and being businesslike.

At the end of the interview, the manager will have an understanding of the employee's grievance and how they would like to see it resolved. If the employee's grievance is, for example, that they have been denied access to a training opportunity then the employee will have explained why they were denied the opportunity and how they wish management to resolve the situation, perhaps by sending them on the next available appropriate training opportunity. The 'why?' question is always the most difficult since an individual always gives a favourable view of their case, withholding information which may weaken it. However, remember the golden rule outlined in Chapter 7, namely that the manager needs to get all the facts, including those that might make the individual's case against management less clear-cut.

The management requires all the facts. They are seeking to reach a decision as to whether the employee's grievance is well-founded and, if so, what action to take. If the grievance interview fails to bring out vital information the manager may conclude, wrongly and with adverse consequences, that the employee does not have a genuine complaint. On the basis of the information gained from the grievance interview the manager makes an assessment of the situation. They decide upon an appropriate course of action explaining to the individual employee, their representative and to managerial colleagues why they have decided upon that action.

Unfounded grievances

At the end of the interview, management may conclude the grievance is unfounded because:

- the real problem is a clash of personality between the individual employee and their immediate manager

- the employee has a misunderstanding (for example, of a works rule)

- the employee is happy management has listened sympathetically to the case and decides to drop the matter because they feel to take it further will only make matters worse.

Grievances can be actual or unfounded and distinguishing between them is an important responsibility of both employer and employee representatives. They have a common interest to avoid wasting time, resources, effort and emotion in putting inappropriate issues through formal procedures. However, all grievances are important and must be treated on their merits. If management receives a complaint which it judges to be ill-founded, it is not good practice to dismiss it in an arbitrary manner. They must:

- find out why and how it has happened

- explain clearly and openly why it is a complaint which merits no action.

This not only sets the record straight but also allows everyone to see that even an imagined rather than a real complaint is being handled seriously. For instance, some organisations have agreed employment conditions which include the option of changing the location at which individuals work. Local authorities, for example, with offices in towns across their areas, sometimes need to move their officers around to cover short- or long-term pressures and this is set out in employment contracts and/or collective agreements. An employee required to move location but who did not wish to would not have a legitimate grievance. However, if they did raise the complaint it would have to be discussed and resolved at the earliest possible stage. This would both clarify the facts of the situation and avoid treating the individual in a way which might lead to long-term resentment and thus damage long-term relationships.

In this case, the grievance is imagined rather than real. Management's action (ie relocation) is within agreed procedures. As nobody is acting in a way contrary to the accepted way of behaving – even though the employee does not like the action which is taking place – there is no real grievance to be handled. However, the employee had to be heard and the issue dealt with if only to clarify the facts. It is important the issue was handled in a way which avoided the possibility of the individual feeling ignored or snubbed in a manner which they felt insulting.

Genuine Grievance

On the other hand, the manager may conclude after interviewing the employee laying the complaint that further information is required about the grievance (for example, what does the agreement say? Are there any witnesses or other people with relevant information that also need to be interviewed?) before management's attitude to the issue can be established. In such circumstances management will make arrangements with the employee and their representative for a further meeting. However, following the grievance interview management may decide the employee's grievance is genuine and it is prepared to seek a resolution to the matter but requires time to prepare its considered response and case. In this situation, management will also agree arrangements as to when and where it will next meet with the employee and/or their representative to resolve the issue.

Planning to meet with the employee and their representatives

There are three main stages to preparing to meet with the individual employee and their representative to negotiate a settlement to the individual's grievance. These are:

- analysis

- establishment of the aims as to how the grievance can be resolved whilst at the same time protecting management's interests

- planning the strategy and tactics to achieve the established aims.

Analysis

The analysis stage involves management collecting and analysing relevant information to substantiate its proposals for resolving the individual employee's grievance. It also includes developing the argument to be put to the employee and their representative to support management's case. In managing grievances the main source of relevant information will be obtained from interviewing management colleagues and employees who are regarded as having relevant information (for example, if they witnessed the incident about which the employee is complaining) to the issue at stake.

This analysis stage also involves management checking whether the subject of the grievance has been complained of previously by employees and, if so, what the outcome was. Knowledge of such outcomes enables management to know whether any 'precedent' exists for dealing with the employee's grievance. Other important management activities in the analysis stage include asking whether:

- there are any relevant company rules

- custom and practice are relevant to the employee's complaint

- any collective or personal contracts are relevant.

The most important activity for management in the preparation stage of handling grievances is the identification of the exact details of the employee's complaint. As we saw earlier in this chapter, the resolution of one grievance is never achieved at the expense of dropping another individual's grievance. In managing grievances the parties concentrate on resolving one grievance before proceeding to resolve the next. However, in handling grievances agreement can be reached by the parties trading the details surrounding the issue but retaining certain principles. In making a decision about which 'details' to trade, management assesses their significance to the complaint of the individual concerned. Having decided which 'details' it is prepared to trade, management then turns to anticipating which 'details' it believes the employee will be prepared to trade.

Let us assume management has suspended an employee for swearing in the presence of a frontline manager for three working days without pay. The individual considers the penalty to be too harsh and with their representative approaches management to register this fact. In analysing the situation, management identifies three issues – suspension, the length of the suspension and no pay for the period of suspension. From a management perspective, given the offence, for the employee to escape any disciplinary penalty would be unacceptable. However, before finally making this decision, management assesses how strongly the individual's work colleagues feel about the harshness of the disciplinary penalty. Would they, for example, be prepared to impose industrial sanctions against the company and, if the answer is yes, how successful might such action be? Management has to weigh up whether, if it persists with retaining the initial penalty, the grievance might not escalate into a collective dispute with all its associated costs. If management concludes the employees would not take the issue to a collective dispute it can be confident in its view that the initial penalty can be upheld. However, if the conclusion is the opposite, then management is likely to take the view that although the principle of the imposition of a disciplinary penalty cannot be compromised, the severity of the penalty might be reduced.

If management comes to this conclusion, it turns to consider the length of the suspension and lost pay. Again, the management is unlikely to see payment of wages during a period of the suspension period as a matter upon which a compromise can be made. If management assesses that to sustain this stance will not provoke a collective dispute then non-payment of wages during a period of suspension will become non-negotiable. However, if management's assessment is that the employees feel strongly about non-payment then they will be prepared to negotiate on the issue.

On the basis of the above analysis, management will see a resolution based on some compromise on the length of the suspension (ie a reduction in its duration from three days) in return for the retention of lost pay and some disciplinary penalty. Management has decided which details it is prepared to trade in the light of assessing its bargaining power relative to the group of workers concerned, should the individual complaint of too harsh a disciplinary penalty develop into a collective dispute. Management has anticipated the employee will accept the principle of suspension but will trade the details surrounding the length of the suspension and the lost pay.

Establishment of aims
Having completed its analysis, management then establishes objectives

for the forthcoming meeting with the individual employee and their representative. Management establishes three aims:

- how would it ideally like the grievance to be resolved?

- how does it realistically think the grievance can be resolved?

- what is the least for which management will settle (the fall-back position)?

Management establishes these three positions for each of the issues involved in the employee's grievance. Having established its own aims/objectives, management turns its attention to anticipating the aims/objectives of the employee making the complaint: what is the individual employee ideally, realistically and minimally expecting to achieve as a resolution to their grievance?

Management can now construct an Aspiration Grid (see Chapter 7) setting the parameters for the expected outcome from the forthcoming grievance handling negotiations. A possible Aspiration Grid for management is shown in Table 38. It shows that management ideally would like to trade no details surrounding the grievance with the employee. However, management knows this is unrealistic and has established, on the basis of its analysis of the situation, a realistic position of some compromise around a retention of the suspension and no pay in return for a reduction in the period of the suspension from three days to two days. Its fall-back position is to retain the suspension and lost pay for a further reduction in the length of the suspension (to one day).

The Grid shows management anticipates that the employee expects them to be unwilling to compromise on suspension and the lost pay accompanying it. It also demonstrates management anticipates the employee will accept a reduction in the length of suspension and, if a mutually acceptable solution is to be achieved, then it will be around this issue. It also shows no problems are anticipated over the loss of pay issue because, although management is not prepared to make compromises on this aspect of the grievance, the employee is.

The Aspiration Grid shows there is a basis for a resolution to the employee's complaint that management has imposed too harsh a discipline penalty. In the fall-back position, although management is not prepared to compromise on the principle of the suspension, it is on its duration. However, it is not prepared to compromise on the 'no

Table 38 Aspiration grid – three days' suspension without pay grievance

Possible Resolution to Grievance	Management			Employee		
	Ideal	Real	Fall–Back	Fall–Back	Real	Ideal
3 days' suspension – pay restored	X	X	X	O	O	X
2 days' suspension and pay restored	X	X	X	O	O	X
1 day's suspension and pay restored	X	X	X	O	X	X
2 days' suspension – no pay	X	X	O	O	O	X
1 day's suspension – no pay	X	O	O	O	O	X

NB: O = prepared to trade
    X = not prepared to trade

pay' during suspension issue. The employee is prepared to make compromises on length of suspension and to accept 'no pay' during the period of suspension. Management will test by the use of appropriate techniques (see Chapter 7) during subsequent meetings that the expected employee (and their representative) negotiating objectives are as anticipated. Management, at the same time, will seek to pass on to the employee, by appropriate coded language and techniques (see Chapter 7), its attitude towards the issues of the length of the suspension and no pay during the period of suspension. Should new information come to light in their subsequent meetings then the management team will have to review and amend its Aspiration Grid.

Strategy and Tactics

Having established its negotiating aims, management now moves to planning its strategy and tactics to realise those objectives. There are a number of issues for management to consider:

- the size of its negotiating team

- who will speak for management and in what order

- communications within the negotiations team (for example, passing of notes)

- anticipation of counter-arguments from the employee to management's arguments and how these can in turn be countered

- anticipation of arguments to be made by employee in support of their case and how these might be countered.

As we saw in Chapter 7, there is no hard and fast rule on the size of a management team in any negotiation situation, let alone a grievance handling one. The quality of preparation rather than the numbers on each side is the crucial factor. Lung power and the quality of preparation are not the same. The size of the management team in a grievance handling situation depends on the circumstances but is likely to consist of a leader, a note-taker and an observer (who listens and watches but does not speak).

The anticipation of the likely arguments to be used by the other side in support of their case and how management might counter these is particularly important. Insights into these sets of counter-arguments can be gained by a member of the management 'playing the devil's advocate' to probe management's case for weaknesses. In the light of this exercise, management can strengthen its case.

The preparation stage is the most important stage in grievance handling negotiations. Why this is so was explained in Chapter 7 where the golden rule in preparing for negotiation is:

> Failure to prepare
> is Preparing to fail

Chapter 7 demonstrated that if management prepares inadequately the situation can be rescued by management reassessing its negotiating analysis, aims and strategy in the light of new information which it failed, for whatever reason, to obtain whilst preparing its original case in response to the individual employee complaint.

Meetings with the Employee and their Representative

As we saw in Chapter 7, in presenting their case to the individual employee and/or their representative, management informs the employee and their representative of the matters it intends to raise and then:

- presents a broad picture of its proposals for resolving the grievance

- gives the details of its proposals backed by supporting evidence

- summarises its proposals to resolve the grievance.

The employee will have stated his or her case at the grievance interview.

The parties now have to move on to seek confirmation of their expected common ground for the basis of a resolution to the employee grievance. As we saw in Chapter 7, there are a number of techniques management can use for this purpose – 'if and then' technique, questioning for clarification, watching, listening, etc. However, information to confirm the expected basis for an agreement will not arise if the meetings with the employee are unconstructive in that the parties merely blame each other for the grievance having arisen, keep interrupting each other, attack personalities on the other side, etc. In most grievance handling negotiations, adjournments are likely to be called to confirm facts or to speak to a witness who can confirm the facts, rather than because of the provision of significantly new information which requires the parties to re-consider their strategy and tactics and their negotiation objectives.

Resolving the grievance

If a manager is unable, after meaningful negotiations, to find a resolution to the grievance, the matter can be referred to the next stage in the procedure where a higher level manager will prepare, present and try to negotiate a mutually acceptable solution. If a grievance remains unresolved and the manager has to pass the matter to the next stage, then they should check this has actually happened.

However, before finally accepting that a resolution to the grievance has been agreed, management needs to:

- be convinced the employee understands what has been agreed

- 'play back' to the employee what management understands the resolution of the grievance actually means, to prevent misunderstanding arising.

If this process reveals misunderstanding by the employee as to what has been agreed and this cannot be cleared up by discussion, then the negotiations will need to restart.

Once management has an oral agreement for the resolution of the employee's grievance, it should be written up. In many grievances this will take the form of an internal memo/letter to another manager and to the employee, recording what has been agreed. For example, if the complaint was one of denial of access to a training opportunity and it is upheld via the grievance handling process, then a manager will write to personnel or the appropriate department, reporting it has been agreed the individual concerned should attend the next available appropriate training course. On the other hand, it can, depending on the issue, take the form of a signed agreement by the manager concerned, the individual employee and their representative. The outcome is then reported to the appropriate interested parties. Clarity is important and the manner in which what has been agreed is recorded should leave no room for doubt.

> Outline the skills required of managers in successfully handling grievances. Which do you consider to be the most important and why?

Specific issues/specific procedures
The grievance procedure deals with the broad range of complaints and problems. However, some issues are related specifically to topics which have their own specific list of issues. These include:

• job grading and evaluation

• complaints by one employee about the behaviour of another

• sexual harassment

• discrimination in promotion and advancement.

So, while some employee complaints remain as general grievances, others are best dealt with by specific procedures designed to deal with the type of difficulties specific to certain issues.

Job evaluation
Job evaluation helps determine the appropriate level of a job as measured against criteria such as decision-making, working conditions (for example, exposure to hazards, working in the open air as against an office, etc), contacts within and outside the organisation, the degree of supervision received, the complexity of the work (for example, gathering data rather than gathering and then manipulating data) within the organisation's structure. The appropriate level in the structure influences the pay level and seniority associated with the job.

A grievance around this issue involves the individual claiming their job has changed relative to when it was last evaluated because it now carries greater responsibility for:

• people (in terms of supervising and training them)

• financial resources (increased budget, financial control)

• physical resources (modern high tech expensive equipment)

and therefore warrants a higher grading and level of remuneration.

On the other hand, management may argue the job has not changed in responsibility and what has changed is an increase in the volume of tasks, at the same level of responsibility. It therefore makes sense in resolving such a dispute to have a procedure tailored to cover the specific circumstances of job grading, including access to specialist and expert individuals.

Job-evaluation appeals procedure

In a typical job-evaluation appeals procedure, the first stage normally involves the individual employee discussing the basis of their appeal with their immediate line manager/team leader. The second stage normally requires the individual to complete a Formal Appeal Form which then goes before a meeting of a Job-evaluation Appeal Panel, which is an internal, not an external, body. The complainant, accompanied by their representative, presents their case to the Appeal Panel, as does the employer. The Appeal Panel will decided either to upgrade the job or to reject the appeal. The decision is usually communicated to the individual through their line manager. If the appeal is upheld, the decision will be implemented from the date of the panel's decision.

If the job holder or manager is dissatisfied with the decision of the Appeal Panel then they may request their case goes to a third stage and be heard by an Independent Appeal Body. At this stage the job holder (assisted by their representative) will present the basis of the appeal. A member(s) of the Appeal Panel will present justification for their decision and the Independent Appeal Body, which is usually chaired by an independent chairperson acceptable to both parties, will make a decision which is final and binding. Thus, in some organisations with job-evaluated pay structures, individual grievances over job gradings are at the end of the day decided by arbitration (see Chapter 4).

A job-evaluation procedure is relatively clear-cut and straightforward. It has the advantage over the standard grievance procedure of building access to experts at each appeal stage and providing more specialist panels to hear the appeals.

Dignity at work

Harassment based on gender, race and bullying at work has received increasing attention in recent years as organisations and worker representative bodies have become more concerned about the dignity of individuals in the workplace. Many organisations have policies and procedures which link the complaints procedure on harassment with the existing grievance procedure rather than establishing separate arrangements for such complaints. Others have treated it as a specific issue. Both approaches work.

In organisations where a harassment policy exists, it is normal for a dual system to operate. The initial action is usually confined to the specifics of the complaint within the procedure laid down for managing sexual harassment. If the problem cannot be resolved within the limits of the policy and is proved to be an issue that merits disciplinary proceedings, then the disciplinary procedure is triggered.

When an employee complains they have suffered sexual harassment from another employee, whether a manager or not, they have a grievance. They are, in fact, making a complaint to management. In dealing with an allegation of sexual harassment, the manager first conducts a thorough investigation to establish whether there is a *prima facie* case of sexual harassment for the accused employee to answer. If the manager decides, on the basis of the investigation, there is a case to answer then disciplinary proceedings will be instigated against the accused employee. However, this is conditional on the 'victim' agreeing the issue be taken to this stage. If the 'victim' refuses to proceed any further with the matter, that is the end of it. If the disciplinary proceedings are started against the accused individual and the charge of sexual harassment is upheld, then an appropriate penalty is imposed including, often as a last resort, dismissal of the employee. If, on the other hand, the manager decides the sexual harassment allegation has no foundation, then they must explain fully to the 'victim' and their representative why this is the case.

So, if a manager is sitting in his or her office and a woman employee comes in claiming she has been sexually harassed and she has witnesses and wants action taken against the individual concerned, then it is clear what the manager should do:

- investigate the claim thoroughly

- decide whether there is a case to answer

- if there is a case to answer and it cannot be settled amicably and the 'victim' insists on pressing their complaint then the disciplinary procedure is triggered

- if there is no case to answer, then this must be explained carefully and sensitively to the 'victim'.

Different organisations define differently their acceptable standards of behaviour, particularly with respect to gross misconduct. In some organisations sexual harassment is regarded as gross misconduct carrying instant dismissal if proven; that this is the case will be spelt out to employees in the organisation's policy statement on sexual harassment and/or dignity at work. This, however, is not the case in some organisations, where lesser penalties can be, and are, imposed on the harasser.

There are therefore good reasons for dealing with sexual harassment complaints outside the general grievance procedure. First, there is a reasonable chance that the person who is the subject of the complaint is the line manager of the employee making the complaint. This makes it difficult to resolve the grievance as near to the point of its origin as possible. Second, there is a link between grievance, discipline and harassment. The role of the employee relations specialist in sexual harassment complaints is to act as a catalyst for line managers to manage the issue by providing them with general expertise and support, including access to training programmes to handle dignity at work issues.

Other areas
Other complex areas of employee complaint which justify having separate grievance procedures include discrimination in promotion and

advancement and alleged unequal treatment in terms of pay, overtime, travel, etc. Each case is unique and requires thorough investigation before deciding whether the grievance is real or imagined, whether the offence is proven and whether an informal response or formal action through procedures is appropriate. All cases of grievance have to be handled with equal care. Procedures offer the means of management behaving in a fair and reasonable way in managing grievances.

SUMMARY

This chapter began by examining the business case for resolving employee grievances, defining a grievance and identifying the issues which are most frequently the cause of employee grievances. It then went on to explain that the effective negotiation of the resolution of grievances, unlike bargaining, excludes a trade-off between different employee complaints about management behaviour. The chapter also explained the extent to which employees took up (or did not take up) grievances, analysed the underlying principles of a grievance procedure and described the main features of a 'typical' procedure (ie the number of stages, time limits, representation of employees, etc).

The chapter also examined the operation of grievance procedures and the role of employee relations specialists in managing employee grievances (for example, the promotion of 'best practice' in managing grievances among line managers). In addition, it outlined the legal framework surrounding grievance handling. The chapter then went on to point out that many grievances are of a simple nature and are resolved quickly, but that this is not always the case. The managing of employee grievances involving a number of stages – hearing the grievance (the grievance interview), preparing to meet the employee (analysis, establish aims, plan strategy and tactics), meeting with the employee and/or their representative, confirming, as the basis for a successful resolution of the grievances, the common ground between the employee and management, resolving the grievance and reporting the outcome. The chapter also explained how a crucial role in managing employee grievances effectively is that a manager should be able to distinguish the genuine employee complaint from the unfounded one.

It was also pointed out in the chapter that the grievance procedure deals with the broad range of employee complaints and problems but that issues are best dealt with by specific procedures designed to deal with specific difficulties that can arise from handling such issues. These include job-grading and evaluation, complaints by one employee about the behaviour of another, sexual harassment, bullying and discrimination in promotion and advancement.

REFERENCES AND FURTHER READING

ADVISORY, CONCILIATION AND ARBITRATION SERVICE (1997) *Guide for Small Firms: Dealing with Grievances*. London, ACAS.

BOUWEN R. *and* SALIPANTE P. F. (1996) 'Behaviour analysis of grievances: episodes, actions and outcomes' *Employee Relations*. Vol 12, No 4.

FOWLER A. (1996) *Negotiation Skills and Strategy*. 2nd edn. London, Institute of Personnel and Development.

HOOK C. M. *et al* (1996) 'Supervisor and management styles in handling discipline and grievance: Part one – comparing styles in handling discipline and grievance'. *Personnel Review*. Vol 25, No 3.

INDUSTRIAL RELATIONS SERVICES (1997) 'Handling employee grievances: Part 1'. *Employment Trends*, No 635, July.

INDUSTRIAL RELATIONS SERVICES (1997) 'Handling employee grievances: Part 2 – collective disputes'. *Employment Trends*, No 642, October.

INSTITUTE OF PERSONNEL AND DEVELOPMENT (1998) *Fairness at Work and the Psychological Contract*. London.

KELLY J. *and* GENNARD J. (1997) 'The unimportance of labels: the diffusion of the personnel/HRM function'. *Industrial Relations Journal*, Vol 28, No. 1.

RENWICK D. *and* GENNARD J. (1999) 'Grievance and discipline: A new set of concerns', in Redman T. and Wilkinson A. (ed) *Human Resource Management: Theory and practice*. Reading, MA, Addison Wesley.

ROLLINSON D. *et al* (1996) 'Supervisor and management styles in handling discipline and grievance: Part 2 – Approaches to handling discipline and grievance'. *Personnel Review*, Vol 25, No 4.

TORRINGTON D. *and* HALL L. (1998) *Personnel Management*. Hemel Hempstead, Prentice Hall.

10 Bargaining

WHAT IS BARGAINING?

Chapter 7 presented an overview of the negotiation process. This chapter looks in more detail at what is involved in bargaining with the workforce. After you have read this chapter, you will be able to:

- define bargaining

- explain bargaining arrangements

- outline the different types of agreements that exist

- understand what is involved in preparation for bargaining

- justify what is involved in conducting and concluding negotiations

- understand what is involved in writing up a collective agreement

- appreciate what is involved in managing conflict.

Bargaining is one of a number of different forms of negotiation and was defined in Chapter 7 as two parties coming together to make an agreement by purposeful persuasion and constructive compromise. It is in a bargaining situation that the buyers and sellers of labour services are in their most adversarial relationship because their representatives are seeking to protect and advance the economic interests of their constituents. Bargaining is a situation where the parties involved have a 'shopping list' of demands of each other.

One party (usually the employees collectively) proposes a list of improvements to pay and other conditions of employment whilst the other (normally the employer) responds with a set of counter-proposals covering changes in working practices. For example, in the 1999 national agreement negotiations between the Graphical, Paper and Media Union (GPMU) and the British Printing Industries Federation (BPIF), the former had the following shopping list:

- a wage increase above 'headline' inflation

- phased improvements in annual holidays starting with the inclusion of one extra day's holiday in 1999 with the ultimate aim of introducing 30 days per year over the medium term

- removal of the overtime clause which states 'the necessity of working overtime as occasion arises is accepted as a necessity to meet production requirements of the industry'

- a parental leave and time-off for domestic incidents clause be inserted into the agreement

- provision of reasonable time off during working hours for local Chapter officials to meet new employees during their first week of employment to inform them about the GPMU and explain the benefits of membership

- the introduction of preretirement leave

- the introduction of a national minimum sick pay scheme

The BPIF presented the following counter shopping list:

- a wage increase of 1.5 per cent (£3.15 per week)

- any additional costs arising from the 1999 national settlement to be recovered in full by efficiency and productivity improvements at company level

- no increase in holiday entitlement

- retention of overtime clause

- no access for the union to new employees to tell them about the union.

A bargaining situation involves issues of collective interest to the workforce, unlike an employee grievance which normally involves an issue of interest only to that individual. Bargaining, unlike grievance handling, involves 'trading' of items in the relative shopping lists with the use of language such as, 'if you drop that part of your claim then we shall drop this part of ours'. The parties to collective bargaining come to an agreement by trading items in their respective shopping lists.

Bargaining is thus about trading with the other party and not about conceding to the other party. In the 1999 national agreement the BPIF traded:

- increases in pay ranging from £5.35 to £4.82 per week for adult workers

- increases in the pay of learners from £2.19 to £4.82 per week

- a millennium Bank Holiday

- introduction of preretirement leave arrangements

- access to new employees

- introduction of a national minimum sick pay scheme from 1 January 2000

- introduction of a parental leave/domestic incident scheme.

In return they received:

- retention of the 'overtime clause'

- the additional costs of the agreement being fully recovered by efficiency and productivity improvements at the workplace

- a lower wage settlement in return for the introduction of a national minimum sick pay scheme.

Such 'something for something' agreements have been traditional in large parts of the manufacturing sector. However, there are situations, especially in the public sector, where it is normal for the employer to give a pay increase to the workforce, perhaps to compensate for an increase in inflation since the last rise, without receiving anything in return.

In most academic literature the words 'negotiation' and 'bargaining' are taken to be one and the same thing. This is incorrect. Bargaining is only one of a number of different types of negotiating situations in which a management might find itself (see Chapter 7). Bargaining is usually a process of changing employment conditions and advancing economic interests. It is a means of creating new employment rules. The tenor and style of negotiations in bargaining is likely to be more adversarial than in grievance handling and group problem-solving situations.

Has there recently been bargaining in your organisation? If yes, what was the outcome? What was traded for what?

BARGAINING ARRANGEMENTS

A necessary condition for the existence of collective bargaining is the recognition for a trade union(s) for this purpose. Multi-union recognition is the norm in UK employee relations. This is because of the large number of trade unions, the structure of the trade unions and the history of employee relations. Apart from multi-union recognition, other characteristics of employee relations where unions are recognised include multiple bargaining units and separate unions for manual and non-manual workers.

Level of bargaining

An important decision for a management which recognises and negotiates with the union(s) is to decide the level at which bargaining is to take place. There are a number of strategic choices of bargaining levels available:

- multi-employer
- single employer
- enterprise
- a consolidation of these three.

Multi-employer bargaining (or industry-wide or national bargaining) is where minimum terms and conditions of employment are negotiated for all employers that are party to the mutual agreement. The bargaining unit (that is the workers covered) is the industry. Multi-employer bargaining, for small companies, offers the advantage that management can concentrate on other aspects of the business as well as preventing employers playing each other off in the wage bargaining process. However, they have the disadvantage of forcing some employers to pay more than they can afford and do not relate changes in employee conditions to local market conditions, employee productivity and employee performance.

Single-employer and company bargaining is where all terms and conditions are negotiated at employer level, in either single site or multi-site organisations. Bargaining at this level enables pay and conditions to be related to the economic circumstances of the company and provides standardised conditions across the company for similar jobs. On the other hand, it exposes the company to isolation from its competitors in an industrial dispute and in multi-site organisation situations does not relate pay and conditions to market forces and ability to pay.

Enterprise bargaining (or plant bargaining) is where terms and conditions are negotiated between management and union representatives locally. It is either autonomous or co-ordinated. In the former case each plant has the authority to settle all terms and conditions locally. In the latter case the negotiations are co-ordinated at plant level within limits set by the centre. Enterprise bargaining has the attraction of enhancing management's ability to respond flexibly to employee relations by introducing pay, conditions and incentives related to local conditions. However, on the downside it requires management to have a competency in negotiation skills which might not exist at plant level and can increase the danger of claims for wage parity by the unions.

Two-tier bargaining is where some aspects of pay and conditions are determined at one level whilst others are decided at another, usually lower level. In some industries industry-wide bargaining determines minimum standards of pay, hours of work, holidays etc but at company or enterprise level agreements are made, related to the ability to pay, that supplement the national minimum standard. In this way it is possible to balance the need for the stability of industry-wide minimum standards with the need for financial flexibility at the company level. In other cases two-tier bargaining takes place with single employer bargaining arrangements. Basic conditions of employment are established at the company-wide level with pay being determined at enterprise level.

MINIMISING MULTI-UNIONISM

In the last twenty years many organisations in the UK, but especially foreign-owned companies establishing a greenfield site, have adopted employee relations strategies of dealing with one union only or a number of unions collectively. The main elements of this strategy have been:

- single union agreements
- single table bargaining
- single union/no strike agreements.

Single union agreements
Single union recognition is where a company recognises only one union for collective bargaining and related purposes. These

agreements have been associated with what some observers have called 'new style' agreements but the newness of such agreements is highly questionable. Single union agreements have long existed in the UK, for example, in the retail sector. However, the number of such agreements is still relatively small compared with the number of employees covered by traditional collective bargaining practices. Their growth has been most prominent on greenfield sites. They have been particularly controversial where an employer has decided to become single union by derecognising existing unions and the preferred union has been chosen after a so-called 'union beauty contest'. Some managers claim that a single union recognition agreement is especially beneficial where an organisation is aiming for teamworking, quality and flexibility amongst its workforce, since the union is seen as facilitating a common purpose within the company.

Single table bargaining

In single table bargaining arrangements unions come together to discuss and agree their position before sending a single team or one bargaining unit to the table. This team negotiates for all employees from every union, which saves management time and resources and minimises interunion strife that can affect the smooth running of the enterprise. It depends on all employees having similar employment deals or it cannot work. Terms and conditions must be at least close in terms of pay, sick leave, holidays, pensions and other fundamentals. Single table bargaining shortens the communications chain and can be used to unify and harmonise working conditions as well as making the introduction of new practices, such as flexible working, easier to achieve.

However, single table bargaining is not an easy principle or practice to introduce. There has to be commitment to the concept from the top management. In addition, it must be remembered there are specific levels of negotiation which have to be maintained for particular groups below the level of the single table. Managers have to be prepared to open up with all employees issues such as fringe benefits, which previously may have been restricted to one or two groups.

In February 1995 the Industrial Relations Services *Employment Trends* published the results of its survey of collective bargaining arrangements in 69 organisations. It found that single table bargaining was in place in less than a quarter of those organisations. It reported that although the introduction of single table bargaining was often a management initiative, it was usually done with the support of the unions concerned. The most common reason given for introducing single table bargaining was

> ... to facilitate the introduction of changes in pay and conditions applying to all or most of the workforce and to help in the harmonisation of the terms and conditions of different groups ...

Management responding to the survey said saving management time and facilitating change were the most common benefits from introducing single table bargaining. The most frequently mentioned disadvantages were problems in ensuring the proper representation of minorities in the workforce and conflict arising from disagreements between the unions involved.

No-strike agreements

A feature of some single union recognition agreements is a no-strike clause. This is precisely what the clause says – an agreement not to use strike action as a sanction in bargaining. This restricts the options of the trade union. In fact, in some greenfield site cases the employer made it a condition of recognition for collective bargaining that the union committed itself to a no-strike agreement. The commitment not to strike is usually replaced by a commitment on the part of both parties that disputes will be solved by pendulum arbitration (see Chapter 4). The final stage of the disputes procedure contained in no-strike agreements provides for disputes to be solved in this way. Single union/no-strike agreements received a considerable amount of publicity but the number of such agreements signed was very small indeed.

Partnership

There is a variety of types of collective agreement. Collective bargaining is an infinitely flexible process of employee relations. In the face of increasing global competition, thriving in business depends upon improvement of conditions and constant change. To achieve this the co-operation of all those involved in the enterprise is required. We saw in Chapter 1 that the idea of management, employees and trade unions working together for their mutual benefit and to secure the future of the business is the very essence of employee relations. The idea has re-emerged onto the employee relations agenda as a result of the Involvement and Participation Association (IPA) publication *Towards Industrial Partnership Report* (1992), the TUC publication, *Partners for Progress – the Next Step for the New Unionism*, and the Government's White Paper, *Fairness at Work*, and has resulted in a number of companies and trade unions signing what have become known as Partnership Agreements. The companies involved include:

- Blue Circle Cement
- Co-operative Bank
- Scottish Power-Generation Wholesale Division
- South and East Belfast Health and Social Services Trust
- Tesco
- United Distillers and Vintners.

Partnership deals operating within the unionised context vary in content and style. However some common themes do emerge and they include:

- new consultation and communication arrangements that are business focused
- setting up of joint working groups
- employee commitment to business goals
- long-term pay deals

- an umbrella of employment security

- sharing of information

- emphasis on training and development

- greater focus on local problem-solving activities

- a move towards harmonisation and single status.

There are six clear principles at work in Partnership Agreements. First, both management and trade union are committed to the success of the enterprise and have a shared understanding of its goals. Second, the agreements recognise each side has legitimate and separate interests (see Chapter 1). This requires trust, respect and a willingness to resolve differences. Third, effective partnerships based on employment agreement have a responsibility to maximise employment security within the enterprise and to improve the employability of their employees via training and development. Fourth, such agreements are designed to improve working life by creating opportunities for personal growth. Fifth, there must be a real sharing of 'hard' information. Consultation must be genuine with a commitment from both sides to listen to the business case for alternative plans. Both signatories to Partnership Agreements have to accept conditions of confidentiality and the need to manage their own communications with their constituents. Finally, an effective partnership adds more to the business by tapping into new sources of motivation, commitment and resources.

There are other factors that are essential for desirable partnerships. One is leadership on all sides. Successful partnerships are often based virtually on the personal leadership skills of a few individuals who often take significant risks in moving relationships onto a new footing. Another factor is a clear understanding of the case for change. Whether the spur is a shift in product markets, the advent of new business goals or the impossibility of continuing a tradition of adversarial industrial relations, it has to be closely understood. Building a relationship requires both employees and managers to invest time and effort. Partnership agreements are by definition high-trust relationships and particularly where they supersede antagonism there is no way to shorten this lengthy process.

Having examined bargaining arrangements and looked at the rise of Partnership Agreements, we now turn to the practice of preparing for bargaining.

PREPARATION FOR BARGAINING

Selection of the bargaining team

The size of the management team will vary but there are advantages in it being small and of an uneven number. If the team is small then it is easier to retain team discipline. An odd number means that if the bargaining team has to take a vote to determine its position there will always be a majority view to prevail. A team of three will always at least split two to one whilst one of five will at least divide three to two. A team of two could divide one and one whilst one of four may split two and two. The management bargaining team should represent all major parts of the business.

There are a minimum of three functions to be covered by a bargaining team. There is a need for a leader who will be the main spokesperson and principal negotiator and who will conduct the negotiations. In addition, the leader will call for an adjournment if management considers one to be necessary and will hold the chair in adjournments. It is the team leader who will enter corridor (private) discussions with the leader of the other side. The leader will also be responsible for finalising the agreement on behalf of management. Leaders require a number of attributes. They require good interpersonal skills to build the team as a coherent whole and they need to be acquainted with the employees' attitudes and, if appropriate, the policies and problems of the trade unions who represent the employees. It is imperative the leader can give leadership and is respected by the other members of the team. In addition, they must be firm, be capable of exercising good judgement, be patient, be a good listener and be skilful in communicating ideas and getting points across.

The bargaining team also requires a note-taker whose role in negotiations cannot be stressed enough. The note-taker's role includes:

- in adjournments, informing the bargaining team whether the negotiations are making progress or just going round in circles

- advising the bargainers whether the agreed strategy and tactics are being observed

- recording the actual proposals made by the other party

- indicating whether the bargaining team has, say, through lack of concentration, missed an offer/proposal from the other side (if this is the case, the bargaining team can return to it in the next or subsequent bargaining sessions)

- ensuring all issues are addressed; the note-taker summarises to the bargaining team what issues have been asked and what are still outstanding and prevents issues that are on the bargaining agenda from being forgotten or overlooked

- supplying the record of what has been agreed, from which management drafts the agreement.

The team also requires a strategist whose role is to monitor the strategies of both sides and to identify and seek to confirm the anticipated basis of common ground and constructive compromise for both sides. The strategist also provides any additional information or details that may be required by the team. In addition, he or she monitors and assesses proposals as and when they are made by the other party.

Some bargaining teams also find it is useful to have a member whose sole purpose is to listen to what is being said and to make no spoken contribution in the bargaining sessions. Some teams also like to have a person whose role is to watch the body and facial reactions of the members of the other side when they are receiving proposals from management or making proposals to management. These reactions can convey useful information and reveal the extent to which the other party is committed to its own proposals and counter-proposals from the other side.

Regardless of the size of the management bargaining team and the division of labour between them, it is imperative, prior to both the first meeting with the other side and to meeting again after an adjournment, that each member of the management team be given the opportunity to contribute to the discussion and agree on the bargaining objectives, strategy and tactics. Ideally, the bargaining team should determine these issues. This provides each team member with an insight into the overall plan and strategy and thereby generates commitment amongst the whole team to its objectives. So while the role of the team leader is most important during negotiations, the role of the whole team is very important in determining policies and strategies.

Team discipline
Members of the management team should conduct themselves during the negotiations in line with the agreed position(s) established in the preparation stage so that the team in the actual negotiations is united and purposeful. It is important before meeting with the other side the team agree only one member should speak at a time in the negotiation sessions and that the team leader should not be interrupted unless it is absolutely necessary. However, all members of the team should be prepared to speak when called upon to do so by the team leader. If members of the team, other than the leader, are to make a spoken contribution during the bargaining sessions then it should be part of a predetermined strategy, the leader having indicated to the other party that they are speaking by invitation from the leader.

It is also important before meeting with the other party that the team remind themselves of the importance of not disagreeing as a team in front of the other side and that if team discipline begins to break down then the leader should seek an adjournment so that the necessary action to re-establish discipline can be taken (even to the extent, if necessary, of excluding a member of the team from participating any further in the face-to-face bargaining sessions). The maintenance of team discipline is easier where all members are fully acquainted with the bargaining objectives, the necessary arguments and tradable items seen as essential to achieving those objectives and that if before meeting with the other side the management team members have agreed a non-verbal method of communicating with each other (eg signals, passing notes, etc) during the negotiation session.

The arguments from the management bargaining team need to be consistent and, no matter how unprofessionally the other side behaves, this should not influence the management side's behaviour as individuals or as a team. If during negotiations the other side attempts to disrupt the discipline of the management team by trying to bring in another speaker from the management side against the planned sequence of contributors, then the team leader must intervene immediately. They should tell the other side to address all their remarks through them as the team leader. If a member of the management bargaining team begins to 'talk out of turn' then the leader will restrain them by the use of appropriate language in the right tone of voice. It may, for example, only be necessary to tell the team member to be quiet or to calm down for discipline to be restored but if this does not work then an adjournment may be necessary during which discipline can be restored.

The members of the bargaining team remain within their agreed roles and only speak when invited to do so unless a change of plan is agreed during adjournments in the negotiations. However, the team members should help each other out of a difficulty and avoid assuming a 'nothing to do with me' expression when the team comes under pressure. This transmits to the other side a clear message that management is not united in its commitment to its case and that unexpected gains may be made by playing on these perceived differences.

> What considerations does management need to take into account in selecting its team for bargaining with its employees' representatives? Justify your answer.

The analysis stage
Source of information
The analysis stage of preparing for bargaining involves management collecting and analysing relevant information to substantiate its claims and/or its proposals to be put to its employees' representatives. In preparing for bargaining situations, management is likely to have to analyse information derived from sources internal and external to the organisation. Internal sources are likely to cover issues such as:

- labour productivity trends
- profitability
- labour turnover
- absenteeism
- total sales
- investment
- pay changes
- orders pending
- cash flow position.

External sources of information for bargaining purposes will include employers' associations, the employee relations 'trade press' and UK Government departments. These external sources maintain national average data and as a result the pay data they contain may not be very useful in local pay negotiations. For local pay negotiations, of much more value are likely to be local pay and salary surveys which the organisation is likely to collect itself.

Employers' associations are an important external source of information. They have records about the types of agreements that exist in an industry and collect data on the size of pay increase settlements being granted by member companies. Many employer associations are also trade associations and, as such, collect information on an industry basis for a number of subjects eg total sales figures, the balance of foreign trade (export/import trends) and unit labour costs.

Industrial Relations Services

An important source of pay information available to those engaged in preparing for bargaining is Industrial Relations Services (IRS). Its twice-monthly Employment Review provides information on employment trends and special features based on a survey of organisations, covering their employment policies and practices. It also contains a Pay and Benefits Bulletin which reviews trends in the general level of pay settlements and reports on pay deals concluded in private and public organisations as well as those involving a whole industry.

It also summarises the latest pay awards showing the name and size of the group of workers covered, the effective date and length of the agreement and brief details of the main changes. Its datafile contains information on price changes (the Retail Price Index), on changes in average earnings (Average Earnings Index), and on future forecasts of annual rates of change in prices and earnings. In addition, it contains a useful summary of the main bargaining statistics (inflation, average earnings, productivity/labour costs, hours worked, unemployment and employment).

The Employment Review also contains an Industrial Relations Law Bulletin which covers European Union Directives, case notes on significant employment law cases and up-to-date news items. Its final section, entitled Health and Safety Bulletin, contains briefings on health and safety issues.

Industrial Relations Services (IRS) also publishes a monthly *Pay Intelligence* updating service. It features key facts and statistics from its pay databank, including settlement levels for the public, private manual, private non-manual, manufacturing and services sectors as well as the whole economy and other analysts' settlement figures. It also contains a summary of the IRS monthly pay analysis and settlement chart and a 'state of play' table detailing news and deals in key negotiations as well as the latest official inflation and earnings figures, together with the predictions of 10 leading forecasting organisations. The IRS pay databank is the only regularly published source of pay statistics independent of employers, trade unions and UK Government. Each year it records the details of pay settlements for some 1,500 bargaining groups covering more than 9 million employees across all sectors of the economy.

Incomes Data Services

Another important independent source of pay statistics for bargainers is Incomes Data Services (IDS) Ltd. Its *Report*, published twice monthly, describes the changes to pay and conditions that are being agreed at company and industry level and reports current developments in collective bargaining, quickly and simply. Pay settlements are given in detail and the latest statistics on wages, earnings and prices are reported and interpreted.

The IDS *Pay Directory* is published three times a year. It lists the wage rates, holidays, shift premium, etc of a wide range of occupations in a variety of companies. It also records the wage rates that apply in selected industries and the public sector. It also publishes Studies twice monthly which report on results of research on single topics such as the pay of a particular group of workers, paid holiday entitlement, sick pay, pensions provisions, shift premium pay, redundancy and absenteeism. Changes to practice are described and explained. Its Top Pay Review, published monthly, monitors the changes to the pay and benefits of executives and professionals and provides a comprehensive briefing on remuneration trends in companies and in the public sector. Its Focus publication is published every quarter and puts forward views on a wide range of issues that influence pay and collective bargaining.

Labour Market Trends

Two important UK Government sources of information for bargainers are *Labour Market Trends*, which incorporates the former *Employment Gazette*, and the *New Earnings Survey*. *Labour Market Trends* provides statistical information on aspects of the labour market, of which the most significant are employment, unemployment, unfilled vacancies, labour disputes, earnings and UK Government-supported training schemes. It also provides regular statistical information on inflation trends, being the official outlet for the Index of Retail Prices. It also provides information on changes in unit wage costs for all employees for manufacturing, energy and water supply, production industries, construction and the economy as a whole.

New Earnings Survey

The richest source of pay data for bargainers is the *New Earnings Survey* (NES). It is the most comprehensive source of earnings information in Great Britain. It is a survey of earnings of employees in employment in Great Britain carried out in April of each year. The survey is based largely on a 1 per cent sample of employees who are members of PAYE income tax schemes and is designed to represent all categories of employees in businesses of all kinds and sizes. The sample each year comprises all those whose National Insurance Numbers end with a specific pair of digits. The same pair of digits has been used since 1975. Employers are then contacted to give details on the identified employees. The method covers about 90 per cent of the sample. The remaining 10 per cent is obtained directly from large employers. This sample can include some employees not in a PAYE scheme. The coverage of full-time adults is virtually complete. But the coverage of part-time employees is not comprehensive.

The NES provides an annual snapshot of earnings and hours worked analysed by industry, occupation, age group, region, county and collective agreement. Its results are published in six parts:

• Part A is a streamlined analysis giving selected results for full-time employees in particular wage negotiation groups, industries, occupations, age groups, regions and sub-regions.

- Part B provides analyses of earnings and hours for particular wage negotiation groups.

- Part C analyses hours and earnings for particular industries.

- Part D provides the same analysis for particular occupations.

- Part E provides the same analysis for regions and counties.

- Part F provides an analysis of the distribution of hours, joint distributions of earnings and hours and an analysis of hours and earnings for part-time women employees.

The earnings data covers the level of earnings, the make-up of total earnings (basic pay, overtime pay, shift premiums, incentive payments, etc) and the distribution of total earnings (by decile, quartile and median).

> Take a look at the *New Earnings Survey*. Write a report on how pay and conditions in your organisation compare with the national average. How would you account for any differences found?

Identification of Tradable Items

However, the most important activity for management in preparing for bargaining, as in grievance handling, is the identification of the key issues involved in the forthcoming negotiations and which of these management is prepared to trade. In making this decision, management weighs up the significance of the issues at stake for its economic interests. In a bargaining situation, for example, the management team may decide changes in paid holidays and reduction in the working week are not tradable items but it is prepared to trade improvements in pay levels and improved childcare facilities in return for greater flexibility between work tasks, the right to recruit part-time labour and to tighten the operational rules surrounding the sick pay scheme.

Having decided which items it is prepared to trade, the management team starts the task of anticipating which issues it believes the employees (the union) will be willing to trade. In doing this it assesses the strength of feeling of the employees about the issues in their shopping list, including whether they feel sufficiently strongly that at the end of the day they would be willing to impose industrial sanctions against the organisation. Taking the above example, the management team might anticipate its employees do not feel particularly strongly about increased holidays and a shorter working week. However, it knows that they feel strongly about a pay increase and improved childcare facilities and will be reluctant to trade these items. The judgement for the management team then becomes, 'will the employees be prepared to trade changes in working practices and changes in the sick pay scheme to achieve improved pay and childcare facilities?' If management decides, after due consideration and analysis,

Table 39 Aspiration grid: bargaining situation

Possible resolution to grievance	Management			Employees and their representative organisation		
	Ideal	Real	Fall–back	Fall–back	Real	Ideal
Increased holidays	X	X	X	0	0	X
Reduced working week	X	X	X	0	0	X
Increased pay	X	0	0	X	X	X
Improved childcare facilities	X	0	0	X	X	X
Greater task flexibility	X	X	X	0	0	X
Tightening the sick pay scheme	X	X	0	0	X	X

that this is the case, then it will see a basis for agreement around increases in pay and childcare provisions in return for changes in working practices and the operation of the sick pay scheme in directions which are more favourable to management.

Establishment of Aims

As in grievance handling, so in bargaining. When management has completed its analysis of the negotiating situation it is about to enter it moves to establish its objectives in terms of what it would ideally like to achieve. What does it realistically expect to achieve? What is the minimum it must achieve? Management's bargaining team will establish these three positions for each of the items in the respective shopping lists of both parties. Having established its negotiating aims/objectives, management's next step is to anticipate the aims/objectives of the representatives of the employees, for example, what do they ideally and realistically want and what is the minimum for which they would settle?

As in a grievance handling situation, the management bargaining team can now construct an Aspiration Grid which sets out the parameters for the expected outcome of the bargaining (see Table 39). The Grid shows that ideally management would like to trade no items with the employees. However, it knows this is unrealistic. The Grid shows management has established a realistic position of wishing to trade increases in pay and childcare facilities for changes in working practices and tightening of the conditions surrounding the sick pay scheme. Management's fall-back position is to improve its pay offer, to provide childcare facilities and reduce the restrictions surrounding the sick pay scheme in return for obtaining changes in working practices. The bottom line for the management negotiating team is to trade pay, childcare facilities and aspects of the sick pay scheme in return for no change in holidays and working hours but alterations to working practices.

The Aspiration Grid also shows management's expected negotiating objectives of its employees' representatives. It expects ideally that the employees' representatives will view this as unrealistic. The Grid, therefore, shows that management expects the employees' realistic position to be one of seeking a deal around increases in pay and childcare facilities and fewer restrictions on the sick pay scheme, in return for no changes in holidays and working hours and some changes to existing working practices. The Grid shows management anticipates that the 'bottom line' for the employees' representatives is likely to be to trade increases in pay and childcare facilities in return for no changes in holidays and hours of work but to accept management's desire for changes in working practices and in the details of the sick pay scheme.

The Grid shows there is a basis for agreement between the parties. This is indicated in that the fall-back positions of the two parties do not have two Xs against the same issue. Management is not prepared to trade holidays, working hours and changes in working practices. Management anticipates that the employees' representatives are prepared to trade these issues. The employees are expected by management not to be prepared to trade increased pay and increased childcare facilities. However, management has evaluated it can live with trading these issues. The management negotiating team now has a structure of how the bargaining can be expected to develop and evolve. In the face-to-face sessions with the employees' representatives it will have to pass information to them as to what issues management is prepared to trade and at the same time seek to gain information from the employees' side which confirms management's expectations as to what the employees are prepared to trade.

Before establishing its aims for the forthcoming bargaining, management will have assessed its bargaining power relative to the group or groups with which it is to negotiate. The outcome of this assessment will be a significant factor in management determining its bargaining objective. In making an assessment of its relative bargaining power, management gives consideration to issues such as:

- Are the employees, at the end of the day, willing to impose industrial action?

- What is the degree of organisation and solidarity amongst the employees?

- What is the quality of the leadership of union/group employees?

- Have the employees imposed industrial sanctions previously and, if so, what was the result?

- What type of industrial sanctions did they use? What tactics did they use?

- What is the degree of substitutability of product/service produced by the employees concerned?

- Can an alternative supply of labour be obtained?

- How crucial is the group of employees in the production/service supply process?

- How long will it take for industrial sanctions, if imposed, to have an adverse effect on the operation of the organisation?

The management bargaining team must take all these factors into account. If the balance of bargaining power favours the employer then the Aspiration Grid will be different to that where the bargaining power lies with the employees and their representative organisation.

Planning strategy and tactics

Having established its negotiating aims on the basis of its analysis of the situation, management now moves to planning its strategy and the tactics it will use to deliver its objectives. This covers some of the issues raised above when discussing the selection of the bargaining team and discipline within the team and the issues raised under this aspect of preparation in the chapter on managing grievances. In bargaining, as in grievance handling, the preparation stage is the longest and most important stage in the process. The golden rule to remember when preparing for bargaining is:

> Failure to prepare is
> Preparing to fail

In bargaining, as in grievance handling, management should keep under regular review its bargaining objectives in the light of information it gains from the face-to-face negotiating sessions with the other party. Any information received that was not known or anticipated during the original preparation stage must be analysed as to its implications for the established bargaining aims and strategy and tactics.

'Failure to prepare is preparing to fail.' Explain the importance of this statement for managers who are involved in bargaining.

PRESENTATION OF PROPOSALS

In presenting its proposals for the first time, the management team will begin by presenting a general summary of the proposals by the use of language such as:

> We want to put to you today proposals in six areas – increased holidays, reduced working hours, increased pay, childcare facilities, changes in working practices and conditions surrounding the operation of the sick pay scheme ...

After stating what it is going to tell them, the management team then moves on and outlines in detail, supported by facts and other appropriate evidence, its proposals in each of the six areas. The team will stress the rationale behind its proposals and give some indication of its strength of feeling on the issues. At the presentational stage management puts its ideal position on the table. The importance of putting all the proposals out on the table has been discussed in Chapter 7.

However, the opening statement is important because it sets the parameters for the bargain, determines the amount of room available for movement and can be used to structure the expectations of the other party. There can be advantages from opening with an extreme position. It provides more scope for movement in the bargaining sessions, allows extra time to identify the position of the other party and avoids the problem of opening too low and passing up an opportunity of maximising possible outcomes. However, these possible advantages have to be weighed up against possible disadvantages. First, extreme demands might be given no credibility by the other side and be ignored. Second, the other party might perceive them as totally unreasonable and question the seriousness with which management is treating the negotiations. There is also the danger the other side might respond with an equally extreme position. In deciding the level at which to pitch its opening demands, the management team would be influenced by what it knows to be the style of the other side. Knowing and understanding the other party is very important for bargainers as it helps the process of predicting how they might react to your proposals and to understand their style of negotiations so that 'ritual' can be distinguished from the real position.

If management is receiving proposals from its employees' representatives then it listens carefully to what is being said and does not interrupt the presentation. After the conclusion of the presentation, the management team should avoid an unthought-out response to the proposals that have just been put before it. Management should limit its response to questions to seek clarification of the employees' proposals so that it can be confident it understands what the other party's proposals actually mean.

CONFIRMATION OF COMMON GROUND

At the completion of the original presentation of proposals by the two parties, all issues/demands/proposals will be out in the open. At this stage, there will be little common ground between the two parties. The bargaining sessions now move to confirm the anticipated common ground from which a basis for a mutually beneficial agreement can be built. The tone of the meetings switches from concentrating on differences between the parties to confirming points of common interest and possible agreement. The management bargaining team acknowledges the point has been reached at which both they and the employees' representatives identify the common ground within and between their positions.

As we have already noted, management's objective is to gain information from the negotiating sessions to confirm its expectations about the areas of common ground between the parties. The implication is that the bargaining sessions must be used constructively by both parties. This is more likely to be the case where management seeks to ascertain relevant information from the other party by:

- listening to the other side no matter how outrageous the statements of the employees' representatives might be; management must hear them out carefully

- questioning for clarification of the other side's position

- summarising issues neutrally eg 'So, what you have been telling us is ...'

- seeking and giving information

- suggesting solutions as to how problems of implementing the proposals might be overcome.

Bargaining sessions taken up with pointless arguments which go nowhere (eg 'It's your fault.' 'No, it's not, it's your fault.' 'We tell you again, it's your fault.'), constant interruptions of contributions, point scoring, attacking personalities on the other side, failing to listen to the other side (talking too much) and shouting down the other side are unconstructive and a waste of time. In such bargaining sessions, it is likely that one side will fail to take up a proposal or accept agreement by the other side to one or more of their proposals. It can be difficult then to get the offer repeated although in a subsequent adjournment the note-taker should point out what has happened and the negotiating team will consider how it can get the other side to repeat its offer or agreement. A golden rule of bargaining is that once the other party makes an acceptable offer to one of the items in your shopping list, it should be agreed immediately. The team having gained its point should then move the negotiations to the next issue(s).

It was demonstrated in Chapter 7 that there are a number of techniques a management bargaining team can use to help confirm, or otherwise, the expected basis for an agreement as outlined in the Aspiration Grid. The most important of these are the 'if and then' technique, interviewing techniques, watching and listening techniques and linking of issues. If you are not familiar with these techniques then you should reread the appropriate sections of Chapter 7. In seeking to identify the common ground, management can also make progress by seeking agreement in principle to trade an item before discussing the details of the trade. For example, it is pointless discussing the details of how a new incentive payment scheme would work if either side is totally opposed to the idea of incentive schemes in the first place. It is also advantageous to seek to confirm the common ground if the management negotiating team adopts the policy of being firm on principles. For example, management might say, 'If we are to agree to this then we must be given greater flexibility in the utilisation of labour.' Management then proceeds to propose particular changes to working practices which can be the basis of discussion and negotiation.

In bargaining situations, listening skills enable the team to decode the hidden language of signals. The examples given in Chapter 7 were:

- 'At this stage, we are not prepared to consider that' means 'that is a tradable item but at this stage it is not thought necessary to trade it'.

- 'We would find it extremely difficult to meet that demand' means 'it is not impossible'.

- 'I am not empowered to negotiate on that' means 'see my boss'.

- 'We can discuss that point' means 'it is negotiable'.

- 'These are company standard terms' means 'they are negotiable'.

- 'It is not our policy to make bonus payments and even if we did they would not be as large as 10 per cent' means 'I'll give you 2 per cent'.

- 'It is not our normal practice to' means 'but we might if you make it worth our while'.

There is significant information to confirm tradable items in these statements. If management does not consider the meaning of these statements very carefully, then it will miss important information.

We saw in Chapter 7 that the confirmation of the common ground between the two parties enables the bargaining sessions to have momentum. If the negotiations get bogged down on a particular item they can be kept going by switching to a new issue. The difficult issue can be returned to later and if it is then the only outstanding issue to an agreement being secured, the parties are likely to readjust their attitudes towards it.

Adjournment
In bargaining the use of adjournments is useful in ensuring the negotiations are proceeding as planned. As Fowler (1996) points out, although adjournments may be suggested at any time, there are at least three other constructive uses of the *ad hoc* (as distinct from scheduled) break:

- to give the parties an opportunity to withdraw and review progress amongst themselves or consider a proposal put by the other side

- to provide a break if the negotiations have reached an impasse or become bogged down in trivia or personal argument such that team discipline is in danger of breaking down or has broken down

- to provide an opportunity for one or two members of each side to talk informally with each other away from the negotiating table in a manner that would not be appropriate in the formal negotiation sessions. This provides an opportunity for the leaders of the two teams to meet away from the negotiating table to discuss, without commitment, what it would take to unblock the impasse. The words 'without comment' are normally used in such situations to reassure the other members of the two teams that their leaders will not strike any formal deal without prior reference back.

Adjournments thus enable one or both parties to reconsider their position in private and are very much part of bargaining and group problem-solving negotiation situations. They are also useful in grievance handling situations. Their main purpose is to review and assess progress against your negotiating objectives and the anticipated objectives of the other party. They provide an opportunity to update the negotiating strategy according to how the negotiations are progressing. There are partial re-preparation sessions for a reconvened meeting. If the adjournment is taken to consider a specific proposal, it is important to bear in mind that such adjournments create expectations of a response in the minds of the other party. Reading what is going on is vital and keeping the mind focused on the negotiation objectives is essential. In such situations, Cairns (1996) offers a warning:

> ... if the adjournment is to consider a new offer, don't take ten minutes to reject it and 50 minutes discussing sport or the previous night's TV. Management may get the signal that if you took an hour to consider their offer they are close to an agreement.

As Fowler says above, adjournments should also be sought by

management wherever they have any doubts about how the negotiating session is progressing or team discipline is about to break down, or has already broken down. The golden rule of management is:

If in doubt, get out.

Concluding the agreement

In pay bargaining where increases in pay and other conditions are being given in return for changes in working practices etc, the last item to be decided is what the amount of the increase in pay will be. There are a number of reasons for this. First, the employer wants to know exactly what they are getting in terms of increased work effort for the pay increase. It is only when an amount is on offer that the employer can make a considered judgement that the 'price' for the changes in practice gained is worthwhile. The same applies to the employees. It is only when they know the things they have to give up (ie the price to be paid) that they can make a considered decision whether the proposed pay increase on offer is adequate compensation.

Second, as we have already seen, if the pay issue is put on the table early in the negotiations, then they are likely to become deadlocked. The momentum of the negotiations will come to a halt. Neither of the parties could accommodate each other's interests because they would not, at that stage, be able to assess whether the 'price' was worthwhile. The employer would not have a complete picture of what they were receiving in return for the proposed pay improvement. The employees, by the same token, would be unable to judge whether they were being asked to pay a fair price in return for their pay improvement.

Third, by bargaining over pay after all other issues have been agreed, the bargainers are faced with a stark choice. If they cannot accommodate each other over pay then the whole agreement collapses. What has been agreed concerning the other items in the respective shopping lists is withdrawn. The parties have to weigh up whether they want to 'throw out the baby with the bath water'. The agreement must cover all the issues raised by both parties unless one or both have agreed to take an issue off the table. The attitude of the parties to accommodate each other over a difficult and basic issue but one which is the only outstanding item of non-agreement, will be favourable and not antagonistic. Neither party will want to see all their previous hard work go to waste. Attitudes are thus more compromising than if there were more than one outstanding issue. Both sides also have to weigh up whether, if an agreement fails to materialise over the one outstanding issue of pay improvement, they are prepared to bear the costs that go with the other party imposing industrial sanctions against them.

Factors to consider in concluding the agreement

There are a number of considerations management should bear in mind in closing the negotiations. First, they need to be satisfied all the issues have been discussed and agreed and that both parties fully understand what they have accepted. If there is any uncertainty about the meaning of the agreed proposals, management should go over its case again with the other party and perhaps explain how they see their proposals working in practice (the so-called play-back technique).

However, if it turns out there is a misunderstanding over what has been agreed, the negotiations must recommence. It is crucial that both sides have the same meaning and understanding as to what they have agreed. If this is not the case then when the agreement is implemented, the parties will become embroiled in frequent disputes over whether one party (or the other) is applying and interpreting the agreement properly.

Second, management has to convince the other party their final offer is final. Management needs to be extremely careful about bluffing that this position is their final one. A series of 'final offers' from management will destroy its credibility with the other party and undermine its ability to convince the workforce the 'bottom line' has been reached. There is little value for management in telling the employees there can be no further improvement on its offer because management has reached its bottom line (ie its fall-back position) if the threat of industrial pressure from the employees, for example, by achieving a successful industrial ballot result, forces a further concession. In such circumstances, management has demonstrated to the other side it has not reached its fall-back position and the employees will begin to expect even further improvement. If management tells the employees that its offer is final, then management must mean that and not give in to the threat of industrial pressure.

The authors once heard a personnel director referring to the fact he always had four sets of final offers, each hidden away in one of his pockets. This may sound amusing but when he pulls out those four offers he will destroy his negotiating credibility with the trade unions. To tell them management has reached its final offer will not be believed because what the director was saying was that he was prepared to raise his final offer three more times. What would he do if the fourth offer were not believed? A management negotiator needs to retain the respect and credibility of the other party. Final/final/final offers will not achieve this.

Third, management should avoid being rushed into concluding a final agreement, no matter how tempting the offer/proposal sounds. They must make sure they have all the information they require from the employees (or their representatives) and then seek an adjournment. This will enable management to examine the final offer and identify any potential problems that may have gone unnoticed before.

Writing up the Agreement

Once management has an oral agreement, it should summarise to the employees' representatives what has been agreed and secure agreement that what has been summarised was agreed. It should then be written up in 'draft form'. The written agreement should state:

- who are the parties to the agreement

- the date on which the agreement was concluded

- the date upon which the agreement will become operative

- which groups/grades are covered by the agreement

- what are the exceptions (if any) to the agreement
- the contents (clauses) of the agreement
- the duration of the agreement
- whether the agreement can be reopened before this finish date and, if so, in what circumstances
- whether the agreement can be terminated if it has no end date and, if so, how
- how disputes over its interpretation and application will be settled (will it be the existing grievance/disputes procedure?)
- which, if any, other agreements it replaces.

The written agreement should contain the signatures of representatives of the parties covered by the agreement.

> Explain why recording of the negotiating process is vital. Outline what techniques can be used for this purpose and what are the advantages of each.

The agreement is usually drafted by management and then sent to the other side who will usually initial the clauses the wording of which they accept. Only when both sides are happy with its wording will the agreement be printed and formally signed. There are some pitfalls that management should avoid when writing up the agreement. First, they should check the wording very carefully. One word can make a big difference to the meaning of a clause in the agreement. There is a big difference in meaning between a clause which states 'the management may provide' and one which states 'the management will provide'. The first implies that in certain circumstances management may not provide. The second leaves no room for doubt.

Second, they should retain full concentration in the latter stages of the bargaining. It is likely the negotiations have gone on for some time. There is a danger the management bargaining team will relax once they have an oral agreement, as they think the hard work is over. However, management should bear in mind that, in a very short time, what was said in negotiations will be forgotten. The agreement will be what is down in black and white on the signed agreement.

Third, the agreement must be clear and easy to understand. Unless the agreement is fully understood by both parties and its wording and intent clear, its operation will cause endless disputes over its interpretation and application. Four, it is important for management to keep an accurate record of what was agreed. This may be management's only protection against the other party attempting to insert into the agreement something that was not agreed during the negotiations. Fortunately, attempts 'to cheat' when writing up an agreement are extremely rare amongst management, employees and employees' representatives. To behave in this way would be to try to 'pull a fast one over the other side'. A party may get away with this type of behaviour once but the cost could be high in terms of lost professionalism and of lost trust with the other party.

MECHANISMS FOR RESOLVING CONFLICT

If agreement cannot be made and a breakdown in negotiation takes place, there are a number of choices available to the employer. First the matter can be referred to the disputes procedures. If this fails to result in a settlement then the parties may consider calling in ACAS which can offer the services of conciliation, mediation and arbitration. These were explained in Chapter 4. What happens if the parties decide to go to arbitration?

Arbitration

Terms of reference

If both parties voluntarily agree to arbitration then the first task is to agree terms of reference for the arbitration. ACAS will assist the parties in this task. The terms of reference are important because they tell the arbitrator what it is the parties wish them to do. It sets limits to the arbitrator's powers which are usually constrained to within the range of the parties' claims. It prevents the arbitrator from wandering into issues that the parties do not wish them to, for example, commenting on the defectiveness of procedures. In arbitration, the terms of reference are usually worded in a simple manner. Typical terms of reference would be:

> ... to decide the daily rate of pay for short-term supply school teachers.

The terms of reference give the arbitrator flexibility within limits.

However, in the case of 'pendulum' (or formal offer) arbitration, the terms of reference confine the arbitrator's award to either the employer's final offer or the employees' (union) final claim. The arbitrator must make an 'either-or' decision, and no other settlement is open to be awarded. This is made clear in the terms of reference. An example of a pendulum arbitration terms of reference is as follows in the case of a dispute between the Isle of Man Post Office and the Communications Workers' Union (CWU):

> The arbitrator is asked to decide between the following differences in the employer's offer and the CWU claim:

The IOM PO Offer	The CWU Claim
From 1 January 1999 a 3.1% increase on basic pay, bonuses, overtime and all allowances	From 1 January 1999, a 4.6% increase on basic pay, bonuses, overtime and all allowances

Pendulum arbitration has been favoured by electronics firms where a strike would run the risk of losing markets because adjustments cannot be made quickly enough to produce services in the light of rapidly changing customer demand and technology. Manufacturing companies whose main customers are the large supermarket chains have also favoured pendulum arbitration, believing a strike runs the risk of a permanent loss of business to what is their main customer.

Pendulum arbitration is usually written in as the formal stage of an agreed dispute procedure. It is argued by those who favour pendulum arbitration that by prohibiting arbitrators from occupying the middle ground between a final employer offer and formal union claim, it encourages the parties to make more reasonable offers and claims, since the alternative is to enter a win/lose situation. Indeed it is argued that eventually both sides will be so close together that the gap becomes bridgeable in negotiation so that arbitration is unnecessary. In other words, the main theoretical advantage of pendulum arbitration is that it so pressurises the employer and trade union to make an agreement that the process is unlikely ever to be used.

A great disadvantage of pendulum arbitration lies in the assumption that one side is 100 per cent right and the other is 100 per cent wrong. Why should compromise be an acceptable and justified principle in the collective bargaining processes and yet be ruled out in the arbitrational process? Second, there are longer-term employee relations consequences if one side is found to be comprehensively right and the other just as comprehensively wrong. There are other disadvantages. An arbitrator may be faced with two complicated packages and unless they are very lucky they will find both packages unsatisfactory. If the arbitrator cannot select the best items from each package and award accordingly they have to weigh the two packages and choose the least objectionable.

Choice of arbitrator

The next stage in the process is for the two sides to agree jointly the name of the independent person to arbitrate on their differences. Again, ACAS facilitates this by making available to the parties its 'panel of arbitrators' but it does not provide any information about previous cases to disputant parties. Sometimes the parties are content to allow ACAS to appoint the arbitrator. Mumford (1996) reports the vast majority of the 94 people on ACAS's panel are academics (or retired academics), over 45 years of age and grammar school-educated, but interested in the practicalities of industry and employee relations. In short, they do not live in 'ivory towers'. ACAS strives to maintain long tenure amongst its arbitrators, thereby providing them with experience which helps them develop the skills in conflict management that greatly aid dispute resolution. The parties thus jointly determine the independent person to whom they are prepared to hand over the decision as to how to resolve their differences.

Written submission to the arbitrator

After the terms of reference and the independent person has been selected, the next step in the process is the setting of the date and the venue for the arbitration hearing.

This is agreed between the parties and the arbitrator, although it is ACAS which implements these arrangements. Before the hearing date, both sides submit to the arbitrator a written statement of their case and arguments. The parties also exchange their respective written cases to the arbitrator before the date of the hearing. It is essential that all information given to the arbitrator be known to the other side. The written statements, together with any supporting documents and a list of those attending the hearing, are submitted to the arbitrator at least one week before the hearing.

Arbitrators reach their conclusion only after considering all the facts and arguments put to them by the parties and they always study the written statements very carefully. The written statement normally covers: the background information about the company and its products, union representation, etc; an explanation of the history and background of the dispute, including an account of the sequence and outcome of any relevant meetings or discussions; the arguments supporting or opposing the claim, and a brief summary of the case which brings together the essential points the arbitrator is being asked to consider. Relevant agreements, procedures or rules are attached as appendices. In the case of a job grading dispute, full details are given of the grading scheme in operation, whilst in a disciplinary case, details of any rules or procedures are provided.

In certain circumstances, before the hearing date, there may also be a site visit. This is highly likely in the case of differences between parties concerning the degree of skill required by a job, the physical conditions under which work is done and the assessment of piece work, prices or times. In all these cases, it is of value for the arbitrator to see the work in progress.

The arbitration hearing
The hearing is informal and confidential with the parties usually being represented by those responsible for conducting normal negotiations. The hearing is usually completed in two to three hours, is held in private and the procedure to be followed is a matter for the arbitrator. However, the stages of a typical arbitration hearing are:

1. Arbitrator explains their role and then reads out the terms of reference to ensure both parties place the same interpretation on their scope or meaning.

2. Arbitrator checks that parties have exchanged their written statements and have had sufficient time to give the statements proper consideration.

3. Arbitrator normally invites the party making the 'claim', or seeking to change the *status quo*, (say, Party A) to put its case uninterrupted and to include a critique of the written submission of the other party (say, Party B). This is usually done by one person but other members of the team may be called upon to give supporting statements.

4. The arbitrator then invites Party B to ask questions about Party A's statement. Such questioning can be done either directly by the leader of Party B to Party A or through the arbitrator.

5. The arbitrator invites Party B to put its case uninterrupted and to include a critique of the written submission of Party A. This again will be done by one person but with other members of the team giving supportive statements.

6. The arbitrator then invites Party A to ask questions on Party B's statement. Again, such questioning can be done directly to the other party or via the arbitrator.

7. The arbitrator will then ask questions of each party in turn or put the same questions to both parties. The party to whom the question is directed may respond through the team leader or nominate another member of the team to respond. The person answering the question may call upon another member of the team to make a supporting statement. If one party responds to a question, the other party is given the opportunity to comment on the response. One party can ask questions of the other through the arbitrator.

8. Before inviting the parties to make formal statements, the arbitrator will normally obtain a formal assurance from each party that everything it wished to say has been said and that it has had sufficient opportunity to comment on or attempt to rebut what has been said by the other side.

9. The arbitrator will then invite each side to make its closing statement. These are taken in reverse order to the opening presentations. The formal (or closing) statement is a summary of the main points the party wishes the arbitrator to take into account in reaching their decision and should contain no new material. The arbitrator cannot accept any further evidence after the hearing.

The award

The arbitrator does not announce the award on the day of the hearing. The arguments of the parties are taken away and given serious consideration. The parties receive the award, via ACAS, usually within two to three weeks of the hearing. All awards are regarded as confidential to the parties and are not published unless the parties agree otherwise. A typical award will be presented as follows:

> The Award
> Having given very careful consideration to the arguments very well presented to me, both orally and in writing, I award that:
> THE JOB OF CLERICAL OFFICER IS CORRECTLY GRADED
> AT LEVEL 4

Arbitrators do not give reasons for their decisions since to do so could give rise to a cause for further dispute between the parties. Nevertheless, arbitrators need to consider many factors, including the need for the parties to continue in a working relationship after the award, the need to bring the dispute to a final conclusion, the potential 'knock-on' effects of an award on other groups of workers, the ability of the employer to finance the award and the credibility of the negotiators, particularly where the employers' pay offer has been rejected in a vote of the employees concerned. In short, these collapse to three major considerations, namely equity, economics and expediency (pragmatism).

A wise arbitrator (C W Guillebaud) once stated about arbitration that:

> If at all possible, neither side should be left with a strong feeling of resentment so that the dispute continues to rankle: for the arbitrator will not then have achieved their objective of settling the matter satisfactorily and improving relations for the future.

In other words, the arbitrator's award should seek to minimise aggregate dissatisfaction. In addition, the parties are not always interested in the rationale behind the arbitrator's decision since they have come to arbitration after a long process and are relieved that the matter has been resolved and satisfied that they have been able to state all the arguments in favour of their position.

The award of the arbitrator is not legally binding but it is virtually unknown for an award not to be implemented by the parties. It would be difficult (or require very exceptional circumstances) for one of the parties not to want to implement the award. They are morally bound to do so. After all, they have gone to the arbitration of their own volition, shaped the terms of reference for the arbitrator, selected the arbitrator and had every opportunity to state their case to the arbitrator.

COPING WITH INDUSTRIAL ACTION

Although your focus will be to concentrate on steps to avoid disputes turning into industrial action with sanctions, they can and do happen. In this event it is essential management implements a strategy and policy that maintains as much normality as possible. There is a set of management strategic options that can minimise the likely disruption from the application of industrial sanctions to the organisation. However not every one applies in every case to every organisation. They are:

- keeping materials and supplies coming in

- finding alternative sources of labour

- maintaining output or a level of service to satisfy demand

- maintaining the distribution of the product or service to the customer.

Management needs to evaluate critically each of these strategic choices. In the case of a retail organisation, in terms of keeping supplies coming in the critical questions that have to be answered are:

- will a picket be mounted?

- who will unload and store the goods?

In the case of an alternative supply of labour the critical question will be whether the organisation can get other staff and new part-timers. With respect to the maintaining of a minimum level of service the vital considerations are:

- can you arrange advance orders?

- is there overstocking that you can run down?

As regards the distribution of the goods operation, issues include whether customers will come to the organisation and, if so, whether there will be pickets. Can we telephone customers and deliver? Can we stay open late?

> Imagine you are the manager of a transport operation. You believe negotiations are going to break down and your employees will impose industrial sanctions upon you. What key questions would you ask yourself with respect to the strategic options open to you?

Keeping supplies coming and going is critical. If you cannot continue to service the market or continue to receive materials, the organisation will have difficulties in maintaining output or some level of service. Recruiting an alternative workforce is more than just getting in extra people. It may be that the alternative workforce is already in your organisation. Managers and team leaders/frontline managers may be able to do the work of the potential strikers. Perhaps the work to be done can be covered by other workers who are members of other trade unions not involved in the dispute or who are not unionised at all. Maintaining output to satisfy demand is often possible in the period before the dispute starts. Overtime can be increased, production switched to other plants or companies and priority tasks be tackled first. However, building up stocks to anticipate demand from customers is not advisable.

SUMMARY

This chapter began by defining bargaining and looking at bargaining arrangements, including single-table bargaining. It also introduced the concept of Partnership Agreements. It then went on to examine what is involved in preparing and conducting bargaining. It drew attention to sources of pay information, particularly the *New Earnings Survey*. The chapter then examined the options available to managers should bargaining break down and the possibility arise of industrial sanctions. These included third party intervention and the chapter explained what happens if the employer and employees decide voluntarily to go to arbitration. Finally the chapter looked at strategic choices available to employers to minimise the impact of the imposition of sanctions on the organisation.

REFERENCES AND FURTHER READING

FOWLER A. *Negotiation Skills and Strategies*. London, Institute of Personnel and Development, 1996.

KENNEDY G., BENSON J. *and* McMILLAN J. *Managing Negotiations*. London, Hutchinson, 1987.

CAIRNS L. *Negotiating Skills in the Workplace*. London, Pluto Press, 1996.

INDUSTRIAL RELATIONS SERVICES *Employment Trends*, published twice monthly.

INDUSTRIAL RELATIONS SERVICES 'Single-table bargaining: an idea whose time has yet to come?, *Employment Trends*, No 577, February 1995.

INDUSTRIAL RELATIONS SERVICES *Pay Intelligence*, published monthly.

INCOMES DATA SERVICE *Report*, published twice monthly.

INCOMES DATA SERVICES *Pay Directory*, published three times a year.

INCOMES DATA SERVICES STUDIES Partnership Agreements, October 1998.

MUMFORD, K. (1996) 'Arbitration and ideas in Britain: a historical perspective'. *British Journal of Industrial Relations*, Vol 34 No 2.

OFFICE FOR NATIONAL STATISTICS *Labour Market Trends*, incorporating *Employment Gazette*, published monthly.

OFFICE for NATIONAL STATISTICS *New Earnings Survey*, 1996, which is published in six parts.

11 | Managing redundancies

INTRODUCTION

Over the past quarter of a century British business has been exposed to ever increasing competition in its own and world markets. In the 1960s, 1970s and early 1980s this tended to impact more heavily on manufacturing industry, which therefore experienced the greatest job losses. However, in the last 15 years this increase in competition has spread to the public and service sectors.

Notwithstanding the significant improvements in competitiveness of many UK businesses in the last decade, Britain has not always been successful in competing in overseas markets nor in defending home markets. The supposed weakness of the British economy has variously been blamed on trade union resistance to change, poor and badly trained management, a financial system that is geared to shareholder reward rather than capital investment, too much or too little UK Government spending and a whole range of other economic and social factors.

It is fair to say no single cause can be blamed, but whatever problems there have been with our economic and competitive performance there is no doubt one of the most significant outcomes in recent years has been an increase in the number of people registered as unemployed. Between 1945 and 1970 unemployment in Britain never rose above 3 per cent. Following oil price rises and other economic setbacks during the mid-1970s the average level of unemployment had risen to just over 5 per cent by 1979. Following a climb during the 1980s to around 13 per cent, levels of unemployment at the end of 1996 were averaging about 8 per cent. However, as Blyton and Turnbull (1994) and other commentators have pointed out, comparisons are hindered by the many changes in the way that unemployment figures are compiled.

INCREASE IN REDUNDANCY

Running parallel with the steadily increasing numbers of unemployed has been a large increase in the number of redundancies. You will be aware of the structural change in our economy from a manufacturing base to a service base and that many of the job losses are the result of this. However, it is not just the decline in the manufacturing sector that has caused an increase in redundancies. Financial services, once considered one of the safest of occupations in terms of job security, has seen a steady rise in job losses. In declaring their 1996 results, National Westminster Bank made it clear that their policy of branch reduction, with the consequent loss of jobs, would continue over the next five years and towards the end of 1998, personnel managers in the City of London were 'preparing themselves for a white-knuckle ride as they gear up for huge job losses caused by turmoil in world markets' (*People Management* 29 October 1998 p12). The problems with foreign economies, especially in South East Asia (see Chapter 2) were predicted to cause up to 50,000 job losses. The impact of the global market is also evident in the energy sector where changes in world oil prices and mergers have caused a number of significant job losses including over 8,000 at Shell.

These major job losses have a cascade effect downwards to smaller businesses who are somewhere in the supply chain or who are affected by changes in consumer spending. Even Marks and Spencer, held up by many as the exemplar employer, cancelled its 1999 graduate recruitment programme. This would have been unthinkable ten years ago. It is for this reason that we are devoting a whole chapter to redundancy issues.

LEGAL REGULATION OF REDUNDANCY

Prior to 1965 employees had no statutory protection in respect of redundancy. The 'right' of organisations to hire and fire at will was seen as one of those inalienable 'management rights' that were necessary if organisations were to compete successfully in a commercial world. However, by the beginning of the 1960s there was a widespread belief that economic growth was being held back because of a lack of labour mobility. The Redundancy Payments Act 1965 was part of the answer to this problem and enjoyed the support of both major political parties as well as both sides of industry; this is a classic example of the post-war consensus that we discussed in Chapter 2. The Act set out for the first time that a worker with a minimum period of service was entitled to compensation for the loss of their job through redundancy. Compensation was decided on the basis of age and length of service and was subject to both a maximum and a minimum amount. The basic law in relation to redundancy compensation has not changed much in the intervening years, but there have been significant developments in respect of consultation, selection and the transfer of undertakings.

Definition of redundancy

In order to properly understand the way in which the law seeks to offer protection to those facing the loss of their employment there are a number of factors which need to be considered. The first of these concerns the definition of redundancy, which is set out in section 139 of the Employment Rights Act 1996. Principally, there are two ways in which a redundancy can occur and these are set out in s139(1) as follows:

(a)   The fact that [the] employer has ceased or intends to cease –

    i)   to carry on the business for the purposes of which the employee was employed by him, or

ii) to carry on that business in the place where the employee was so employed, or

(b)   The fact that the requirements of that business –

i) for employees to carry out work of a particular kind, or

ii) for employees to carry out work of a particular kind in the place where the employee was employed by the employer, have ceased or diminished or are expected to cease or diminish.

To put that in everyday language: redundancy occurs when the employer closes down completely, moves premises, requires fewer people for particular jobs or requires no people for particular jobs. Redundancy can also occur when an individual has been laid off or kept on short time for a period that is defined in sections 147 to 152 of the 1996 Act. Assuming that the reason an individual's employment comes to an end is within one of the statutory definitions, or that they have been laid off or kept on short time and assuming that they have a minimum period of qualifying employment, then they are entitled to a statutory redundancy payment.

Redundancy 'can mean different things to different people. Even as a specific legal concept, it has been the subject of differences and errors of interpretation' (Fowler 1993). For that reason it is an area in which the employee relations specialist must develop their skills.

When you have completed this chapter you will be able to:

• understand the connection between redundancy and the management of change

• be able to produce a redundancy policy and associated procedures

• explain the legal framework in respect of redundancy, in particular the requirements on consultation

• understand the need to have clear policies for managing the 'survivors' of a redundancy exercise.

Need for redundancy policy and procedures
For personnel professionals, job security policies and the avoidance of redundancy are an increasingly important part of the employee relations framework. In Chapter 5, in discussing the management of change we said that organisations have a continuing need to evolve and to search constantly for their distinctive capabilities. This in turns means a continuing process of change and leads to the inevitable weakening of employees' confidence in their employer's ability to maintain job security. Where redundancy is unavoidable, 'best practice' dictates that organisations have in place policies and procedures that enable them to deal with a difficult situation with sensitivity and equity. The employee relations specialist has a key role to play in this process in advising managerial colleagues as to the scope and extent of any policies and in advising them how to manage the redundancy process.

Policies and procedures are important, not only because the law dictates certain minimum requirements, but because, like most activities connected with employee relations, there is a good business case for having them. An important part of any policy is the need to provide effective counselling and support for the redundant employee, support in terms of job seeking and outplacement, but it is also important to ensure that those who are to remain in employment, and may be fearful for their future, are not ignored. Ignoring the 'survivors' is likely to produce a demotivated workforce that is prone to conflict with management.

REDUNDANCY AND THE MANAGEMENT OF CHANGE

In the context of redundancy we need to look at what it is that causes firms to need to change and ask whether job losses have to be the inevitable result. In many cases, organisations have had no option but to declare redundancies, for example, because of an urgent need to cut costs or the failure to win an important contract. But redundancies could sometimes have been avoided if organisations had invested more time in human resource planning, training or skills development.

Case example

Towards the end of 1994, Clamason Industries, a medium-sized company producing high-precision metal pressings and associated electrical assemblies, was on a slippery downward slope.

The family-owned business had just recorded an operating loss in excess of half a million pounds and was haemorrhaging cash. Very few orders were delivered on time and at the end of each month around £250,000 worth of orders were waiting to be delivered.

The directors admit that the company was providing a poor service to its customers and would have eventually gone into liquidation. Redundancies would have been the inevitable outcome. But, with external assistance they set about turning the company round and, unlike many organisations, their first thought was not to dispense with the workforce.

There were redundancies, around a dozen out of a workforce of over 200, but because they were short of money the rescue plan relied on investment in existing employees, not wholesale job cuts. While the business was being restructured, a training and development initiative – without which the transformation could not have been managed – was set in motion.

There have been other job losses along the road to recovery, but by the end of the 1999 financial year the company expects to have returned to profitability. While there is much more to the Clamason turnaround than simply investing in the workforce, it does point up some valuable lessons, not least that re-deploying the skills and talents already available to a business can have beneficial effects, whereas simply pruning does not always work.

For a full account of the Clamason story see *People Management* 11 February 1999 p50.

While the Clamason case illustrates that businesses can be improved and changed without wholesale job losses we have to recognise that business change will continue to lead to reduced workforces. This is because organisations are under continuous pressure to:

• improve their effectiveness

• increase profitability

• reduce costs

• remain innovative.

Changes in markets have created a need for organisations to be much more responsive to their customers' requirements. In manufacturing, for example, consumers demand higher and higher quality standards combined with better value for money.

In Chapter 5 we looked in detail at the need for organisations to develop clear business strategies which would, in turn, help to identify what their people strategies ought to be and how they should manage change. For many, the answer has been to downsize the organisation or to introduce flexible working practices. These responses 'raise questions about the most appropriate organisational form ... Under the burden of economic and competitive pressure, a range of organisational strategies is aimed at competing not just on cost, but on quality and speed of response' (Sparrow and Marchington 1998). Certainly, the problems that Clamason encountered had their origins in a failure to respond.

The growth in unemployment since the late 1970s has had a number of causes, but there is some evidence to suggest that had alternatives to redundancy been at the top of everybody's agenda some jobs might have been saved. For many senior managers the need to deliver very large productivity increases and cost savings made redundancy the only option (P. Lewis 1993). While this lack of choice needs to be acknowledged there are two reasons why employers need to be considering the alternatives to redundancy. One is that every organisation needs to maintain some form of competitive advantage. Two, it is a reasonable assumption to say that competitive advantage is unlikely to be achieved and maintained without a committed and motivated workforce.

Decisions about redundancy, because they are often made to address an immediate and short-term problem, can create the entirely opposite wrong effect. They can engender a mood of disillusionment and cynicism which, if allowed to fester, can destroy any of the short term financial gains of a redundancy exercise, together with any hope of gaining employee commitment to the future. Sparrow and Marchington (1998) make the point that, in relation to downsizing and de-layering, 'immediate financial and performance measurements made today cannot assess the implications of correct or incorrect decision-making, as such decisions now tend to operate and be proved effective over a longer time-span'.

Employee commitment

If employee commitment is to be obtained, together with high levels of motivation, then employees need to feel secure in their employment, not afraid for their future. In 1983, when unemployment was running at over 3 million, Ron Todd, then General Secretary of the Transport Workers Union (TGWU) commented that there are 3 million people on the dole, and another 23 million who are scared to death (Blyton and Turnbull 1994). There is little evidence to suggest that the fear factor has gone away. In its 1996 report, *Statement on Employee Relations*, the IPD stated that 'insecurity has damaged people's commitment', a state of affairs that, if not remedied, has the potential to damage competitive performance. While we acknowledge that all businesses have to worry about competition, about retaining their competitive edge, about growth and even survival, these worries can be eased if they know they have a committed and loyal workforce. The challenge is how to overcome the 'fear factor' and achieve the necessary commitment which is so important.

There is no magic formula for achieving commitment, but the 1995 survey by the IPD and Templeton College, Oxford, Issue No. 12 *The New Employment Relationship: Examining the Psychological Contract*, identifies some important elements which can help management achieve this objective. One of these is trust, on which must rest, says the survey, the 'psychological contract' that the employer has with employees. The employees will have trust if they are confident that the employer will continue to search for new customers and new markets, thus making it possible for their talents to be employed. Clearly, as the survey points out, 'trust is vulnerable to the incidence of redundancy in an organisation' and serious questions are now being raised about some of the cost reduction, redundancy and downsizing policies that have been prevalent in recent years. This, said the survey, had caused some employers to declare that they would offer continual employment except in the most exceptional circumstances. Where businesses find it impossible to underwrite job security they should commit to consulting on those strategic issues that can affect security of employment.

> Whether or not there have been redundancies in your own organisation, what do you think is the current position in respect of employee security? Do you and your colleagues feel secure, or is there some concern about the future?

Much depends on the interaction that can be created between managers and the workforce as a means of fostering the levels of commitment and loyalty that are being sought. These sorts of imperative are the major reason that there has been such a concerted push by human resource specialists to integrate people management issues into strategic management. As Pettigrew and Whipp (1993) argue, one of the central contributing factors to competitive performance is the way in which people within a firm are managed. In employee relations terms this means creating a partnership between workers and their managers which is collaborative, not adversarial. There are a number of examples where employers and employees are prepared to negotiate and make agreements over job security, although these tend to be in unionised environments.

At the end of 1993 a pioneering agreement on 'worksharing', cutting hours and pay to save jobs, was negotiated by Volkswagen, the German car manufacturer. Since then, such arrangements have gained an increasing profile in German industrial relations (*European Industrial Relations Review* 254, March 1995) and in the UK, Sheffield City Council employees voted for a worksharing deal intended to avoid around 1,400 redundancies (*Personnel Management Plus*, January 1994). Another example of a job security agreement, although not 'worksharing', can be found in the deal negotiated in January 1997 between Blue Circle, the cement manufacturer, and the GMB and TGWU unions.

> Are you aware of any other arrangements of this kind? Is it something your organisation has considered?

POLICIES AND PROCEDURES

No matter what sort of strategic vision an organisation employs there will sometimes be no alternative to reducing the numbers employed. The possibility of this occurring is much higher now than it was 20 years ago. Nowadays good employee relations practice dictates a need for clear policies and procedures which allow redundancy situations to be dealt with in a professional and equitable manner. Not only are there legal regulations to be taken into account, but the 'psychological contract' needs to be maintained.

Policy

A statement of policy on redundancy might, in some ways, be better classified as an organisation's statement of intent in respect of maintaining employment. For example, a policy statement on redundancy might be set out as follows:

> The company intends to develop and expand its business activities in order to maintain its competitive advantage within our existing marketplace. It is also our intention to seek new products and markets providing they have a strategic fit with the rest of the business. To achieve these objectives we need the active co-operation and commitment of the whole workforce. In return our aim is to provide a stable work environment and a high level of job security. However, we also need to ensure the economic viability of the business in the competitive world in which we now have to operate. In such a world changes in markets, technology or the corporate environment may cause us to consider the need for reductions in staffing levels. In order to mitigate the impact of any reductions in staff the following procedure will be adopted.

Such a policy statement does not make any commitment to no compulsory redundancies, but it is an important first step in recognising people as an important asset. Evidence is already beginning to suggest that the downsizing, re-engineering culture of the late 1980s and early 1990s can have a detrimental affect on businesses that are seeking to grow. A study by International Survey Research cites responses from a number of senior human resources managers which found that downsizing went too far and the overall effect was negative (*People Management* No 22 November 1996 p15). We have already quoted the Sparrow and Marchington view that decision-making needs to be evaluated over a longer time-scale and many organisations are now beginning to recognise that they have lost valuable experience and skills which are proving difficult to replace. Local UK Government, which has seen its share of downsizing in recent years, has been accused by the Audit Commission of knee-jerk restructuring and delayering which has exposed them to fraud and poor management (*People Management* No 23 November 1996 p11).

Mumford and Hendricks, in charting the rapid rise and fall of the re-engineering concept (*People Management* May 1996), argue that it has failed as a technique because many of its followers did not understand people and change management techniques. They point to evidence that re-engineering always took longer than expected, involved more resources than were available and presented unforeseen problems. Developing a redundancy policy, or statement of intent, as described above, should be driven by an organisation's overall business strategy and can be an important first step in building that important management/workforce partnership. But, even in the most strategically-aware organisations, not everything is predictable and there may be situations in which job losses cannot be avoided. This is where the procedure, mentioned in our example of a policy statement, comes into play.

Procedure
The first thing to say about a redundancy procedure, as with any other procedure, is that it needs to fit the business. That is, it needs to be written and designed to cater for the individuality of each organisation. Draft procedures can be obtained from professional bodies like the IPD, but they should always be treated as guidelines or templates and be amended to meet individual organisations' requirements.

As a basic minimum, there are a number of things that a redundancy procedure should cover, starting with alternative courses of action. Where the possibility of a reduction in employee numbers arises, management should begin a process of consultation. There are a number of legal rules relating to consultation, which must take place with either trade unions, elected workplace representatives or individuals. The purpose of this consultation is to establish whether any potential job losses can be achieved by means other than compulsory redundancies. Some of the factors that would normally be considered at this juncture would be:

• a ban on recruitment (unless unavoidable)

• retraining of staff

• redeployment of staff

• restrictions on use of subcontract labour, temporary and casual staff

• reductions in the amount of overtime working.

Depending on the nature of the business, other considerations might include temporary lay-off, short-time working or even job sharing.

Early retirement

If there are any employees who are over normal retirement age it may be necessary to insist on their immediate retirement and, at the same time, it may be appropriate to ask for volunteers for early retirement. This is only an option if the business has its own regulated pension scheme and does need careful consideration. Early retirement, if it is to be a serious option, needs to carry some form of financial inducement. As an absolute minimum the pension scheme must allow for the payment of pensions early on grounds of redundancy. In effect, the potential retiree is credited with more years of pensionable service than they have actually worked. The question of how many extra years to credit will depend on how near to normal retirement age a particular employee is. It is possible that the employer might have to make a payment into the pension fund to ensure there is no detriment to the early retired employee or to provide a lump sum that will take the employee up to an agreed date for receiving their pension.

It is important that these financial considerations are taken into account by the employee relations specialist when they are asked, as they often are, to cost the available options for reducing the workforce. A further point to remember in considering early retirement is the position of pension trustees. Following the 'Maxwell' scandal trustees now have much more responsibility for the management of individual schemes. Whether to allow early retirement on redundancy grounds or to enhance the value of an individual's pension, are not management decisions. They are trustee decisions. For the employee relations specialist, all of this means that the question of early retirement as an alternative to compulsory redundancy needs to be carefully costed and researched.

When management has given very careful consideration to the alternatives discussed above but concludes that the need for redundancies still remains, the next step in the procedure is for them to give employees or their representatives written details of their proposals. These would include details of the criteria that management proposes to use for selecting individuals for redundancy.

Voluntary redundancy

Management may indicate at this stage that it is prepared to accept volunteers, but this must be subject to the company's need to retain a balanced workforce, with the appropriate mix of skills and knowledge. As P. Lewis (1993) and others have identified, the concept of voluntary redundancy has become the most widely acceptable method of dealing with redundancy and there are obviously a number of advantages in adopting the voluntary approach. Firstly, it can help to avoid some of the demotivating effects that redundancy inevitably has on an organisation. Secondly, it can be cost-effective. While persuading people to go, rather than forcing them to leave, will probably require higher individual payments (possibly in pension costs), the financial benefits of a redundancy exercise can begin to impact much earlier if a costly and time-consuming consultation exercise can be avoided. It may be possible to reduce the workforce by a higher number than was originally envisaged if a voluntary approach is adopted, as British Telecom found with its 'Release 92' scheme which was considerably oversubscribed. Accepting more people in this way obviously has unbudgeted cost implications and it is important, before paying extra costs in this way, that a comprehensive human resource planning exercise has been carried out in order to assess future labour requirements.

Compulsory redundancy

If the voluntary option was not feasible because the wrong people were volunteering or insufficient numbers came forward the next step would have to be compulsory redundancy. At this point in the procedure there would be an acknowledgement that the organisation would, as far in advance of any proposed termination date as possible, notify all employees that compulsory redundancies are proposed and that a provisional selection has been made. This part of the procedure fulfils a statutory requirement. The easiest and most non-contentious method of selection is last in first out (LIFO), but this can have significant negative effects. Using LIFO can, for many organisations, mean that they are losing their youngest employees or those with the most up-to-date skills. For this reason many organisations have adopted a selection system that is based on a number of criteria such as attendance records, range of work experience, disciplinary records etc. Such criteria, which need to be as objective as possible, and be based on a system of points scores, tend to be looked on very favourably by tribunals. It is important to stress that any selection is provisional and subject to change following consultation with the employees affected.

Creating a points score

Once management has determined what criteria should be used, it is suggested that each employee should be scored by an appropriate number of points for each criterion (usually on a scale of 10). There should be clear guidance given to the manager/managers who are asked to make the decision on the number of points each individual will receive and some thought should be given to weighting each criterion by a factor which would take into account the importance of that factor to the employer. For example, you should decide which particular attribute or criteria is the most important and then multiply that score by a factor of, for example, five. The criterion which has the lowest importance might be multiplied by a factor of, for example, one.

It is important that great care is taken in setting scoring guidelines. When all the scores have been calculated, those employees with the lowest scores will be the ones who should be selected for redundancy, but it is often the case that companies produce scores in this way but still feel unhappy about the results. In other words, they feel unhappy about dismissing certain employees even though those employees have scored badly. In such cases the employers should consider very carefully why they would be unhappy about selecting those employees. There may be an objective reason why they should be retained and, had the selection criteria been drafted to take that reason into account, those employees would have scored more highly. An employee may be engaged in a particular project (eg to introduce information technology into the workplace), and as such the employer may be loath to choose that employee for redundancy. For this reason, the selection criteria should include whether or not someone is engaged on a particular project, and that particular criterion should be assigned an appropriate weighting factor. Alternatively, employees who have some unique or special skill which it is essential that the employer retain could be taken out of the pool for selection completely.

In summary, therefore, an employer should make a note of those objective criteria which it considers appropriate, decide upon a scoring system, and then decide upon the weighting factor for each criterion. A specimen matrix and score sheet is set out in Table 40.

Assistance to redundant employee
Once the selection of individuals has been confirmed it is important, particularly if the procedure is to be consistent with the policy, that if possible an offer is made in respect of alternative employment. Of course, alternative employment is not always possible, nor is it always desired by those to be made redundant. Nevertheless, it is incumbent on the employer to make every effort to look for alternatives and where they exist, to consider redundant employees for suitable vacancies. Where the organisation or the number of jobs to be reduced is very small, options in respect of alternatives are very rare.

Table 40 **Specimen Matrix and Score Sheet**

Name:	Age:
Date of Birth:	Years of service:
Department:	Job role:

Employee Assessment			
Criteria	Score out of 10	Weighting (maximum 5)	Total
		x	
Skills		x	
Attendance		x	
Flexibility		x	
		x	
		x	
		x	
		x	
	Grand Total		

Assessed by ....   Checked by ....

Source: IPD Employment Law Service.

Nevertheless, the procedure needs to set out the basis on which employees will be interviewed for any vacancies and the terms and conditions on which alternative jobs will be offered. Terms and conditions may be the standard terms for the job in question. They may be the terms previously enjoyed by the individual concerned or there may be some form of transition. These are all issues that the employee relations specialist needs to consider. Naturally, the procedure needs to say something about trial periods.

It would be normal practice for a redundancy procedure to set out what steps the organisation proposed to take in assisting the redundant employee who could not be found alternative employment within the business. Such steps should include provisions for paid time off to attend interviews, to seek retraining opportunities or to attend counselling sessions. This latter point will be dealt with in more detail later in the chapter.

Compensation for redundancy

Finally the procedure might set out the basis on which employees will be compensated for the loss of their employment. There is a statutory entitlement to a minimum amount of redundancy pay which is set out in Section 162 (2) of the 1996 Act as follows:

- one and a half week's pay for each year of employment in which the employee was not below the age of 41

- one week's pay for each year of employment that the employee was between the ages of 22 and 40

- half a week's pay for each year of employment under the age of 22.

No more than twenty years' service can be taken into account in calculating an individual's redundancy payment and there is also a maximum weekly amount that an individual can receive, irrespective of how much they earn. This maximum amount is reviewed by the UK Government on an annual basis, but this does not always mean the maximum weekly amount taken into account will be automatically increased. However, some organisations are prepared to make enhanced payments in order to ease the trauma that redundancy can cause or to encourage volunteers to come forward. They can also pay for more than twenty years' service if they so wish, but it is important to remember that any enhancements, to either amounts or length of service, are entirely at the employer's discretion, unless there is a specific contractual arrangement. Employee relations specialists who are charged with drawing up a procedure should be warned of the pitfalls of setting out too much detail on compensation. It is important to ensure that the organisation retains some flexibility on the issue of enhanced payments. Whatever motives lie behind paying more than the statutory amount, no organisation can predict the future or the circumstances in which redundancies may occur. It is important, therefore, to ensure that any payments set out in a procedure document are not considered to be contractual.

Entitlement to compensation

In the context of redundancy payments, the definitions of redundancy can be of particular importance. Before 1990, an employer had certain rights to reclaim part of any redundancy payment made to an individual employee and while this rebate only applied to the statutory part of a redundancy payment, it was an important factor for an employer to take into consideration when considering an enhanced payment. With the ending of the rebate, employers now have to meet the total cost of all redundancy payments and, as a consequence, have become much more concerned with ensuring that any loss or diminution of work does actually justify a payment.

Business reorganisation

There are three sets of circumstances which an employer might argue create no entitlement to a redundancy payment. In the context of so much change management an employer might say that the events which led to an individual leaving employment had nothing to do with redundancy, but were simply the consequences of a legitimate and lawful business reorganisation which were unacceptable to the employee(s) concerned. In such circumstances it is likely that the employee will argue that the 'work of a particular kind' which they had been carrying out had 'ceased or diminished' and that they are entitled to their statutory rights. This would then need to be resolved by a tribunal which D. Lewis (1997) describes as one of their more difficult tasks. In the case of *Lesney Products* v *Nolan* (1977) IRLR 77, Nolan and some of his colleagues argued that the change from a long day shift with overtime to a double day shift was a diminution in the employer's requirements for work of a particular kind and that they should have received a redundancy payment. The Court of Appeal held that such a change was a legitimate reorganisation, based on efficiency, and that therefore no payment was due.

The employee's workplace

The second set of circumstances in which an employer might refuse to make a redundancy payment concerns the words 'in the place where the employee was so employed'. This raises the whole question of mobility clauses in the Contract of Employment and how much the employer can rely on them. For example, if the contract required that an employee be required to work anywhere, a refusal to do so could lead to a dismissal for misconduct, but not for redundancy. For the employer to rely on the terms of a mobility clause to rebut a claim for a redundancy payment there must be an express clause in the contract which allows an employer to ask an employee to work at a different location or locations. Even then it is by no means certain that the employer will win the argument.

In 1995, the Court of Appeal held that a clause contained in a contract of employment requiring an employee to work in such parts of the UK as her employers might dictate, constituted unlawful sex discrimination within the Sex Discrimination Act 1975. The case in question, *Meade-Hill and Another* v *British Council*, revolved around the British Council's decision to require Ms Meade-Hill to accept the incorporation of a mobility clause into her contract as a consequence of a promotion. While this particular case, which was decided in Ms Meade-Hill's favour, was more concerned with sex discrimination than redundancy payments, it is important because of statements made by the Court of Appeal in respect of mobility clauses generally. They commented that even if it (this particular mobility clause) could not be justified in its present form, the objectionable aspects would disappear if it were modified in a relatively minor respect. In the court's view there was no great cause for celebration by employees as a result of this particular decision.

For most employee relations specialists the question of mobility is more likely to arise when the whole or part of a business is moving, either to a new geographical location some distance from the present workplace or to new premises broadly within the existing geographical location. In order that an organisation can retain a degree of flexibility in terms of its location it is important to be clear about an employee's place of work. For this reason it is important, when drawing up the employee's 'Statement of Terms and Particulars of Employment' as required by the Employment Rights Act 1996, to identify whether 'the employee is required or permitted to work at various places' (s1 (4)(h).

> What does your contract say about mobility? Are there any circumstances in which the current wording could bring you into conflict with an employee?

Alternative employment

The third set of circumstances that might lead to refusal to make a redundancy payment is when the employee refuses an offer of 'suitable alternative employment'. In circumstances when the employee is offered a new contract of employment, to begin immediately or within four weeks of the termination of the old contract, and the offer is unreasonably refused, there is no entitlement to a redundancy payment. However, the burden of proving that an offer is suitable lies with the employer. If the employee were to express the view that the proposed new job was inferior to the old one it would be for the employer to demonstrate that it was not and how they can do this has been the subject of many industrial tribunal cases. In *Hindes* v *Supersine Ltd* (1979) IRLR 343 it was argued that whether the proposed employment was 'substantially equivalent' to the former job was as objective an assessment as any. In *Cambridge & District Co-op* v *Ruse* (1993) IRLR 156, the Employment Appeal Tribunal held that 'it is possible for an employee reasonably to refuse an objectively suitable offer of alternative employment on the ground of his personal perception of the job offered'. In this case Mr Ruse had refused an alternative job because he considered it represented a demotion and a loss of status.

It is very difficult to give absolute advice on such matters as alternative employment. The sensible employee relations specialist will deal with each case individually and on its merits. It may be that what is suitable for one employee may be totally unsuitable for another. One alternative is the provision within section 138 (3) of the legislation that allows for a 'trial period'. This gives the redundant employee an opportunity to try a new job for a period of four weeks, or such longer (specified) period as may be agreed to allow for retraining. If, having opted for a trial period, the employee decides at the end of it that the job is not suitable, then a redundancy payment is still payable.

THE LAW AND CONSULTATION

Since the mid-1970s all member states of the European Union have been required to enact legislation which obliges employers to consult with workers' representatives about redundancy. This was generally assumed to mean consultation with recognised trade unions and was first implemented into our legal framework by sections 99 to 107 of the Employment Protection Act 1975. The relevant provisions are now contained in sections 188 to 198 of the Trade Union and Labour Relations (Consolidation) Act 1992.

During 1992, the European Commission claimed that there were imperfections within the UK legislation because:

- there was no provision for consulting with employees in the absence of a recognised trade union

- the scope of the UK legislation was more limited than was envisaged by the original European Directive (75/129/EEC)

- there was no requirement that an employer considering collective redundancies had to consult workers' representatives with a view to reaching agreement in relation to the matters specified in the Directive.

The Commission complaints were considered to be well-founded and amendments made by the Trade Union Reform and Employment Rights Act 1993 made it a requirement that consultations about proposed redundancies must include discussion and consultation about ways of avoiding dismissals altogether. This change to the legislation was considered to be insufficient and in 1994 the European Court of Justice ruled that the UK could not limit the right to be consulted to representatives of recognised trade unions. As a response to this, additional regulations, the Collective Redundancies and Transfer of Undertakings (Protection of Employment) (Amendment) Regulations 1995, were introduced and took effect from March 1996.

There are further changes from the European Commission in the pipeline. Consultation has been taking place with the Social Partners, which is likely to lead to further EU legislation on minimum standards for worker information and consultation. The main purpose of such legislation would be to:

- recognise at an EU level the fundamental rights of employees to be informed and consulted on any decisions likely to affect them significantly

- develop arrangements for anticipating and forestalling the social consequences which may arise from changes in the life, organisation and running of a company

- strengthen the link between information and consultation on strategic and economic issues and consultation on how to address the social consequences arising therefrom.

The Commission has therefore made the following suggestions as to the content of possible legislation covering three main fields:

- the establishment of forward-planning mechanisms for employment management, allowing early identification of any negative social consequences of change, particularly on employment, and effective provision to protect the jobs or enhance the employability of those affected

- the establishment of permanent, structured mechanisms for informing and consulting employees on firms' strategic and economic decisions

- the introduction of effective sanctions, of a proportional and dissuasive nature, to be applied in case of violation of workers' fundamental rights to be informed and consulted.

In the event that the Social Partners reach agreement, this would then be implemented as a Directive. If not, the Commission has indicated that it will, itself, draft a legislative proposal under the Social Chapter provisions, taking into account any views expressed by the Social Partners.

Irrespective of what may or may not be on the horizon, what does this plethora of Directives, legislation and regulation mean in practical terms for the employee relations specialist? What is an employer required to do if there is a possibility that employees will be made redundant? The question needs to be considered from two angles: collective redundancies and individual redundancies.

Collective redundancies
The Trade Union and Labour Relations (Consolidation) Act 1992, together with the 1995 Regulations, obliges any employer wishing to make 20 or more redundancies to consult with 'appropriate representatives'. These appropriate representatives do not have to be union representatives, even where there is a recognised union in the workplace, but may, if the employer so decides, be employee-elected representatives. The regulations have never been particularly easy for employers to understand, for example, they were silent on how many representatives can be elected or how they are to be selected, but following a consultative exercise carried out by the Department of Trade and Industry new regulations were introduced. Their general intention is as follows:

- employers will have to make suitable arrangements for the election of employee representatives which ensure that an election is carried out sufficiently early to allow for information to be given and consultation to take place in good time

- the number of representatives to be elected and the terms for which they are to be elected will be matters for the employer to determine, so long as the number of employee representatives is sufficient to represent all employees properly and the period of office is long enough to complete the consultation

- the candidates for election must be members of the affected workforce at the date of election

- no-one who is a member of the workforce may be unreasonably excluded from standing for election

- everyone who is a member of the affected workforce at the date of election must be entitled to vote and each person may cast as many votes as there are representatives to be elected

- the election should be conducted in such a way that those voting do so in secret and that the votes given at the election are fairly and accurately counted

- in the event of any dispute as to the validity of the election, any of the affected employees may complain to a tribunal and the burden shall be on the employer to show that the election conditions were complied with.

The timetable for consultation

Section 188(2) of TULR(C)A 1992 requires consultation about proposed redundancies to begin at the earliest opportunity, but in cases involving 20 or more people minimum time periods are a necessity. If the employer is proposing to dismiss over 100 employees then the consultation process must begin at least 90 days before the first dismissal takes effect. If the proposal is to dismiss less than 100, but 20 or more, then the consultation process must begin no later than 30 days before the first dismissal. Some commentators have expressed doubt about how the phrase 'proposing redundancies' should be interpreted, particularly as the Collective Redundancies Directive uses the phrase 'contemplating redundancies'. There is a degree of agreement that the Directive requires consultation at an earlier stage than TULR(C)A. There is very little case law which helps to clarify the problem and the safest course for any employer is to start the consultation as soon as possible.

Information required by employee representatives

The timetable described above can only start to run once employees or their representatives have been provided with certain information:

- the reasons for the employer's proposals

- the numbers and descriptions of the employees to be dismissed

- the method of selection the employer proposes for dismissal

- the method of carrying out the dismissals the employer proposes having due regard to any procedural agreement that might be in existence

- the period of time over which the programme of redundancies is to be carried out

- what method the employer intends to use in calculating redundancy payments unless the statutory formula is being applied.

Should an employer fail to provide any or all of the information required, or if the information that is provided is insufficient, then the consultation period will be deemed not to have started. In such circumstances the employer faces the risk of a penalty being imposed (see below) for failing to consult at the earliest opportunity. It is difficult to give precise guidance on what, and how much, detail must be provided, but vague and open-ended statements will not be acceptable. For the employee relations specialist there has to be an acceptance that every case must be decided on its merits and will need to be researched.

It is no good relying on 'what happened last time'. In *MSF v GEC Ferranti (Defence Systems) Ltd* (1994) IRLR 113 the Employment Appeal Tribunal held that 'whether a union has been provided with information which is adequate to permit meaningful consultation to commence is a question of facts and circumstances. There is no rule that full and specific information under each of the heads [of the legislation] must be provided before the consultation period can begin'. It went on to confirm an earlier judgement which held that a failure to give information on one of the heads may be a serious default, but that there is nothing to say that it must be treated as a serious default.

Consultation must be genuine

For consultation to be deemed genuine it has to be conducted with a 'view to reaching agreement' with employees' representatives. Three things have to happen. An examination has to take place on ways of avoiding dismissals. If this is impossible, ways of reducing the numbers to be dismissed should be looked at. Finally, ways should be found of mitigating the consequences of any dismissals. How tribunals will measure whether these obligations have been fulfilled is open to question. It would be strange if the legislation, as amended, meant that the employer and the representatives had to reach an agreement. What is more likely is that employers must approach the discussions with an open mind and where possible take account of any proposals put to them by the representatives.

Penalties for failing to consult

If there has been a failure to follow the proper consultation process an application can be made to an Employment Tribunal for a declaration to this effect and that a 'protective award' should be paid. This is an award requiring the employer to pay the employee remuneration for a protected period. The legislation relating to protective awards is quite complex, but some of the important elements are:

- the affected employee receives payment at the rate of one week's gross pay for each week of the 'protected' period

- unlike some compensatory awards there are no statutory limits on a week's pay

- subject to certain maximums, the length of a protected period is at the Employment Tribunal's discretion; the test is, what is just and equitable having regard to the seriousness of the employer's default

- the maximum periods are 90 days when 90 days should have been the consultation period and 30 days when 30 days should have been the consultation period; in any other case the maximum is 28 days.

As P. Lewis points out (1993) the financial implications of protective awards can be quite significant as there are often substantial numbers of employees involved and yet, according to a report commissioned by law firm Nabarro Nathanson, around one in five companies was unsure about the requirements of the legislation (*People Management* No 25 December 1996 p7).

For employers with well-established redundancy procedures it is unlikely that they will come into conflict with the law over a failure to consult. Notwithstanding this, the prudent employee relations specialist will keep the procedure under review in the light of any relevant tribunal decisions. The real problems arise for those organisations that do not have a procedure or who try to put together a procedure in a hurried or casual manner when redundancies are imminent. Such organisations might find that the price they pay for a lack of preparedness is extremely high. Tribunals have shown an increasing tendency to take a very narrow view of any special pleading by employers that there was no time to consult, and the guidelines set out by the Employment Appeal Tribunal in 1982 are still of very great relevance.

CASE EXAMPLE

The EAT has stressed (*Williams* v *Compair Maxam* {1982} ICR 156, EAT) that:

- the employer should consult the union as the best means by which the management result can be achieved fairly and with as little hardship to employees as possible

- the employer should try to agree with the union the criteria to be applied in selecting the employees to be made redundant

- when a selection has been made, the employer should consider with the union whether the selection has been made in accordance with these criteria.

To be acceptable, non-consultation would have to be the result of some event that was quite out of the ordinary, but it would be very unwise to believe that circumstances which you believe to be 'out of the ordinary' would be accepted as such by a tribunal.

Individual consultation
Consultation with trade unions and now with the wider constituency of 'employees' representatives' has tended to attract most of the attention in studies of redundancy and there is certainly a good deal of case law on the subject, but the necessity for individual consultation must not be overlooked. Many managers have fallen into the trap of assuming that when only one or two individuals are to be made redundant there is no obligation to consult or that consultation can be cursory. This is an incorrect assumption and although there is no statutory framework for individual consultation as there is when

collective redundancies are on the agenda, tribunals can still intervene. The Employment Rights Act 1996 identifies redundancy as a fair reason for dismissal (section 98 (2) (c)), providing that the employer has acted 'reasonably'. This requirement opens the door for an employee to claim unfair dismissal on grounds that the employer, by failing to consult, had not acted reasonably.

Most claims for unfair dismissal in respect of redundancy are in two areas :

- unfair selection

- lack of consultation.

Many employers have argued that because the redundancy only affected one or two individuals, consultation would not have made any difference. This defence has been virtually closed to employers since the decision of the House of Lords in *Polkey* v *A. E. Dayton Services Ltd* (1987) IRLR 503, but unwise and unprofessional employers still try to use it. In *Polkey* the House of Lords did not say that consultation was an absolute requirement, but that the onus is on the employer to demonstrate that consultation would have been 'utterly useless'. In the majority of cases it would be difficult to demonstrate the uselessness of something that had not been tried.

By far the best option for employers is to recognise that good employee relations would be best served by adopting a systematic approach to consultation whether the proposed redundancies are going to affect five people or fifty people. This means that you should always allow enough time for a proper consultation exercise even when only one or two people are to be made redundant. You should give very careful consideration to the possibilities of alternative employment, even lower paid alternative employment. You must allow people time to:

- consider their options

- challenge the need for redundancy

- propose their own alternatives.

The employer does not have to go along with any alternatives proposed, but they must be able to demonstrate that they gave them careful and objective consideration.

Are you confident, having read the sections on consultation, that you fully understand the legal requirements? Do you need to advise any of your colleagues of their obligations?

Transfers of undertakings

When the ownership of a business transfers there is always the possibility that redundancies will be one of the results that flow from such a transfer. Under the Acquired Rights Directive of the European Union (Directive 77/187/EEC) member states are required to ensure, in broad terms, that all employees who are covered by employment protection legislation should receive additional protection in respect of job security if the identity of their employer changes. This does not mean that an employer who acquires a new business is obliged to retain all the inherited employees irrespective of the commercial realities, but equally the new employer cannot just dispense with those employees without just cause. Should employers find that, on the transfer of a business, there are sound commercial reasons for reducing the headcount, then subject to the normal rules on consultation and the operation of a fair selection procedure, the law will not stand in their way. What the law does insist on, however, is that the transferred employees' rights are retained. This means if they had the requisite period of service with their old employer to qualify for a redundancy payment, then the new employer cannot avoid making a redundancy payment to them. In the context of consultation, all the issues of representation and the right to information that we have discussed above in respect of collective redundancies apply equally to transfers of undertakings.

POST REDUNDANCY

The massive rise in unemployment in recent years has meant that more attention is now paid to the needs of redundant employees. In this section we look at the growth in both counselling and outplacement services and, in addition, the position of those employees that remain in employment. This is the so-called 'survivor syndrome'.

Counselling

We have decided to examine counselling and outplacement separately, notwithstanding that they overlap in many ways. In this section we analyse talking about counselling in the sense of helping employees come to terms with the fact that they have lost their job. Counselling in respect of personal skills, job search and financial planning will be dealt with under 'outplacement'.

Although redundancy has become part of everyday life, the loss of one's job usually comes as a tremendous personal blow. Even when 'the writing is on the wall' and the prospect of job losses in the organisation is inevitable, individuals still hope that they will be unaffected. To paraphrase an advertising slogan made famous by the national lottery, they hope 'it will not be them'.

There can be a tendency for employers to want a redundancy exercise to be forgotten as quickly as possible and this can manifest itself in a very uncaring attitude. The employee relations specialist should be reminding managerial colleagues that they have a continuing responsibility for their redundant employees and, as the IPD *Guide on Redundancy* says, be providing displaced employees with a counselling service. Redundant employees can feel anger, resentment and even guilt, emotions which, if not carefully managed, can inhibit an employee from moving forward to the next phase of their career. This is where effective counselling becomes crucial. However, it is important to proceed cautiously, and earlier in this book in another reference to counselling we stressed the need for proper training. 'Handling the first stage of redundancy counselling requires considerable skill, and should not be attempted by anyone who does not, as a minimum, understand the general principles of all forms of counselling' (Fowler 1993).

Not every redundant employee will agree to or want counselling, but nevertheless it is important to understand its key purpose. If you talk to redundant employees, as we have done, you are struck by the violent mood swings that can occur during the initial post-redundancy phase. Depending on the personality of the individual concerned, the mood can swing from pessimism about the future to unfounded optimism and from anger at the former employer to a feeling that they have been given an opportunity to do something different. The objective of counselling is to bring all these emotions out into the open and to help individuals to make decisions about their future. It is not a panacea, it will not stop people being angry or feeling betrayed, but it might help them to view their future constructively.

For the employee relations specialist, there is a further dimension to the provision of counselling. Not only is there a moral imperative, but there are sound business reasons. Unless the organisation is closing down completely, there will be other employees left around whom you will want to build the organisation. Richard Baker, Director of Human Resources at Hoechst Roussel, made a very valid point when he said, 'people ... never forget the way they are treated when they are made redundant, and neither do the friends and colleagues who remain behind' (*People Management* No 2 January 1996 p31).

Outplacement
Outplacement is a process where an individual or individuals who have been made redundant by their employer are given support and counselling to assist them in achieving the next stage of their career. There are a large number of organisations offering outplacement services, but the range and quality of their services varies greatly and the employee relations specialist needs to research carefully prospective suppliers if a decision to use outplacement is taken.

Broadly, outplacement consultancies will offer services on a group or individual basis which fall into the following general categories:

• CV preparation

• researching the job market

• communication techniques

• interview presentation

• managing the job search.

Each organisation will operate differently, but in the best organisations the process would probably start with a personal counselling session with a trained counsellor. Once this has been carried out, the next step would be the preparation of the CV. This involves identifying key skills and past achievements so that the job hunter can self-market from a position of strength. Step three would be to make decisions about job search methods (cold contact, advertisement, recruitment consultants etc) and contact development, for example, networking. Step four would be to ensure that the key communication skills of letter writing, telephone techniques and interview presentation were of a sufficiently high standard to enhance the job search. Where skills need to be improved, the better consultancies will provide the necessary training at no extra cost. The final step is managing the actual job search, setting personal targets, keeping records of letters and phone calls, maintaining notes of interviews and carrying out a regular job search evaluation.

Running alongside these basic services will be a range of support services, such as secretarial help, free telephone and office space and financial planning advice. What an individual gets will depend on the particular package that the former employer purchases on their behalf.

> Does your organisation have any sort of policy on counselling and outplacement? If not, who would make the decisions about what level of support to offer?

Survivor syndrome

When people are forced to leave employment because of redundancy, those that are left behind can be affected just as much as those that have left. Anecdotal evidence we have gathered from the finance sector and local UK Government indicate that disenchantment, pessimism and stress are the likely result of even a small scale redundancy exercise. Survivor syndrome, as it is called, can be minimised if, as we pointed out above, those who are to be made redundant are treated fairly and equitably and there is a decision made to invest in an effective post-redundancy programme. This usually means a time commitment from senior managers and a good communication process.

The feelings referred to above are the result of two factors. One, that the remaining employees are often asked to 'pick up' the work of their former colleagues either directly or indirectly as the consequence of a reorganisation. In one local authority individuals had to reapply for their own jobs three times in three years following a series of redundancies and reorganisations. The second factor concerns communication. The anecdotal evidence that we have suggests that in many organisations the remaining employees are not always communicated with effectively, thus providing the opportunity for rumour and disenchantment to thrive. Getting the message across about why redundancies were necessary and what happens next is vitally important and yet most people we have spoken to identify poor communication as one of the principal causes of their dissatisfaction.

Blakstad and Cooper (1995) identify three sets of stimuli which can interfere with communications, one of which is internal stress. Internal stress can be caused by a number of variables, but one of the causes identified is 'group concerns'. The aftermath of a redundancy exercise is a classic example of 'group concerns' and yet many managers do not take this into account when communicating with the survivors. For the professional manager who wishes to minimise the effect of survivor syndrome, communication and communication methodology need to be carefully worked out. 'While it is usually impossible to understand the individual concerns of each member of the [group], structuring the communication around an awareness of group tensions can be used to strengthen retention of messages' (Blakstad and Cooper 1995).

SUMMARY

Redundancy is one of the most emotive issues that any manager can be called upon to deal with. Calling an individual into your office and informing them that they no longer have a job is never easy. For the employee relations specialist who is at the beginning of their career, managing a redundancy exercise can be just as traumatic for them as for the redundant employee.

No matter how experienced you become, managing redundancy is never straightforward, but in this chapter we have attempted to set the process into some sort of organised framework. Most redundancies occur because organisations need to change and although we have recognised this, we nevertheless feel it is important that employee relations specialists recognise that there should be alternatives to reducing an organisation's headcount. In particular we stressed that in an era of constant change businesses need to retain their competitive advantage. This is unlikely to happen if their employees are constantly looking over their shoulders, fearing for their jobs. One of the challenges that all managers, whether or not they are personnel practitioners, will face in the twenty-first century is how to reconcile the need for organisational change with the individual's need for contentment and security at work.

Despite our plea for managers, at all levels, to consider the alternatives to redundancy we do recognise the realities of organisational life. For this reason we have devoted a considerable part of this chapter to the need for effective policies and procedures for dealing with a redundancy situation. We would particularly draw to the attention of employee relations specialists the dangers of not having a policy and procedure.

In the section that dealt with the legal framework we identified the costs that could accrue to an organisation that did not fulfil its statutory obligations. Evidence from numerous tribunal cases demonstrates that the most expensive failure is that of not consulting. The fact that so many organisations still fall into this trap is a direct consequence of not having an appropriate policy and procedure.

The final section of the chapter dealt with the way in which employers should deal with both redundant employees and those that remain in employment. The words of Richard Baker of Hoechst Roussel which we quoted are very pertinent. People do not forget how a redundancy exercise was handled and the professional personnel practitioner will take care to ensure that any redundancy exercise considers the needs of all individuals, as well as those of the organisation.

REFERENCES AND FURTHER READING

BLAKSTAD M. *and* COOPER A. *The Communicating Organisation.* London, Institute of Personnel and Development. 1995.

BLYTON P. *and* TURNBULL P. *The Dynamics of Employee Relations.* London, Macmillan. 1994.

FOWLER A. *Redundancy.* London, Institute of Personnel Management. 1993.

HAMMOND SUDDARDS *Redundancy.* London, Institute of Personnel and Development, 1999.

HENDRICKS R. *and* MUMFORD E. 'Business process re-engineering RIP'. *People Management.* Vol 2, No 9, May 1996 pp22–29.

KAY J. *Foundations of Corporate Success.* Oxford, OUP, 1993.

LEWIS D. *Essentials of Employment Law.* London, Institute of Personnel and Development, 1997.

LEWIS P. *The Successful Management of Redundancy.* Oxford, Blackwell, 1993.

PETTIGREW A. *and* WHIPP R. *Managing Change for Competitive Success.* Oxford, Blackwell, 1995.

SPARROW P. 'New Organisational forms, processes, jobs and psychological contracts' in Sparrow P. and Marchington M. *Human Resource Management: The new agenda.* London. Pitman Publishing, 1998.

SPARROW P. *and* MARCHINGTON M. *Human Resource Management: The new agenda.* London. Pitman Publishing/Financial Times. 1998.

SUMMERFIELD J. 'Lean firms cannot afford to be mean'. *People Management,* Vol 2, No 2, January 1996 pp30–32.

Part 5

REVIEW

12 Examination questions and advice

INTRODUCTION

The purpose of this final chapter is to review readers' knowledge and understanding of the major issues dealt with in the book. The chapter should prove especially useful for those students preparing for the IPD Professional Standards in the Generalist Module, Employee Relations, in that it provides questions which are similar to those likely to be found on the nationally-set examination paper. At the same time, however, it should also prove beneficial to readers who are studying for internally set examinations, since it provides a framework for revision, as well as for those who are interested in posing questions about employee relations in their own organisation.

The chapter comprises two sections which follow the format of the IPD national examination paper in employee relations and a third section which provides general advice on how to tackle the paper. The first section includes three cases similar to the one which is set in the national examination. If students are trying to simulate examination conditions, each of these questions should take about one hour to complete. In the second section there are 32 questions which aim to test knowledge and understanding through short answers, typically one paragraph in length, which can be completed in 5 to 10 minutes. This style of question forms a common element of the IPD assessment portfolio under the Professional Qualification Scheme, not just the Generalist Module, Employee Relations, but throughout the whole set of modules.

SECTION A: CASE STUDIES

Case 1 : relocation of employment

ABC is an organisation located in the middle of the UK. Although the product market is highly competitive, the organisation is successful. It is a progressive company which is always looking for new opportunities but it is also aware of its workforce responsibilities.

ABC employs 85 workers (manual and non-manual), the bulk of which are full-time and are currently housed in premises which it owns in an expensive part of the city centre. The majority of the workforce live within easy travelling distance of the firm.

ABC is not a member of an employers' organisation. The delivery of the personnel function is line-management centred. There is only a small personnel department with two personnel officers to advise and assist line managers. There is, however, a personnel director who sits on the highest policy-making body of ABC.

The working hours for manual employees are 36 hours per week but 35 hours for non-manual. Paid holiday entitlement for all employees is four weeks. There is a company pension scheme. Enhanced maternity leave arrangements exist. ABC maintains regular communications with its employees and has grievance, discipline, job grading and redundancy procedures.

However, ABC is concerned about:

a) the city centre location hampering expansion and the ability to invest in new technology

b) problems of recruiting and retaining highly skilled employees

c) suppliers are relocating outside the city centre assisted by Government and European Commission funds.

ABC has, therefore, decided to relocate its establishment to a new site outside the city centre. The new location is some 50 minutes' travelling distance from its present location. ABC would like to transfer to the new site as many of its existing employees as possible. The employees are understandably concerned and some of the more skilled employees have already started to look for alternative employment.

Explain how you think ABC can relocate its present operation but continue to achieve its employee relations objectives. How might some of the problems that you envisage will arise be overcome and how might commitment from your managerial colleagues be gained?

Case 2 : threats from the corporate environment
XYZ is an organisation located in south-east England. It employs 400 people. Two hundred and fifty are manual employees, of which half are male and the other half female. There are 100 administrative, clerical, technical and professional staff and the gender balance within these groups is appropriate. The remaining 50 employees are at senior, middle and supervisory levels of management. The bulk of employees work full-time, although there are some part-timers amongst the clerical staff.

XYZ is not a member of an employers' organisation. The delivery of the personnel function is highly structured. There is a relatively large personnel department with a number of personnel assistants, officers and managers. There is, however, a personnel director who sits on the highest policy-making body of XYZ.

The working hours for the manual employees are 37 hours per week but 35 hours per week for all other employees. Paid holidays for manual employees are five weeks but six weeks for other employees. There are pay differentials between and within the main occupational categories at XYZ. There is a company pension scheme. XYZ maintains regular communications with its employees. XYZ has the usual procedures to be found in an employing organisation – grievance, discipline, promotion, job grading and redundancy – and these work satisfactorily. Indeed, relationships with the employees have been good and employees regard employment at XYZ as relatively secure. This has been helped in that the pace of change in the organisation has been slow and evolutionary. It has certainly not been revolutionary.

However, XYZ is becoming anxious about the future. There are no crises at present but management is giving thought to how the following might affect XYZ's activities in the future:

a) the organisation is becoming exposed to greater product market competition

b) the Social Dimension of the European Union is moving forward at a relatively slow pace but there are pressures from Member States for this to be accelerated

c) technology is changing as computers, lasers and telecommunications continue to develop. It is clear the rate of change at XYZ in the future will accelerate significantly.

Explain how you think these changes in the external environment in which XYZ operates will impact upon its employee relations strategy and policies. How might some of the problems you envisage be overcome and how might commitment be gained from your managerial colleagues and from the workforce?

Case 3 : gaining the confidence of the employees
You are employed as a personnel-HRM specialist with a large multi-plant private sector company which has just purchased a formerly central government-owned establishment in the manufacturing sector.

As part of the management, you face many problems at the establishment you have just acquired. The chief ones are:

a) The government is not promising to guarantee any work to your newly-acquired establishment and the industry in which you operate is depressed. The workforces fear your first decision will be to declare redundancies.

b) There are pre-privatisation day grievances, particularly the dismissal of half a dozen employees, which are festering and if not handled carefully will further alienate the workforce.

c) The workforce feels the management of the acquiring organisation will have no commitment to their new establishment and will see working in the former government establishment as a staging post en route to more senior management positions in the main organisation.

d) All trade unions were hostile to the privatisation, fearing job insecurity and the abolition of civil service employment conditions. However, they accept the need for improved efficiency. There are two main trade union groups. Three represent administrative employees and five represent the manual workers. Union density is high and each union jealously guards its autonomy and bargaining rights. Although strikes have occurred in the past they were infrequent and involved small numbers of employees of one union. There are two nation-wide collective agreements which were negotiated by central government and the Civil Service unions. One agreement covers manual employees and the other non-manual. There are two separate sets of negotiations and single-table bargaining arrangements operate.

e) The personnel management function is underdeveloped and mainly administrative in operation. Policies merely stemmed from the acquired establishment's sponsoring Ministry. There has also been a rapid turnover of personnel managers at the site.

All these problems mean your company has taken over a demoralised workforce. You have been asked to produce a personnel/HRM strategy and related policies to gain the confidence of the employees and to demonstrate there is a 'stake' for them in the new privatised establishment which is superior to that of the 'old' Civil Service world.

Provide a report outlining the personnel/HRM strategy and policies to achieve this objective.

SECTION B: QUESTIONS REQUIRING SHORT ANSWERS

1 Explain the main components of a grievance procedure.

2 Outline the main services ACAS provides to employing organisations.

3 Why might organisations wish to be members of an employers' association?

4 Outline the main functions of the State in employee relations.

5 What do you understand by the term, the European Union 'Social Dialogue'?

6 Briefly outline the key principles underpinning a disciplinary procedure.

7 Explain three management skills required by an effective employee relations specialist.

8 Explain the difference between bargaining and grievance-handling.

9 Explain the difference between qualified majority voting and unanimous decision-making in the European Union.

10 Outline the main roles of the law in regulating the employment relationship.

11 Explain the difference between conciliation, mediation and arbitration.

12 What are the main principles that should underlie employee relations procedural arrangements?

13 List at least four ways in which employee relations negotiating situations are different from commercial negotiations.

14 Explain the importance of interviewing skills in handling employee grievances.

15 Outline at least three pitfalls a management should avoid in disciplining employees.

16 Explain briefly the process you would adopt when dealing with a case of alleged sexual harassment or bullying by one employee against another.

17 What factors determine the balance of bargaining power between the buyers and sellers of labour services?

18 What constraints does the Working Time Directive impose on a business wishing to change its pattern of working hours?

19 List at least four reasons either (a) why an organisation may wish to manage with trade unions or (b) wish to manage in a union-free environment.

20 Explain the differences between joint consultation and collective bargaining.

21 Explain the terms 'substantive' agreement and 'procedure' agreement.

22 Identify and explain a minimum of three 'core skills' required by an employee relations manager when handling employee grievances.

23 Why is the *New Earnings Survey* a publication with which every employee relations manager should be familiar?

24 In handling disciplinary matters, how does management demonstrate 'fair' and 'reasonable' behaviour?

25 List at least three pitfalls a management should avoid in managing a redundancy situation.

26 Explain, with examples, how the Social Chapter of the Treaty of Rome has impinged on the day-to-day activities of personnel managers.

27 Identify the pressures that lead the buyers and sellers of labour services to reconcile their different labour market interests.

28 List, with justification, the criteria you would use to evaluate whether procedural arrangements were operating satisfactorily from a management perspective.

29 Explain briefly the terms 'quality circles', 'team briefing' and 'profit-related pay'.

30 In managing a redundancy situation, list the information that the employer concerned must make available to the employees or their representatives or both.

31 List at least four employee relations advantages that might arise

from the implementation of employee involvement and commitment schemes.

32 Explain the difference between 'pendulum' arbitration and so-called 'conventional' arbitration.

EXAMINATION GUIDELINES

The purpose of this final section is to provide students with some guidance about the way in which to tackle examination questions on the Employee Relations (Generalist Module) paper. A number of general comments are appropriate, given that students tend to make mistakes on each part of the paper, but these are supplemented with more specific reservations relating to each part of the paper.

Four general points can be made:

1. Many candidates fail to answer all parts of a multi-part question and this is often the case on the compulsory case study. Typically, the majority fail this question because they do not:

    (1) outline the problems the case study poses for management

    (2) provide specific proposals to overcome these problems. Often the proposals are far too general with no specifics

    (3) provide a rationale for their proposals. Candidates do not explain what problems their proposals are designed to overcome. Too many candidates produce 'wish lists'

    (4) discuss the resource implications of their proposals

    (5) provide an implementation plan with timescales

    (6) discuss how they would gain the commitment of their managerial colleagues and, if appropriate, the workforce to their proposals.

2. Many candidates fail to address the question that has been set, preferring to tell the examiner all they know about the subject matter of the question. While this can be very interesting it demonstrates that the student has not read and/or understood the question set. Candidates must read the questions and then answer the question set. Similarly, it is common for candidates to write an essay rather than a report or draft training programme when this is requested. One of the skills that examiners are trying to assess in the paper is the ability of candidates to write in a clear, concise and convincing manner. You are advised to produce a shorter answer which is well planned and reveals knowledge and understanding of the subject matter of the question rather than a long, unstructured answer which produces the relevant points by accident rather than by design.

3. Many candidates seem to lose sight of the overall objectives when answering a question and provide an unbalanced answer which devotes far too much time to one part of the question to the detriment of others. Clear planning before starting to write an answer can obviously reduce the probability of this problem

arising. On many occasions, candidates seem to believe that making references to well-known academics demonstrates knowledge and understanding of the principal issues surrounding the subject matter of the question. This is all very well if the references are relevant and appropriate, and do not appear to be bolted on to a somewhat peripheral answer.

4. Many candidates fail to locate their answer in the wider commercial and environmental context, showing little appreciation of national or European Union-wide trends or longer-term developments in the economy as a whole, the legal framework surrounding management employee relations strategies and policies, or in employee relations in particular. There is often a temptation to assume that current fads and fashions represent a superior solution to organisational problems and little recognition that they may be superficial and trite. Candidates must demonstrate when discussing current 'new' management practices (sometimes referred to as 'fads') that they are capable of analysing and evaluating whether the success (or alleged success) of the introduction of such practices in one organisation is relevant and capable of being successfully transplanted into another organisation. Candidates all too often fail to recognise the force of existing cultural norms and traditions when putting forward recommendations, somehow assuming that all options are feasible. It is important to demonstrate an awareness of the constraints (financial, resistance from one's managerial colleagues etc) as well as the opportunities when answering questions. One of the things which the Professional Qualifications Scheme aims to develop in candidates is the ability to persuade line managers of the usefulness of employee relations strategy, policies and practices in solving specific organisational problems.

Taking a more positive stance, there are certain guidelines which students might like to bear in mind when preparing for the examination, some of which build upon what has been said in the previous paragraphs. These are:

1. Make sure that the material in the whole syllabus is understood, otherwise you may have difficulty in providing answers to the eight compulsory questions in Section B of the paper. In addition, when addressing the case study in Section A, students need to be able to demonstrate a holistic appreciation of employee relations.

2. Provide examples, as appropriate, to support a particular answer and arguments. These may be drawn from any organisation, not only the one for which the candidate currently works, and it is useful if contemporary examples are provided as these show that the candidate is up-to-date and is reading the professional journals.

3. Write concisely and clearly, providing signposts to an answer. There is nothing worse for an examiner than having to reread an answer several times in order to try to identify precisely what the candidate is trying to say. A clear introduction stating explicitly what will be contained in the answer helps considerably in this respect, as does the use of paragraphs, sections and numbering; the precise technique which is used matters less than the overall impact, and

candidates should therefore use the approach with which they feel most comfortable.

4. Ensure that the examination is timed so that an attempt can be made at all questions. It is worthwhile repeating that approximately one hour should be allocated to each section in the examination paper. This means that in Section B, each question should be answered in 5 to 10 minutes.

These guidelines should not be seen as an attempt to impose unrealistic professional standards on IPD students. Rather, these skills are central to all aspects of managerial work, namely addressing the question which is posed; choosing from alternatives to formulate a realistic answer; justifying recommendations; and writing in a clear and well-structured manner which manages to persuade the reader.

There are a number of more specific comments relating to each of the sections. When addressing the case study, candidates need to ensure they understand the case as a whole and are able to identify the key points within it. In suggesting solutions to the problems posed in the case study, candidates should demonstrate:

a) they can integrate the different aspects of employee relations

b) they can discuss policy options including the pros and cons of each, which on balance they would select, and why

c) if 'new' management practices (fads) are relevant, explain why this is so but more importantly explain how their adoption would help solve the organisation's problems and how they could be successfully introduced

d) how the employee relations solution would contribute to the achievement of the organisation's objectives

e) they understand commercial realities. Candidates frequently argue they would reduce an organisation's headcount by early retirement schemes but without telling the examiners whether the organisation's pension fund scheme could finance such a policy or without recognising that early retirement is a matter for the fund's trustees and not the chief executive. Candidates have also demonstrated that they do not realise the implementation of technological change takes time as well as money in that the technology has to be ordered, delivered, installed and technical problems ironed out.

Section B comprises a number of questions which require short paragraph-length answers. These can be drawn from all parts of the syllabus and require candidates to present fairly basic core information in order to demonstrate their knowledge and understanding of the topics under consideration. The answers in this section need to be concise, but can usefully be supplemented with examples to illustrate the candidate's knowledge and understanding of the issue. It is important that all questions in this section are answered.

Index